IRSH 3475
OP 50

25_
ES

RESHAPING CONFEDERATION

Books of Related Interest

Political Support in Canada

The Crisis Years

Edited by Allan Kornberg *and* Harold D. Clarke

The Politics of Canadian Airport Development

Lessons for Federalism

Elliot J. Feldman *and* Jerome Milch

Influence in Parliament

Canada

Allan Kornberg *and* William Mishler

The Influence of the United States on Canadian Development

Eleven Case Studies

Edited by Richard A. Preston

Influence in Parliament: Canada was published as a part of a series from the Consortium for Comparative Legislative Studies. All other titles were published for the Duke University Center for Commonwealth and Comparative Studies, or for its successor, the Duke University Center for International Studies.

RESHAPING CONFEDERATION

*The 1982 Reform
of the Canadian Constitution*

Edited by

Paul Davenport *and* Richard H. Leach

A Duke University Center for International Studies Publication

Duke University Press

DURHAM, NORTH CAROLINA   1984

The text of this book was originally published without appendix or index as Volume 45, No. 4, of the journal *Law & Contemporary Problems.*

Library of Congress Cataloging in Publication Data
Main entry under title:

Reshaping confederation.

(Duke University Center for International Studies publications)
Includes index.
1. Canada—Constitutional law—Congresses. I. Leach, Richard H.   II. Davenport, Paul.   III. Series.
KE4218   1984   342.71′03   83-20665
ISBN 0-8223-0578-X   347.1023

CONTENTS

INTRODUCTION

PAUL DAVENPORT

The twelve papers that follow were presented at the McGill-Duke Symposium on *The 1982 Reform of the Canadian Constitution*, held at Duke University on April 26 and 27, 1982. The Symposium was organized jointly by Richard Leach, Director of the Canadian Studies Center at Duke University, and Paul Davenport, Chairman of the Canadian Studies Program at McGill University. The participants included seven McGill academics and five academics from Duke, covering the disciplines of Political Science, Economics, History, and Law. The conference was thus explicitly interdisciplinary in nature: the purpose was to bring together scholars from different disciplines and backgrounds, so that they might compare their academic theories and personal insights into the constitutional reform process which culminated in the Canada Act of 1982.

The process and the reformed constitution itself will undoubtedly play a central role in reshaping Confederation in the decades to come. The new provisions of the reformed constitution include many which will change the workings of Canada's federation: the expansion of provincial powers with respect to resource taxation and management; the entrenchment of language rights, particularly with regard to schooling; the Charter of Rights and Freedoms, which will certainly afford better legal protection of individual rights than the Canadian Bill of Rights; and the increased importance of the courts, especially the Supreme Court of Canada, in the interpretation and protection of individual rights. The process by which the reform was adopted will also influence the workings of Confederation. In particular, the failure to win approval from the Government of Quebec, and Quebec's subsequent feelings of betrayal, may complicate or indeed poison federal-provincial relations for some time to come. Finally, the new amending formula, which does not require unanimity of the provinces for constitutional amendments, may open the door to a more fundamental reshaping of Confederation, including a new distribution of powers between the federal and provincial governments. The distribution of powers, which has been at the center of constitutional debates over the last two decades, was one of the major issues left unresolved by the constitutional reform of 1982.

Just nine days before the McGill-Duke Symposium, on April 17, 1982, Queen Elizabeth II proclaimed the Canada Act in a ceremony in Ottawa. The event ended several decades of unsuccessful attempts to make Canada legally independent of the United Kingdom. Some 17 months earlier, in October 1980, the Government of Canada had presented a draft of a proposed constitutional reform to the House of Commons. The draft was opposed by all the provinces except Ontario and New Brunswick. Manitoba, Newfoundland, and Quebec took their objections to the courts, with the result that the Supreme Court of Canada issued a judgment on September 28, 1981. The Court held that although the proposed constitutional changes were legally proper they violated a constitutional convention which required substantial provincial consent for constitutional changes; the Court did not, however, indicate how many provinces would define substantial provincial consent. The federal government then re-opened negotiations with the provinces, and on November 5, 1981, all the provinces except Quebec agreed to a revised draft of the constitutional reform. The revised draft allowed provinces to opt out of future amendments and of many of the provisions concerning individual rights; these were the most important of several concessions made by the federal government to reach agreement. In the following month the resolution to send the constitutional changes to the United Kingdom was approved by the House of Commons and the Senate of Canada.

The Canada Act was given Royal Assent in the United Kingdom Parliament on March 29, 1982, and proclaimed in Canada three weeks later. Schedule B of the Canada Act comprises the Constitution Act, 1982, which had been earlier approved by the Parliament of Canada. Part I of the Constitution Act is the Canadian Charter of Rights and Freedoms, including thirty-four sections which deal with fundamental freedoms, democratic rights, mobility, equality, legal rights, official languages, minority language educational rights, and enforcement and application of the Charter. The remaining twenty-six sections of the Constitution Act are divided into five parts, dealing with aboriginal rights; equalization and regional disparities; a future constitutional conference; the procedure for amending the Constitution; amendments to the British North America Act of 1867 with respect to natural resources; and general provisions.

The Canada Act of 1982 represented the culmination of a century of constitutional wrangling and will likely be the prelude to another century of legal and political infighting in Canada. The constitutional debates of the first 115 years of Confederation are reviewed in Filippo Sabetti's paper. Sabetti demonstrates that constitutional change in Canada can be divided into three periods. The first, extending from the 1870's to 1927, witnessed the growth in power of the provincial governments; the second, which extends into the late 1970's, involved the growth of federal and provincial institutions to deal with constitutional problems, short of actual constitutional change; and finally comes a third phase, involving the reform of the Constitution itself, which began in 1980 with the federal government's decision to attempt to reform and patriate the constitution—unilaterally, if necessary. Canada is still in this third phase and the results of the constitutional reform which the Trudeau government achieved in the short space of two years cannot yet be determined. Sabetti describes the historical background surrounding the great constitutional issues of the last few years, including six that deserve special mention: (1) the question of whether Confederation was a compact-of-provinces or a compact-of-peoples, the latter involving an implicit covenant between the French and English communities; (2) the importance of politics in constitutional change, including the difficulties of reconciling the objectives of many different political jurisdictions, each with its own independent base of support; (3) the great Canadian dilemma of how to protect the French language and culture, while at the same time protecting minority rights; (4) the economic issues underlying many of the disagreements between the federal government and the provinces, and the implications of constitutional arrangements with respect to the distribution of income and the distribution of regulatory powers; (5) the essential issues of the rights of individuals as opposed to the rights of society, particularly with regard to language, culture, civil liberties, and the like; and (6) the fundamental issue, which was left completely unresolved at Confederation, of how the Canadian Constitution might be amended. These are the issues treated in the other contributions to this volume, to which Sabetti's paper serves as a very effective introduction.

The British North America Act of 1867 followed the American Constitution by some eight decades and represented a vastly different type of document in both style and content. These differences are the subject of Clark Cahow's paper. Cahow argues that constitutional change and agreement has been particularly difficult in Canada because the country lacks a national ethos, which might provide a framework for agreement and compromise. He traces the development of what he deems the American ethos from the New England Puritans of the Massachusetts Bay Colony through to the Civil War. Cahow finds that Americans were united in their belief that government received its authority only from the consent of the people and that this national belief, once enshrined in the new Constitution, was a unifying force, even in the face of such a shattering experience as the Civil War. He then follows the growth of Canadian political institutions from New France to Confederation and concludes that the lack of a national identity or spirit has been a continual obstacle to constitutional change in Canada. Some readers may disagree with this thesis, or find that the lack of an overriding national ethos in Canada has been desirable: it is, perhaps, the strength of Canadian regional and linguistic identities that has enabled the country to maintain a very diverse and unique character. Nevertheless, Cahow's interpretation of the Canadian identity and its manifest importance to the political process is a challenging one, in part because it brings to the fore the different meanings attached to such concepts as "nationalism" and "national identity," north and south of the 49th parallel.

Constitutional change in Canada has always been principally a political process involving governments who must please their electorates and stand for re-election. J.R. Mallory surveys the political aspects of constitutional change from both an historical and an analytical perspective. He reveals that the economic collapse of the 1930's and the mobilization for World War II created dramatic changes in federal-provincial relations, culminating in the period of "cooperative federalism" after the war, in which federal funding was used to promote social programs in areas of provincial jurisdiction. The distribution of powers, particularly in areas of social and economic administration, is undeniably one of the great pieces of unfinished business with which future constitutional change will have to cope. Mallory reviews many other issues which the reform of the Canadian Constitution left unsettled including: the question of Quebec's place in Confederation, and whether any sort of special status is possible or desirable; the issue of the optimal amending procedure for the new constitution, and whether the "opting out" clause with regard to amendments in the reformed Constitution will create a "checkerboard" of constitutional rights, as Prime Minister Trudeau has warned; the growing importance of courts and particularly the Supreme Court of Canada in constitutional change, and the fascinating question of how the Supreme Court will interpret the Charter of Rights in the decades to come; and finally the institution of federal-provincial conferences, which has become an essential but expensive way of exchanging information and reaching policy compromises on areas of disagreement involving the two levels of government.

Mallory addresses at length the increasing difficulties encountered in conflict resolution between the federal government and the provinces since World War II. These difficulties arise in part from the growing power of the provinces, the increasing militancy of Quebec nationalism, and the inability of the federal government to manage the economy, especially over the last decade.   A further problem is that while the accommodation of differences through federal-provincial negotiation was relatively uncomplicated in the early years when the objectives of both levels of government were congruent and complementary, accommodation quickly becomes nearly impossible when the objectives are in direct conflict, as in the case of energy, foreign investment, and industrial strategy.   The emergence of a large degree of overlapping jurisdiction has led to a growing conflict over jurisdictional "space."

The constitutional accord of 1981 involved the federal government and nine provinces. The resulting package of changes was sent to London despite the bitter opposition of the Quebec government. One of the unresolved questions of this process is whether the reformed constitution and the manner of its adoption will increase support for political independence among Quebecers. The paper by Allan Kornberg and Keith Archer investigates sources of support for the various constitutional options in Quebec, including the status quo, renewed federalism, special status for Quebec, sovereignty association, and independence. Kornberg and Archer attempt to explain constitutional preferences through a multiple regression analysis. Five variables are found to be significant determinants of support for sovereignty association and independence: identification with the Parti Québécois, indifference toward Canada, orientation toward provincial rather than federal politics, belief that Quebec does not benefit in fiscal terms from federalism, and the age of the respondent. Moreover, once these five variables are controlled the remaining variables are relatively insignificant: ethnicity, education, socioeconomic status, and the person's judgment of his own costs or benefits from a particular constitutional option. A fascinating question remains at the end of the Kornberg-Archer paper. Will the young Francophones of today, who are heavily in favor of sovereignty association and independence, change their views as they age? If they do not, and if young Francophones continue to support independence, the years ahead will witness a growth in support for sovereignty association and independence in the province.

The constitutional discussions of the past decade have often seemed like a kind of open-air market, with eleven participants haggling over terms, each concerned only with his own self-interest and oblivious to any higher principles. Bill Watson reviews constitutional reform in just these terms, by making use of the emerging economic literature on the behavior of politicians and bureaucrats. Watson considers not only the normative question of what *should* be the division of powers in an optimal federal state, but also the positive question—which he considers more interesting—of how the self-interested behavior of politicians and bureaucrats will bring about a particular division of powers. Not surprisingly, he finds that the behavior of politicians and bureaucrats often will *not* produce an optimal division of powers, a situation that leads him to question the usefulness of economic models of federalism that focus on optimal jurisdictional arrangements. He concludes that constitutional change is generally continuous, consisting of a never-ending series of deals and temporary arrangements. This process will be affected, but by no means terminated, with the constitutional reform of 1982.

The paper by Paul Davenport also treats of economic matters, in this case the sharing of wealth in Canada, particularly among the provinces. The difficulty of achieving a proper balance of personal income and government revenue among the provinces has been a pervasive constitutional problem in Canada since the British North America Act of 1867. During Canada's first nine decades, an interprovincial balance of sorts was achieved by ad hoc federal subsidies and lump-sum payments to provinces experiencing short or long term difficulties. In 1957, a formal system of equalization was adopted, in which the provinces with below average government revenue were paid subsidies by the federal government. This scheme was expanded in 1967, but it encountered trouble with the unexpected large jump in oil prices in 1973. Although the Canada Act of 1982 entrenches the principle of equalization in the Constitution, the equalization formula itself has been changed so frequently in recent years that the significance and effect of entrenchment is uncertain. Wealth sharing in Canada has been greatly complicated by the problems inherent in dividing the very large revenues from oil and gas production among the producing companies, the producing provinces, nonproducing provinces, and the federal government. Davenport suggests that many of the problems associated with equalization could be resolved with a re-structured equalization formula, based on total provincial income rather than simply government revenue, as is currently the case. These challenging issues will undoubtedly confront Canadian policy makers.

One of the crucial, yet unanswered, questions about the constitutional reform of 1982 is its long-term effect on the balance of power between the provinces and the central government within Confederation. This federal-provincial political balance is the subject of Richard Leach's paper. Leach reviews the history of the ebb and flow of political power between the provinces and the federal government after 1867, focusing on the notion of Confederation as a compact among the provinces. Provincial power tended to grow at the expense of the federal government from Confederation to World War II. While the size and importance of the federal government grew dramatically during the war, over the last three decades there has been a fairly steady erosion of federal power to the benefit of the provinces. Leach also considers the unfinished business of constitutional reform, including the constitutional conference on native rights called for in Section 37 of the Constitution Act, 1982; the conference on the review of the amending formula, referred to in Section 49; the reform of the Senate, perhaps to make it representative of regional interests; the possibility of a proportional representation scheme for the House of Commons; reform of the cumbersome and often ineffective institution of federal-provincial conferences; and, finally, changes in the appointment of Supreme Court justices. Leach declares that it would be premature to conclude whether the Canada Act itself, and the reform that may follow it, will lead to a strengthening of the federal government, or a continuation of the trend toward greater provincial power within Confederation.

Daniel Latouche also analyzes the impact of the Canada Act on Canadian federalism. Latouche finds that the constitutional reform represents a crushing defeat for those Québécois who wanted to negotiate an independent country and for those who wanted to negotiate renewed federalism. Their error, in both cases, was the mistaken assumption that there existed a unified English group in Canada prepared to negotiate with Quebec on the central issue of the role that our two great linguistic communities would have in Confederation. The enthusiasm and pomp with which the Canada Act was greeted outside Quebec is a measure for Latouche of the failure of Canadian federalism. Instead of obtaining an equal or a special status, Quebec finds its political powers actually reduced, so that in the future the protection of the French language and culture will be largely at the discretion of federal officials and institutions, particularly the federally appointed judges who will interpret the linguistic sections of the Charter of Rights. Although Latouche believes that the linguistic and cultural heritage of French Canadians can best be protected by recognition of Quebec's status as a distinct nation, he concludes that there is no significant group within English-speaking Canada amenable to granting that recognition. Even among those English-speaking Canadians most sympathetic to Quebec's unique linguistic and cultural needs, there remains an overriding and uncompromising vision of a single Canadian nation with diverse provinces and cultures. There is no single English Canada with which Quebec can negotiate a new political arrangement—this for Latouche is the central lesson of the constitutional reform. The English Canadian majority was willing to entrench a special status for the French language, but not for the Government of Quebec.

William Tetley surveys the historical and political background to Sections 16 to 23 of the Constitution Act, 1982, which establish and clarify language rights. Tetley reveals that the British North America Act failed to protect the French language and culture outside Quebec, as evidenced in Manitoba by the Official Language Act and the School Acts of 1890, and in Ontario by Regulation 17, introduced in 1913 to curtail the use of French in Catholic schools. He traces in detail the evolution of language legislation in Quebec during the 1960's and 1970's, with the special insights and knowledge of one who served as a cabinet minister in the Bourassa government from 1970 to 1976. Tetley discusses in depth the political, constitutional, and practical difficulties of language legislation in Quebec in a number of areas: the language of the courts and National Assembly; the use of language in commerce and marketing; the language of instruction in schools; and the linguistic composition of school boards. Tetley clearly demonstrates that the language problems to which Quebec is now searching for a solution have been intensely debated for at least twenty years. He compares the spirit and letter of language legislation under the Liberals with that of the Parti Québécois, with special reference to the differences between the Liberals' Bill 22, passed during the summer of 1974, and Bill 101 of the Parti Québécois, which became law just three years later. Tetley concludes by deploring the fact that the English and French languages, two great cultural assets for Canada, have more often been a source of disunity than unity in the country, and by urging greater linguistic cooperation and tolerance throughout Canada in the years to come.

One of the most controversial parts of the Canada Act is the Canadian Charter of Rights and Freedoms, which was criticized by the provinces as an unwarranted intrusion upon provincial jurisdiction over property and civil rights, and by various special interest groups as too weak and vague. A. Kenneth Pye's paper closely examines the likely impact of the Charter on the rights of persons accused of crime. Pye concludes that the Charter represents a significant improvement in legal protection over the Canadian Bill of Rights which has been a disappointingly ineffectual document. Nevertheless, in many areas the protections afforded by the Canadian Charter appear to be significantly less than those available in similar circumstances in the United States. For example, although the Charter provides for the right to retain and instruct counsel without delay when a person has been arrested, it is unclear how that will afford protection to poor people in provinces and regions where legal aid is inadequate. Furthermore, in many cases the real impact of the Charter will become clear only as the courts give life to its provisions through judicial interpretation. Thus, while the Charter prohibits unreasonable search or seizure, there is no way of predicting what will be interpreted as "unreasonable." Difficult decisions will have to be made with respect to electronic surveillance and writs of assistance, or general search warrants, which may be several years old and not relate to any specific person or offense. In large measure, therefore, the responsibility for protecting individual rights and liberties has passed from Parliament and the provincial legislature to the courts. Pye points out that if this transfer is perceived as successful, Canadians may wish to strengthen the provisions of the Charter itself.

During the past several decades of constitutional debate involving the provinces and the federal government, one of the most difficult areas in which to reach agreement was the amending formula. The amending procedures actually adopted in part 5 of the Constitution Act, 1982, are subject to a searching analysis by Stephen Scott. Under the British North America Act, the provinces had the right to amend their own constitutions (with the exception of the office of lieutenant-governor) and the federal parliament had the power to make amendments affecting the institutions of central government. Other amendments, however, such as those affecting the distribution of legislative power, remained victim to the exclusive province of the British Parliament at Canadian request. In general, the practice was that such amendments would not be pursued without unanimous provincial consent, even though it was not clear whether this was a binding constitutional convention. Under the Constitution Act, 1982, the general procedure for amendments affecting the distribution of power now requires the assent of Parliament together with the assent of two-thirds of the provincial legislatures representing at least fifty percent of the population. Any amendments so passed will have no effect in those provinces which did not support them, although the provinces may at any later date remove their dissent with a majority vote of the legislature. Prime Minister Trudeau argued that this opting-out provision would produce a "checkerboard" Canada, but he reluctantly agreed to it in his effort to win provincial support for the entire constitutional package.

In addition to this general procedure, however, the Act enumerates four other procedures for amending the Constitution. The consent of the Senate, the House of Commons, and of all the provincial Assemblies is required for certain sorts of amendments, including those dealing with the office of the Queen, membership in the House of Commons, the use of the English and French languages, and the composition of the Supreme Court; amendments to provisions that apply to some but not all of the provinces require the consent of the affected provinces; Parliament may act unilaterally to amend the constitution in relation to the executive government of Canada, the Senate, and the House of Commons; and finally, each province may unilaterally amend its own constitution. Scott shows lucidly that the scope of these various procedures is not always clear, nor is their apparent relation to each other. Ultimately, much will hinge on how the terms "the Constitution of Canada" and "the constitution of the Province" are interpreted. Scott argues that the provincial constitutions should be interpreted as part of "the Constitution of Canada," but whether this interpretation will prevail remains to be seen.

Walter Dellinger's paper also scrutinizes the amending formula in the Canada Act, comparing it to the amending process in Article 5 of the United States Constitution. Dellinger points out that in a federal system of government the division of powers between the federal government and the provinces is absolutely crucial. According to Dellinger, it is necessary to agree not only on an initial division, but also on an amending process through which that division can be altered. Where there is a disagreement on the initial division, as there is in Canada, agreement on the amending process will be manifestly more difficult. It is significant that the American Constitution was drawn up by a special convention chosen for that purpose and was submitted for ratification to similar special conventions in the states. Conversely, in Canada it has been the existing legislatures which have drawn up the constitutional reforms; this creates a problem if the legislatures themselves are in need of reform.

Dellinger reviews the rather complicated amending formula contained in the Constitution Act, 1982, and praises it for addressing specifically many questions that are not adequately considered in Article 5 of the American Constitution. The Canadian Constitution, for example, clearly indicates how and when those provinces which dissent from amendments may change their dissent to approval. It also unambiguously indicates which parts of the Constitution require unanimous agreement—for example those parts dealing with representation in the legislation of the central government. Despite these salutary provisions, Dellinger does criticize the Canadian Constitution for limiting future constitutional changes to those suggested by the national government or the provinces. He suggests that alternative means of constitutional amendments, such as a national referendum or specially elected conventions in each province, might provide for amendments that would have wide popular support but would be opposed by existing legislatures. Finally, Dellinger comments on those provisions that allow provinces to opt out of constitutional amendments with which they disagree and to override the Charter of Rights. Even though they may seem objectionable to those familiar with U.S. constitutional law, these provisions accurately embody the current character of Canadian federalism.

For those concerned with the future of Canada's federal system, the twelve papers in this volume provide ample scholarly thought on the subject for both the layman and the academic. The past decade has been a tumultuous one for Canadian federalism, which has been forced to cope with the conflicts engendered by prolonged and seemingly insoluble economic problems, the strains of western alienation, an *independentiste* government in Quebec, and the bitter divisions produced by the constitutional reform process itself. These salient problems have reacted with each other in a manner that makes the interpretation and analysis of any one of them very difficult. Thus, the constitutional reform of 1982 and its implications for Canada's future represent a remarkably broad and variegated landscape, of which the papers that follow can of necessity give only a partial view. Yet by their interdisciplinary nature, the papers emphasize one essential aspect of the process of constitutional reform: the complex interweaving of political, economic, linguistic, and legal issues that make up the fabric of Canadian federalism. Whether that fabric will hold together, or be torn asunder, is a question implicit in all of the papers, and one which only the future can answer.

THE HISTORICAL CONTEXT OF CONSTITUTIONAL CHANGE IN CANADA

FILIPPO SABETTI*

Ut incepit fidelis sic permanet?†

The British North America Act (BNA Act)[1] has been "patriated." At last, Canadians have their own basic law. The historical context of this constitutional change is the history of a political system that did not work as its creators had intended, of constitutional reform efforts that ended in stalemate, and of analysts "fallen into speaking the language of doubt when describing their society."[2] Why, then, should we bother about the past? The past is important for three simple reasons: 1) A large proportion of the reasoning still employed in the analysis of contemporary government and politics rests explicitly or implicitly on an interpretation of the historical record of constitutional change; past experience could discredit this current reasoning; 2) The modelling and remodelling of constitutional arrangements are well enough documented to suggest conclusions which could become plausible working hypotheses about constitutional choice; and 3) The Constitution of 1982[3] could be checked against the working hypotheses about past experiences in order to explain its successful patriation and to predict its applicability for resolving old problems. But the method of the attack of the historical record will determine the utility of the analysis.

First, the importance of constitutionalism for a liberal democratic society is well enough established to require no extended elaboration or defense.[4] Laws, regulations, organizations, and property rights—the institutional arrangements in society that create incentive systems through which citizens and public officials

---

* Associate Professor of Political Science, McGill University. Many essential ingredients to the preparation of this article have been contributed by the intellectual exchange I have shared with colleagues associated with the Workshop on Covenant and Politics organized by Daniel J. Elazar at the Center for the Study of Federalism, Temple University, with colleagues participating in the McGill-Duke Symposium on the Reform of the Canadian Constitution in 1982 organized by Paul Davenport and Richard H. Leach at Duke University, and Charles Tilly's work on European state making. I am particularly grateful to Christopher Armstrong, Marcel Caya, J.R. Mallory, Kenneth H. Norrie, Mario R. Pietrangeli, David E. Smith, Mark Sproule-Jones, and John H. Thompson for suggestions. Vincent di Norcia was especially thoughtful in his extended comments. This article draws on research supported by a sabbatical leave fellowship from the Humanities and Social Science Research Council of Canada in 1980-81, help which I also wish to acknowledge.

† "As loyal she began, so shall she remain?" With apologies to the Province of Ontario.

1. British North America Act, 1867, 30 & 31 Vict., ch. 3 [hereinafter cited as BNA Act].

2. D. BELL & L. TEPPERMAN, THE ROOTS OF DISUNITY, A LOOK AT CANADIAN POLITICAL CULTURE 6 (1979).

3. Constitution Act, 1982.

4. *See generally* Maddox, *A Note on the Meaning of 'Constitution'*, 76 AM. POL. SCI. REV. 805 (1982); Sartori, *Constitutionalism: A Preliminary Discussion*, 56 AM. POL. SCI. REV. 853 (1962).

operate and think politically—are, in the final analysis, established and maintained by constitutional arrangements. These constitutional arrangements determine who may exercise governmental authority, what limits (if any) are placed on this authority, and the kinds of agreements which must exist between government decisionmakers before laws, regulations, and organizations are changed.[5] "The study of politics must, therefore, very largely consist of the examination of the ways in which constitutional and political institutions, and the social forces and movements in a particular society, interact with each other; of the limits upon the extent to which stable constitutional modes of behavior can be developed and maintained; of the effects they can have on moulding behavior."[6] By drawing upon the distinction between individuals engaged in constitutional decisionmaking and individuals pursuing their relative advantages within institutions, modern public choice scholars have been able to resolve several paradoxes inherent in collective or social choices and to provide a better understanding of the strategic opportunities afforded to future individual decisionmakers by different types of decision rules or decisionmaking structures.[7]

Second, the historical context of the Canadian Constitution of 1982 must be defined. If the span of time is very long, it is possible to bias the analysis toward evolutionary and deterministic explanations that are very difficult to confirm or disprove. Almost all the work on Canadian development before World War II is plagued with these difficulties.[8] If the span of time is very short, it is impossible to detect trends. It was not too long ago that distinguished students of Canadian history and politics were dismissing both "provincial rights" as a passing phase in national development and the Supreme Court as a useful agency for conflict management in federal-provincial relations. Beginning the analysis with the constitutional settlement of 1867, known as Confederation, seems appropriate on at least two counts. The span of time involved, being neither very long nor very short, avoids the two extremes. Moreover, Confederation was, *all at once*, the constitutional change that ended the deadlocked union of 1841 and the status quo that triggered (or deadlocked) constitutional changes for more than a century.

Third, the object of this article is not simply to explain why, almost since Con-

---

5. *See, e.g.,* Kiser & Ostrom, *The Three Worlds of Action: A Metatheoretical Synthesis of Institutional Approaches,* in STRATEGIES OF POLITICAL INQUIRY 179-222 (E. Ostrom ed. 1982); Sproule-Jones, *Institutions, Constitutions and Public Policies: A Public Choice Overview,* in CANADIAN PUBLIC POLICY: A COMPARATIVE APPROACH 38 (M. Atkinson & W. Chandler eds. 1983).

6. M. VILE, CONSTITUTIONALISM AND THE SEPARATION OF POWERS 314 (1967).

7. *See, e.g.,* J. BUCHANAN & G. TULLOCK, THE CALCULUS OF CONSENT (1962); V. OSTROM, THE INTELLECTUAL CRISIS IN AMERICAN PUBLIC ADMINISTRATION (2d ed. 1974); Sproule-Jones, *Public Choice Theory and Natural Resources: A Methodological Explication and Critique,* 76 AM. POL. SCI. REV. 790 (1982). Buchanan and Tullock were able to show that it would be a Pareto-efficient move for individuals at the constitutional stage to opt for a set of decision rules that *does not* meet the condition of Pareto efficiency in taking collective actions. Ostrom has advanced the argument regarding democratic administration as an alternative to bureaucratic administration. Sproule-Jones has placed in sharp relief the methodological criterion of logical consistency for the impetus behind the growth of the public choice paradigm at the interface of political science, economics, public administration, and law. J. RAWLS, A THEORY OF JUSTICE (1971) may be viewed as a more philosophic treatise of this paradigm.

8. *See, e.g.,* C. BERGER, THE WRITING OF CANADIAN HISTORY, ASPECTS OF ENGLISH HISTORICAL WRITING: 1900-1970 (1976).

federation, Canadians have been in the midst of some form of constitutional crisis—what historian Goldwin Smith in 1891 characterized as "the Canadian question."[9] It is also to evaluate that chain of crises. As Mark Sproule-Jones suggests, "The challenge is not only to explain who wins and who loses, but to develop new norms to assess the place of the individual in the organization of the state."[10] The principal problem that confronts people in the design and redesign of constitutional arrangements is to determine how values and principles articulated in correlative forms can be expected to yield different results. The attempts of many revolutionaries to create new societies and new social orders suggest that it is entirely possible for fallible human beings to formulate explanations and to use those explanations for undertaking political and social experiments that do not work in anticipated ways. The reiteration of unitary and hierarchical principles of organization led de Tocqueville in his recollections of the 1848 revolt to the conclusion that "in France there is only one thing that we cannot make: a free government; and only one thing that we cannot destroy: centralization."[11] But this is no argument for skepticism, merely one against pretensions to omniscience. By disaggregating the problem of social organization between constitutional choice and governmental decisionmaking, Hobbes was able to anticipate the implications that this distinction has for the way evaluative analysis is conducted. Hobbes observed that when constitutional failures occur "the fault is not in men, as they are the *matter*; but as they are the *makers* and orderers of [commonwealths]."[12]

The remainder of the article will proceed as follows. First, the Canadian political tradition and the making of Confederation is discussed. Then, the factors that led to the remodelling of the 1867 constitutional settlement are traced and examined. This remodelling suggests three broad phases of constitutional change. The first phase, beginning in the 1870's and ending in 1927, led to the transformation of provincial governments from glorified municipalities to agents of constitutional choice placed alongside the federal government. The second phase, beginning in 1927 and ending in the late 1970's, involved efforts by the provincial and federal governments to determine jointly constitutional arrangements for both the full patriation of the BNA Act and the provision of public services. The third phase, beginning in 1980 with the attempt by the federal government to unilaterally patriate the constitution and continuing to date, led to the proclamation of the new Canadian Constitution in 1982. The first and second phases of constitutional change are assessed. Finally, the significance of the Canadian Constitution of 1982 for the resolution of old problems and issues while critical features of Canadian governance remain unchanged is explored.

I

THE CANADIAN POLITICAL TRADITION AND CONFEDERATION

As Frank R. Scott, a leading student in Canadian federalism and for many

---

9. G. SMITH, CANADA AND THE CANADIAN QUESTION (1891).
10. Sproule-Jones, *supra* note 5, at 28.
11. A. DE TOCQUEVILLE, RECOLLECTIONS xviii (J. Mayer & A. Kerr eds. 1971).
12. T. HOBBES, LEVIATHAN 237 (M. Oakeshott ed. 1962)(1st ed. London 1651).

years professor of constitutional law at McGill University, suggests, "Like most
political events in which the chief actors profess high aims, Confederation had its
more materialistic aspects."[13] These ranged from the need to provide a more
secure basis to certain financial and railway interests and the desire to facilitate the
westward expansion of Upper Canada, to the threat to survival engendered by the
vicissitudes of the American Civil War. "Yet even when all allowances necessary
(to take these factors into account) are duly made, the political fact of the 1867
union remains. A new country was created . . . ."[14]

The terms of the 1867 constitutional settlement combined federal and unitary
principles of organization while the settlement itself was created by a statute of the
imperial parliament, the BNA Act.[15] "[T]he Canadian Constitution at the time of
its creation presented to the world of political science a novel combination of constitutional principles—a monarchical federation based upon legislative supremacy
under a single external sovereign."[16] It is probably true that without the
Francophone community, the creation of this new country would have proceeded
along centralized lines—in the words of Sir John A. Macdonald, "one government
and one parliament, legislating for the whole of these peoples . . . the cheapest,
the most vigorous, and the strongest system of government we could [have]
adopt[ed]."[17] As Ormsby suggests, "[T]he survival of French Canada, despite the
deliberate attempt to overwhelm it in a union of the two Canadas, demanded the
emergence of a federal concept."[18]

But Confederation was not a sharp break with the history of British North
America since the conquest of New France in 1763. It took place within the
British Empire and the North American Loyalist tradition to the Crown—with a
particular twist. The mixed and balanced nature of parliamentary sovereignty
that was the hallmark of English constitutional tradition and thought did not have
time to emerge as a practice and doctrine in Canada.[19] The colonial governmental system was replaced in the 1840's by "responsible government," the so-
called Westminster model of government.[20] As a result, choices about basic policies and the availability of different organizational arrangements for pursuing new
developmental opportunities continued to reside with members of the executive in
control of the House of Commons. Research for *The Developing Canadian Commu-*

---

13. Scott, *Political Nationalism and Confederation,* in ESSAYS ON THE CONSTITUTION: ASPECTS OF CANA-
DIAN LAW AND POLITICS 4 (1977).

14. *Id.*

15. *See supra* note 1.

16. Scott, *The Development of Canadian Federalism,* in ESSAYS ON THE CONSTITUTION: ASPECTS OF
CANADIAN LAW AND POLITICS 35 (1971). *See also* Hodgins, *The Plans of Mice and Men,* in FEDERALISM IN
CANADA AND AUSTRALIA—THE EARLY YEARS 3, 13 (1978).

17. John A. Macdonald, *quoted in* THE CONFEDERATION DEBATES IN THE PROVINCES OF CANADA,
1865, THE CARLTON LIBRARY NO. 2, at 40 (P. Waite ed. 1963).

18. W. ORMSBY, THE EMERGENCE OF THE FEDERAL CONCEPT IN CANADA, 1839-1845, at 36 (1969);
see id. at 120-21.

19. M. VILE, *supra* note 6, ch. 8.

20. *See generally* Mallory, *Responsive and Responsible Government,* 12 TRANSACTIONS OF THE ROYAL
SOCIETY OF CANADA, SERIES IV, at 207 (1974); Mallory, *Conflict Management in the Canadian Federal System,*
LAW & CONTEMP. PROBS., Summer 1981, at 231-32.

nity [21] led S.D. Clark to conclude that

> what has been thought of in Canada as an orderly process of adapting political institutions
> to changing circumstances has actually represented an effort to hold in check the kind of
> democratic forces which were growing up from within the Canadian community. Respon-
> sible government developed in reaction rather than in response to the true democratic spirit
> of the Canadian people.[22]

Just as the emergence of the federal concept assured the survival of French
Canada, so the reiteration of responsible government in 1867 assured the continuation of the executive-centered system of government of colonial times.

The fusion of different and antithetical constitutional principles suggests in
part that the Confederation Fathers did not give adequate consideration to the
relationship between the principles and forms used to fashion a united Canada nor
to the consequences that were apt to follow. An examination of some of the fundamental features of the 1867 constitutional settlement suggests why there was little
awareness that the "novel combination of constitutional principles" could give rise
to consequences that radically deviated from expectations.

First, the Canadian constitutional system through sections 40, 90, 91, 92, 93,
95, and 132 of the BNA Act gave the national government formidable power and
influence over provincial governments to place the latter in a colonial subordina-
tion to the national government. Why did Upper Canada Fathers of Confederation like George Brown, who were so pro-Upper Canada localism,[23] choose to
support this system of government?

Christopher Armstrong, in his recent book on Ontario's relations with the federal government between 1867 and 1942, suggests possible reasons.[24] It is true that
Brown spoke for the businessmen of Toronto who saw in a strong central government a prerequisite for economic growth and western expansion, as well as for the
Upper Canada farmers. But Brown was convinced that the strong Ontario representation in the Senate and the House, to which a rising population entitled the
province, and the prospects of sending loyal Reformers to both chambers provided
sufficient safeguards for the vital interests of their locality. Institutions and individuals would see to it that Ontario's local intersts were not neglected. But the
Upper Canada Reformer did not adequately consider that the powers of a prime
minister over his cabinet and party and the convention of collective responsibility
and party solidarity could render Ontario's representation in Parliament almost
nugatory. "As a result, George Brown and his Reform supporters had no qualms
about leading Upper Canadians into a highly centralized union, almost a legislative union of the type desired by John A. Macdonald."[25]

Alternatively, "a Constitution similar in Principle to that of the United
Kingdom"[26] combined with federal arrangements meant, in effect, legislative and

21. S. CLARK, THE DEVELOPING CANADIAN COMMUNITY (2d ed. 1968).
22. *Id.* at 208.
23. *See generally* Jones, *Localism and Federalism in Upper Canada to 1865*, in FEDERALISM IN CANADA AND
AUSTRALIA: THE EARLY YEARS 19 (1978).
24. *See* C. ARMSTRONG, THE POLITICS OF FEDERALISM: ONTARIO'S RELATIONS WITH THE FEDERAL
GOVERNMENT, 1867-1942 (1981).
25. *Id.* at 12.
26. BNA Act, *supra* note 1, preamble.

administrative supremacy at the provincial as well as the federal level of government. But the powers of the federal government over the provinces served to obscure and confound the implications of provincial legislative supremacy for national government dominance. As a result, "no one realized that [this constitution] contained in embryo a principle of the 'co-ordinate sovereignty' of general and local governments, the inevitable result of which would be sovereign provincial powers and the political cry of 'provincial rights.' "[27]

Second, though French-speaking communities existed, and were recognized as such beyond Quebec, French received no written guarantee outside Quebec. The absence of such guarantee has often been used by most Anglophone analysts to support the claim that Confederation did not represent the conscious effectuation of a compact between the English and the French as the two founding peoples of Canada. Some Anglophone analysts have, however, noted that "[t]he argument from evidence (or rather from lack of it) that the fathers [of Confederation] made no open and acknowledged commitment to give legal status to the French language from coast to coast has not and cannot lay to rest the idea of the 'spirit of Confederation' " as an implied bicultural compact.[28] This implied bicultural compact received, it is further alleged, confirmation in the 1870 Manitoba Act[29] and the 1875 Act establishing the Northwest Territories.[30] Unfortunately, the existence of a bicultural compact between the English and the French is difficult to confirm or disprove.[31] Covenantal or providential theology did not even provide the basis for an emergent English Canadian nationalism.[32] Other, less controversial, factors can be adduced to account for the absence of a written guarantee for the French outside Quebec. These are: 1) section 93 of the BNA Act, entitling the national parliament to enact remedial legislation in support of the educational rights of a provincial denominational minority; 2) at the time "minorities were more concerned about potential threats to religious rights than to linguistic rights;"[33] and 3) religious rights were then in part perceived as cultural rights.[34]

Third, the BNA Act contained no formula or machinery for its own amendment. The standard explanation is that by the 1860's the British Parliament "still regarded itself as the supreme constituent power in the British Empire, and it would not lightly have been persuaded to grant a wholly Canadian procedure of

---

27. W. MORTON, THE CRITICAL YEARS, THE UNION OF BRITISH NORTH AMERICA, 1857-1873, at 177 (1964).

28. Heintzman, *The Spirit of Confederation: Professor Creighton, Biculturalism, and the Use of History*, 52 CAN. HIST. REV. 245, 249 (1971); *see also* Stanley, *Act or Pact: Another Look at Confederation*, 1956 REP. ANN. MEETING CAN. HIST. A. 1.

29. The Manitoba Act, 1870, 33 Vict., ch. 3.

30. Act to amend and consolidate the Northwest Territories, 1875, 38 Vict., ch. 49.

31. *See generally* F. Sabetti, Covenant Language in Canada: Continuity and Change in Political Discourse 4-12 (1980) (Workshop on Covenant and Politics Working Paper No. 37, Temple University Center for the Study of Federalism).

32. Wise, *God's Peculiar Peoples,* in THE SHIELD OF ACHILLES: ASPECTS OF CANADA IN THE VICTORIAN AGE 36, 59 (W. Morton ed. 1968).

33. R. COOK, *French Canada and Confederation: The Quest for Equality,* in THE MAPLE LEAF FOREVER, ESSAYS ON NATIONALISM AND POLITICS IN CANADA 68, 72 (1971).

34. *See generally* A. SIEGFRIED, THE RACE QUESTION IN CANADA 19-105 (1906 & photo. reprint 1966).

amendment."[35] The absence of an amending procedure was no problem as long as Confederation worked as its creators intended.

For these reasons, Confederation did not appear at creation to be "the ambiguous bargain" it was later thought to be.[36] Led by the prevailing conception of political rule and biased toward hierarchical arrangements, Confederation Fathers expected the 1867 constitutional settlement to work as it should.

II

THE FIRST PHASE OF CONSTITUTIONAL CHANGE

The rising dominance of provincial legislatures and parliament by disciplined mass parties strengthened simple majority rule and legislative supremacy of the executive. By the 1870's, federal and provincial autonomy joined with federal and provincial supremacy to reveal critical shortcomings in the design of Confederation. Pressures for changing the 1867 constitutional settlement came from provincial governments and interests. In the absence of an amending formula, the compact of provinces emerged as "the political formula"[37] for changing the 1867 constitution. The consequences of the compact of provinces for the Francophone communities outside Quebec led, in turn, to other pressures for change, using "the compact of peoples" as the moral and metaphysical foundations of Confederation.

A.   The Compact of Provinces

Judge T.J.J. Loranger in his *Letters upon the Interpretation of the Federal Constitution Known as the British North America Act*[38] offered one of the most articulate and well-known elaborations of the compact of provinces as the legal basis for constitutional change. Loranger's contention was grounded on the fact that the central government was the creation of the provinces which existed before Confederation; they were certainly not abolished by it. Hence, it followed that "[t]he Confederation of the British Provinces was the result of a compact entered into by the provinces and the Imperial Parliament, which in enacting the British North America Act, simply ratified it."[39]

The compact of provinces as the political formula for constitutional change has continued to receive theoretical exposition among Francophone analysts and politicians.[40] But it was the government of the Province of Ontario under Oliver Mowat that, between 1872 and 1896, took the lead in giving practical expression

---

35.   J. MALLORY, THE STRUCTURE OF CANADIAN GOVERNMENT 24 (1971); *see also* P. GÉRIN-LAJOIE, CONSTITUTIONAL AMENDMENT IN CANADA 33, 37-39 (1950).

36.   *See generally* Mallory, *Confederation: The Ambiguous Bargain,* J. CAN. STUD., July 1977, at 18.

37.   G. MOSCA, THE RULING CLASS 70 (H. Kahn trans. 1st ed. 1939). *See also* Sabetti, *Mosca in Canadian Social Science,* in STUDIES ON THE POLITICAL THOUGHT OF GAETANO MOSCA 165-80 (A. Albertoni ed. 1982).

38.   T. LORANGER, LETTERS UPON THE INTERPRETATION OF THE FEDERAL CONSTITUTION KNOWN AS THE BRITISH NORTH AMERICA ACT (1884).

39.   *Id.* at 61.

40.   *See, e.g.,* R. ARES, DOSSIER SUR LE PACTE FÉDÉRATIF DE 1867, LA CONFÉDÉRATION: PACTE OU LOI? (1967); B. BISSONNETTE, ESSAI SUR LA CONSTITUTION DU CANADA (1963); G. RÉMILLARD, LE FÉDÉRALISME CANADIEN 26, 79-122, 165-66 (1980).

to that formula. The work of Christopher Armstrong[41] provides a careful and updated analysis of Ontario's relations with the federal government and offers plausible answers to several questions.

Why did Ontario, rather than another province, take the lead in altering the constitutional settlement? Why was Ontario's influence in such remodelling so paramount? As Armstrong suggests,

> Mowat recognized that the province occupied a unique place within the Canadian federation, owing to its size, its wealth, and its population. The poorer provinces might look upon federalism as a means of overcoming regional disparities, but Ontario politicians have always valued autonomy more than equality. The province wished to be left alone to develop its bountiful resources, provided that national policies guaranteed it access to markets in other parts of the country. Leaders from Mowat onward, therefore, set out to extend the sway of 'Empire Ontario' and in so doing increase their own power and authority.[42]

The Interprovincial Conference of 1887—hailed by the attending provincial premiers as a new 1864 Quebec conference[43]—suggests the point of convergence between Ontario and the other provinces. Whereas all the other premiers, including Quebec's Honoré Mercier, sought economic assistance from the national government, the Ontario premier sought autonomy, though in the interest of maintaining a united provincial stand he went along with their requests for economic concessions.[44]

What factors account for the pressures to remodel the 1867 constitution? First, there was the propensity of provincial leaders to strengthen and increase their own power and authority. In the case of Ontario, this struggle for provincial executive supremacy focused on specific but also "universalistic" issues: 1) boundary disputes with Manitoba; 2) whether the lieutenant-governor was to continue to be a sort of prefect of the national government in the province or whether he should be simply the representative of the monarch in the province as the governor general was in national affairs; 3) the control of patronage; 4) the exercise of the dominion power of disallowance over the provincial laws that placed the provincial government under the tutelage of the federal government; and 5) the maintenance of clearly defined, or "water-tight," dual sovereignty jurisdiction in several policy areas over time.[45] This struggle for jurisdiction was fueled by two other factors: the ability of businessmen to mobilize government for their own ends—propelling the two levels of government into conflict with one another regardless of ties of party solidarity, and the tendency of provincial bureaucrats to defend their sphere of authority against what they saw as federal interference.[46] Ontario civil servants, fearful that federal government might encroach upon their power to license, regulate, and monitor private companies, "enlisted in [their] battle both their political superiors, who feared the loss of authority and revenues, and certain private interests who, for reasons of their own, preferred to come under [provincial] rather than

---

41. C. ARMSTRONG, *supra* note 24.

42. *Id.* at 4.

43. R. COOK, PROVINCIAL AUTONOMY, MINORITY RIGHTS AND THE COMPACT THEORY, 1867-1921, at 41-42 (Studies of the Royal Commission on Bilingualism and Biculturalism No. 4, 1969).

44. *Id.*; *see also* C. ARMSTRONG, *supra* note 24, at 27-30.

45. *See, e.g.,* C. ARMSTRONG, *supra* note 24, at 14-27.

46. *Id.* at 85.

national jurisdiction."[47] Moreover, the decisions of the Judicial Committee of the Privy Council in favor of provincial jurisdiction and Mowat's political skills and canniness helped to raise the compact of provinces to a first principle of constitutional choice.[48]

The end of the Macdonaldian Constitution[49] was thus evident well before John A. Macdonald died. French-Canadian Prime Minister Wilfrid Laurier expressed the prevailing view in 1907 when he said that "Confederation is a compact, made originally by four provinces, but adhered to by the nine provinces who have entered it, and I submit to the judgment of this House and to the best consideration of its members, that this compact should not be lightly altered."[50] By that time "provincial rights and the compact theory [had] attained a position close to motherhood in the scale of Canadian political values. It would be difficult to find a prominent politician who was not willing to pay at least lip-service to the principle of provincial rights and its theoretical underpinning, the compact theory."[51]

Two qualifications must be noted here. First, "[t]here was not the slightest vestige of a 'compact'" in the Acts of Parliament that created the provinces of Alberta and Saskatchewan in 1905.[52] Second, although Laurier agreed to hold a federal-provincial conference in 1906, to discuss the revision of financial subsidies to the provinces, other constitutional amendments involving the Senate and the House of Commons continued to be made at the behest of the federal parliament alone as late as 1916.[53] And yet, the fact remains that as Canada emerged from World War I "close to an independent state,"[54] it became exceedingly difficult for the federal government to ignore or disregard the constitutional demands of the provinces. As Donald Creighton, a leading historian of Confederation, disparagingly characterized federal-provincial relations of that period:

> The 1920's was a great era for the ventilation of provincial rights. Ontario reaffirmed the Compact Theory of Confederation—the theory, that is, that any change in the British North America Act requires the unanimous consent of the provinces. The west contributed the doctrine that the beneficial control of natural resources is historically and constitutionally vested in the provinces—a doctrine which meant that the Dominion, having assumed control of the lands of the western provinces, should now restore what remained of them with compensation. The Maritimes, on their part, presented the thesis of Maritime Rights, in which it was asserted that the Atlantic provinces had been induced to enter Confederation on the strength of certain representations and promises, which had never been fulfilled

---

47. *Id.*

48. *See* the now classic article: Cairns, *The Judicial Committee and Its Critics,* 4 CAN. J. POL. SCI. 301 (1971).

49. *See generally* Morton, *Confederation, 1870-1896: The End of the Macdonaldian Constitution and the Return to Duality,* J. CAN. STUD., May 1966, at 11, *reprinted in* CANADIAN HISTORY SINCE CONFEDERATION, ESSAYS AND INTERPRETATIONS 189 (B. Hodgins & R. Page eds. 1972).

50. Wilfrid Laurier, *quoted in* CONSTITUTIONAL ISSUES IN CANADA, 1900-1931, at 16 (R. Dawson ed. 1933).

51. R. COOK, *supra* note 43, at 44.

52. A. LOWER, COLONY TO NATION, A HISTORY OF CANADA 432 (4th ed. rev. 1964).

53. G. STEVENSON, UNFULFILLED UNION: CANADIAN FEDERALISM AND NATIONAL UNITY 210 (1979).

54. A. LOWER, *supra* note 52, at 474; *see also* O. SKELTON, THE CANADIAN DOMINION, A CHRONICLE OF OUR NORTHERN NEIGHBOR 271-74 (The Chronicles of America Vol. 49, 1919).

and must now be carried out. Broadly speaking, the Dominion surrendered its position in all these matters.[55]

At the Dominion-Provincial Conference of 1927, the sixtieth year of Confederation, the federal government, through Justice Minister Ernest Lapointe, formally recognized and conceded that the provinces had to be consulted about the formula for amending the BNA Act.[56]

The compact of provinces as a political formula accomplished a veritable constitutional revolution in at least three ways. First, the provincial governments were converted from glorified municipalities into coordinate sovereignties in matters of public policy. Second, the provinces acquired the right to be consulted about, and to share in the choice of, the formula for amending the BNA Act. Finally, and most important for future constitutional changes, these transformations gave provincial governments and the federal government authority to determine or set jointly constitutional *and* institutional arrangements for the provision of public services—in effect, making the process of constitutional decisionmaking virtually indistinguishable from that whereby intergovernmental policy is made in a federal system.

B.   The Compact of Peoples

While the compact of provinces theory of Confederation emerged as an attempt to provide legal support for checking and minimizing the federal government's tutelage over provincial governments and affairs, the compact of peoples theory of Confederation emerged as an attempt to provide moral support for checking and minimizing the consequences of the compact of provinces for the Francophone communities outside Quebec—in essence, to sustain what Mr. Justice Berger of the Supreme Court of British Columbia has recently referred to as "fragile freedoms."[57] The emergence of "provincial rights" gave rise to powerful incentives for a strict application of provincial majority rule and "responsible government"—paralyzing both the BNA Act and the courts as instruments of juridical defense of minority rights. In such circumstances, neither the Monarchy nor its representatives in Canada could act as they were intended to—as a check on the ultimate power of elected politicians and provincial governments. As the settlement of the West transformed the delicate population balance of Canada, Arch-

---

55.   Creighton, *Federal Relations in Canada Since 1914,* in CANADA IN PEACE AND WAR, EIGHT STUDIES IN NATIONAL TRENDS SINCE 1914, at 29, 46-47 (C. Martin ed. 1941).

56.   This is how the Report of Dominion-Provincial Conference, 1927, phrased it:

In order that adequate safeguard should be provided it was proposed that in the event that ordinary amendments being contemplated the provincial legislature should be consulted, and a majority consent of the provinces obtained, while in the event of vital and fundamental amendments being sought involving such questions as provincial rights, the rights of minorities, or rights generally affecting race, language, and creed, the unanimous consent of the provinces should be obtained.

CONSTITUTIONAL ISSUES IN CANADA, 1900-1931, *supra* note 50, at 22. The report, *id.* at 23-24, also makes clear that the Conference divided sharply on the proposal. Some provinces were entirely opposed to the procedure, others either approved of the Minister of Justice's proposal in its entirety or with minor modifications. Although the Dominion government under Mackenzie King decided, as a result, to let the matter drop, the principle that provinces were entitled to be consulted about the formula for amending the BNA remained. *See also* P. GÉRIN-LAJOIE, *supra* note 35, at 228-30.

57.   T. BERGER, FRAGILE FREEDOMS: HUMAN RIGHTS AND DISSENT IN CANADA (1981).

bishop Tache, the ecclesiastical and national leader of the French Canadians in Manitoba, foresaw the outcome: "Number is going to make us weak, . . . and since *under our constitutional system number is power,* we are going to find ourselves at the mercy of those who do not love us."[58]

Beginning in New Brunswick in the 1870's, in Manitoba in the 1880's, then in the newly created provinces of Alberta and Saskatchewan in 1905, and finally in Ontario in 1912 and Eastern Canada as a whole by 1920, the linguistic and educational rights of the various French Catholic communities were challenged by responsible government, with relative immunity.[59] In an effort to minimize or prevent this tyranny of the majority or privileged minority, Francophone lay and religious leaders turned to the compact of peoples as the implied moral and metaphysical base of Confederation.

Henri Bourassa, a Catholic thinker and founder of the influential Montreal newspaper *Le Devoir,* emerged as the most eloquent user of this political formula as a means to insure the survival of Canadian duality.[60] He frequently asserted that mutual respect was "the only ground upon which it is possible for us to meet so as to work out our national problems. There are here neither masters nor valets; there are neither conquerors nor conquered ones; there are two partners whose partnership was entered into upon fair and well-defined lines."[61] He averred that the making of Canada in 1867 represented, in the final analysis, "the free and voluntary association of two peoples, enjoying equal rights in all matters."[62] Bourassa warned that "[i]f the Canadian constitution is to last, if the Canadian Confederation is to be maintained, the narrow attitude towards minorities which increasingly manifests itself in the English provinces must disappear, and we must return to the original spirit of the alliance."[63] The original spirit of Confederation was, for the founder of *Le Devoir,* best exemplified by what was taking place in Quebec:

> The vast majority of its people speak French, but they grant to the English-speaking minority the right to speak English freely, and they accord them in the local administrations, municipal or provincial, those facilities which we ask in federal affairs, not merely as a matter of right—I would never put the question on that narrow basis—but as a matter of

58. R. COOK, CANADA AND THE FRENCH-CANADIAN QUESTION 183 (1966)(emphasis added); *see also* R. BROWN & R. COOK, CANADA 1896-1921, A NATION TRANSFORMED 2-5, 60-73 (1974); Cook, *The Paradox of Quebec,* in ENTERING THE EIGHTIES: CANADA IN CRISIS 49-51 (R. Carty & W. Wards eds. 1981).

59. *See generally* T. BERGER, *supra* note 57, at 19-21, 26-89; R. BROWN & R. COOK, *supra* note 58, at 12-18, 75-78; L. CLARK, THE MANITOBA SCHOOL QUESTION: MAJORITY RULE OR MINORITY RIGHTS? (1968); R. COOK, THE POLITICS OF JOHN W. DAFOE AND THE FREE PRESS 69-70 (1963); A. LOWER, *supra* note 52, at 399-402, 421; W. MORTON, THE KINGDOM OF CANADA 371-72, 380-81, 432-35 (1963); W. MORTON, *supra* note 27, at 259, 269; Staples, *Consociationalism at Provincial Level: The Erosion of Dualism in Manitoba, 1870-1890,* in CONSOCIATIONAL DEMOCRACY, POLITICAL ACCOMMODATION IN SEGMENTED SOCIETIES 288 (K. McRae ed. 1974); M. WADE, THE FRENCH CANADIANS 1760-1967, at 433-40, 537-45 (rev. ed. 1975).

60. The following works provide a helpful introduction to Bourassa's thought and action: Davenport, *Nationalism and Conciliation: The Bourassa-Hertzog Posture,* 44 CAN. HIST. REV. 193 (1963); Laurendeau, *Henri Bourassa,* in OUR LIVING TRADITION, FOURTH SERIES 135-58 (R. McDougall ed. 1962); Levitt, *Henri Bourassa and Modern Industrial Society,* 50 CAN. HIST. REV. 37-50 (1969); O'Connell, *The Ideas of Henri Bourassa,* 19 CAN. J. ECON. & POL. SCI. 361 (1953); 2 M. WADE, *supra* note 59, at 617-65.

61. R. COOK, *supra* note 58, at 107.

62. *Id.* at 51.

63. 2 M. WADE, *supra* note 59, at 618.

common sense, and true Canadian spirit, so as to spread out into every province of Canada the same spirit of Canadian citizenship which exists in Quebec, and should exist everywhere in the Dominion.[64]

The history of Quebec is not free of ethnic prejudice, nativistic discrimination, and religious intolerance—at times even against non-French Catholics. But this history does not greatly undermine Bourassa's compact of peoples. As André Laurendeau, a committed Quebec nationalist and co-chairman of the Royal Commission on Bilinguilism and Biculturalism of the 1960's, noted, "Bourassa defended the rights of his own . . . [, the] French Canadians; but he always chose to do so in terms that were valid for all."[65]

Bourassa's appeal to an implied covenantal base of Confederation was not heeded, however. Protestant and English Canadians, well familiar with covenantal thought, failed to extend that tradition to French Canadians. As Ramsay Cook explained in *Provincial Autonomy, Minority Rights and the Compact Theory, 1867-1921,*[66] Bourassa's compact of peoples formula for constitutional choice

> had on its side none of the powerful influences which had played so large a part in gaining wide acceptace for the theory of the compact of provinces. No political party adopted it as part of its platform . . . . Nor did the theory win the whole-hearted approval of powerful provincial governments; indeed to the extent that it implied a limitation on provincial powers, it went against the views of most of the provinces. Not even the province of Quebec . . . adopted the theory in any consistent fashion. Finally, the compact of [peoples], unlike the theory of the compact of provinces, won no support from the Judicial Committee of the Privy Council . . . . In light of these observations, it is not surprising that the concept of the cultural compact of Confederation remained the possession of only a small minority of Canadians.[67]

What became known as "the Anglo-Saxon Kulturkampf" followed, sweeping away French-language rights outside Quebec[68]—in effect, lending credence to de Tocqueville's observation that "the extension of judicial power in the political world ought . . . to be in the exact ratio of the extension of elective power. If these two institutions do not go hand-in-hand, the state must fall into anarchy or into servitude."[69]

It has been suggested that French Canadians then had "the proof that the English Canadians—at least a noisy and powerful group among them—did not accept French Canada as an equal partner."[70] Yet, at least until World War II, most French-Canadian nationalists clung to the hope that some day they would receive equitable treatment outside Quebec.[71] It is fair to recall another item of "proof:" Quebec's failure to adopt the compact of peoples in any consistent fashion gave English Canadians "proof" that the Quebec governing class was like

64. *Quoted in* R. COOK, *supra* note 58, at 39.
65. Laurendeau, *supra* note 60, at 135, 145.
66. R. COOK, *supra* note 43.
67. *Id.* at 63.
68. *See supra* note 59.
69. 1 A. DE TOCQUEVILLE, DEMOCRACY IN AMERICA 77 (P. Bradley ed. New York 1954)(1st ed. Paris 1835).
70. Brunet, *The French Canadians' Search for a Fatherland,* in NATIONALISM IN CANADA 47, 55 (P. Russell ed. 1966).
71. *See* ROYAL COMMISSION OF INQUIRY ON CONSTITUTIONAL PROBLEMS, THE TREMBLAY REPORT (D. Kwavnick ed. 1973).

that of all other provinces.[72] Against this backdrop of Confederation transformed, the second phase of constitutional change occurred.

III

THE SECOND PHASE OF CONSTITUTIONAL CHANGE

The "agreement" reached at the 1927 federal-provincial conference[73] ended the first phase of constitutional change. But it also virtually insured that no area of public economy could not henceforth be potentially subject to "federal-provincial diplomacy"[74] and be dealt with on the basis of unanimous consent. As a result, the search for an amending formula for the constitution that could at the same time appropriately locate and fix "power somewhere"[75] in the face of changing public economies and changing political contingencies proved to be exceedingly difficult and costly in time and effort.

A. Attempts to Amend the Constitution

The 1927 federal-provincial conference was followed by others in 1931, 1933, 1934, 1935, 1936, 1941, 1945, 1950, 1955, and 1957, to reach an unprecedented number, activity, and scope in the 1960's and 1970's. The "category" approach to constitutional amendments adopted in 1927[76] was refined in the 1935-36 negotiations. Constitutional provisions were divided into four categories: 1) those affecting the Dominion alone would be amended by Parliament; 2) those affecting the Dominion and some but not all the provinces would be amended by the consent of the parties involved; 3) those affecting fundamental rights such as civil law in Quebec and linguistic and educational provisions would require the unanimous consent of Parliament and all the provincial legislatures; and 4) all other matters would need the approval of six of the nine provinces, and those six must contain fifty-five percent of the total population.[77] This category approach became the basis of all subsequent federal-provicial negotiations and was further refined between 1960 and 1966 by what became known as the Fulton-Favreau Formula.[78]

---

72. *See generally* G. GLAZEBROOK, A HISTORY OF CANADIAN POLITICAL THOUGHT 328 (1966).

73. *See supra* note 56.

74. *See generally* R. SIMEON, FEDERAL-PROVINCIAL DIPLOMACY: THE MAKING OF RECENT POLICY IN CANADA (1972).

75. For evidence of this tradition of thought and action among students and practitioners of Canadian politics see, e.g., Cairns, *Alternative Styles in the Study of Canadian Politics,* 7 CAN. J. POL. SCI. 101 (1974); Sproule-Jones, *An Analysis of Canadian Federalism,* PUBLIUS 110-13 (1974); Sabetti, *Reflections on Canadian Urban Governance Research,* 8 COMP. URB. RESEARCH 87-112 (1981).

76. The standard account for this history is P. GÉRIN-LAJOIE, *supra* note 35, at 234-49; *see also* C. ARMSTRONG, *supra* note 24, at 199-206.

77. C. ARMSTRONG, *supra* note 24, at 205-06.

78. The post-World War II search for an amending formula that culminated in the Fulton-Favreau Formula is aptly traced in J. MALLORY, THE STRUCTURE OF CANADIAN GOVERNMENT 379-86 (1971). Mallory described the Fulton-Favreau Formula in the following terms: the formula "dealt with the problem of section 91(1) of the BNA Act (the 1949 amending formula) by revising it and incorporating it, together with a revised form of the provincial amending power in section 92(1), into the proposed amending procedure. The power of Parliament to amend the constitution was more specifically defined as applying to 'the Constitution of Canada in relation to the executive Government of Canada and the Senate and the House of Commons.'" *Id.* at 384. Some additions were also inserted to protect provincial representation in the Senate and in the House of Commons.

The category approach failed to reform the constitution but it did produce ad hoc financial arrangements for unemployment and relief in the Depression[79] and, by 1940, a national unemployment insurance plan.[80] After the war, the same approach served to introduce considerable flexibility and adjustment in intergovernmental relations concerned with the provision of public services.[81] The earlier ad hoc arrangements for employment and relief grew into conditional and unconditional grants to provinces. This federal spending, together with the delegation of federal powers to provincial agencies and the creation of ad hoc or standing intergovernmental committees, created the basis of what, particularly under the Pearson government, became known as "cooperative federalism."[82] This cooperative federalism overshadowed the constitutional impasse but made it more difficult to overcome, because the federal government, in its desire to accommodate the Quebec government under Jean Lasage, acted as if almost everything was negotiable—even what seemed, to some, essential to the effective functioning of Canadian federalism. Little wonder, then, that by the time the centennial of Confederation approached there was in many quarters considerable skepticism about the very credentials of Canadian constitutional arrangements. As one observer noted, "By . . . 1966, the Canadian federal system had reached one of the most severe crises in its history."[83]

The failure of the piecemeal approach to constitutional change led in the late 1960's to a more comprehensive approach under the new Liberal and more centralist Prime Minister, Pierre Elliot Trudeau, whose task was in turn made easier by successive changes in the Quebec premiership after Lesage—Daniel Johnson, Jean-Jacques Bertrand, and Robert Bourassa. This approach involved the entrenchment of official language rights, a bill of rights, and equalization payments to provinces. This comprehensive approach helped to produce what became known as the Victoria Charter Formula between 1968 and 1971.[84] But its very comprehensiveness could not obscure the fact that it ignored or glossed over division of power questions so crucial to Quebec. As the then Quebec Deputy Minister of Intergovernmental Affairs later explained Quebec's veto: "The charter completely missed the real Canadian problem, that of the place of Quebec and the Quebec nation in Canada. What is more, Quebec's acceptance would have

---

79. C. ARMSTRONG, *supra* note 24, at 148-59.

80. *Id.* at 209-12, 219-20.

81. *E.g.,* D. SMILEY, CONSTITUTIONAL ADAPTATION AND CANADIAN FEDERALISM SINCE 1945 (1970).

82. Cooperative federalism is defined in the Canadian context as a series of pragmatic and piecemeal responses by the federal and provincial governments to the provision of public services involving mutual interdependence. *See generally* D. SMILEY, *supra* note 81, at 111-28.

83. D. SMILEY, THE CANADIAN POLITICAL NATIONALITY 84 (1967).

84. In addition to the points mentioned in the text, the Victoria Charter had a procedure whereby the most important parts of the Canadian Constitution could be amended by resolution of the Senate and House of Commons and of at least a majority of the provinces which included: (1) each province with a population of at least 25% of the population of Canada (in effect, Ontario and Quebec); (2) at least two of the Atlantic provinces; and (3) at least two of the western provinces having together at least half of the population of all western provinces. In brief, the procedure of the Victoria Charter diverged from both existing practice and the Fulton-Favreau Formula by *not* requiring unanimous provincial consent for important amendments.

amounted to a denial of the problem's very existence."[85] Thus the Victoria Charter failed to receive the needed consensus to make it operational, closing yet another round of constitutional negotiations.

The end of the Trudeau minority government in 1974 was accompanied by renewed intergovernmental efforts to patriate and amend the BNA Act, lasting until the very end of the 1970's. But the flurry of activities that accompanied the accession to power of the *independentiste* Parti-Québécois in 1976,[86] the rise of the "New West" in Alberta,[87] the success of the Progressive Conservative party defeat of the Liberal party in the 1979 federal elections, and the return to power of the Liberal party under Trudeau in the January 1980 federal elections[88] could neither lessen nor overcome the constitutional stalemate. Conjectures that Canada would be entering the eighties in crisis[89] did not seem too inappropriate or exaggerated.

Thus the second phase of constitutional change was plagued by insurmountable difficulties in amending and patriating the constitution and by intergovernmental instability in the provision of public services. Little purpose will be served here by tracing *ad plenum* the tangled federal-provincial diplomacy that shaped and accompanied constitutional negotiations and intergovernmental relations between 1927 and 1980 and the many-colored reports of government commissions, task forces, and political parties that the not-so-successful federal-provincial diplomacy generated.[90] Instead, the answers to the following set of questions will be attempted: Why did the great quantity of energy devoted to constitutional decisionmaking over the course of about fifty years produce minimal results? What factors account for the difficulties and deadlocks in constitutional negotiations? What reasons best explain the instability of intergovernmental arrangements for the provision of public services?

B.   Sources of Instability and Stalemate

Several plausible factors causing the deadlock in constitutional negotiations

---

85.   C. MORIN, QUEBEC VERSUS OTTAWA: THE STRUGGLE FOR SELF-GOVERNMENT 1960-72, at 69 (1976). *See also* E. McWHINNEY, QUEBEC AND THE CONSTITUTION 1960-1978, at 24-26 (1979).

86.   As the independentist Quebec government began preparations for how Quebec could peacefully become a sovereign nation-state, in association with or independent from Canada, the Trudeau government in 1977 established a Task Force on Canadian Unity headed by a former Liberal federal cabinet minister from Quebec and a former premier of Ontario, while the Quebec provincial liberals eventually chose Claude Ryan, a much respected and highly regarded editor for *Le Devoir,* to lead them and, in effect, to thwart separatist designs. Academicians also joined in these events by providing analyses and proposals such as those in MUST CANADA FAIL? (R. Simeon ed. 1977).

87.   *See generally* Pratt, *The State and Province-Building: Alberta's Development Strategy,* in THE CANADIAN STATE: POLITICAL ECONOMY AND POLITICAL POWER 133-64 (L. Panitch ed. 1977).

88.   *See generally* CANADA AT THE POLLS, 1979 AND 1980, A STUDY OF THE GENERAL ELECTIONS (H. Penniman ed. 1981).

89.   *See* ENTERING THE EIGHTIES: CANADA IN CRISIS (R. Carty & W. Wards eds. 1981).

90.   In addition to R. SIMEON, *supra* note 74, *see also* TASK FORCE ON CANADIAN UNITY, A FUTURE TOGETHER (3 vols. 1979); blue colored GOVERNMENT OF QUEBEC, QUEBEC—CANADA: A NEW DEAL: THE QUEBEC GOVERNMENT PROPOSAL FOR A NEW PARTNERSHIP BETWEEN EQUALS: SOVEREIGNTY ASSOCIATION (1979); Smiley, The Association Dimension of Sovereignty-Association: A Response to the Quebec White Paper (Discussion Paper No. 8 of the Institute of Intergovernmental Relations, Queen's University, Kingston, Ontario, 1980); and CONSTITUTIONAL COMMITTEE OF THE QUEBEC LIBERAL PARTY, A NEW CANADIAN FEDERATION (1980).

loom large. These factors can be divided into two interrelated but analytically distinct categories: extrinsic reasons which are outside of constitutional arrangements proper, and intrinsic reasons which are due to defects or shortcomings in constitutional arrangements themselves. The principal extrinsic factors were identified by the Task Force on Canadian Unity with the following statement and prognostication: "Duality and regionalism lie at the heart of the Confederation crisis [and] . . . any general reform effort, however well intended, which fails to enhance duality or which offends the principle of regionalism is unlikely to increase harmony and unity in Canada."[91] The principal intrinsic factor was suggested by Mark Sproule-Jones's question: "What consequences are likely to ensue when constitutional arrangements are jointly determined by an exclusive group of eleven governments, governments that individually act as 'teams' . . . ?"[92] Each of these three factors is considered below.

1. *Canadian Duality.* Canadian duality is a summary phrase which stands for mutually proper, fair, and just political relationships between English-speaking and French-speaking Canadians. The Anglo-Saxon *Kulturkampf* against the French and the rejection of the compact of peoples during the first phase of constitutional change seriously undermined Canadian duality, with little threat to the territorial integrity of Canada. But the French *Kulturkampf* for survival since then has posed and continues to pose a serious threat to the territorial integrity of Canada.

It has often been asserted that "[t]he refusal of the majority in English-speaking Canada to uphold the linguistic rights and therefore the cultural integrity of the minority led that minority to assert that it should have, indisputably and where it could exercise it, the political power necessary to insure its survival. If [Georges Etienne] Cartier became [Henri] Bourassa, Bourassa, owing in part to the fate of the bicultural idea in English Canada, became Michel Brunet."[93] The identification by French Canadian nationalists of their country with the province of Quebec alone contributed, no doubt, to what Michel Brunet (a Quebec nationalist historian) called the end of the French Canadians' long search for a fatherland.[94] But the end of this long search was empirically grounded and manifested in the social, economic, and political transformations that reached unprecedented levels with the end of the Duplessis regime in 1959.[95]

The societal transformations were encouraged, sustained, and given purpose by the bureaucratic and political imperatives of provincial state building and omnicompetence.[96] These transformations not only led to a new "language ques-

91. 1 TASK FORCE ON CANADIAN UNITY, A FUTURE TOGETHER 36 (1979).
92. Sproule-Jones, *supra* note 75, at 109, 123; *see also* Sproule-Jones, Public Choice and Federalism in Australia and Canada (Canberra Center for Research on Federal Financial Relations Research Monograph No. 11, 1975)
93. Smith, *Metaphor and Nationality in North America,* 51 CAN. HIST. REV. 247, 269 (1970).
94. Brunet, *supra* note 70, at 60.
95. *E.g.,* C. BLACK, DUPLESSIS (1977); K. MCROBERTS & D. POSGATE, QUEBEC: SOCIAL CHANGE AND POLITICAL CRISIS (1976).
96. Bolduc & Gow, *Environment and Administration: Quebec, 1867-1980,* in THE ADMINISTRATIVE STATE IN CANADA 31, 46-56 (O. Dwivedi ed. 1982); *see also* K. MCROBERTS & D. POSGATE, *supra* note 95, at 96-129.

tion" in Quebec itself that revealed fully the precarious freedoms of access to equal public services enjoyed by Canadians of non-French and non-English origin.[97] But they also created an almost unprecedented case for "Quebec versus Ottawa"[98] that neither the federal nor the other provincial ruling classes of Canada could ignore or deny without danger. In the course of the 1960's and 1970's, there thus developed a situation whereby, as the ten governments tried to accommodate Quebec's struggle for jurisdiction in several policy areas, the Quebec government, under different parties and leaders, came to view the very patriation and reform of the Canadian Constitution as potential checks on Quebec's own "unfinished revolution."[99] The decisional rules that applied to federal-provincial negotiations ultimately served to insure that the Fulton-Favreau and the Victoria Charter formulae would remain just that. The defeat of the Parti Québécois Proposal of a sovereignty-association between Quebec and Canada in the 1980 May referendum could neither remove Canadian duality from question nor finish "Quebec's unfinished revolution."

2. *Regionalism.* It is generally recognized that regionalism was and has been one of the most consistent and hardy factors for "limited identities"[100] in Canada since Confederation. Although the roots and strength of regionalism are difficult to measure and although regional interests may not be the same as provincial government interests,[101] provincial governments have historically been important agencies for regional movements, demands, and protests.

As we have already seen, the compact of provinces was used as a political formula to justify and effect a veritable revolution in federal-provincial relations. As a consequence, even the Depression failed to persuade many provincial leaders that the problem of the modern, industrial state could be met only through the centralization of power in Ottawa.[102] More recently, interprovincial conferences have become important forums for interprovincial bargaining and for developing joint positions to take to Ottawa.[103] The growth of what has been called "prairie capitalism"[104] is one of the most powerful expressions of regionalism since World War II. The defeat of the Social Credit government of Alberta in 1971 by the Progressive Conservative Party brought to an end a long period of government conservatism and began a new era of "interventionist, 'positive' government . . . employed to nurture the development, and to defend the province-building interests, of an ascendant class of indigenous business entrepreneurs, urban profes-

97. Some of the consequences of the French-language legislation (Bills 22 and 101) are traced and discussed throughout S. ARNOPOULOS & D. CLIFT, THE ENGLISH FACT IN QUEBEC (1980).

98. *See generally* C. MORIN, *supra* note 85.

99. *See generally* L. DION, QUEBEC: THE UNFINISHED REVOLUTION (T. Romer trans. 1976); *see also* the article by Daniel Latouche in this issue of LAW & CONTEMP. PROBS.

100. Careless, *"Limited Identities" in Canada,* 50 CAN. HIST. REV. 1 (1969).

101. Simeon, *Intergovernmental Relations and the Challenges to Canadian Federalism*, 23 CAN. PUB. AD. 14, 26 (1980).

102. *See generally* J. MALLORY, SOCIAL CREDIT AND THE FEDERAL POWER IN CANADA (1st ed. 1954).

103. *See* Leach, *Interprovincial Co-operation: Neglected Aspect of Canadian Federalism*, 2 CAN. PUB. AD. 83 (1959); Simeon, *supra* note 101, at 21.

104. *See* J. RICHARDS & L. PRATT, PRAIRIE CAPITALISM: POWER AND INFLUENCE IN THE NEW WEST (1979).

sionals, and state adminstrators."[105] As a result, the post-Victoria rounds of federal-provincial negotiations were characterized by a considerable struggle for jurisdiction over culture, communications, and the federal spending power, as well as natural resources. Alberta and Quebec were not the only provinces to engage in this struggle for jurisdiction with Ottawa.[106]

The growth of regionalism necessarily implied an increasing interdependence and sharing of responsibilities with the federal government. But federal-provincial negotiations were structured so as to hinder rather than facilitate federal-provincial interdependence and partnership.

3. *Constitutional Arrangements as Executive-Determined Facilities.* Standard accounts of Canadian federal-provincial instability and constitutional stalemate start with the assumption that constitutional arrangements are *as a rule* set jointly by the executive-dominated governments acting individually as constitutional decisionmakers. As the writings of Alan Cairns[107] indicate, the shortcoming in this approach is to take as given what should be taken as problematic. The chief value of Sproule-Jones's analysis of Canadian federalism[108] consists in *reversing* the order by considering what consequences are likely to ensue when constitutional arrangements are jointly determined by an exclusive group of eleven governments requiring unanimous consent.

First, the provincial and federal governments of Canada resisted all attempts to include other public or private persons from sharing in the setting up of constitutional arrangements. Exclusion was rigidly maintained. The controversy surrounding the Statute of Westminster[109] in 1930-1931 is a case in point. By removing all constitutional limitations on the sovereignty of the British Dominions, the Statute of Westminster appeared, in effect, to transfer the power to amend the BNA Act from the British Parliament to the parliament of Canada without necessarily the consent of provincial legislators. Provincial governments successfully pressured the national government to secure a clause in the Statute of Westminster exempting the BNA Act from the effect of the Statute and thereby maintaining their role as agents of constitutional choice.[110] Another example is furnished by the Royal Commission on Dominion-Provincial Relations, the Rowell-Sirois Commission, mandated by the federal government in 1937 to examine the economic and financial basis of Confederation, the distribution of legislative responsibility, and the financial relations between governments.[111] For their centralist bias on many policy issues, members of the commission were hailed in some quarters as "the new Fathers of Confederation"[112] but this view was stren-

---

105. Pratt, *supra* note 87, at 133.
106. *See* J. MEEKINSON, CANADIAN FEDERALISM: MYTH OR REALITY 140-87, 280-365 (3d ed. 1977).
107. *See* Cairns, *The Other Crisis of Canadian Federalism*, 22 CAN. PUB. AD. 175-95 (1979); Cairns, *The Governments and Societies of Canadian Federalism,* 10 CAN. J. POL. SCI. 695-726 (1977).
108. *See* M. SPROULE-JONES, *supra* note 92; Sproule-Jones, *supra* note 75, at 109.
109. The Statute of Westminster, 1931, 22 Geo. 5, ch. 4.
110. *See* C. ARMSTRONG, *supra* note 24, at 146-48.
111. THE ROWELL-SIROIS REPORT, THE CARLETON LIBRARY NO. 5 (D. Smiley ed. 1963)(an abridgment of Book 1 of the Royal Commission Report on Dominion-Provincial Relations, 1940).
112. *See, e.g.,* Creighton, *supra* note 55, at 56. *See also* Alway, *Hepburn, King, and the Rowell-Sirois Commission,* 48 CAN. HIST. REV. 113 (1967). Smiley, *The Rowell-Sirois Report, Provincial Autonomy, and Post-War*

uously opposed in words and deeds by several provincial premiers. More recently, attempts to entrench a bill or charter of human rights by Prime Minister Diefenbaker in the late fifties and by Trudeau in the late sixties and seventies failed to secure unanimous consent because such charters transferred, or appeared to transfer, a substantial amount of authority from the legislatures to the courts.[113]

A second consequence of the joint supply of constitutional arrangements by the exclusive club of eleven governments was put in this way by one observer: "[R]edrafting [the constitution] is hard enough in Canada. It becomes immensely more complicated when too many people want to use the occasion to solve all the country's political problems at the same time—as well as design new rules for determining the framework for tackling these very problems."[114] Several other consequences occurred when the governments attempted formal or tacit coordinated behavior. Each government had an incentive to be the sole supplier (i.e., exclude each other from the provision) of public services within its jurisdiction, while enlisting the other governments in sharing the costs of programs. At the same time, each government had an incentive to prevent another from raiding its treasury to provide services that are nonconsumable within its own jurisdiction. As a result, each government had to ensure that new or extended programs undertaken by other governments met with its own willing consent. There must either have been unanimous approval or no coordinated action was viable.[115]

Sproule-Jones noted three other consequences that flowed from the logic requiring unanimous consent for federal-provincial initiatives. As the history of the different patriation formulae between 1935 and 1979 suggests, one consequence of unanimous consent was to grant any holdout extraordinary bargaining power.[116] As a condition of giving its consent, any holdout government was able to demand a much larger than proportionate share of its payoffs from the group activity. Quebec has not been the only government to engage in frequent holdout tactics,[117] although its reasons differ from those of the other provinces. The result in the post-World War II period was a series of complex and evolving fiscal arrangements and equalization schemes, as well as the establishment of the "welfare-state"—whose eventual modifications, subject as they were to other rounds of bargaining costs, plus any side payments to take account of holdout strategies of one or more governments, carried with them their own source of instability.[118]

Another consequence was the prevalence of logrolling.[119] Governments were willing to give consent on certain matters strongly preferred by other governments, in exchange for their support on matters which the first government preferred

Canadian Federalism, 28 CAN. J. ECON. POL. SCI. 54 (1962), notes correctly that "[i]n spite of the scope and quality of the commission's work, its analysis of federal-provincial relations has had surprisingly little influence on the direction that the theory and practice of Canadian federalism have taken since 1945."

   113. Sproule-Jones, *supra* note 75, at 124. See Laskin, *An Inquiry into the Diefenbaker Bill of Rights*, 37 CAN. B. REV. 77 (1959).

   114. Black, *Federal-Provincial Conferences and Constitutional Change*, 78 QUEEN'S Q. 298, 298 (1971).

   115. Sproule-Jones, *supra* note 75, at 124-25.

   116. *Id.* at 125.

   117. *Id. See also* C. MORIN, *supra* note 85, at 69 and E. MCWHINNEY, *supra* note 85, at 24-26.

   118. Sproule-Jones, *supra* note 75, at 125, and nn. 54, 55 & 56 cited therein.

   119. *Id.* at 126.

intensely. The Canada Pension Plan of 1966 and the different opting-out procedures were some of the most evident results.[120]

The final consequence of the unanimous consent procedure is the bargaining
costs in time and effort that each government was forced to bear over the course of
fifty or more years.[121] The institutionalized machinery of federal-provincial relations become more and more complicated by the 1960's.[122] Formal meetings, conferences, and committee meetings among civil servants and occasionally ministers
of the eleven governments became frequent occurrences—increasing the bargaining costs. Sproule-Jones suggested that another reason for the increase in bargaining costs was that each government had an incentive to monitor the
operations and initiatives of the other governments, for fear of being left out from
future deliberations.[123] The growth of provincial intergovernmental relations min-
istries was, no doubt, partly due to this. The outcome was an increased size of the
bargaining costs encountered by each government as time progressed.

As a result, the joint supply of constitutional arrangements by the exclusive
groups of governments led to the rigid exclusion of other individuals or collective
bodies from sharing in the setting of constitutional arrangements. It led to a
variety of ways in which public goods and services were delivered and amending
formulae conceptualized. The post-fifties period was characterized by an une-
qualed level of federal-provincial negotiations and relations. But the dictates of
federal and provincial bargaining, together with the pressures of Quebec nationalism and regionalism more generally, insured that none of the ways in which
collective services were delivered and constitutional changes proposed would
remain stable or secure for too long. Minimal results in constitutional reform and
inherent instability in intergovernmental relations have been the signal features of
some fifty years of attempted constitutional change in Canada.

IV

IMPLICATIONS FOR THE THIRD PHASE OF CONSTITUTIONAL CHANGE

The making of Canada was one of the most notable achievements in the nineteenth century. Unlike some other countries, Canada was established by peaceful
means within an international *imperium*. A new political economy experiment was
created by fusing together two seemingly antithetical principles of organization:
federalism and responsible government. The novelty of this experiment attracted
the attention of an Italian publicist, Enea Cavalieri,[124] who in 1876 travelled
throughout most of what was then Canada to see how the new social, economic,
and political order worked. He remarked in his travel notes that all the reading he

---

120. *Id.*
121. *Id.*
122. *Id.*
123. *Id.*
124.   Enea Cavalieri is perhaps best known for the work he did with L. Franchetti and Sidney Sonnino
on Sicilian rural conditions in 1876. In fact he left Sicily to visit Canada and the United States. His book
on North America is entitled IN GIRO DEL MONDO: OSSERVAZIONI ED APPUNTI (1880) and is divided into
two parts: Part I, consisting of 17 chapters, deals with Canada; Part II, consisting of 20 chapters, deals with
the United States.

had done on North America had not prepared him for what he found: a union of various colonies and peoples in a single and great Dominion. Europe paid little attention to this new country, but, suggested Cavalieri, its constitutional development, public economy, and law were worth knowing and studying. Canadian Confederation signalled the beginning of a new political economy equilibrium in North America and presaged the possibility of novel solutions to contemporary problems in Europe.[125]

Flaws in its original creation made Canada highly unstable in some important respects. Yet, the flaws that made Confederation highly unstable also served to insure its very existence. Such was the view of Andrew Pattullo, an Ontario journalist and legislator, as he praised Mowat's leadership in pressing for constitutional change between 1872 and 1896.[126] Contemporary historians of Canadian federalism tend to side with Pattullo. They suggest that previous generations of historians and political scientists have dealt too harshly with the compact of provinces theory of Confederation and with premiers such as Ontario's Mitchell Hepburn.[127] But, as we have hinted in the discussion of the compact of peoples and the second phase of constitutional change, the benefits from the first phase of constitutional change are not easy to reckon.

Trudeau's last attempt to patriate and amend the BNA Act succeeded in overcoming the stalemate, in part because it began unilaterally and in part because it was achieved without unanimous consent (Quebec dissenting). To be sure, there had been threats of unilateral action before by Trudeau and other prime ministers. What factors account for Trudeau's urgency to press ahead? Why did he succeed when all others failed?[128] No doubt, these are features of the Trudeau partriation package that will receive considerable scholarly attention in the future—as they should. But other features of Trudeau's patriation package appear equally worthy of study.

The proclamation of the Canadian Constitution of 1982 ends a long phase of crisis, stalemate, and minimal results and begins a phase of constitutional decision-making that seems to bear little relationship to the past. What implications, if any, do the previous phases of constitutional change have for the new one?

Canadian dualism or the place of Quebec in Confederation will continue to tax the new constitutional arrangements as will the forces of regionalism or provincial state building. More fundamentally, as long as federal and provincial executives continue to jointly determine constitutional arrangements, and as long as the present practice of parliamentary government continues, the third phase of constitutional change will be characterized by considerable institutional weakness and failure. Robin W. Boadway and Kenneth H. Norrie in their recent analysis of "Constitutional Reform Canadian-Style" warned of somewhat similar consequences:

---

125. *Id.* at 196-97.

126. *See* C. ARMSTRONG, *supra* note 24, at 32.

127. *Id. See also* Mallory, *Style and Fashion: A Note on Alternative Styles in Canadian Political Science,* 7 CAN. J. POL. 129 (1974).

128. D. SMILEY, CANADA IN QUESTION: FEDERALISM IN THE EIGHTIES 88 (3d ed. 1980).

[B]y turning the task over to the first ministers we are *necessarily* severely restricting the kind of constitutional change we might expect. We are guaranteeing that the process will be one of strategic bargaining by eleven self-interested participants. There will be no opportunity to present and discuss alternative constitutional arrangements that might more effectively provide public goods to the population. This is especially true of proposals that would significantly alter the authority of both existing levels of government. Not only does the process itself preclude other options, however, but it also seems slated to deliver us a result that might actually be undesirable.[129]

The Charter in the 1982 Constitution may, however, open up the process of participation in constitutional change through citizen litigation which may, in turn, enhance the role of the courts in conflict management.[130] This means that the Charter could become an important source of instability and crisis for "parliamentary majoritarian democracy" *à la* McRuer Report[131] in, and outside of, Ontario.

There is no interest in straitjacketing, albeit if only with the power of words, Canadian constitutional development. As Milovan Djilas has observed, "History does not exactly abound with instances of thinkers' predictions having come true, least of all those relating to social patterns and people's attitudes and ways of life."[132] The adaptive potential of the Canadian people encourages "a bias for hope."[133] And yet, the preceding analysis suggests that there is little or no prospect for changing the executive-centered system of government in Canada. At the same time, knowledge of the basic rules that are applicable to the governance of Canadian society may be lost as people become spectators of federal-provincial conflict and state pageantry. A situation may develop whereby as Canadians become increasingly prone to speak the language of doubt when describing their society,[134] they will be unable to conceptualize political solutions appropriate to their exigencies. But, it is precisely here that political scientists can make a contribution. Their task is not to tend to the system, but rather to assess its performance.[135] For this reason there is much to learn or unlearn from the study of the historical context of the Constitution of 1982. A new understanding of Canadian Federalism is needed before contemporary problems can be resolved.

---

129.   R. Boadway & K. Norrie, *Constitutional Reform Canadian-Style: An Economic Perspective,* 6 CAN. PUB. POL'Y 492, 494 (1980).

130.   *See generally* Mallory, *Conflict Management in the Canadian Federal System,* LAW & CONTEMP. PROBS., Summer 1981, at 231. *See also* T. BERGER, *supra* note 57, at 258, 260-262.

131.   *See generally* Smiley, *The McRuer Report: Parliamentary Majoritarian Democracy and Human Rights,* J. CAN. STUD., July 1970, at 3.

132.   M. DJILAS, THE UNPERFECT SOCIETY 150 (1969).

133.   A. HIRSCHMAN, A BIAS FOR HOPE (1971)(to borrow a phrase from another context).

134.   D. BELL & L. TEPPERMAN, *supra* note 2, at 6. The authors noted:

A group of Western and Maritime Canadian intellectuals brooded over the "burden of unity"; at the same time, their colleagues from Ontario asked the ominous question "Must Canada fail?" A philosopher has offered a "lament" for Canada, an economist has documented its "silent surrender," and a political scientist has called into "question" Canada's continued existence. According to other writers, Canada is a "nation unaware" of its past and uncertain of its future. Our legendary capacity for "survival" stands threatened by internal strains, "divided loyalties" and foreign "dominance."

Id. Bell and Tepperman themselves contributed to this list by entitling their book THE ROOTS OF DISUNITY.

135.   For a beginning in this direction see especially Cairns, *supra* note 75, and Sproule-Jones, *supra* notes 5, 75, and 92.

COMPARATIVE INSIGHTS INTO CONSTITUTIONAL HISTORY: CANADA, THE CRITICAL YEARS

BACKGROUND OF CANADIAN CONSTITUTIONALISM

When Her Majesty Queen Elizabeth II presented the Canada Act[1] to the people of Canada, they alternately hailed the process as the patriation of the existing British North America Act (hereinafter "BNA Act") and the formation of a new Canadian Constitution. Actually it is both, because the Canada Act significantly modifies the BNA Act and very nearly establishes an entirely new constitutional order. The Canada Act will not slow the debate on the efficacy or efficiency of Canadian federalism, nor will concerns for protecting the language and cultural heritage of Quebec be diminished in the minds of the Parti Québécois. The promulgation of the Canada Act, however, with its entrenched Charter of Rights and language guarantee, will significantly alter the terms of the debate about Canadian federalism and its French connection. Now the debate will take place under the aegis of a document which Canadians hope will be a real national constitution, that is, a constitution that embodies the legitimizing First Principle of national sovereignty.

Canadians have had something they call a national constitution since the enactment of the BNA Act by the British Parliament in 1867. By American standards, however, the BNA Act was less than a constitution, because it was not a fundamental charter containing specific provisions that effectively defined the limits of the courts and legislatures with respect to human rights, nor did it embody the essence of national ideals and sovereignty. But to assume that Canada has not had a constitution for the past 115 years misunderstands the Canadian perception of constitutional process, for Canadians place great stock in British notions of constitutionalism.

This misunderstanding has deep historical roots as old as the first conflict between American and British notions of constitutionalism. As historian Bernard Bailyn has noted:

> The word "constitution" and the concept behind it was of central importance to the . . . minds of both English and Americans, and so great was the pressure placed upon it in the course of a decade of pounding debate [the 1770's] that in the end it was forced apart, along the seam of a basic ambiguity, to form the two contrasting concepts of constitutionalism that have remained characteristic of England and America ever since . . . .

* Faculty of Arts and Sciences, Duke University. The author wishes to thank Harold D. Tallant, doctoral candidate in history, for his help in preparing the bibliography and editing this paper.
    1. The Canada Act, 1982, ch. 11.

. . . [None of the American] writers who touched on the subject, meant to repudiate the heritage of English common and statutory law. Their claim was only that the source of rights be recognized, in . . . "the laws of nature" . . . but what was the ideal? What precisely were the ideal rights of man? They were, everyone knew, in some sense life, liberty and property. But in what sense? Must they not be specified? Must not the ideal now be reduced from a radiant presence and a conglomerate legal tradition to specific enumerated provisions? Must not the essential rights of man be specified and codified if they were to serve effectively as limits on the actions of courts and legislatures?[2]

Americans answered these questions with notions of constitutionalism that were far different from those of their British predecessors. Canadians, too, have struggled with these questions. Unlike the United States, however, Canada has never resolved them to its satisfaction. Indeed, a central theme of Canadian constitutional history under the BNA Act is the existence of a tension between these two concepts of constitutionalism. Canada has had a written charter which served, in some ways, as an American-style constitution. At the same time, it is clear that British concepts of constitutionalism abound in Canadian thought, and statements to this effect can be found throughout the writings of Canadian constitutional authorities.

Professors R. I. Cheffins and R. N. Tucker contend that the BNA Act "was in no way intended to be a definitive statement of Canada's constitutional functioning. . . . To read the British North America Act [in isolation] would be to get a totally misleading impression of the Constitution."[3] The authors contend that the "document is still the most important one relating to the constitutional process in Canada,"[4] but that, "there are other aspects of law within the constitutional framework regulated by conventional practice."[5] The same position is taken in Professor Frank R. Scott's description of the BNA Act as creating "central and local legislatures which were confined strictly to their prescribed spheres of action by the binding force of the doctrine of Imperial sovereignty. The federal Parliament in Canada cannot invade the provincial sphere, nor the provincial legislature that of Parliament."[6] Having established the ground rules for a division of powers, Scott goes on to argue that "convention has long since tempered the rigidity of this fundamental doctrine and the Statute of Westminster of 1931 made some breaches in the actual law." "Convention," he argues, "provides that the unlimited lawmaking power of the United Kingdom Parliament is a ritual or process to be employed at the request of any Dominion for the giving of legal validity to decisions already arrived at in that Dominion. . . . Hence Canada possesses, by convention, a most flexible Constitution."[7] Alan C. Cairns adds to the potential confusion in the American mind by arguing that the Canadian Constitution is "in essence not a document but a living institution built . . . around a particular document."[8] It seems apparent that Canadians conceive of "the Constitution" as

---

2. B. BAILYN, THE IDEOLOGICAL ORIGINS OF THE AMERICAN REVOLUTION 67, 188-89 (1967).
3. R. CHEFFINS & R. TUCKER, THE CONSTITUTIONAL PROCESS IN CANADA 7, 10 (1976).
4. *Id.* at 20.
5. *Id.* at 11.
6. F. SCOTT, ESSAYS ON THE CONSTITUTION: ASPECTS OF CANADIAN LAW AND PRACTICE 245 (1977).
7. *Id.*
8. Cairns, *The Living Canadian Constitution,* 77 QUEEN'S Q. 483, 486 (1970).

something broader than the BNA Act. The key question, then, becomes, how can Canada blend these two notions? How can the nation achieve a constitution of statutory law, common law, and convention within the framework of a written charter?

The tension between these competing ideas has compounded several of Canada's political issues, including those issues connected with federalism. When provincial interests collide with Ottawa or with each other, the issue frequently becomes whether a solution will be found in judicial interpretation or constitutional amendment, or whether it will be found in convention or "extraconstitutional" legislation.

In many ways the new Canada Act speaks to this issue by opting for the American formula. The new Constitution is a document which guarantees citizens rights against government encroachment; changes in governmental structure are to be made by amendment and judicial interpretation; and the Supreme Court of Canada has been given the power to declare legislation unconstitutional, not merely *ultra vires*.[9]

The incorporation of American-style ideas of constitutionalism into the new Canada Act also speaks to nationality, an issue that is perhaps more fundamental than federal questions. Is the adoption of an American-style constitution necessary for Canada to conceive of itself as a truly independent and Canadian nation? Do independence and full sovereignty mean, almost by definition, the psychological rejection of England's constitutional system? If this is the case, it remains to be seen whether an American-style constitution will provide Canada with the legitimizing First Principle of national sovereignty any more than the BNA Act. It is one thing for the Canada Act to rest on the sovereignty of the Canadian people; it is another for the people to accept the document as the *grundnorm* or fundamental law. Ultimately, the quest for a Canadian national identity may require Canadians to find a new notion of constitutionalism as Americans found it necessary to replace the Articles of Confederation with a constitution that established a national identity.

AMERICAN CONSTITUTIONALISM

The quest for a constitution expressing national identity and sovereignty has perhaps been easier and more successful in the United States than in Canada. America's success in developing a national spirit is largely rooted in the evolution of American colonial settlements during an age of restless Protestantism which provided Americans with a world view that both promoted settlement and offered a model for developing new American societies. The secularized version of this world view became a large part of the evolving American national identity, and the experience of the American Revolution and the formation of the Constitution in 1787 solidified this fact. While the key ingredients of the emerging American identity were present in the thought of most colonial American Protestants, they are most clearly seen in the thought of the New England Puritans.

---

9. THE CONSTITUTION AND YOU 8, 12 (Ottawa 1982).

As historian Edmund S. Morgan has noted, the Puritans' ideas about politics and government centered around three ideas: the calling, the covenant, and the special relationship between Church and State.[10] The calling was, perhaps, the most important part of Puritan political thought and was rooted in the Puritans' concept of salvation: that man's total depravity prevented him from effecting his own salvation and only God's selective grace promised salvation to a few "elect" souls. Man, however, could and should strive to be righteous so that he would receive assurance of his own salvation. Those who were not chosen by God for salvation would also benefit from the quest of assurance, for they would place themselves in agreement with God's plan for human society. Each man was "called" by God to fulfill a divinely appointed role. The Puritan idea of the calling could have quite conservative implications when applied to the social realm. As the Puritan governor of the Massachusetts Bay colony, John Winthrop, argued, "God Almightie in his most holy and wise providence hath soe disposed of the Condicion of mankinde, as in all times some must be rich, some poore, some highe and eminent in power and dignitie; others meane and in subieccion."[11] The Puritans believed that just as God called men, he also called nations of men to fulfill his divine appointment, and that just as the Israelites were God's chosen people in Biblical times, so the Puritans were now God's chosen people. Their calling was to separate themselves from the corrupted Christians of the world so that their righteous example would purify these Christians. As Winthrop wrote, "All other churches of Europe are brought to desolation, and it cannot be, but the like judgment is comminge upon us: and who knows, but that God hath provided this place, to be a refuge for manye, whom he means to save out of the general destruction."[12] The settlement of Puritans in New England became vested with the idea of a divine calling, a unique mission to become "a city on a hill" which would shine the light and way of salvation to the rest of the world.

If God's chosen people accepted their calling they were placed in a special relationship with God, from which accrued the benefits of His blessing. Just as the Puritans modeled their notion of the calling after the Biblical Israelites, they modeled their notion of their relationship with God after the Israelites' Covenant. The Puritans believed that God would bless and use His chosen nation as long as it fulfilled His calling. So pervasive was the Puritans' notion of the covenant that

---

10. E. MORGAN, PURITAN POLITICAL IDEAS xiii-xlvii (1965). The introduction to Morgan's book is a good, brief synthesis of what has become the standard interpretation of the Puritans' political ideas. For a more detailed discussion of Puritans' thought, see PERRY MILLER, ERRAND INTO THE WILDERNESS (1956). For a recent reappraisal of these ideas, see Bercovitch, *New England's Errand Reappraised,* in J. HIGHAM & P. CONKIN, NEW DIRECTIONS IN AMERICAN INTELLECTUAL HISTORY 85-104 (1979). Bercovitch writes:

> What first attracted me to the study of Puritanism was my astonishment, as a Canadian immigrant, at learning about the prophetic errand of America. Not of America, for the prophecies stopped short at the Canadian and Mexican borders, but of a country that, despite its arbitrary territorial boundaries—despite its bewildering mixture of race and genealogy—could believe in something called America's mission, and could invest that patent fiction with all the emotional, spiritual, and intellectual appeal of a religious quest.

Id. at 87.

11. Winthrop, *A Modell of Christian Charity, reprinted in* THE PURITANS 195 (1938).

12. *Quoted in* E. MORGAN, THE PURITAN DILEMMA: THE STORY OF JOHN WINTHROP 40 (1958).

they believed it extended to include not only man's relationship to God, but also man's relationships with other men. Indeed, when John Winthrop and other Puritan leaders discovered that the charter of the Puritan-dominated Massachusetts Bay Company allowed the company's colony to be governed from the New World, they saw that fact as God's calling to establish a unique form of government made up of righteous men banded together to fulfill God's calling in a colony free from control by the corrupt, old world. The Company's charter itself became a sacred covenant, binding God's chosen people together in a government which would help the people fulfill their calling. As Winthrop stated:

> [W]ee are entered in to Covenant with him for this worke, wee have taken out a Commission, the Lord hath given us leave to drawe our owne Articles . . . if the Lord shall please to heare us, and bring us in peace to the place wee desire, then hath hee ratified this Covenant and sealed our Commission, [and] will expect a strickt performance of the Articles contained in it.[13]

By possession of the Charter, the colonial leaders were able to use it as the cornerstone of the colony's constitution free from interference of England.

According to the Puritans, this sacred government of God's chosen people called forth a special relationship between Church and State. Since the government of God's chosen people was instituted to help them fulfill their calling, and since the Puritans believed that the power of governance was delegated by God, they thought the ultimate role of government was to further God's kingdom. As Puritan teacher and writer John Cotton noted, "It is better that the commonwealth be fashioned to the setting forth of Gods house, which is his Church: than to accommodate the church frame to the civill state."[14] The Puritans, however, did not seek to establish the dominance of the church in governmental affairs. Rather, they hoped that in a commonwealth of God's chosen people, church and state would use different means and powers to achieve the same result, furthering God's kingdom. As John Cotton noted:

> [M]agistrates are neyther chosen to office in the church, nor doe governe by directions from the church, but by civill lawes, and . . . by the governors and assistants. In all which, the church (as the church) hath nothing to doe: onely, it prepareth fitt instruments both to rule, and to choose rulers which is no ambition in the church, nor dishonor to the commonwealth
> . . . .
> . . . Purity, preserved in the church, will preserve well ordered liberty in the people, and both of them establish well-ballanced authority in the magistrates.[15]

In the Puritan's view, secular leaders were to further the kingdom of God. Like everything else, the Puritans believed these leaders were called by God to govern the people, as indicated by a vote of the "elect" church members of God's commonwealth. Thus John Winthrop declared:

> It is yourselves who have called us to this office, and being called by you, we have our authority from God, in way of an ordinance, . . . the contempt and violation whereof hath been vindicated with examples of divine vengeance . . . . The covenant between you and us . . . which is to this purpose, that we shall govern you and judge your causes by the rules

---

13. Winthrop, *supra* note 11, at 198.
14. Cotton, *Copy of a letter from Mr. Cotton to Lord Say and Seal in the Year 1636, reprinted in* THE PURITANS 209 (1938).
15. *Id.* at 210-212.

of God's laws and our own, according to our best skill.[16]

The idea of divine calling of rulers, like the concept of the calling in general, could have very conservative implications. As Winthrop argued in his Journal:

> [W]hen the people have chosen men to be their rulers, and to make their laws, and bound themselves by oath to submit therto, now to combine together . . . in a public petition to have any order repealed, which is not repugnant to the law of God, savors of resisting an ordinance of God; for the people, having deputed others, have no power to make or alter laws, but are to be subject.[17]

Yet, this doctrine could also have radical implications, because the Puritans held that it was the duty of God's people to remove a ruler who ignored his calling. Indeed, perhaps the most pressing reason why the Massachusetts Bay colony allowed for frequent elections was to protect God's people from rulers who violated their calling.

Given the basic views outlined above, the leaders of Massachusetts Bay held a tight reign. Nevertheless, in the process of practical governance one hundred new freemen were admitted to the colony in 1631. Each town was established by law in 1635, as an independent entity with powers to decide all local matters.[18] The town meeting was granted authority to establish and maintain all laws pertaining to the community, to elect deputies to the legislature, and to elect magistrates. John Cotton preached the 1634 election sermon advocating that magistrates be elected for life. The same year, the freemen repudiated this notion by turning Winthrop out and electing Thomas Dudley as governor.[19] In 1635, the secret ballot was instituted upon demand of the freemen.[20] The *Body of Liberteyes* were established in 1641 as the first written law code of Massachusetts, and in 1644, upper and lower houses of the legislature were established.[21] The legislature passed the Township Act in 1647 which granted the franchise to nonfreemen on all local matters, thus extending the influence of the already established town meetings.[22] This new and wholly secular institution was the vehicle for transferring Puritan religious conviction to political ideology so that by the middle of the eighteenth century "emphasis shifted from the government's obligation to please God to the government's obligation to protect life, liberty and property . . . to please the people."[23]

The upshot of the political thought of the Puritans and other American Protestants of the period was the establishment of ideas which became the foundation of the American national ideal. Rulers were to be called to office through the voice of the people and allowed to remain in office only as long as the people believed the rulers were fulfilling that calling. The people and their rulers were to be united together in a special and sacred covenant, an agreement free from outside control,

---

16. Winthrop, *Speech to the General Court, July 3, 1645, reprinted in* THE PURITANS 205, 206 (1938).
17. Winthrop, *Journal entry for May 22, 1639, reprinted in* THE PURITANS 202, 203 (1938).
18. R. WALL, MASSACHUSETTS BAY: THE CRUCIAL DECADE, 1640-1650, at 6 (1972).
19. *Id.* at 9-10.
20. S. MORISON, BUILDERS OF THE BAY COLONY 86 (1930).
21. R. WALL, *supra* note 18, at 17 and 63-64; B. LABAREE, COLONIAL MASSACHUSETTS: A HISTORY 74 (1979).
22. R. WALL, *supra* note 18, at 228.
23. E. MORGAN, *supra* note 10, at xlii.

in which the people united mutually to pursue their common calling. That calling, or mission, was to institute a righteous and uncorrupted society which would be a light to show the world God's plan for man and, thus, be the instrument of man's salvation. The concept of divine mission, established in the colony, would be a factor in the later acceptance of the American Constitution as a secular article of faith.

Indeed, the evolving world view held by Americans gave them an outlook on public events which made it increasingly difficult for them to remain a part of the British Empire. When Britain began to tighten its governance of the colonies, Americans began to doubt that the British people and government were really the upholders of liberty and republican government. Throughout the crisis which led to the Revolution, Americans began to think of themselves as the only upholders of liberty in a world of corrupt men. Americans saw themselves as a light of liberty, a beacon which would save the empire from corruption. In the early years of the conflict, Americans thought that their example would save the empire from forces which threatened to corrupt it and would touch off an empire-wide reaffirmation of liberty. Separation from the empire came only after the colonists feared that the British people were so hopelessly corrupted that a continued connection with them would destroy the American commonwealth of liberty.

The problem after independence was to establish a government for these apostles of liberty which would secure the mission of these people. The experience of the Revolution taught Americans how easily rulers could violate their calling and abuse the very liberty they were to protect. From this experience Americans wrote their first national constitution, the Articles of Confederation. It established a national government which was intentionally weak.

For all intents and purposes, authority to govern the new nation rested in the states. Americans believed that exercise of power by the states would lessen the danger of tyranny and corruption and thereby preserve republican government. Ultimately, though, the Articles proved to be an insufficient covenant. The Articles were designed to protect liberty from the encroachments of a strong national government. The events of the years after the Revolution, however, convinced many men that the greatest threat to republican government and to a sound exercise of liberty came from the anarchy of competing state interests. Thus, to these men the Articles were responsible for threatening the fruits of the Revolution itself. The solution was to create a new mode of government which received its authority from the sovereignty of the people, not from the state governments. The reformers believed that by establishing a new covenant directly between the people of the nation and the national government, the nation could truly achieve its calling to preserve liberty and republican government. Ultimately, this was to be the success of the American Constitution. It grew out of a concern to protect the national calling, and by institutionalizing the people's image of themselves as a nation, the Constitution quickly became accepted by almost everyone as the embodiment of the national idea.

The new constitution was not, of course, without opponents. Yet, the remarkable fact about the American Constitution is that even its original opponents

quickly came to view it as an article of national faith. The Antifederalists originally had doubts about the ability of the Constitution to implement the national
calling to republican government, because their classical republicanism had
trained them to view departures from established republican constitutions as
decay, which they saw as the ultimate threat to republicanism. While the Antifederalists were not satisfied that the Constitution was the best possible foundation for
the national ideal, their fear of decay encouraged them to uphold the standard of
the Constitution against any change. The process encouraged men to transform
their doubts about the Constitution into the fear of rulers who seemed to threaten
the established republican order. Former Antifederalists became, in the words of
historian Lance Banning, "an opposition party which would quickly elevate the
Constitution as the palladium of American liberty."[24]

In becoming "an opposition that claimed to be more loyal than the government itself,"[25] the Antifederalists set the pattern for opposition to governmental
policies which has prevailed throughout American history. In this way the American Constitution has become the article of faith of the nation, the vantage point
and justification for all actions.

Even in cases where a real governmental crisis called the Union itself into question, Americans found little reason to go outside the Constitution to justify their
positions. In the crisis surrounding the passage of the Alien and Sedition Acts in
1798, Thomas Jefferson justified the nullification of federal laws by states by
arguing that the Alien and Sedition Acts were "so palpably against the Constitution as to amount to an undisguised declaration, that the compact is not meant to
be the measure of the powers of the general government, ... [The Alien and
Sedition Acts] surrender the form of government we have chosen."[26] Later, William Harper of the South Carolina Supreme Court made the same point to justify
his state's nullification of the tariffs of 1828 and 1832: "[Congress] hath exceeded
its just powers under the Constitution . . . and hath violated the true meaning
and intent of the Constitution."[27]

Such appeals to the Constitution were apparent in the most serious of all
American crises, the secession crisis and Civil War. The citizens of Floyd County,
Georgia, were just one of many groups of Southerners who voiced constitutional
arguments in the midst of the crisis. The North, they declared, had waged "cease-
less war upon their plainest Constitutional rights; . . . an open and shameless nullification of that provision of the constitution intended to secure the rendition of
fugitive slaves."[28] The actual secession of the South was not the result of dissatisfaction with the Constitution itself; rather the South left the Union because it felt

---

24. Banning, *Republican Ideology and the Triumph of the Constitution,* 31 Wm. & Mary Q. 167, 179 (1974);
see also Berens, *The Sanctification of American Nationalism,* 3 Can. Rev. of Stud. in Nationalism 172 (1976).

25. Banning, *supra* note 24, at 168.

26. Kentucky Resolutions (Nov. 16, 1798) (Drafted by T. Jefferson), *reprinted in* H. Commager, Documents of American History 178, 181 (1968).

27. South Carolina Ordinance of Nullification (Nov. 24, 1832) (Drafted by W. Harper), *reprinted in* H.
Commager, *supra* note 26, at 261.

28. Resolutions on Secession from Floyd County, Georgia (1860), *reprinted in* H. Commager, *supra*
note 26, at 362.

that the political structure of the nation had placed it in a position of a permanent minority, a political position from which it could not adequately protect its "peculiar" interests. The South, in fact, retained a strong loyalty to the Constitution as an article of faith; even after secession had divided the nation, the South made the Constitution of the Confederate States an almost exact replica of the American Constitution.

In this way the South sought to separate the Constitution and the national ideals it represented from the actual Union of states whose political structure seemed to threaten the interests of the South. In this struggle the South not only employed the text of the American Constitution but also adapted the canon of American heroes and ideals to support its cause. George Washington, Thomas Jefferson, and Andrew Jackson became the forefathers of the Confederacy; the American Revolution became the model for action. Jefferson Davis, the president of the new Confederation, called on Southerners "to perpetuate the principles of our Revolutionary fathers, . . . to maintain our ancient institutions, . . . to renew such sacrifices as our fathers made to the holy cause of constitutional liberty, . . . [and] [t]o show ourselves worthy of the inheritance bequeathed to us by the patriots of the Revolution."[29]

The North, too, found reason to call on Washington, Jefferson, and the Constitution to support its cause. For Northerners the question was, will the legacy of the Revolution survive? Will the national calling be fulfilled? "What is now combated is the position that secession is consistent with the Constitution—is lawful and peaceful, . . ." wrote Abraham Lincoln. "On the side of the Union it is a struggle for maintaining in the world that form and substance of government whose leading object is to elevate the condition of men—to lift artificial weights from all shoulders; to clear the paths of laudable pursuit for all; to afford all an unfettered start, and a fair chance in the race of life."[30]

It should be emphasized that in 1861 the North did not fight the South to wage a war against slavery. They were fighting to preserve the Union. Even Lincoln, though affected by the pall of slavery, thought that "partial and temporary departures"[31] from the national ideal might be acceptable, and, indeed, that the preservation of the Union might ultimately require the preservation of slavery. He wrote editor Horace Greeley in 1862 that:

> I would save the Union. I would save it the shortest way under the Constitution. The sooner the National authority can be restored, the nearer the Union will be 'the Union as it was.' If there be those who would not save the Union unless they could at the same time *save* slavery, I do not agree with them. If there be those who would not save the Union unless they could at the same time *destroy* slavery, I do not agree with them. My paramount object in this struggle *is* to save the Union, and is *not* either to save or destroy slavery. If I could save the Union without freeing *any* slave, I would do it; and if I could save it by

---

29. Inaugural Address of Jefferson Davis (Feb. 22, 1862), *reprinted in* H. COMMAGER, *supra* note 26, at 407, 408-09.

30. Lincoln's Message to Congress in Special Session (July 4, 1861), *reprinted in* H. COMMAGER, *supra* note 26, at 393, 395.

31. *Id.*

freeing *all* the slaves, I would do it.[32]

By 1863, Lincoln found that the preservation of the Union required the elimination of slavery; and the subsequent course of events cemented the union of what became the North's dual war aims, union and abolition. Beyond the moral effect of freeing four million individuals from slavery, the linkage of union and abolition had profound implications for the future of the American nation. For years before the war slavery was the one continuing irritant on the American political scene. By successfully removing the irritant and at the same time defeating the only successful effort to divide the Union, the American nation seemed to have permanently repudiated secession as a recourse for disgruntled states. Further, by tying the repudiation of secession with the Civil War amendments to the Constitution, the nation seemed to reaffirm its calling and renew its covenant to be a light of liberty to the world. Indeed, some Americans saw the Civil War as God's retribution; the United States, they believed, had betrayed its sacred covenant of liberty and must pay for its violation in blood. God, though, stood ready to forgive His chosen people and renew His covenant with them and bless His nation if they would repent. "Let then no sordid interests or vile prejudices prevent us from a magnanimous, humane and vigorous effort to secure now to four millions of our fellow-men their natural and God-given rights," wrote one American, "then shall war cease, peace and harmony return, and a measure of prosperity such as has never marked the history of our once prosperous but now distracted country."[33] The Civil War became a renewal of the American ideal, an event some have considered the Second American Revolution.

THE DEVELOPMENT OF THE CANADIAN CONSTITUTION

If the growth and development of a national ethos has been a central fact of American history, the comparative lack of a national ethos has been a central theme of Canadian history. The closest parallel in Canada to the strong American sense of national identity has been the nationalism of French-Canadians. It is ironic, though, that the sort of national spirit that became the glue of the American nation is the solvent of the Canadian nation. Though French-Canadian nationalism began in the same period of colonial development as American nationalism, its political and cultural roots differed remarkably from those of American nationalism. While the American variety began as an expression of restless Protestantism, the French-Canadian variety began as an expression of zealous Catholicism. The American ethos tended to be "modern," the French-Canadian ethos tended to be "traditional." While the American spirit was nurtured by representative political institutions, the French-Canadian spirit was nurtured by an authoritarian administrative structure. Yet, both the American and French-Canadian national identities grew out of the process of seventeenth-century colonization. They both represent an adaptation of Old World ideas to the conditions of

32. President Lincoln's Letter to Horace Greeley (Aug. 22, 1862), *reprinted in* H. COMMAGER, *supra* note 26, at 417-18.
33. J. FEE, WHY AGITATE THE SLAVERY QUESTION? (1862).

the New World, which was encouraged by the colonial political structure. In both cases this adaptation resulted in the growth of an enduring national identity.

For French-Canadians, the process of developing a national ethos began in 1602, with the grant of a series of monopolies to French fur traders. These monopolies set the stage for a mercantilist industry that became the dominant economic force throughout the entire history of New France. In the same period the church established a foothold through the missionary efforts of the Society of Jesus, which sent the first Jesuit missionaries to New France in 1625. The two groups, one bent on economic gain for France, the other on establishing a Catholic French civilization, supported each other's efforts and were relatively free from crown control until 1663, when Louis XIV established New France as a royal province. Administrative control of public offices passed from the companies to the Crown under the direct authority of a superior council charged with the responsibility of implementing edicts of the king's council in France. Professor Kenneth McNaught points up the administrative arrangement of the council:

> Within the superior council of Quebec three figures of power dominated the proceedings: . . . the governor, with primary responsibility for defense and external relations; the intendant, like his counterpart in old France, with special concern for the maintenance of royal power and the administration of justice and economic growth; and the bishop, who wielded considerable authority due to the early groundwork of religious influence laid by the Jesuits. . . . [W]hile it [the council] provided scope for men of outstanding capacity and determination, it failed to develop a body of political representatives with a growing sense of community, such as appeared in the English colonies to the south. Whether one sees in English colonial representative government the beginnings of democracy or simply the advent of Whiggish mixed government, the contrast with New France is nonetheless striking. The tendency of local interests to look to particular men of influence in the government and to think of them as *chefs* with a natural right to patronage was one that grew steadily in New France.[34]

The administrative structure of the superior council, the influence of the church, the insistence that the *raison d'être* of the colony was to provide profit for France under a mercantilist system, and the French legal code that included the seignorial system combined to establish an authoritarian political structure and attitude that, according to McNaught, has not "disappeared in the democracy of present-day French Canada."[35] The net result of implicitly uniting the effort to extend the power of Catholic France, the royal goverment, the seignoirs, and the church kept the loyalty of the colonists directed toward a higher authority embodied in the monarchy.

Whether one accepts the view of historians who argue that the defeat of France in the Seven Years' War and the surrender of New France to England were catastrophes that shattered opportunities for self advancement of the French-Canadian society or were merely incidents that "did not cause any profound changes in the fabric of French-Canadian society,"[36] the fact remains that the significant elements of the religion, law, and custom of French Canada were preserved with the

---

34. K. MCNAUGHT, THE PELICAN HISTORY OF CANADA 27 (1973); *see also* W. ECCLES, THE CANADIAN FRONTIER, 1534-1760, at 10 (1969).
35. K. MCNAUGHT, *supra* note 34, at 28.
36. K. MACKIRDY, J. MOIR, & Y. ZOLTVANY, CHANGING PERSPECTIVES IN CANADIAN HISTORY: SELECTED PROBLEMS 62 (1971).

ultimate implementation of the Quebec Act in 1774. While the Quebec Act was passed because of the need for "some imperial apparatus to govern and control the French and Indian frontier incorporated into that empire by the Treaty of Paris,"[37] the Act was designed to accomplish more than the establishment of an effective imperial adminstration. The British Parliament was persuaded in its deliberations by the crisis brewing in the American colonies; they hoped that by satisfying French-Canadian hopes for a return to authoritarian local government which would be in the hands of a governor and an appointed council the American rebellion would not spread to Canada.

By speaking to French-Canadian aspirations, however, the Quebec Act precluded any possibility of developing a uniform colonial constitutional structure. Under the Act a dual system of English criminal and French civil law was established in Quebec. The seignorial system of tenure and the authority of the Catholic church were retained. These traditional forms of French-Canadian government were incorporated into the Quebec Act upon the recommendation of Sir Guy Carleton, the governor of Quebec, who "was convinced that the Canadians could best be ruled by a feudal authoritarian system."[38]

The Quebec Act was promulgated as a matter of administrative convenience, and it was accepted initially as such by most Canadians. Within seventeen years, however, the impact of the American Revolution and the influx into Canada of some 10,000 American Loyalists transformed the colony. The Loyalists wanted to own land without the restrictions of the seignorial system and they wanted legal protection under the British system. Further, the migration of American Loyalists swelled the ranks of the already disgruntled English merchants of Montreal. Although the Quebec Act contained provisions aimed at conciliating these merchants, namely, implementing elements of English commercial law, including "the grant of *habeas corpus*" and "the use of juries in civil suits,"[39] Carleton's refusal to enforce such provisions precipitated several political struggles during the period of the Revolutionary War. By 1790, the hostility of English-Canadians to the Quebec Act made it apparent that "the basic assumptions on which the Quebec Act had been founded now lay in ruin."[40]

The British response was, again, an administrative action of convenience. Rather than attempt to alter the Quebec Act to conciliate the English-Canadians at the risk of alienating the French majority, Parliament found at least a temporary solution to the problem by enacting the Constitutional Act of 1791. The colony was divided into the two provinces of Upper and Lower Canada. Lower Canada retained the basic form of government established by the Quebec Act except for the provision that new land grants could be made in freehold at the request of the landowner. Upper Canada was to enjoy the benefits of the English common law and criminal code, and land was to be granted in freehold. A bicameral assembly, with an elective lower house and an appointed upper house, was

37. W. MORTON, THE CANADIAN IDENTITY 19 (1972).
38. E. McINNIS, CANADA: A POLITICAL AND SOCIAL HISTORY 160 (1969).
39. *Id.* at 185.
40. *Id.*

established in each province. The provincial government's authoritarian structure was retained by giving the governor the power to veto or reserve bills, and the British Parliament retained the right to disallow all measures. In an effort to provide some equity to the Church of England, Parliament established the right to collect tithes and required the provincial governments to establish land reserves equal to one-seventh of future land grants for support of the clergy. The new government was described by Sir John Graves Simcoe, the governor of Upper Canada, as "the very image and transcript of the English constitution."[41] The obvious intent of the Constitutional Act was to assure a peaceful political cohabitation of the French and English within the colony. In spite of earlier failures to assimilate the French into the British system, some British leaders, notably William Pitt, continued to believe that gradual assimilation would occur. Instead of providing a basis for uniting the colony, however, the Constitutional Act served to generate dissension.

Professor McInnis' summary of what he calls the "vain illusion of unity" best describes the new difficulties that plagued the colonists and the British Parliament.

> The French found in the new system new opportunities to consolidate their racial and religious separatism. The seeds of racial friction were not eliminated by partition of Canada. The older mercantile groups were left within the bounds of Lower Canada, whose essentially French character was acknowledged by the new measure. The merchants had gained their demand for an assembly, but this was completely stultified by the division of the province, which left the English of Lower Canada in a hopeless minority. Yet their economic and political ambitions were not abandoned; and the result was a steadily increasing friction between the two races in that province and the complete failure of the grant of representative government to solve the problems of Canada.[42]

The period from 1791 to 1840 was marked by growing discontent in both Upper and Lower Canada centered on the lack of any connection between the elected assemblies and the appointed governors and councils, the issue of language in Lower Canada, and an animosity, bordering on hostility, between Protestant church groups and the Church of England over the latter's income from one-seventh of all surveyed land. Warnings to the Foreign Office that all was not well went unheeded until brief but open rebellions occurred in both Upper and Lower Canada in 1837. The investigation that followed under Lord Durham's leadership prompted a report calling for uniting the two Canadas into one province in which Francophone Canada East and Anglophone Canada West could share equal representation and abandoning the principle of oligarchy in favor of responsible government.

The British government, however, adopted only a part of the Durham Report; according to Professor Morton, Lord John Russell, the British colonial secretary, "continued the old Whig policy of making over the colonial constitutions."[43] The Union Act of 1840 united the two Canadas as Durham had recommended, but it did not grant responsible government to Canada. The British government had again taken an action of administrative convenience that was short-lived. The

41. *Id.* at 191.
42. *Id.* at 192.
43. W. MORTON, *supra* note 37, at 38.

movement toward responsible government was not easily quieted; Lord Russell was either unwilling or unable to recognize that a "truly representative system was bound to move flexibly from one area of authority to another."[44] Russell's own instructions to the first governor of the united province began the shift toward responsible government; he wrote that the governor, Lord Sydenham, should in most cases choose as ministers men whose "principles and feelings were in accordance with the majority."[45] The move toward responsible government continued under Governor Charles Bagot, who installed a ministry led by reformers when they achieved a majority in the assembly. Though this was not a complete acknowledgement of the principle of responsible government since there were still conservatives in the cabinet, Bagot could report by 1841 that "[w]hether the doctrine of responsible government is openly acknowledged, or is only tacitly acquiesced in, virtually it exists."[46] Bagot defended his concession of accepting five reformers into the ministry as the only possible course, and, according to McInnis, "the home government reluctantly accepted his view."[47]

Responsible government was formally acknowledged in 1847 when the governor, Lord Elgin, asked Louis H. Lafontaine and Robert Baldwin, the leaders of the reformist majority, to form a cabinet. Lord Elgin then set the precedent of not attending cabinet meetings or taking a direct hand in establishing policy. The governor, however, still retained the authority of government set forth in the Union Act.

Professor Morton makes the point that "[i]n achieving self-government, Canadians all unwittingly had set out to be an associated, but equal, nation within the British Empire. No explicit formulation was given to this determination; its revelation was left to the working of time and event." He further points out that "self-government was not a condition but a process. Durham's easy formulation of the subjects to be reserved for Imperial control was . . . easily eroded by the ever-advancing claims of the colonies to ever more powers of self-government."[48]

Matters of local concern rested with the united province, and as McInnis points out, "[t]he lack of a clear dividing line between imperial and provincial topics resulted in a wide flexibility which allowed the colonies to extend their activities into ever-broadening fields."[49] The hope of achieving harmony between Canada East and Canada West through legislative union was, however, false. Aspects of the political, economic, and religious life of the two provinces became seedbeds of dissension. Representation of the two provinces, one of the most serious points of conflict, was anything but equal when critical issues before the legislature were decided on the principle of the "double majority." The advocacy of representation by population—"rep by pop"—by Upper Canadian radicals threw the French into the position of defending the Union Act. A brief lull in sectional ten-

---

44. K. McNaught, *supra* note 34, at 97.
45. *Id.* at 96.
46. E. McInnis, *supra* note 38, at 277.
47. *Id.*
48. W. Morton, *supra* note 37, at 40.
49. E. McInnis, *supra* note 38, at 299.

sion achieved by Lafontaine and Baldwin and continued into the Morin-McNab ministry allowed the Union to carry forward a relatively effective, if tenuous, existence until the fortunes of the moderates collapsed in the election of 1854. The issues of church land reserves, seignorial tenure, and the location of the provincial capital all served to return sectional differences to the breaking point. Political difficulties threatened the recently secured responsible government with destruction. From 1861 to 1864, there were two elections and three changes of administration. Political struggles for power within the two provinces spilled over to sectional issues in the assembly to such an extent that by 1864 Canada faced a political and sectional deadlock.[50]

By this time it was apparent that measures would have to be taken to secure the unity of Canada. The solution which Canadian political leaders eventually rallied around was to unify all of British North America into a federal system. The impetus for such a movement came from George Brown, the leader of the Upper Canada reformers and an early advocate of "rep by pop." Brown believed that some form of federation might free Upper Canada from French-Canadian political domination and hoped that French-Canadians might support a new governmental structure which freed them from the constant struggle to preserve their special interests. Likewise, some Confederationists believed that other British North Americans could find reasons to be interested in forming a political union. By uniting the power of all British North America in a strong central government which was given charge of developing the Canadian economy, various provincial aspirations might be served. A governmentally sponsored transcontinental railroad, like that being built in the United States, might secure the prosperity of the Maritime provinces, give Montreal businessmen a chance to compete with their New York rivals, and open the West up for settlement by hemmed-in Upper Canadian farmers. Finally, many Canadian politicians were concerned that the increasing diplomatic troubles between Great Britain and the United States might again spill over into Canada, and with Britain increasingly cool to the defense of its colonies, it seemed to many that Canada's very existence as a political entity required the formation of a government which had the power to defend itself.

Such considerations increasingly influenced Canadians to support Confederation as a solution to their problems and an expression of their aspirations. The details of the new Confederation were ironed out between May 1864 and March 1867, and full political acceptance of the idea was hammered out by the efforts of Liberals and Conservatives alike. The result of their efforts, the British North America Act, was enacted by Parliament and went into force on July 1, 1867. It united the four provinces of Nova Scotia, New Brunswick, Ontario, and Quebec into the new Dominion of Canada.

The Confederation addressed many concerns of Canadians of the 1860's. Yet, the act of confederation created new concerns and increased some very old ones. The Fathers of Confederation hoped to address provincial aspirations by creating a strong central government while drawing a sharp line between the interests of

---

50. *Id.* at 325.

that government and the interests of the provinces. But could such a federal mechanism work? Previous attempts to reform the relationship between the two Canadas had not worked as expected. Now with the introduction of even more diversity by the inclusion of the Maritime provinces in Canada, would the new mechanism work any better? More importantly, if British North Americans created a new nation with Confederation, would the BNA Act so embody the ethos of the new nation that it would serve to bind the nation together despite its diversity?

The new nation would be tested and these questions answered during the next thirty years, a period dominated by the leadership of John A. Macdonald, the Father of the Confederation. This was, indeed, the critical period for the BNA Act, a period when its meaning and the identity of the new nation were to be defined. As one group of Canadians asked, "What is a Canadian? Where is Canada going?"[51] Macdonald himself hinted at this problem when he spoke of the need to create a "great nationality—forming a great nation" and "joining these 5 people into 1 . . . to take our position among the nations of the world."[52] Other Canadians echoed this concern. One wrote of "the new nationality that is to be created" and of the problems of creating a Canadian nation when Canadians were "cut into many struggling nationalities."[53] Sir John Rose, the Canadian Finance Minister, spoke of the "vague aspirations of a new nation."[54] Their concern was well founded, because it was doubtful whether Canadians possessed the sort of national spirit which Macdonald hoped would bind the nation together. "It is a fact," wrote the Ottawa *Free Press*, "that there is not in Canada that national spirit."[55] The *Montreal Gazette* agreed with this assessment, writing that "this Canadian national spirit is undoubted[ly] the great want . . . of the Canadian people."[56] And, as one modern writer has noted, in the years following Confederation, "[n]ational sentiment was still a distinctly secondary factor . . . and only a few of the leaders betrayed in their speeches evidence of a broad vision of Canadian nationhood . . . [or support for the] nebulous goal of promoting national patriotism."[57]

The failure of Canadians to forge a distinctive national ethos in the post-Confederation years can be seen in the two preeminent nationalist movements which arose during the period, the Canada First Movement and Macdonald's Conservative political coalition. The deeply problematic nature of Canadian nationalism can be seen most clearly in the Canada First Movement. "Canada First . . . was a group of nationalists who represented one particular section; . . . it was composed of imperialists who believed in everything from independence to annexation."[58] Thus, while Canada First claimed its platform was the only one which truly repre-

51. *Quoted in* Farrell, *The Canada First Movement and Canadian Political Thought,* J. OF CAN. STUD., November 1969, at 16, 17.
52. *Quoted in id.* at 16.
53. *Quoted in id.*
54. *Quoted in id.*
55. *Quoted in id.* at 18-19.
56. *Quoted in id.*
57. Hougham, *Canada First: A Minor Party in Microcosm,* 19 CAN. J. OF ECON. & POL. SCI. 174 (1953).
58. Farrell, *supra* note 51, at 25.

sented the whole nation, the group was little interested in addressing the concerns of Quebec or the Maritimes; it "looked to the West for Canada's future,"[59] but had little notion of the West as anything but an extension of English central Canada. Further, the members of Canada First could never decide what Canada's relationship to the British Empire and the United States should be. They spoke of their desire to see an autonomous Canada within the British Empire, yet they wondered whether that autonomy could be obtained. Some members of Canada First supported a complete break with the empire, an American-style independence. Yet, at this time independence was often a catchword for annexation by the United States, and some members of Canada First seemed to support annexation as the true expression of Canadian nationalism.

Even Macdonald's political coalition was not immune from the problems of Canadian nationalism. From 1867-1873 and again from 1878-1896, Macdonald and his Conservative successors tried to govern in a manner consistent with the principles of nationalism which they thought the BNA Act expressed. The keystone of their policies was the National Policy, a program of national economic development based on protective tariffs and transcontinental railroads. Macdonald also sought and, to a considerable extent achieved, a broadly based national political coalition. If any group should be expected to absorb the national spirit which Macdonald hoped the BNA Act expressed, it should have been his party. But by the late 1890's Macdonald's coalition had foundered on the rocks of provincial interests. The Northwest Territories challenged the Dominion's authority in the Second Riel Rebellion; the Maritimes were near rebellion over federal fiscal policies with Nova Scotia contemplating secession; and Quebec was upset over the government's handling of the Manitoba schools issue.

The failure of Macdonald's coalition to transcend provincial interests in favor of national goals was symbolic of the broader failure of the BNA Act to become the embodiment of any sort of national ideal, the national ethos upon which all actions are justified. In the crucial period following Confederation, Canadians failed to discover exactly what it meant to be a Canadian, and the BNA Act, the founding document of the nation, failed to become the supreme expression of the national ethos.

The lack of a distinctive Canadian identity embodied in a constitution is the root of many of the political problems faced by Canada today. It is significant that today's Canadians felt a need to address these problems by writing a new constitution, for these problems reach beyond the scope of normal political issues to involve the very essence of nationhood. The first of these problems involves the question of the process of amending the Constitution. Until the passage of the Canada Act, the ultimate authority for amending the BNA Act rested with the British Parliament, a fact that concerned Canadians for many years. Although British law and practice allowed Canada to have effective control of the BNA Act, a concern about the symbolism of the arrangement remained. Could Canada

---

59. *Id.* at 20.

truly be a sovereign and independent nation in her own eyes and in the eyes of the world if her fundamental law could be changed by a British statute?

Professor Frank Scott succinctly spoke about the Canadian concern by posing the question of sovereignty in an address at the 1950 annual meeting of the Royal Society of Canada. "Does it make any difference," he asked, "whether a British statute can extend to Canada whenever the preamble says Canada has requested it, or whether no such statute can have the force of law unless it has been enacted in identical terms by the Canadian Parliament?"[60]   For Scott, and for Canadians generally, the answer was that there is a great difference:

> It is all the difference between the theory that the American constitution rests on the sovereignty of the people—the American people, and the theory that the Canadian constitution rests on the sovereignty of the Parliament—the British Parliament. It is all the difference between having a constitution that is your own and a constitution that belongs to somebody else. . . . We should have no certainty or stability, unless the entire constitution were to become a Canadian constitution, binding on all future Canadian legislatures, and incapable of being altered save by a process which derives its validity from the will of the Canadian people alone.[61]

It is significant that Canada could not assert its nationality by patriating the Constitution because it lacked the depth of national spirit necessary to patriate the Constitution. Provincial concerns for their own well-being always confounded the assertion of a national spirit by preventing the enactment of a Canadian amendatory process. Further, despite the fact that Britain had not exercised its right to legislate for Canada without the permission of the Ottawa government since 1931, many provinces looked to this right as the ultimate guarantee of their interests. With the passage of the new Constitution, Canadians have tried to lay aside these concerns. The question remains, though, whether these concerns will be laid aside in an assertion of national spirit.

Another issue involves what it means to be a Canadian. Do citizens have certain rights which a constitutional government may not violate without trampling upon its own founding principle? Should these rights express the founding principle and extend to all parts of the nation? Should different Canadians have different rights? These questions became increasingly prominent as Canadians watched the explosion of concern for civil liberties in the United States since the 1960's and thought about the significance of civil liberties in their own nation. The traditional Canadian concept of civil liberties revolved around politics. Ultimately, preservation of civil liberties depended on the will of the majority; when rights were infringed, Canadians traditionally sought political rather than judicial remedies. Civil liberties were thought of as the rights of political association: parliamentary democracy, the right to vote, and freedom of speech and press. This conception of civil liberties stemmed from the continuing presence of the Crown in Canadian life. In a fundamental way, civil liberties in Canada represented the people's rights against their sovereign to replace the monarch's unworthy ministers. Increasingly, however, as the Crown's presence in Canada became less pronounced, and effective sovereignty came to rest in the Canadian people, civil

---

60. F. SCOTT, *supra* note 6, at 248.
61. *Id.*

liberties came to mean persons' rights against the majority. How then could civil liberties be protected under the BNA Act? Paul C. Weiler described "the nature of the problem" when he stated that:

> The major impetus in Canada for a constitutional Bill of Rights is concern for Canadian unity when challenged by cultural dualism. One important reason why Pierre Trudeau has always insisted on a new Bill of Rights has been his commitment to guarantee language rights to all French Canadians and thereby to defuse the threat of Québécois nationalism.[62]

Quebec objected to the constitutionally entrenched Bill of Rights that now supersedes the legislative Bill of Rights which it supported in 1960. In spite of the difficulties which arose out of the objections, Professor Weiler argued that "[w]e should entrench our fundamental rights in the Canadian constitution in order to give them the legal and symbolic authority which could be conducive to their flourishing."[63] But what will the new guarantee mean? Will it embody Canadians' concept of themselves? Will this expression of national citizenship be accepted?

The final issue of language and culture involves both civil liberties and the nature of the Union. Previous constitutional settlements attempted to determine to what extent Canada would be a bicultural nation. None of these settlements ever satisfactorily determined the level of Canada's biculturalism nor answered the question of what biculturalism meant to Canadian nationality which helped lead to the failure of each. The BNA Act, for instance, provided for definite but "limited bilingualism and biculturalism,"[64] but by the 1890's this settlement was already inadequate. Later attempts to address the inadequacy through the politics of convention were transitory, and the ferment of the Quiet Revolution in Quebec only deepened the problem. Canadians now seem so far apart on the issue of bilingualism and biculturalism that achieving a new constitutional settlement is harder than ever.

Symbolic of the divergent outlooks on the issue is the rift between the two French Canadians who are now the chief protagonists of the language issue, Pierre Elliott Trudeau and René Lévesque. Both men agree that Canada should be a bicultural nation, as probably do most Canadians, but they differ widely about what the nature of such a society should be. Trudeau is interested in building a nation in which each individual's language and culture are respected by society and guaranteed by the government. He argues that "certain fundamental rights and freedoms should, in a democratic society, be reserved to individuals and minorities and be untouchable by the state."[65] Trudeau's position is that language rights of minorities should be protected wherever they may be found, a position which serves to protect English language rights in Quebec. It is at precisely this point that he conflicts with Lévesque. The Quebec premier's primary concern is

62. Weiler, *Of Judges and Rights, or Should Canada Have a Constitutional Bill of Rights?* 60 DALHOUSIE REV. 205, 207 (1980).
63. *Id.* at 231.
64. Forsey, *The British North America Act and Biculturalism,* 71 QUEEN'S Q. 141 (1964).
65. Pierre Elliott Trudeau, "Prime Minister's Reply to the Letter Addressed to Him on September 9, 1977, by the Premier of Quebec," in Canada, Office of the Prime Minister, "Prime Minister's Letter to the Premier of Quebec and Position of the Federal Government on Quebec's Bill 101, October 6, 1977," Ottawa, 1977 (typescript).

the building of a French-Canadian nation. Thus, his concern for minority language rights extends only to the rights of Francophones. He sees Trudeau's desire to protect English minority language rights in Quebec as "a threat to the very survival of the Francophone community through assimilation,"[66] and he opposed the entrenchment of such rights in the constitution. The question for Canada as its new constitution enters the critical years is whether men like Trudeau and Lévesque will be able to settle the language issue and make the Canada Act succeed where previous constitutional settlements have failed.

Canadians stand, just as they did in 1867, at the dawning of a critical period in their history where they can forge a national identity or repeat the failures of the past. The authority that once rested with the British Parliament as the ultimate guarantor of provincial interests now rests with the sovereignty of the Canadian people. The certainty and stability that Professor Scott speaks of must rely on a "process which derives its validity from the will of the Canadian people"[67] and their sense of nationhood. Likewise, the new Canada Act must embody this sense of nationhood before it can be the structure, the *grundnorm,* through which the nation's problems are solved. For the new process to be a success, it must rest on the national ideal to accommodate sectional differences. Only time will tell if Canadians will find a national ethos in this critical period that will provide the glue of legitimacy for the new Constitution.

---

66. René Lévesque, Letter to Pierre Elliott Trudeau, September 9, 1977 (typescript); for the views of one academician who supports Lévesque's position, *see* Beaujot, *A Demographic View on Canadian Language Policy,* 5 CAN. PUB. POL. 16 (1979).
67. F. SCOTT, *supra* note 6, at 248.

THE POLITICS OF CONSTITUTIONAL CHANGE

J. R. MALLORY*

One of the most useful characteristics of federalism is that it makes it possible to offload some issues which produce conflict in the system onto regional units, where local majorities can achieve policies never acceptable to the country as a whole. The persistence of such conflict if they cannot be hived off in this way can overload the system, poison its politics, and reduce it to the immobility of a political stalemate. It is well known that the political leaders in the province of Canada attempted to overcome such avoidable conflict through the device of federation with the other provinces of British North America. The most troublesome conflict was the schools question. In Lower Canada (which became Quebec) the substantial Catholic majority was content with nothing less than a Catholic school system, an anathema to the Protestant majority in Upper Canada (which became the province of Ontario). The best way to resolve this divisive struggle was to make education a provincial responsibility, while at the same time inserting a guarantee in the constitution protecting the right to separate schools to "the Queen's Protestant and Roman Catholic subjects" in both provinces. Similarly, the historic right to preserve the civil law, rather than the common law, in Quebec made it essential that civil law and procedure should be a provincial concern.

All federal constitutions have a certain rigidity, necessary to protect the perceived interests of their component parts. Through time the environment changes, demands on government alter, and later generations may find the old form irksome and possibly irrelevant. How can they be changed without generating conflicts which put excessive strain on the system? This is a perennial problem with federations, amplified in the last hundred years by the rapid changes brought about by modernization. In Canada the pressure for change has reverberated through the political system, colouring the motives of politicians and governments, and inevitably involving the courts in the task of discerning and redefining the original bargain in contemporary terms.

* * *

The framers of the Canadian Constitution thought that they had designed a flexible constitution with a strong and adaptable role for the central government. To them the lesson of the American Civil War was that the existence of strong and immutable states' rights threatened the survival of the whole enterprise. This was a mistake that the framers had no intention of repeating. They envisaged a strong and dominant role for the central government, endowed with ample powers to carry out the great task of expansion and development. Many of the framers

---

* Emeritus Professor of Political Science, McGill University.

would have preferred a unitary form of government, but "they could not ignore the social forces rooted in the history of the colonies any more than they could presume to bind the future indefinitely to the past."[1] The result of the framers' effort was a strongly centralized union in which provincial powers and functions were strictly limited and confined, it was thought, to issues of local importance which would have produced irreconcilable divisions at the national level.

It was thought that rigidly confining jurisdiction in separate spheres would reduce conflict to manageable issues, reconcilable within one or the other of the jurisdictions. In the ideal form of classical federalism each level of government can go on serenely cultivating its own jurisdiction almost as if the other did not exist. The real world, however, does not seem able to adjust itself to this model. Conflict emerges between the two levels of government, and some way has to be found to settle such conflict. At bottom, this political conflict is the result of the actions of political men intent on defending political space, which to them in a federal system is largely defined in jurisdictional terms. If jurisdictions do not seem adequate to this territorial imperative, there will be pressure to redefine the boundaries of the constitution. Where formal amendment is too difficult to achieve, political bargaining and/or litigation over jurisdiction may achieve nearly the same result.

The initial method of conflict management, which frequently involved constitutional issues, sheds a strong light on the nature of the system the founders had put together in the British North America Act. It was based more on a colonial than a federal model. This is not surprising. The Canadian statesmen who founded the union had grown up in a colony in which they enjoyed limited powers of self-government under controls operated by the British government. These controls were both executive and legislative. Colonial governors were armed with elaborate instructions as to which measures they were free to approve and which should be referred to the Colonial Office for final action. This was called the power of reservation, by which the governor, instead of giving assent to a bill, could reserve it "for Her Majesty's pleasure" so that the final decision to approve the bill was taken by the British Colonial Secretary. If a governor was sufficiently lacking in vigilance that he failed to reserve such a bill, the act itself could be nullified within two years by the British government exercising the power of disallowance. These powers over the new government of Canada were retained in London, but in fact they rapidly fell into desuetude.

In the provinces, similar powers of reservation and disallowance were vested in the lieutenant-governor of the province and the governor general of Canada respectively, but from the beginning the powers were exercised on the constitutional authority of Canadian ministers. Accordingly, Ottawa had the same "imperial" powers over the provinces that the British government had over the Dominion of Canada. But while the British powers of control atrophied, the powers of the central government were strongly asserted. Sir John A. Macdonald,

---

1. I ROYAL COMMISSION ON DOMINION-PROVINCIAL RELATIONS [ROWELL-SIROIS] REPORT Book I, 36 (1940).

who led the federal government as Prime Minister for many years before his death in 1891, initially also held the portfolio of Minister of Justice. In that capacity he announced in 1869 "that the Federal Government would be called upon to consider the propriety of allowance or disallowance of provincial enactments much more frequently than the Imperial Government had done in the recent past."[2] Over the next thirty years fifty-one bills were reserved and sixty-five acts were disallowed.[3] The federal government

> claimed the substantially judicial function of deciding whether provincial legislation was ultra vires. It stood ready to invalidate provincial enactments which it thought unjust or contrary to sound principles of legislation. It was prepared to veto legislation which, according to its view, conflicted with imperial treaties or policies, or with Dominion interests and policy.[4]

Such a one-sided method of dispute settlement was not likely to sit well with provincial governments, and it did not. In 1887, the premier of Quebec summoned a conference of his fellow premiers, and also invited Prime Minister Macdonald. The latter refused to attend, on the ground that the legitimate representatives of the provinces were the members of parliament at Ottawa. The political overtones of the meeting were obvious; two of the five provincial premiers did not attend, and the premiers who did were not of Macdonald's party. The conference resolved that the disallowance power should be taken away from the federal government and that resort to the courts was a better method of settling such disputes.[5]

By this time Confederation was twenty years old. One of the effects of the great world depression, which began in the 1870's and lasted for over twenty years, was the weakening of the authority of the federal government. Provincial resistance to national policies was fueled by regional discontent. The role of the provinces as agencies of government was greatly strengthened by two other factors. One was the growing importance of extractive industries, such as forestry and mining, heavily dependent on provincial governments both for the infrastructure of roads and of electric power, and for the allocative role of granting leases on provincially controlled natural resources. The second factor, a consequence of growing urbanization and industrialization, was the new demands on government for alleviative measures which could be achieved under provincial jurisdiction. Such measures at the time of Confederation were inhibited by the dominant doctrine of laissez-faire, but thereafter a growing role for the state in the social sphere became increasingly respectable.[6] New roles for government in federal systems raise questions of which level of government is to carry them out. These questions may be settled authoritatively by the courts, which thus legitimize constitutional adjustments and, in this manner, act as part of the machinery of constitutional amendment.

---

2. *Id.* at 49.
3. *Id.*
4. *Id. See also* G. LaForest, Disallowance and Reservation of Provincial Legislation (1955); J. McHenry, Memorandum on the Office of Lieutenant-Governor of a Province (1955).
5. LaForest, *supra* note 4, at 58-59.
6. *See* J. Mallory, Social Credit and the Federal Power in Canada (1954).

The courtroom battles of this era can be seen as political in the sense that the vested interests which initiated them—having lost the battle at the ballot-box and in lobbying ministers against regulations they did not like—were continuing the political contest by other means. This was certainly true of some of the earlier cases. In the landmark case of *Russell v. the Queen*,[7] the federal government did not appear in the case even though it involved a jurisdictional question that disputed the general power of parliament to legislate even in areas which appeared to fall under provincial jurisdiction over property and civil rights.

In later cases the politicians were not so innocent, and the courts became an important arena of federal-provincial conflict. One of the most important of these cases was the "Local Prohibition Case."[8] In *Russell* the court had upheld a federal statute permitting local areas to impose prohibition of the sale of alcoholic beverages. In the Local Prohibition Case the question was whether, notwithstanding *Russell*, a province possessed the power to regulate the liquor traffic in a variety of ways. This case was a direct confrontation between the province of Ontario (with Quebec and Manitoba as intervenors) and the Government of Canada. The court upheld the provincial power, and in so doing strictly limited the general legislative power of parliament. The decision meant that, except in unspecified extraordinary situations, parliament's general legislative power could not be exercised in any of the enumerated fields of provincial jurisdiction. The effect of the decision in the Local Prohibition Case and others was to shift the balance of Canadian federalism toward the provinces.

As the depression receded, much of the energy of the federal government was absorbed by the completion of the transcontinental railways, the management of land settlement on the prairies, and the development of the wheat economy. In the meantime, provincial governments steadily expanded their own responsibilities in their own spheres. The result was a federal system much closer to the classical model, in which each level of government functioned autonomously in its own sphere of activity. Inevitably there were conflicts of jurisdiction, which were resolved by the courts. By the beginning of the first World War, thirty years of constitutional interpretation had created a situation in which each level of government was reasonably capable of meeting the demands laid upon it by the political system.

The depression of the 1930's put a severe strain on the constitutional arrangements which had developed as a result of the judicial interpretation of the past. The enhanced provincial jurisdiction over welfare and social policy, which the courts not unreasonably confirmed in the simpler days of the nineteenth century, proved to be an unhappy legacy when the provinces and municipalities staggered under the burden of providing relief for the unemployed and the destitute. The distribution of financial resources in the constitution had now become totally inadequate to meet provincial requirements. Provincial revenue sources were limited and inelastic, insufficient for even the richest provinces. On the other hand, the

---

7. (1882) 7 App. Cas. 829.
8. Attorney-General of Ontario v. Attorney-General of Canada, [1896] A.C. 348.

federal government, which possessed the major sources of revenue, lacked the jurisdiction necessary to deal directly with the social and economic problems created
by the depression.

At first the government in Ottawa extended financial aid to the hard-pressed
provinces, albeit on a scale inadequate to meet the problem. Inevitably it was
driven to enlarge its jurisdiction to fill the gap. In part inspired by the example of
the New Deal in the United States, Prime Minister Bennett's Conservative government belatedly introduced its own measures, including the regulation of hours of
labour and the introduction of a plan for unemployment and social insurance.
These measures were held by the Judicial Committee of the Privy Council to be
beyond the federal government's legislative powers.[9] The rulings created a virtual
no-man's land in the constitution. The federal government had the resources to
deal with problems now national in scope, while the provinces had the jurisdiction
but neither the financial means nor the bureaucratic capacity to deal with the
problems effectively.

Some provinces, notably Alberta, intervened directly to deal with the pressing
problems of farm debt through the creation of debt-adjustment legislation, and to
deal with the more general problem by seeking to institute a regime based on
Social Credit doctrines. The federal government considered this legislation an
infringement upon its territory. Its sacred jurisdiction over interest rates, banking,
and monetary policy was strongly defended in the courts, initially by the mortgage
and lending interests, and the federal power was further defended by the revival of
disallowance.[10] Federal-provincial conflict thus emerged as a dominant theme of
the 1930's.

* * *

The liberal government of Mackenzie King responded with typical caution.
At the same time it was defending its essential jurisdiction against provincial
inroads, it appointed a royal commission of enquiry to investigate the whole field
of federal-provincial relations. The Commission took three years to complete its
hearings and to ponder a substantial volume of research. Basically its report reaf-
firmed its faith in the federal system, but some important modifications of jurisdiction were recommended. These included the transfer to the federal government of
jurisdiction over unemployment insurance, which was considered administratively
inappropriate for provincial jurisdiction. The most important recommendation
was for a major revision of federal-provincial financial relations, with the creation
of an impartial grants commission to administer the transfer of funds to "have-
not" provinces so that they could provide reasonable levels of service within their
jurisdictions at reasonable levels of taxation. The Commission rejected, largely on
the grounds of inefficiency and lack of accountability, jointly-financed programs.
The result of implementing the Commission's recommendations would probably

---

9. Attorney-General of Canada v. Attorney-General of Ontario, [1937] A.C. 326 (P.C.); Attorney-
General of Canada v. Attorney-General of Ontario, [1937] A.C. 355 (P.C.); Attorney-General of British
Columbia v. Attorney-General of Canada, [1937] A.C. 377 (P.C.).

10. *See* MALLORY, *supra* note 6.

have been to reduce federal-provincial conflict by making the provinces more financially secure in their own jurisdictions.

The apparent inadequacies of government in the 1930's led to increased awareness that some constitutional amendment reallocating power between the two levels of government seemed unavoidable. The question of the procedure of formal amendment, which had long remained dormant, suddenly became an issue. For reasons which are not entirely clear, the Canadian Constitution did not include a complete amending procedure in 1867. In most major areas, amendment to the British North America Act legally remained with the British Parliament. This arrangement became increasingly incongruous with the growth of dominion status and the formal legal equality between the self-governing dominions and the United Kingdom proclaimed by the Statute of Westminster.

As a result of provincial protests it became necessary to insert a section in the Statute of Westminster exempting the British North America Acts from its effect. It was assumed that an appropriate amending formula would be found. It was not. While apparently all that was necessary for the British Parliament to amend the British North America Act was a joint resolution of both Houses of the Canadian Parliament, prudence dictated that provincial consent was necessary where a reallocation of powers was concerned.[11] Provincial premiers learned to barter their consent at a high price, so that numerous attempts to find an acceptable amendment formula, and to "patriate" the constitution, failed.

The attempt of the Royal Commission on Dominion-Provincial Relations to rewrite a truly federal constitution in the light of twentieth-century demands on government also failed. The Dominion-Provincial Conference, called to discuss the report on January 14 and 15, 1941, broke up without agreement. However, a totally different approach to the problem emerged as a result of the wartime arrangements for economic management. The impact of total war had the incidental effect of reducing provincial governments to spectators since many of their normal fields of jurisdiction were assumed by the federal government under the War Measures Act. Scarcity of materials ensured that some of their most visible activities, such as public works, ceased. Wartime full employment solved the problem of relief for the unemployed. Under wartime taxation agreements achieved in 1942, the provinces temporarily surrendered the income, corporation, and succession duty taxation fields to the federal authorities in exchange for guaranteed revenues.

Other factors contributed to a major change in the Canadian federal system. The skillful application of the doctrines of Keynesian economics by the Department of Finance seemed to demonstrate that the management of the economy could be achieved largely by fiscal and monetary means. Consequently, the need for jurisdictional reallocation in favour of the central government receded. Constitutional revision, with all its divisive implications, could wait. Nevertheless, it was clear that public expectations of an expanded role for government in the fields of

---

11. P. GÉRIN-LAJOIE, CONSTITUTIONAL AMENDMENT IN CANADA (1950); G. FAVREAU, THE AMENDMENT OF THE CONSTITUTION OF CANADA (1965).

social security, health care, and the like, had risen sharply. The British Beveridge Report, with its promise of social security "from the cradle to the grave," was echoed in Canada by similar proposals for post-war reconstruction.

The problem facing the federal government at the end of World War II was to find a way of managing such policies within the framework of the federal constitution. The innovative capacity of federal politicians and civil servants, sustained by the high prestige of the federal government from its management of the war economy, suggested a way to achieve the result without noticeable constitutional change. The provinces had the jurisdiction, but not the administrative and fiscal capacity, to undertake post-war measures of full employment and social security. All that was necessary was for the federal authorities to define the policy objectives, set the administrative norms, and offer financial incentives to get the provinces to join in unified measures to tackle the problems. Though this approach would probably lead to prolonged negotiation between the levels of government, the chances of serious conflict were initially slight. Federal proposals had the initial momentum of strong public support, which made them difficult to resist, while the provincial governments, with anemic bureaucratic support, had little capacity to resist.[12]

* * *

There is a danger that complex intergovernmental arrangements will run afoul of the constitution. The strict "water-tight compartment" view taken by the courts in the 1930's could easily have frustrated attempts to achieve common policy objectives. As Lord Atkin observed,

> Unless and until a change is made in the respective legislative functions of Dominion and Province it may well be that satisfactory results for both can only be obtained by co-operation. But the legislation will have to be carefully framed, and will not be achieved by either party leaving its own sphere and encroaching upon that of the other.[13]

It must be remembered, however, that the courts are essentially passive instruments of conflict resolution. If nobody wants to go to court, the constitution ceases to be an active ingredient in the situation. This was largely true in the years immediately following the war. The great corporations, many of whose officers had been wartime civil servants, had learned the benefits of government control of the marketplace and had little disposition to fight last-ditch battles in the courts. Similarly, provincial governments at that time were generally hesitant to start a challenge in the courts which might have large and unforeseen effects on the whole edifice of post-war economic and social policy. Furthermore, perhaps in part because the Supreme Court Act amendment of 1949 made the Supreme Court the court of last resort in Canada, the courts proved to be more accommodating than before to the imperatives of government, even when the bending of constitutional rules was involved. Thus, in *P.E.I. Potato Marketing Board v. H. B. Willis, Inc.,*[14] the Supreme Court upheld the provisions of the Agricultural Products Marketing Act

---

12. *See* D. SMILEY, THE CANADIAN POLITICAL NATIONALITY (1967), for an excellent discussion of the developments, and R. SIMEON, FEDERAL-PROVINCIAL DIPLOMACY: THE MAKING OF RECENT POLICY IN CANADA (1972), for an analysis of the process.

13. Attorney-General of British Columbia v. Attorney-General of Canada, [1937] A.C. 377.

14. [1952] 2 S.C.R. 392.

of 1949 which empowered the federal government to delegate to a provincial board the power to make and enforce regulations. This decision neatly got around the constitutional difficulty which confined federal jurisdiction to international and interprovincial trade, but excluded it from wholly intraprovincial trade.

* * *

The federal-provincial conference, whether of first ministers, of ministers in a particular field, or even of officials, thus emerged as the dominant method of conflict resolution in this period. It was the era of "cooperative federalism" in which the two levels of government combined federal funding and initiatives with provincial administration in an incestuous relationship which seemed to make constitutional disputes largely irrelevant. Of course, there were conflicts, mostly about details and funding, but they were manageable when the policy objectives of the two levels of government were complementary. Only the Province of Quebec, which until 1960 preserved an implacable hostility to federal-provincial cooperation of this sort, stayed out of joint programs altogether, evidently willing to pay a high price in funding in the interests of constitutional purity.

The increasingly intimate relationships between the two levels of government in cooperative programs led to conflicts over both ends and means. Many of these conflicts were a consequence of the entry of Quebec into active participation in federal-provincial programs. It was a time of furious activity in Quebec—a "Quiet Revolution" in which politicians and bureaucrats steadily expanded the reach of government activity in order to modernize Quebec society. To the Quebec negotiators the new cooperative program modes that satisfied most of the other provincial governments did not take account of the special needs of the different social and cultural milieu of Quebec. This led them to seek a "special status" for Quebec, which would retain full powers over programs subject to uniform treatment in the rest of Canada. Throughout the 1960's and 1970's a significant political issue was the pressure to incorporate a "two-nation" concept into Canadian federalism.

By this time nearly all provincial governments had developed a sophisticated planning and bureaucratic capability, shifting the level of expertise at federal-provincial conferences away from the federal side. Among other things, better provincial capability meant that real conflicts emerged when conflicting priorities surfaced in the negotiation of jointly financed programs. The emollient style of Prime Minister Pearson, while achieving solutions to differences as they arose, threatened to erode federal powers in key areas. This became an urgent problem in the late 1960's when the declining economy put a limit to federal largesse. No longer would it be possible to fund new programs out of federal revenues which grew automatically with a rising gross national product. If, increasingly, the federal government's role was merely to administer fiscal transfers to fund provincial programs, the federal government would be perceived as a tax-gatherer which conferred no visible benefits on the electorate—a prospect which alarmed federal politicians.

Nevertheless, intergovernmental negotiation and cooperation continued to be the mode of political life which provincial governments preferred. To them it was a much better means of conflict settlement than resort to the courts, the outcome of which had all of the disadvantages of a zero sum game. Thus, when the federal government referred a jurisdictional dispute over offshore oil to the courts, "it was widely interpreted as a violation of the rules of the game since the matter was a political conflict which should be settled politically."[15] A decade later the government of Saskatchewan felt equally injured when, in two disputes over mechanisms of provincial management of oil and potash, which some of the affected companies had contested in court, the federal government appeared at the side of the companies as intervenor to protect its own jurisdiction.[16]

The decline of the role of the courts in constitutional adjustment was only partially the result of the political bargaining method of settling federal-provincial conflicts. It also stemmed from a provincial distrust, largely but not wholly in Quebec, of the impartiality and authority of the Supreme Court of Canada. The Court was a creation of the federal parliament, which could modify its jurisdiction, alter its composition, or even abolish it at will. The judges are appointed by the federal government, which means that critics unfamiliar with the obtuseness, independence, and unpredictability of judges will suggest that the Court will have a centralist bias in constitutional cases. As Premier Lévesque is fond of saying, the Court is like the leaning tower of Pisa, which always leans the same way. Provincial governments have thus become reluctant to use the court to settle disputes. Only the present Quebec government has the opportunity to have it both ways. If they prefer negotiation to litigation they usually gain more, while if they resort to litigation and lose, it only proves their point that the present federal system is unworkable.

* * *

Of all the federal-provincial negotiations of the last twenty years, perhaps the most intractable has been the impasse over the amending procedure in the constitution. Perhaps because it was perceived as a divisive issue at Confederation, the procedure had been left undefined. The provinces had the right to amend their own constitutions except in regard to the office of lieutenant-governor, but a number of important matters, such as the division of legislative powers between the two levels of government, were left to the British Parliament. Even before the Statute of Westminster of 1931, it was generally assumed that the role of the British government and Parliament in this matter was purely formal, and the necessity of occasionally amending the British North America Act was an anomaly which would be removed as soon as agreement on an appropriate form of amending procedure could be reached in Canada. Such an agreement had been tantalizingly unattainable for over fifty years.

The matter has taken so long, partly because constitutional adaptation by either judicial interpretation or intergovernmental agreement has sufficed. Since

---

15.   R. SIMEON, *supra* note 12, at 30. *See also* In re Offshore Mineral Rights, [1967] S.C.R. 792 (Can.).

16.   Canadian Indus. Gas and Oil Ltd. v. Saskatchewan, 65 D.L.R. 3d 79 (Sask. Ct. App. 1975); Amax Potash Ltd. v. Saskatchewan, [1976] 6 W.W.R. 61 (Can.). At the moment a dispute over which government has authority to certify unions working on oilrigs has escalated the conflict between Newfoundland and the federal government over offshore oil.

the achievement of an amending formula—like any other constitutional amendment—has always proceeded on the assumption that agreement of all of the provinces was necessary, attempts to achieve a more flexible formula were difficult. In large measure this was because no provincial government could readily agree to a formula by which any of its powers could be altered without its consent. In the case of Quebec there was the further fear that the achievement of "special status," which could imply an increase of its particular powers, would be vetoed by some of the other provinces.

The campaign to persuade Quebec voters to vote against the 1980 provincial referendum on sovereignty-association gave much added impetus to the desire for "constitutional renewal," especially among those federal ministers (including the Prime Minister) who came from Quebec. Negotiations were intense at the ministerial and official level as a prologue to the First Ministers' "summit" in September of 1980. Progress was made, but the summit failed. At that stage the objectives of the two sides were too far apart. The federal government wanted a reasonably flexible amending formula, which the provinces were willing to accept, but only at a price. Prime Minister Trudeau wanted above all to enshrine a Charter of Rights in the constitution in order to protect not only the usual political and legal rights, but also linguistic and educational rights for both French- and English-speaking Canadians. The eight dissenting provinces adopted the position that they would accept a flexible amending procedure, provided that each province had the right to "opt out" of any amendment which it did not like. This would not only meet the objectives of Quebec, but it would also satisfy those provinces which objected on principle to the idea of a bill of rights, or which were reluctant to concede language rights as a matter of law. This position was unacceptable to the Prime Minister, who felt that it would produce a checkerboard of different constitutional provisions applying differently in every jurisdiction.

Negotiation having failed, the federal government decided to go it alone, and it proceeded unilaterally to propose to the Canadian Parliament a package which included an amending formula, "patriation," and the Charter of Rights. This action was supported by only two provinces (Ontario and New Brunswick) and was bitterly opposed, for a variety of reasons, by the others. The federal government had armed itself with an outside legal opinion that in strict law there was no barrier to such action, and, when challenged in the House and elsewhere, ministers insisted that their proposal was not a constitutional issue but rather essentially a political one. They asserted that in the past the federal government, in seeking amendments, had always maintained the position that there was not a convention of the constitution which bound them to consult the provinces.

Even if there was a convention, what legal remedy existed for a breach of it? All legal authorities agreed that the convention was a nonlegal norm, the breach of which could not give rise to a remedy in the courts. In general, the courts in both Britain and Canada had taken the position that they were not concerned with conventions but only with interpreting the law. Presumably they would do so again. Nevertheless three provinces proceeded, by way of reference to their courts of appeal, to challenge the federal action on both legal and conventional grounds.

Two provincial courts (Manitoba and Quebec) upheld the federal position, while one (Newfoundland) found against it.

The matter went to the Supreme Court of Canada, which heard arguments in April 1981. On September 28 the Court delivered judgment.[17] A minority of the Court, led by the Chief Justice, argued in essence that conventions were not a justiciable matter, and, in any event, the precedents were so uncertain that it was not possible to discover whether there was in fact a clear-cut convention. However the majority, while concluding that the federal initiative was legal, nevertheless maintained that there was a convention requiring provincial consent, so that the federal action was unconstitutional in the sense that it did not comply with the convention. The questions posed in the various references had only asked whether provincial consent was needed. No one had asked whether less than unanimous consent would suffice. And yet this is the question which the majority answered. It was not for them to specify what the convention was, they said, but clearly the support of only two provinces was not enough. There should be substantial provincial agreement. But what was substantial agreement? They did not say.

However bizarre the majority decision was as a piece of jurisprudence, it had a catalytic effect. A further First Ministers' Conference in November, after again coming very close to impasse, did in fact produce an agreement between the federal government and nine of the provinces. Quebec remained an outraged dissident. The new formula in effect took the "provincial" amending formula (two-thirds of the provinces having more than fifty percent of the population), and included provisions by which provinces could override the guarantees of the Charter. In effect Quebec had bargained away its presumed veto on constitutional change in April by joining the dissident provinces in proposing the flexible amending formula with the accompanying right to opt out of amendments they did not like. Now its former allies had closed a deal with the federal government involving a less palatable and sweeping opting out formula. The prospect that Quebec will thus be reduced to the position of just another province may have profound political consequences for the future of Quebec-Canada relations. What the effects will be cannot now be readily foreseen, but this particular outcome could not have been expected unless the majority decision of the Supreme Court had taken the form that it did.

* * *

What does this episode tell us about the courts as arbiters of federal-provincial conflict? Up to a point the courts are necessary referees who can determine authoritatively what the constitution means. However, the law is an instrument for achieving precise answers to conflict. Two contradictory rights cannot coexist, and someone must determine which one prevails. Moreover, while federal-provincial conflict involves vague and complex issues, it is essentially a political conflict. The evidence of history suggests that democratic constitutionalism cannot tolerate an unbalanced diet of win-all/lose-all situations. Most of the time the system is better off with political compromises which are tolerable to all significant interests.

---

17. Reference Re Amendment of the Constitution of Canada, 125 D.L.R.3d 1 (1981).

Consequently, strain on the system is minimized when there are effective political instruments to handle most kinds of conflict. But what if these institutions exacerbate conflict rather than contain it? One must then look at the system of government itself, the party system which underpins it, and the intergovernmental machinery which deals with federal conflicts.

Written constitutions—particularly federal ones—are notoriously hard to amend. Nevertheless, though their words may be difficult to change, their meanings change in response to changing conditions. As Dicey pointed out, these changes in accepted meanings—which are tantamount to constitutional amendments—become part of the constitution when they are sanctified by the courts.[18] Political adaptations from intergovernmental bargaining can only go as far as the courts allow. The extent to which the courts are asked to adjust novel political arrangements into the framework of the constitution also depends on the extent to which these arrangements are challenged in litigation.

Resort to the courts can thus be seen as part of the political game of constitutional amendment. During the 1970's the Supreme Court of Canada was confronted with less than three cases a year having significant constitutional importance.[19] The action was elsewhere, involving federal-provincial bargaining over a wide range of issues, such as joint programs, the renewal of five-year agreements covering fiscal transfers to the provinces, and shared fields of taxation. There were also discussions on the perennial question of constitutional amendment, including the achievement of a formula as well as the transfer of jurisdiction from one level of government to the other. To most provincial governments all of these issues were linked together, so that they would hold out hope of agreement on one if concessions could be made on some other issue. This explains the sense of outrage felt by the majority of provincial governments when the federal government seemed intent on proceeding unilaterally with its constitutional proposals whether they agreed or not. In that single gesture the federal government had nullified the provinces' strongest bargaining card—agreement on the constitution in exchange for jurisdictional or other concessions.

When normal bargaining fails to produce satisfactory solutions, there is a tendency for one or the other of the parties to escalate the conflict by resort to a more dangerous but possibly more effective weapon. Thus, collective bargaining can lead to strikes or lockouts, and diplomatic negotiations to war. In Canadian federal-provincial relations the next step is resort to the courts. Generally speaking, during the period of "cooperative federalism" neither the federal government nor the provinces deliberately sought to involve the courts, though from time to time jurisdictional conflicts were generated as a byproduct of some other conflict in society.[20]

---

18. A. DICEY, INTRODUCTION TO THE STUDY OF LAW OF THE CONSTITUTION 179 (10th ed. 1961).

19. Hogg, *Jurisdiction of the Court: The Supreme Court of Canada*, 3 CAN.-U.S. L.J. 44 (1980).

20. A recent example concerns the jurisdiction over offshore oil in relation to Newfoundland. The federal and provincial governments have been negotiating this issue for years, tacitly avoiding a final settlement in the courts in the hope of a political compromise. An application for union certification on the oil-rigs raised the question of whether this fell under the jurisdiction of the Canadian or Newfoundland labour relations boards. The government of Newfoundland demanded that the federal government stop the liti-

The abrupt change in their bargaining position which followed the federal threat of unilateral action on the constitution led the dissident provinces to open a second front in the courts by referring the constitutionality of the federal action to their own provincial courts of appeal. The whole process of constitutional amendment in Canada involves a number of informal steps which might or might not be based on conventions of the Canadian or British Constitutions. The only certain area governed by constitutional law is that covered by the Statute of Westminster. The courts have generally been reluctant to address conventions of the constitution. In their hearts the dissident provinces probably expected to lose, but the litigation would delay the process, just as parliamentary obstruction by their allies, the Conservative opposition in the House of Commons, had done when the federal government sought to push its resolution through parliament. By buying time they hoped to sway public opinion enough to shake the federal government's resolve, and, to an extent, they succeeded. The Supreme Court judgment was announced on September 28th. A further First Ministers' Conference reached a compromise on November 5th, clearing the way for the revised constitutional resolutions to go through both Houses of Parliament in time to be transmitted to the United Kingdom before Christmas.

However much the issue was settled in the rest of Canada, it had been settled without the participation of the province of Quebec, and this again raised a serious political issue with possible constitutional implications. The province of Quebec responded by yet another reference to its Court of Appeal, seeking to resolve the question whether sufficient provincial agreement necessarily involved the consent of Quebec. In part, this was intended as a delaying tactic, but it also raised one of the persistent ambiguities of the Canadian federation: are all provinces alike, or does Quebec—representing one of the "two nations"—have a special place which entitles it to veto issues deemed vital to French Canada? There have been political controversies in Canada in the past when Quebec has been in opposition to the rest of the country, from the controversy over the execution of Louis Riel in the wake of the Northwest Rebellion of 1885, through the issue of participation in imperial wars from the Boer War, to the conscription crises of both World Wars. Because one of the perennial preoccupations of Canadian statesmen has been to avoid or defuse such conflicts, there seems to have been a tacit recognition that the minimal unity necessary for Canadian survival depends on a series of special accommodations to recognize the existence of a "two nations" concept of federalism. Since the 1960's the conflict between Quebec and the federal government has been the most clear-cut of the issues which have strained the capacity of the Canadian political

---

gation and, when that was refused, referred the jurisdiction question to the Newfoundland Court of Appeal. On March 15, the Premier of Newfoundland called a general election on the issue, which he subsequently won by a large majority, as a means of putting further pressure on the federal government. Meanwhile, the Federal Court of Appeal managed to decide the labour relations case in favour of federal jurisdiction without addressing itself to the wider question of the oilfields. Shortly thereafter, on May 19, the federal government itself referred the question of jurisdiction over the Hibernia field to the Supreme Court without waiting for the decision of the Newfoundland Court of Appeal. This provoked cries of outrage in Newfoundland. This episode reveals how a conflict can escalate rapidly when the channels of negotiation do not work.

system. The isolation of Quebec on the constitutional question may greatly enlarge this conflict.

The most visible actors in the process of constitutional readjustment are the governments, both federal and provincial. These governments, it should be noted, are more than the spokesmen of the sectional and national interests which they represent. They have interests of their own which are distinct from, and often more influential than, the people themselves. "[F]ederalism, at least in the Canadian case," as Alan Cairns has argued, "is a function not of societies but of the constitution, and more importantly of the governments that work the constitution."[21] In other words, constitutional change is not merely a predictable response to wider societal changes, but a product of the interaction of the governments and bureaucracies that are strategically placed to shape the process of change. These governmental bodies command large resources of funds and programs, they constitute in their own right a substantial part of the population, and they are able to assert a territorial imperative without apparent support or interest from the public. The basic division of state functions in a federal system has also led political parties and interest groups to conform to this pattern as they play out their roles within the system. Cairns adds,

> Contrary to all predictions, post World War II Canadian politics has not displayed an irreversible trend to centralization, nor the manifestations of capitalist contradiction in polarized class politics, creative or otherwise. Instead, the provinces, aided by secular trends which have enhanced the practical significance of their constitutionally-based authority, and by the deliberate improvement of their own bureaucratic power and capacity, have given a new salience to the politics of federalism and territorially based diversities it encompasses, reflects and fosters.[22]

This has imposed almost intolerable strain on the mechanisms of conflict resolution in the system. When the provincial governments—and for its own reasons the federal government—found that conflict resolution by the courts was an enterprise that was too risky to contemplate, they increasingly put their faith in the federal-provincial conference. Nevertheless this system itself has been less and less effective in recent years.

> Unfortunately [says Cairns], the contemporary search for intergovernmental coordination confronts a set of conditions inimical to conflict resolution. Reconciliation of federal and provincial objectives is facilitated when one or the other level of government is passive, when one level of government is clearly dominant, when the scope of government activity is minimal, or when the two levels deal with discrete, separable sections of society and economy.[23]

This leads Cairns to the conclusion that there were few conflicts over jurisdiction in the early years after Confederation. Nevertheless there were far more conflicts than he suggests, but they were managed successfully, partly because nearly all of his conditions for resolution existed. Furthermore, in the nineteenth century, when Canada was still a subordinate part of the British Empire, the authority of the Judicial Committee of the Privy Council was much greater than that of any judicial body since.

---

21. Cairns, *The Governments and Societies of Canadian Federalism,* 10 CAN. J. POL. SCI. 698, 698-99 (1977).
22. *Id.* at 720.
23. *Id.* at 721.

At the present time most of the conditions for conflict resolution are adverse. Conflicts over jurisdiction reflect real differences in policy objectives, making compromise difficult. The format of the federal-provincial conference also tends to enhance disagreement. Whereas in the early years the meetings were closed, and a provincial premier was normally accompanied only by his attorney-general, they are now vast conclaves, jammed into what was once the magnificent concourse of the Ottawa Railway Station. Participants are constantly distracted by the steady flow of memoranda, every line of which is carefully analyzed for hidden meaning. Meanwhile, at the opening and closing sessions, the principals are pinned under the television lights as they read discourses intended to be consumed by their own electorates, who need to be reassured that their champion is posturing for their benefit and protection. Even the press interviews of each head of government are carefully monitored by the others so that a response can be mounted at once. The atmosphere is that of a summit of great powers, rather than of a closed diplomatic conference seeking diplomatic solutions. When the participants finally withdraw from the public, their attitudes and positions have hardened to the point where negotiation is almost impossible.

If in fact the machinery for the negotiation of constitutional change is faulty, what are the prospects for constitutional adjustment in the future, and how will the changes materialize? The great patriation exercise involved a concentrated effort of time and energy which will not be easy to mobilize again. Both levels of government have strongly held views on the subject matter of Round Two of the constitutional talks, which will involve the thorny question of the repartition of jurisdiction. However necessary this may seem to the principals in the discussion, it is questionable whether they can summon the sense of urgency to begin negotiations all over again. Furthermore, delay might have a calming effect on the relations between Quebec and the rest of Canada. The urgent practical problems of economic recovery are likely to engage the full attention of all governments, and a renegotiation of the five-year fiscal agreements will compel the parties to concentrate their resources on that issue.

It seems likely that a much greater part of the process of constitutional adjustment will take place in the courts. Ten years ago it was possible for Richard Simeon to say that the "Canadian Supreme Court . . . has not so far established itself as an important factor in federal-provincial relations. . . . It appears unlikely the Court will play a much larger part in the future."[24] One of the reasons why one cannot say the same today is the inclusion of a Charter of Rights in the new constitutional document. Challenges to federal and provincial legislation can be expected from individuals and groups on the new ground of infringement of the Charter, which inevitably will raise side issues of jurisdiction as well.

In the past the principal actors in constitutional cases have been the governments and corporations with long purses and substantial financial interests at stake. There has been little participation of concerned citizen groups which loom so large in litigation in the United States, where so many constitutional issues arise

---

24. R. SIMEON, *supra* note 12, at 30.

from the Bill of Rights. In Canada, part of the reason for this low individual participation level has been the existence of very strict rules governing *locus standi,* so that a litigant has needed to demonstrate a direct and usually pecuniary interest in the outcome in order to be heard. One of the few exceptions that come to mind is the case of *Co-operative Committee on Japanese-Canadians v. Attorney-General of Canada.* [25] A much more usual type of intervention is illustrated by the Canada Temperance Federation (which seems to have been a lobby for the liquor interests) or by the Distillers and Brewers' Association of Ontario, which intervened in the Local Prohibition Case in 1896.[26]

In recent years the Supreme Court of Canada has given a much wider interpretation to the *locus standi* rule, thus opening a way for "concerned citizens" to launch court challenges to laws to which they object on general constitutional grounds.[27] Such interventions are likely to be much more numerous on issues raised by the Charter, while governments will be dragged into the process to defend their jurisdictions. In practice the application of the Charter will incidentally raise the older questions of jurisdiction again, so that however much governments in recent years have preferred negotiation to battles in the courts, they will now be even less able to make the choice themselves. This will bring us back to what Dicey identified as one of the principal methods of constitutional adjustment in federal states: substituting litigation for formal amendment. The fact that the Supreme Court is entrenched in the new constitution is likely to strengthen its authority at a time when its role is enhanced.[28]

Of course no one knows how the Court will handle the new Charter. They have felt comfortable for so long with the same old questions of jurisdiction that it will require a considerable intellectual effort for them to see constitutional law in an enlarged perspective. There was little evidence that their horizon was enlarged by the 1960 Bill of Rights, which merely sought to impose new norms on federal legislation. As Walter Tarnopolsky has shown, the majority of the Court shied away from the general propositions of the Bill of Rights whenever possible.[29] Whenever they could decide a case on some narrower ground—such as the safeguards already in the Criminal Code—rather than on the wider and vaguer principles of the Bill of Rights, they did so. Because the Bill of Rights asserted that the rights specified "have existed and shall continue to exist" it was more comfortable to assume that parliament had always legislated with these principles in mind, so that statute law necessarily conformed to its norms. The only thing new was a directive to the courts to interpret the law beneficially in accordance with its principles. If the

25. [1947] A.C. 87.

26. *Cf.* Attorney-General of Ontario v. Canada Temperance Federation, [1946] A.C. 193; Attorney-General of Ontario v. Attorney-General of Canada, [1896] A.C. 348.

27. Thorson v. Attorney-General of Canada, [1975] 1 S.C.R. 138. For a general discussion of this point see Johnson, *Locus Standi in Constitutional Cases after Thorson,* 1975 PUB. LAW 137.

28. For a discussion of the limits on the capacity of the Court to make authoritative decisions on divisive constitutional questions see Mallory, *Constraints on Courts as Agencies for Constitutional Change: The Canadian Case,* 1977 PUB. LAW 406.

29. W. TARNOPOLSKY, THE CANADIAN BILL OF RIGHTS (2d ed. 1975).

same attitude persists, the net effect of the Charter and its vaunted liberties will be minimal.

What will be the result of the pressures for constitutional change in Canada in the foreseeable future? Alan Cairns has no doubt that the trend is towards greater decentralization, partly because of the growing significance and visibility of provincial activity, partly because of the apparent incapacity of the central government to carry out its role of central economic management, and not least because of the increasing difficulty of accommodating the highly self-conscious Quebec nationalism within the bounds of an otherwise uniform system. How far either the Supreme Court or the concerted efforts of government can find a way out of these contradictions is not a question to which a confident answer can be given.

A NOTE ON QUEBEC ATTITUDES TOWARD CONSTITUTIONAL OPTIONS

ALLAN KORNBERG*

AND

KEITH ARCHER†

I

INTRODUCTION

In a recent essay, Alan Cairns observed that the making of a new Canadian constitution has been an elite activity characterized by the assertion of blatant self-interest on the part of key political actors and by strenuous attempts to manipulate public opinion in support of their respective interests.[1] For example, the suggestion that popular referenda be used in constitutional amending procedures appears to have been motivated by self-interest and the tactical advantage this device might provide political elites, rather than by genuine concern over providing the public with an opportunity to express its policy preferences. Paradoxically, the electoral imperative—the need to harvest votes—appears to have led elected public officials at both levels of the federal system to curry favor with their constituents by representing themselves as their true "champions" despite an increasing contempt for their opinions. However, rather than focusing on their rhetoric or on their attempts to secure tactical advantages in the struggle over the new constitution, this paper examines public opinion on five possible constitutional arrangements: the status quo, renewed federalism, special status for Quebec, sovereignty association, and Quebec independence. Since the last three options have more than a modicum of support *only* in Quebec, the analysis is restricted to opinions in that province.

An examination of those opinions will indicate that the parameters structuring the debate over Quebec's future constitutional status have changed. The status quo no longer is a viable option. Instead, the choice is between moderate and radical change. The analysis also will indicate that variations in Québécois positions on constitutional options are most strongly associated with age, direction and intensity of provincial partisanship, degree of affection for the Canadian political community, extent of orientation to federal as opposed to provincial politics, and assessments of the relative costs and benefits of federalism to Quebec.

Two conclusions are drawn from the analyses. First, despite the ambiguity surrounding concepts such as special status, sovereignty association, and renewed

---

* Professor of Political Science, Duke University.

† Department of Political Science, Duke University.

1. Cairns, *Constitution-Making, Government Self-Interest and the Problem of Legitimacy in Canada,* in POLITICAL SUPPORT IN CANADA: THE CRISIS YEARS (forthcoming).

federalism, the Quebec electorate appears to have become increasingly knowledge-able about these concepts in the period between the May 1979 national election and the May 1980 Quebec Referendum on Sovereignty Association. Second, despite the enactment of a new constitution, the constitutional crisis is likely to continue because the strongest support for options such as sovereignty association or outright independence for Quebec comes from a segment of Quebec's popula-tion which is likely to remain an important part of the electorate in the foreseeable future.

II

MEASURES AND METHODS

The data presented in this paper are derived from the May 1979 national elec-tion study and a special referendum study conducted by Harold Clarke and his associates in May 1980.[2] The analysis proceeds in two stages. In the first stage, the 1979 and 1980 distributions of Québécois positions on the five constitutional options are cross-tabulated with their ethnicity, age, direction and intensity of pro-vincial partisanship, socioeconomic status, and level of education.

Analyses of bivariate relationships such as are conducted in stage one at times can make individual independent variables appear to be statistically significant predictors. However, when all of the independent variables are considered simul-taneously, and the covariance among them is taken into account, ones that ini-tially appeared significant can become trivial. Conversely, some that were not initially significant can become so. Given this possibility, the second stage of the investigation involves the entry of only the 1979 data[3] in a regression analysis.[4] In this procedure the dependent variable—constitutional options—is a factor score derived from a factor analysis of the structure underlying Québécois responses to the questions on constitutional alternatives.[5] The independent variables are the

---

2. The 1974, 1979, and 1980 Canadian National Election studies and the Quebec Referendum Study combine national cross-sectional and panel data to study short and long term forces affecting voting and other types of political behavior in Canada. The 1974 study entailed post-election personal interviews with a national sample of 2562 respondents. Of those interviewed shortly after the July 8, 1974, election, 1295 were reinterviewed after the May 22, 1979, federal election. Interviews also were conducted with a new representative cross-sectional sample of 1467 respondents, yielding a total sample of 2762 cases. Following the February 18, 1980, federal election, 1748 respondents in both the panel and cross-section samples were contacted by telephone and reinterviewed. Quebec respondents again were contacted by telephone during the period immediately before and after the May 20, 1980, Referendum and 325 of these were successfully reinterviewed. Technical information on the design of the studies can be found in H. CLARKE, J. JENSON, L. LEDUC & J. PAMMETT, POLITICAL CHOICE IN CANADA 397-400 (1979) [hereinafter cited as CLARKE]; and LeDuc, Clarke, Jenson & Pammett, *A National Sample Design*, 7 CAN. J. POL. SCI. 701 (1974).
3. Only the 1979 data are used because they contain responses to questions that are not included in the 1980 study.
4. Regression analysis is a widely used statistical technique for estimating the functional relationships of a number of independent variables to a dependent variable. It is particularly useful for current purposes since it enables us to isolate the effects of individual independent variables, by controlling their shared variation. For a more extensive illustration of the usage of this technique, see S. CHATTERJEE & B. PRICE, REGRESSION ANALYSIS BY EXAMPLE 1-18 (1977).
5. Factor analysis enables an investigator to reduce a large number of variables into a much smaller set of factors. More specifically, "[g]iven an array of correlation coefficients for a set of variables, factor analytic techniques enable us to see whether some underlying pattern of relationships exists such that the data may be 'rearranged' or 'reduced' to a smaller set of factors or components that may be taken as source

aforementioned predictors (i.e., ethnicity, age, partisanship, socioeconomic status, and level of education) and four attitudinal variables—perceptions of government's impact on one's well-being, perceptions of costs and benefits of federalism to Quebec, federal-provincial orientations, and affective feelings toward the Canadian political community.

Age is measured in years and education in terms of years of schooling completed. The latter has three categories—elementary school, high school, and university. The ethnicity variable has two categories, Francophones and non-Francophones. The socioeconomic status variable is a scale estimated by Bernard Elishen ranging from 14.41 to 75.32.[6] The federal-provincial orientation variable derives from responses to two questions regarding the level of government (federal versus provincial or local) considered by the respondent to be most important and closest to him and his family.[7] The variable assessing perceptions of government's impact on one's well-being is derived from responses to a series of questions that produce an index assigning lowest scores to respondents who are very dissatisfied with their general and material well-being and hold government responsible for their condition. Highest scores are given to people holding the opposite views.[8] The costs and benefits of federalism variable is derived from responses to questions about the manner in which the federal system is perceived to distribute costs and benefits to the several provinces. An index of costs and benefits was constructed by summing the number of times a respondent stated that Quebec bears unfair costs or receives less than a fair share of benefits.[9] The partisanship variable is a measure of the direction and intensity of provincial partisanship and was generated from responses to standard Michigan Center for Political Studies-type questions. The partisanship scale ranges from "very strong Parti Québécois" to "very

---

variables accounting for the observed interrelations in the data." N. NIE, C. HULL, J. JENKINS, K. STEIN-BRENNER & D. BENT, STATISTICAL PACKAGE FOR THE SOCIAL SCIENCES 469 (2d ed. 1975) [hereinafter cited as NIE].

6. Blishen & McRoberts, *A Revised Socioeconomic Index for Occupations in Canada,* 13 CAN. REV. SOC. & ANTHROPOLOGY 71-80 (1976).

7. Responses to the following two questions were used: (1) As far as you are concerned personally, which government is most important in affecting how you and your family get on, the one in Ottawa, the provincial government here in Quebec, or the local government in ———? (2) Would you say that you feel closer to the federal government in Ottawa, or to the provincial government here in Quebec? For each of these questions, federal responses were scored +1, provincial responses -1, and other responses (local, both, etc.) were scored 0. Scores were summed to yield a 5 point index (+2 to -2).

8. Judgments of government's impact on personal well-being were measured by asking respondents whether: (a) they were satisfied or dissatisfied with their economic condition and lives more generally; and (b) government had any effect on their condition. Satisfaction-dissatisfaction responses were scored as follows: very satisfied = +2; fairly satisfied = +1; a little dissatisfied = −1; very dissatisfied = −2. These scores were multiplied by government's perceived impact responses, which were scored as follows: a great deal = 2; some = 1; not much = 0. The resulting index that was generated ranges from +4 to −4. A comparable index was generated for general life satisfaction, and the two measures were summed to yield an overall index with scores ranging from +8 to −8. *See* Kornberg, Clarke & Stewart, *Federalism and Fragmentation: Political Support in Canada,* 41 J. POL. 889 (1979) [hereinafter cited as Kornberg].

9. Assessments of the distribution of costs and benefits of federalism were solicited with the following questions: (1) In your opinion, are some of the provinces bearing more of the costs of governing Canada? (If "yes") Which provinces are these? (2) What about benefits? Would you say that some provinces receive more than their fair share of the benefits of being part of Canada? (If "yes") Which provinces are these? For further details, see Kornberg, *supra* note 8, at 893-94.

strong other".[10] Finally, affective feelings for the Canadian political community are ascertained by a thermometer scale. Respondents are given a picture of a thermometer that is a 100-point scale and asked how favorably they feel about Canada. On the thermometer the 50 degree mark is designated as the neutral point with scores above and below reflecting positive and negative feelings. Since respondents may use the thermometer scale somewhat differently, the scores are standardized.

III

EXPECTATIONS

Initial expectations were that Francophones, especially younger Francophones who were identified with the Parti Québécois, would be most in favor of sovereignty association or outright independence and most opposed to the status quo and renewed federalism. Older Québécois who were neither Francophones nor Parti Québécois partisans would hold the opposite views. It further was assumed that Québécois who were attuned to both federal politics and the federal government, felt that the federal system had not adversely affected Quebec's fortunes, were satisfied with their economic and more general life statuses and felt that government had had a positive impact on them, and ascribed strong support to Canada as a political community also would be most in favor of renewed federalism and the status quo and most opposed to sovereignty association and independence. Finally, no assumptions were made about the impact of education and social class because the effects of those factors on Québécois constitutional positions might be mediated by Parti Québécois partisanship.[11]

IV

FINDINGS

Even a cursory inspection of the data derived from the 1979 national election and the 1980 referendum studies suggests that the Parti Québécois leaders, if they have accomplished nothing else, have successfully shifted the parameters of the debate over Quebec's future. For a majority of the population, the issue is not whether Quebec's status in confederation should change (60% were opposed to the maintenance of the status quo in 1979 and 67% in 1980) but, rather, how extensive the change should be. Particularly striking is the fact that in 1979, 54% of the non-

---

10. For provincial partisan identification, respondents were scored in the following manner: very strong Parti Québécois identification = 3; fairly strong Parti Québécois identification = 2; weak Parti Québécois identification or "leaning" toward the Parti Québécois = 1; non-identifier = 0; weak identification with or leaning toward another party = −1; fairly strong identification with another party = −2; and very strong identification with another party = −3.

11. Previous studies have indicated that the Parti Québécois is to some degree a coalition of "top" and "bottom"—of young, well-educated, upper-middle class professionals and managers and older, less educated, lower status white and blue collar workers. *See, e.g.,* Hamilton & Pinard, *The Bases of Parti Québécois Support in Recent Quebec Elections*, 9 CAN. J. POL. SCI. 3 (1976); Pinard & Hamilton, *The Independence Issue and the Polarization of the Electorate: The 1973 Quebec Election,* 10 CAN. J. OF POL. SCI. 215 (1977); Pinard & Hamilton, *The Parti Québécois Comes to Power: An Analysis of the 1976 Quebec Election,* 11 CAN. J. POL. SCI. 739 (1978).

Francophone proportion of the population were opposed to the status quo.[12] (See Table 1.)

It is clear that sovereignty association and independence are much more popular options among Francophones, the young, and those who identify with the Parti Québécois than they are among other elements in the population. (See Tables 1, 2 and 3.) It is also noteworthy that although approximately equal proportions of the population favor renewed federalism and special status for Quebec in 1979, the percentage favoring the latter option remains relatively constant in the interim between the 1979 national election and the 1980 referendum, whereas the percentage favoring renewed federalism increases significantly during the same period. (See Table 1.) Growth in support for sovereignty association also outstrips growth in support for special status. For example, 61% of the Parti Québécois identifiers favor sovereignty association in 1979 and by 1980 fully 88% are in favor. In addition, Francophone support for sovereignty association increases from 29% to 51% during the year. (See Table 1.) In contrast, support for special status remains unchanged among "Pequiste" identifiers and increases by only 8% among Francophones.

---

12. Although opposition to the status quo among non-Francophones declined somewhat at the time of the Referendum (48%), it seems clear that this option will become increasingly less viable in the future.

TABLE 1

Attitudes toward Constitutional Options among Francophones and Non-Francophones

(in percentages)

PANEL A 1979

	Status Quo			Renewed Federalism			Special Status			Sovereignty Association			Independence		
	Franc.	Other	Total*	Franc.	Other	Total	Franc.	Other	Total	Franc.	Other	Total	Franc.	Other	Total
Favor	32	41	33	36	51	38	34	43	35	29	15	27	18	4	16
Oppose	60	54	60	26	17	25	30	42	32	41	64	44	54	89	76
No Opin.	8	5	7	38	31	37	36	16	33	30	22	29	8	7	8
N=	(643)	(103)	(753)	(643)	(103)	(753)	(641)	(103)	(753)	(642)	(103)	(753)	(643)	(103)	(753)

PANEL B 1980

	Status Quo			Renewed Federalism			Special Status			Sovereignty Association			Independence		
	Franc.	Other	Total	Franc.	Other	Total	Franc.	Other	Total	Franc.	Other	Total	Franc.	Other	Total
Favor	25	47	28	57	86	62	42	35	41	51	15	45	28	6	25
Oppose	71	48	67	34	12	31	36	50	38	45	82	51	68	94	72
No Opin.	4	5	5	8	2	7	22	16	21	4	4	4	4	0	3
N=	(283)	(51)	(335)	(283)	(51)	(335)	(283)	(51)	(335)	(283)	(51)	(335)	(283)	(51)	(335)

* Total calculations include missing data

TABLE 2

Attitudes toward Constitutional Options by Age

(in percentages)*

PANEL A 1979

	Status Quo				Renewed Federalism				Special Status				Sovereignty Association				Independence			
	1	2	3	4	1	2	3	4	1	2	3	4	1	2	3	4	1	2	3	4
Favor	24	24	35	46	28	33	45	42	33	37	35	35	40	37	24	12	31	24	7	7
Oppose	70	73	55	46	32	36	17	20	33	35	30	32	28	42	47	56	57	71	85	86
No Opin.	6	4	10	9	40	31	37	39	34	28	35	33	32	22	29	32	12	5	8	8
N=	(171)	(153)	(236)	(187)	(171)	(153)	(236)	(187)	(171)	(153)	(234)	(187)	(171)	(153)	(235)	(187)	(171)	(153)	(236)	(187)

PANEL B 1980

	Status Quo				Renewed Federalism				Special Status				Sovereignty Association				Independence			
	1	2	3	4	1	2	3	4	1	2	3	4	1	2	3	4	1	2	3	4
Favor	21	18	34	39	49	55	69	73	50	44	41	25	72	56	35	19	49	34	10	10
Oppose	80	77	61	54	45	39	27	12	32	40	35	48	27	42	63	69	50	65	87	82
No Opin.	0	5	5	8	6	7	5	15	18	16	24	27	1	3	3	12	1	1	4	10
N=	(79)	(77)	(112)	(67)	(79)	(77)	(112)	(67)	(79)	(77)	(112)	(67)	(79)	(77)	(112)	(67)	(79)	(77)	(112)	(67)

*1= 18-25 years
2= 26-35 years
3= 36-55 years
4= over 55 years

TABLE 3

Attitudes toward Constitutional Options among Parti Québécois and "Other" Party Identifiers

(in percentages)

PANEL A 1979

	Status Quo		Renewed Federalism		Special Status		Sovereignty Association		Independence	
	PQ	Others	PQ	Others	PQ	Others	PQ	Others	PQ	Others
Favor	18	40	25	46	44	31	61	12	44	4
Oppose	78	52	48	14	35	32	22	55	48	89
No Opinion	4	8	27	40	21	37	17	33	8	7
N=	(231)	(485)	(231)	(485)	(231)	(483)	(231)	(484)	(231)	(485)

PANEL B 1980

	Status Quo		Renewed Federalism		Special Status		Sovereignty Association		Independence	
	PQ	Others	PQ	Others	PQ	Others	PQ	Others	PQ	Others
Favor	9	40	38	78	43	38	88	18	56	5
Oppose	91	53	58	12	41	37	10	76	41	92
No Opinion	1	7	4	10	16	25	2	6	3	4
N=	(132)	(195)	(132)	(195)	(132)	(195)	(132)	(195)	(132)	(195)

When positions on constitutional options are cross-tabulated with two measures of social class (i.e., socioeconomic status and level of education), the data indicate that in 1979 respondents with lower socioeconomic status and education levels were more likely to have no opinions on such relatively vague options as renewed federalism and sovereignty association. In 1980, however—probably as a consequence of the vigorous referendum campaign—the percentage of respondents without opinions on these alternatives declined dramatically. (See Tables 4 and 5.)

Some interesting differences emerge in the associations between socioeconomic status and level of education on the one hand, and constitutional options on the other, when the effects of the ethnic backgrounds of respondents are controlled. Among non-Francophones, increases in socioeconomic status and educational levels are accompanied by a corresponding increase in opposition to sovereignty association. Among Francophones, however, higher socioeconomic status and educational levels are associated with an increased preference for the independence option.[13] These cross-tabulations complete the first stage of the investigation. The results of the second stage, employing a regression analysis, are presented below.

TABLE 4

Attitudes toward Constitutional Options by Socioeconomic Status (Blishen Score)*

(in percentages)

PANEL A 1979

	Status Quo		Renewed Federalism		Special Status		Sovereignty Association		Independence	
	Low	High	Low	High	Low	High	Low	High	Low	High
Favor	35	26	31	49	29	40	17	33	11	19
Oppose	53	72	20	32	23	45	36	55	74	77
No Opin.	12	2	49	19	47	15	47	12	14	4
N=	(189)	(137)	(189)	(137)	(189)	(137)	(188)	(137)	(189)	(137)

PANEL B 1980

	Low	High	Low	High	Low	High	Low	High	Low	High
Favor	34	16	51	68	34	38	39	46	17	30
Oppose	58	83	34	30	40	45	51	53	76	66
No Opin.	8	1	14	1	25	17	10	1	7	4
N=	(71)	(77)	(71)	(77)	(71)	(77)	(71)	(77)	(71)	(77)

* The middle categories have been omitted for clarity

---

13. Data are not presented in tabular form.

TABLE 5

Attitudes toward Constitutional Options by Level of Education

(in percentages)

PANEL A 1979

	Status Quo			Renewed Federalism			Special Status			Sovereignty Association			Independence		
	Elem	H.S.	Coll	Elem	H.S.	Coll	Elem	H.S.	Coll	Elem	H.S.	Coll	Elem	H.S.	Coll
Favor	41	33	27	34	37	42	32	35	38	19	25	36	8	14	23
Oppose	45	61	69	16	24	33	24	30	41	39	46	46	80	80	69
No Opin.	14	6	3	50	39	25	45	35	21	43	29	18	12	5	8
N=	(216)	(256)	(275)	(216)	(256)	(275)	(215)	(256)	(274)	(215)	(256)	(275)	(216)	(256)	(275)

PANEL B 1980

	Status Quo			Renewed Federalism			Special Status			Sovereignty Association			Independence		
	Elem	H.S.	Coll	Elem	H.S.	Coll	Elem	H.S.	Coll	Elem	H.S.	Coll	Elem	H.S.	Coll
Favor	39	32	20	57	64	63	40	35	45	36	41	54	11	24	33
Oppose	50	64	79	26	29	35	29	44	39	55	54	46	82	73	66
No Opin.	11	4	1	17	7	2	31	21	16	10	5	1	7	3	1
N=	(84)	(101)	(150)	(84)	(101)	(150)	(84)	(101)	(150)	(84)	(101)	(150)	(84)	(101)	(150)

V

REGRESSION

The regression technique enables an investigator to assess net relationships between each of a number of predictors and a dependent variable under a condition in which the effects of all other predictors are controlled. As noted above, in the current investigation the predictor variables are age, ethnicity, education, socioeconomic status, provincial partisanship, affective feelings for Canada, federal-provincial orientations, perceptions of government's impact on personal well-being, and perceptions of the costs and benefits to Quebec of federalism. The dependent variable is generated by a factor analysis which produces two scores with Eigen values greater than one which measure the attitudinal structures underlying Quebecers' positions on constitutional alternatives.[14] The first factor score loads most heavily on three options: renewed federalism, sovereignty association, and independence. The second score loads heavily only on special status.

An examination of the results obtained when the first factor score is used as the dependent variable indicates that together the several predictors are able to explain 49% of its variance. Age, provincial partisanship, feelings toward the Canadian political community, perceptions of the costs and benefits of federalism to Quebec, and orientations to federal as opposed to provincial politics are all significant predictors of people's constitutional preferences. Interestingly, however, ethnicity is not a significant predictor. Neither are levels of education, socioeconomic status, nor perceptions of government's impact on personal well-being significant predictors when the effects of the other variables are controlled. (See Table 6.)

The direction of the signed Betas[15] indicates that older Quebecers, people oriented towards federal politics, those who feel Quebec has paid and received its "fair share" of federal costs and benefits, people who feel positively about the Canadian political community, and who are not identified with the Parti Québécois, are most in favor of renewed federalism and, to a lesser extent, the status quo. Conversely, younger elements in the population, those oriented toward provincial politics, who feel federalism has impacted negatively on Quebec, have neutral or negative feelings about the Canadian political community, and are identified with the Parti Québécois, are also the strongest supporters of sovereignty association and, to a lesser extent, of outright independence.

---

14. An Eigen value is a measure of the relative importance of a particular factor (unobserved variable) in an explanation of the total variance of the observed variables. Since the variance explained by any single variable will have a minimal value of one, the general rule for the retention of factors is that they explain more variance than any single variable, and hence have an Eigen value greater than one. For an elaboration of this point see NIE, *supra* note 5, at 468-514; J. KIM & C. MUELLER, INTRODUCTION TO FACTOR ANALYSIS 49 (1978).

15. In multiple regression analysis, a Beta weight (standardized regression coefficient) is calculated to estimate the amount of variance in the dependent variable that is explained by any one of several independent variables, with each of the latter being assigned a unique Beta. Since multiple independent variables are often measured in different units, standardizing the regression coefficients by assigning them each a unit of one facilitates comparison of their relative effects. The sign of the Beta refers to the direction of the relationship. For example, a positive Beta indicates that high values on an independent variable correspond to high values on the dependent variable. For further details see NIE, *supra* note 5, at 325.

TABLE 6

Multiple Regression Analysis of Attitudes toward Constitutional Options

Predictor Variables	(Factor 1) Constitutional Options Scores	
	r	Beta
Provincial Partisanship	.64	.38*
Affect for Canada	−.52	−.19*
Federal-Provincial Orientations	−.49	−.14*
Perceptions of Costs and Benefits to Quebec of Federalism	.37	.12*
Age	−.35	−.13*
Ethnicity	.19	.02
Education	.17	.02
Socioeconomic Status	−.09	−.05
Perception of Gov'ts Impact on Personal Well Being	−.02	−.01
	R= .70	R²= .49

*   p ≤ .001

The second factor score was subjected to a similar analysis. Virtually none of the variance in the dependent variable is explicable, however, because none of the predictor variables—not even provincial partisanship—is a statistically significant correlate. One explanation for the lack of correlation is that the factor analysis employs a varimax rotation.[16] Because of this rotation, significant predictors of first factor scores cannot be similarly strongly correlated with second factor scores. A second reason for the lack of correlation is suggested by the cross-tabulations presented in Tables 1-5. The data in these tables indicate that special status is an option that receives approximately the same degree of minority support from every group in Quebec. Hence, there is relatively little variance in the dependent variable for the regression analysis to explain.

To recapitulate, data derived from a 1979 national election study and a 1980 referendum study were used to assess a number of expectations regarding the distribution of Québécois support for five constitutional alternatives. The data indicate a sharp increase in support for renewed federalism and sovereignty association

16.   In factor analysis, one has the option of specifying either unrotated or rotated factors. If the unrotated factors are expected to be theoretically meaningful, which is usually not the case, then no rotations are performed. However, the rotation of factors is usually desirable since it simplifies the factor structure. NIE, *supra* note 5, at 482. Varimax rotation, the most commonly used, maximizes the variance of the squared loadings in each column; the axes are rotated at a 90 degree angle (on the assumption that the factors are uncorrelated) until they more closely intersect the clusters of variables, thereby producing a simpler solution. J. KIM & C. MUELLER, *supra* note 14, at 49-50. Part of the results are a statistical artifact because each of the factors after the first explains only residual variance.

during the year, a more modest increase in support for independence and special status for Quebec, and a decline in support for maintaining the status quo. The results of a regression analysis are consonant with most of the initial expectations. Thus, the greatest support for renewed federalism and, to a lesser degree, the status quo, comes from Québécois who: identify with other than the Parti Québécois; are older; have strong, positive feelings about the Canadian political community; are oriented toward federal rather than provincial politics; and perceive that Quebec has paid its fair share of the costs and has received its fair share of the benefits of federalism. In contrast, strongest support for sovereignty association and, to a lesser degree, independence, comes from Québécois with the opposite attributes.

VI

DISCUSSION

The analyses above suggest a number of conclusions, two of which are particularly noteworthy. First, it seems clear that the Quebec electorate is not a kind of *lumpenproletariat*. Supporting this conclusion is the dramatic decline during the year in the proportion of respondents without an opinion on the two most ambiguous constitutional options, renewed federalism and sovereignty association. Moreover, the decline occurred even among the least educated segment of the public. For example, in the 1979 survey, 50% of the respondents with an elementary school education or less had no opinion about renewed federalism and 43% had no opinion about sovereignty association. By 1980, however, the proportion without an opinion on those two options had declined to 17% and 10%. (See Table 5.) Thus, it can be inferred that the Quebec electorate, including the segment which in most democracies is least attentive to and knowledgeable about politics,[17] became increasingly politically sophisticated as it was exposed to information during the course of the referendum campaign. Adding force to this conclusion is the result of the factor analysis. The latter indicates—despite any confusion that may have resulted from receiving conflicting information from political leaders[18]—that there is a definite underlying structure to Québécois positions on

---

17.   There is a large body of literature documenting the relationship between education, on the one hand, and political interest, sophistication, and activity, on the other. One of the earliest and clearest expressions of this relationship was presented by Almond and Verba. They argued that "[a]s in most other studies of political attitudes, our data show that educational attainment appears to have the most important demographic effect on political attitudes. Among the demographic variables usually investigated— sex, place of residence, occupation, income, age, and so on—none compares with the educational variable in the extent to which it seems to determine political attitudes. The uneducated man or the man with the limited education is a different political actor from the man who has achieved a higher level of education." G. ALMOND & S. VERBA, THE CIVIC CULTURE 316-16 (1965). For a discussion of the effects of education on levels of political information and sophistication, see Converse, *The Nature of Belief Systems in Mass Publics,* in IDEOLOGY AND ITS DISCONTENTS 206-61 (1964). Regarding the former, Converse notes that "[i]t is well established that differences in information held in a cross-section population are simply staggering, running from vast treasuries of well organized information among elites interested in the particular subject to fragments that could virtually be measured as a few bits in the technical sense . . . . Of course, the ordering of individuals on this vertical information scale is largely due to differences in education." *Id.* at 212. For Canadian data, see CLARKE, *supra* note 2, at 288.

18.   For example, in his paper, Alan Cairns observes that when federal and provincial political leaders refer to a concept such as renewed federalism, they are talking about quite different things. To provincial leaders, renewed federalism is regarded as a constitutional status that will provide them with the opportu-

the five constitutional alternatives.

A second conclusion that merits comment is rather ominous for the future of a Canadian political community that includes Quebec. Analyses indicate that the strongest support for sovereignty association and independence, the two constitutional options posing the greatest threat to the Canadian political community, comes from a segment of the public which is young, cares little about federal politics and is disenchanted with the operation of the federal system. Since Québécois with these attributes[19] also tend to be disproportionately identified with a political party whose avowed raison d'être is independence—outright or in stages—it can be argued that their disaffection with current arrangements goes beyond unhappiness with the political regime and extends to the national political community itself.

Of course, it is arguable that these data reflect a life cycle rather than an age-cohort effect.[20] Therefore, as this group ages, its affection for the Parti Québécois and for sovereignty association or independence could wane, while its support for system-maintaining options such as renewed federalism could increase. Although the necessary longitudinal data from which reliable estimates could be drawn are lacking, a life-cycle interpretation would be congruent with the finding that the strongest support for renewed federalism and, to a lesser extent, the status quo, comes from older Francophones who are oriented toward federal politics, feel the costs of federalism to Quebec have not been excessive, are identified with the provincial Liberal party, and feel strongly and positively about Canada.

However, a life cycle interpretation, although plausible, is not likely to be accurate because it rests heavily on the assumption that support for the Parti Québécois will erode in the future. As a recent analysis by Harold Clarke makes abundantly clear, the opposite has been and will likely continue to be the case.[21] Employing panel data gathered in a series of surveys conducted since 1974, Clarke's analysis reveals that the Parti Québécois has more than doubled its percentage of partisan supporters since 1974.

> It has achieved these substantial net gains in the size of its group of party identifiers by two processes: by converting former adherents of all other major parties, and by *benefitting hand-*

---

nity to expand their influence over the operation of the federal government. For archetypal federalists such as Prime Minister Pierre Elliot Trudeau, renewed federalism means a condition under which Canadians, irrespective of their province of residence, will regard Ottawa rather than their provincial capitals as "their government." Cairns, *supra* note 1.

19. For an extended discussion of the relationships among these variables and their likely impact on the politics of Quebec, see Clarke, *The Parti Québécois and Sources of Partisan Realignment in Contemporary Quebec*, 45 J. POL. 64 (1983).

20. The impact of the Depression on young Americans is frequently cited to illustrate an age cohort effect. For example, a substantial proportion of the people who came of age during the Great Depression retained throughout their lifetime many of the attitudes (including their Democratic partisanship) and opinions they had formed as young people, despite the fact that in many cases their socioeconomic status improved significantly as they aged. Moreover, through the process of socialization, they transmitted many of these attitudes and opinions to their children. In Quebec's case, one might assume that the younger supporters of an independent Quebec will transmit their preferences to their children, while the natural attrition that occurs in any population as it grows older will increasingly diminish the level of support for a federal state in which Quebec remains an integral part. A discussion of the techniques necessary to separate life cycle, cohort, and period effects can be found in N. GLENN, COHORT ANALYSIS (1978).

21. CLARKE, *supra* note 2, at 82-84.

somely by the replacement of older generations of Quebecers by younger cohorts of newly eligible voters who are favorably disposed toward the party and its goals.[22]

Therefore, it would appear—despite the impressive April 17, 1982, ceremonies on Parliament Hill and the subsequent adoption of a new constitution—that the constitutional crisis will continue.

---

22. CLARKE, *supra* note 2, at 67 (emphasis added).

THE ECONOMICS OF CONSTITUTION-MAKING

WILLIAM G. WATSON*

[W]e've always accommodated jurisdictional intrusions in the past by agreement . . . . I come out of the private sector. I've had success as defined by my ability to agree—that's called making deals. Successful businessmen always know when the time has come to make a deal.[1]

I

INTRODUCTION

Despite a reputation as the only provincial premier who speaks neither of the official languages of Canada, William Bennett, in the interview quoted above, provides a succinct rationale for the economic analysis of constitution-making, a theme for this article, and an accurate paraphrase of the history of Canadian constitutional affairs over the last twelve decades. Although there have been occasional court cases and preemptive intrusions, the dramatic realignment of responsibilities across the three levels of government since 1867 has been accomplished mainly by intergovernmental negotiation. As Alan Cairns has argued, "[m]uch of the change which has occurred has not been formally designated as constitutional, and it has not been accompanied by fanfare. It has simply represented the handiwork of busy men attempting to work an on-going system of government."[2] Humble tools sometimes accomplish great things, however, and the metamorphosis of Canada's Constitution has been remarkable.[3]

Since, in large part, economics is the study of exchange, the negotiation of constitutional accommodations seems a natural subject for economic analysis. The purpose of this article is to see what light an economic analysis may throw on the process by which constitutions are made and remade. The term "constitution" is used here to mean the rules, written and unwritten, that govern the division of responsibilities among the different levels of government in a federal state,[4] while "economic analysis" refers to an approach based on the assumption that people's main motivation, at least in their public relations, is to "maximize their utility."[5] The actors whose "utility maximization" is examined in this article are politicians,

---

* Assistant Professor of Economics, McGill University.

1. The Financial Post, Oct. 31, 1981, at 3, col. 1. (Interview with the Hon. William Bennett).

2. Cairns, *The Living Canadian Constitution,* in CANADIAN FEDERALISM: MYTH OR REALITY 143, 144 (J. Meekison ed.) (2d ed. 1971).

3. As Professor Sabetti correctly notes, John A. Macdonald's constitution predeceased its author.

4. Indeed, a crucial question discussed in what follows is whether a state should become federal in the first place.

5. *See generally* G. BECKER, THE ECONOMIC APPROACH TO HUMAN BEHAVIOR (1976).

bureaucrats, and ordinary citizens.[6]

The idea that economic analysis can be used in the study of politics is of course not new.[7] In the last twenty years, large numbers of economists have ventured into areas that traditionally had been the exclusive preserve of political scientists. Whatever effect this may have had on political science, it has greatly increased the sophistication of economic analysis. Economists no longer content themselves with seeking out market failures which they then leave to government to remedy. Instead, they have taken up the twin concerns of how political systems actually work and how they can be made to work in ways more consistent with economic efficiency.[8]

Until recently, however, the economic study of the problem of federalism has been conducted largely in the traditional manner. Economists have focused on the problem of precisely which distribution of powers and responsibilities would maximize overall utility, and they have paid scant, if any, attention to how such distributions actually are decided. In other words, the economic analysis of constitution-making has been almost exclusively normative; in fact, one recent reviewer of the literature on "fiscal federalism" concluded that "[t]he distinction between the positive theory of fiscal federalism and the normative theory tends to become blurred since governments are treated as if they behave optimally."[9]

To a great extent, this shortcoming has been removed by the recent work of Breton and Scott, who, in addition to a new elaboration of the normative treatment of the "assignment problem," offer a positive discussion of the pressures that bear on constitutional dealmakers.[10] Still, as will be argued below, even Breton and Scott tend to blur the distinction between positive and normative in the theory of federalism.[11]

This article sets itself three tasks: (1) a discussion of the traditional (normative) economic approach to the problem of the assignment of jurisdictions and responsibilities, (2) a critique of Breton and Scott's critique of the traditional approach, and (3) an elaboration and application to the Canadian case of Breton and Scott's positive theory of constitution-making. One conclusion emerging from this exercise is that, following "patriation," there probably will not be a second round of constitutional revision dealing with the division of powers and responsibilities.

---

6. Perhaps it is best to make clear at the outset that the subject here is what economics has to say about how constitutions are made, and not what the present (or any future) Canadian Constitution has (or will have) to say about the conduct of or division of responsibilities for economic policies. Although occasion to comment on the appropriate or likely division of purely economic responsibilites may arise, the purpose here is to illuminate the process by which jurisdictional assignments—whether of responsibility for economic, social, or any other policies—are made.

7. Although the intensive use of economic analysis as a tool for the study of politics is fairly recent, dating from Downs, A. Downs, An Economic Theory of Democracy (1957), the notion that rulers pursue their own interests is a constant theme in a literature to which Macchiavelli is the most famous though not the original contributor.

8. E.g., Wolf, A Theory of Nonmarket Failure: Framework for Implementation Analysis, 22 J. Law & Econ. 107 (1979).

9. R. Boadway, Public Sector Economics 407 (1979).

10. A. Breton & A. Scott, The Economic Constitution of Federal States (1978).

11. Their blurring of the two is explicit, however.

Rather, the process of constitution-making is now likely to proceed, much as it has for a century or more, on an almost daily basis.

II

THE NORMATIVE THEORY OF FEDERALISM

A. The Traditional Analysis

The traditional (normative) economic analysis of federalism consists of a straightforward extension of the economic literature on "externalities" and "public goods," especially "local public goods." In economic parlance, a "private good" is a good whose consumption affects only its consumer. A "public good," by contrast, is a good which, if consumed by one person, is consumed by all. The traditional example of a public good is a lighthouse. If person A puts up a lighthouse, person B can navigate by it, and so can C, D, E, and many others, even though they have made no contribution to its finance. Public goods pose a "free-rider" problem; everyone will wait for someone else to purchase them. Thus, despite the widespread benefits such goods can produce, the market may fail to provide sufficient amounts of them. Only by collective and presumably coercive action (i.e., tax-finance) will public goods be supplied in efficient amounts.[12] Thus, the usual economic rationale for the existence of government is the need to provide public goods.

The usual economic rationale for federalism is a simple extension of this argument, focusing on the problems posed by "local public goods." A "local public good" is a public good whose "publicness" is confined to a given area. For example, malaria spraying is of use only over the region sprayed, and the services of a policeman are of use only along his beat. "Local public bads" exist as well; pollution is the most obvious example. The analysis is the same, however, whether "goods" or "bads" are being dealt with: consumption is more or less "joint" within the locality, while outside the locality no effect is felt.

The existence of local public goods may make it difficult for society to achieve an optimal allocation of resources. One of the necessary conditions for such an optimum is that goods with any publicness be produced only to the point where the sum of the benefits brought about by further production is just equal to its costs. If these costs increase with each extra unit of output, and the corresponding benefits decline, then once equality of marginal costs and benefits is reached, producing either more or less of the good in question will involve losses of utility. The difficulty with local public goods is that when their effects extend beyond the jurisdiction making the consumption decision these spillovers will not be taken into account. More precisely, too few resources will be invested in activities that create benefits outside the jurisdiction of origin, while too many will be invested in activities that create "external" costs.

---

12. The "free-rider effect," however, does not suggest that the market will not provide any of the public good. If, for instance, a firm suffers expected shipping losses greater than the cost of a lighthouse, it may decide to put one up on its own. There is also the possibility that people will behave altruistically, though this renders economic analysis difficult.

One obvious solution to this problem is to try for a perfect mapping of jurisdictions against local public goods, so that for each good there is a jurisdiction that completely includes the area over which its spillover effects are felt.[13] A second solution is to establish some fairly small number of jurisdictions and to provide for interjurisdictional subsidies and/or taxes designed to control the external effects of the public goods in question.[14] Subsidies to the "emitting" jurisdictions would encourage the production of goods with positive external effects, while taxes on the output of offending goods would discourage their production. In this way, all external effects could be "internalized;" the producers of harmful externalities would suffer as a result of these externalities and presumably would cut back on them, while producers of beneficial externalities would be encouraged in their (theretofore unintended) good deeds.

The logical awkwardness of the traditional approach to federalism was first pointed out by J. C. Weldon.[15] The trouble is that a prescription for assigning responsibilities across jurisdictions that relies solely on internalizing external effects offers too many solutions to the problem. In fact, with such an approach, the number and size of jurisdictions is indeterminate. External effects can be internalized with many levels of government, with only one government per country, or even with a single world government; for, in principle, a world government can see to it that spillovers are corrected. Thus, the local public goods problem provides no guidance to the would-be constitution writer. In and of itself, the existence of goods with external effects does not require the existence of separate jurisdictions within a society.[16]

B.   Transaction Costs As a Further Necessary Condition for Determinacy: Breton and Scott's Normative Model

A natural objection to this line of thought, even for the noneconomist, is that complete centralization may be overly expensive. A single national government may find it more costly than some hierarchy of governments to undertake the allocations described above. In fact, Breton and Scott argue that it is only in a world in which transactions are costly that the problem of optimal jurisdiction will have a determinate solution.[17] So long as government is costless, however, there is no reason to prefer one constitutional assignment over another. One big government could acquire all the information required to produce the optimal amounts of all local and pure public goods, or many small governments could trade happily among each other to adjust their outputs to the optimal level. The world would be

---

13. *See* Breton, *A Theory of Government Grants,* 31 CAN. J. ECON. POL. SCI. 175 (1965).

14. *See id.*

15. Weldon, *Public Goods (And Federalism),* 32 CAN. J. ECON. POL. SCI. 230 (1966).

16. It should be noted that even the argument of Tiebout—that if different local governments can provide different levels of public goods, and citizens move to satisfy their preferences, this will provide an optimal allocation of local public goods, Tiebout, *A Pure Theory of Local Expenditures,* 64 J. POL. ECON. 416 (1956)—is not sufficient to establish the need for separate jurisdictions. In theory, a central decisionmaking agency could arrange matters so that different quantities of local public goods were provided in different areas of even a very large jurisdiction.

17. A. BRETON & A. SCOTT, *supra* note 10, at 47.

entirely indifferent to the structure of government. Indeed, government itself would not be necessary:

> [W]ith organization costs equal to zero, individuals will not be asked to register their preferences by voting, since these preferences are known or can be known without effort. Furthermore, no other decision rule can exist except unanimity. The entire notion of representative democracy is therefore superfluous and must be discarded.[18]

The reference to unanimity is mysterious—clearly all decisions *could* be unanimous, but *must* they be?—but the rest of the citation is true to the literature on transactions costs. As George Stigler has written, "The world of zero transaction costs turns out to be as strange as the physical world would be with zero friction. Monopolies would be compensated to act like competitors, and insurance companies would not exist."[19] Without transactions costs, public agencies clearly need not exist. Spontaneous coalitions of citizens would purchase those goods more easily consumed collectively and, with all preferences fully known, free-riding and games-playing on the public goods question would be impossible.[20]

That the existence of transactions costs is necessary for a determinate solution to the assignment problem is the central theme of Breton and Scott's work.[21] Of course, the existence of transactions costs is necessary for most economic problems to become interesting. In the frictionless world of Arrow and Debreu,[22] which so amuses noneconomists when they hear about it, a grand tâtonnement takes place on the first day of existence and the entire economic future is predetermined by means of elaborate contingent contracts. To say that Arrow and Debreu's world is different when foresight is imperfect and transactions consume resources is true, no doubt, though not especially provocative. In fairness to Breton and Scott, however, it is only recently that economics has granted transactions costs the attention due them.

The force of Breton and Scott's criticism of the traditional theory of federalism is undercut more severely by the fact that without local public goods any determinate solution to the assignment problem will normally involve the existence only of a national government. This point is important if their purpose is—as they declare it to be—to investigate the optimal structure of government.[23] Unitary government is obviously one such structure. However, the traditional preoccupation of

---

18. *Id.* at 35.

19. Stigler, *The Law and Economics of Public Policy: A Plea to the Scholars,* 1 J. LEGAL STUD. 1, 12 (1972).

20. Dahlman cites Calabresi's axiom on this point, which bears repeating: "[A]ll externalities can be internalized and all misallocations, even those created by legal structures, can be remedied by the market, except to the extent that transactions cost money or the structure itself creates impediments to bargaining." Calabresi, *Transaction Costs, Resource Allocation, and Liability Rules: A Comment,* 11 J. LAW & ECON. 67, 68 (1968), *quoted in* Dahlman, *The Problem of Externality,* 22 J. LAW & ECON. 141, 142 n.3 (1979). Dahlman develops the point about public goods as a corollary of this axiom. It may be more useful, however, to appeal to recent literature on the public goods question that provides several methods for dealing with the free-rider problem. *See, e.g., supra* note 12 and accompanying text. The common denominator of these methods is that they are all very costly, though in a world of zero transactions costs this obviously is not a problem. *See* R. BOADWAY, *supra* note 9, at 143-49 (1979), for a review of this literature.

21. *See* A. BRETON & A. SCOTT, *supra* note 10.

22. *See* Arrow, *An Extension of the Basic Theorem of Classical Welfare Economics,* in PROCEEDINGS OF THE SECOND BERKELEY SYMPOSIUM ON MATHEMATICAL STATISTICS AND PROBABILITY 507 (1951); Debreu, *Valuation Equilibrium and Pareto Optimum,* 40 PROC. NAT'L ACAD. SCI. 588 (1954).

23. *See* A. BRETON & A. SCOTT, *supra* note 10, at 4-5.

the literature, of which their work is an extension, is to try to explain why federalism may be an optimal governmental structure. An argument based solely on transactions costs is not sufficient to accomplish this purpose. Both transactions costs and the existence of local public goods will be necessary, for without local public goods there is no reason—and perhaps no way—not to make all decisions at the national level. Thus, Breton and Scott's essential contribution to the literature is to demonstrate that the existence of local public goods is neither a necessary nor a sufficient condition for determinacy of the governmental structure. Rather, the existence of both local public goods and transactions costs in government is necessary, though, as will be seen, even this is insufficient for determinate federalism. Figure 1 summarizes the discussion of conditions for determinacy.

Figure 1

Necessary and Sufficient Conditions for (Normative) Determinacy

	Necessary	Sufficient
Determinate governmental structure	Non-neutral transactions costs in government	Non-neutral transactions costs in government
Determinate federalism	Non-neutral transactions costs in government and local public goods	Local public goods and particular non-neutral transactions cost functions in government

Perhaps a more interesting proposition about transactions costs is that only some of the costs of conducting government contribute to the determinacy of the governmental structure. Breton and Scott distinguish four costs of government, or "organizational costs:" the costs of administration, coordination, signalling, and mobility.[24] The first two are incurred by governments themselves, though the bill is picked up by the taxpayer. The second two, citizens incur directly.

Administration costs are "the costs of setting up governmental institutions and of running them," while coordination costs are those "that apply to the task of co-ordinating activities between governments."[25] Signalling involves lobbying, "joining social movements, . . . regulating one's own private economic behaviour, . . . voting," and like activities.[26] Mobility refers to "the act of moving from one jurisdiction to another"[27]—the ultimate recourse of dissatisfied citizens.

Breton and Scott argue that the existence of administration costs does not contribute to the determinacy of the governmental structure.[28] This runs contrary to a common line of argument in the literature on federalism that increasing (or decreasing) returns in the provision of goods and services will require greater (or lesser) centralization.[29] Breton and Scott's reason for disagreeing is that it is pos-

---

24. *Id.* at 7.
25. *Id.*
26. *Id.* at 32.
27. *Id.*
28. *Id.* at 41-47.
29. The few existing studies suggest there may be constant returns to scale in the provision of many

sible to imagine one big government deciding to operate in a decentralized way.[30] While the actual provision of goods would be undertaken by departments or administrative units large (or small) enough to take advantage of the economies (or diseconomies) of scale, the overall pattern of consumption could be determined by a unitary government. With the cost of plumbing consumers' preferences still zero, there obviously would be no efficiency loss to making decisions at the center.

This reasoning serves also to illustrate precisely what Breton and Scott mean by "coordination costs." These clearly are not the costs of sending directives between different departments of government. If they were, the unitary government run on divisional lines might well be more expensive than a hierarchical system designed to take advantage of the diseconomies of scale. Rather, by arguing that administration costs leave the assignment indeterminate, Breton and Scott imply that coordination costs do not include the costs of sending orders to local administrative divisions of a unitary government, but instead are the costs incurred in coordinating the activities of different decisionmaking units.[31] Thus, coordination costs only exist when the plans of different jurisdictions have to be made consistent.[32]

The obvious question, then, is why a country would decide to incur coordination costs by setting up different jurisdictions. The answer Breton and Scott provide is that setting up different jurisdictions may reduce the signalling and mobility costs incurred by citizens.[33] Although in a world in which all four kinds of transactions costs exist, the least-cost governmental structure may be the unitary state, it is possible that a more elaborate structure will save resources in the conduct of government. As a corollary to this argument, it appears that the true necessary condition for a determinate, nonunitary governmental structure is the existence of signalling and mobility costs.[34] Otherwise, there would be no incentive to incur coordination costs. Of course, if signalling and mobility costs are low, there may be situations in which incurring coordination costs does not cause savings sufficient to justify an extra level of government.

In the final analysis, many observers are likely to be inherently uncomfortable with an analysis of federalism running along these lines. Breton and Scott phrase their rejection of the argument that administration costs are a sufficient condition for the determinateness of a multilevel solution in a telling way: "Would such costs really give rise to a public sector with a structure in a world in which signalling and mobility costs were zero, and in which, therefore, preferences were known

---

public services, so that on empirical as well as theoretical grounds the existence of administration costs leaves the governmental structure indeterminate. *See, e.g.*, W. Hirsch, The Economics of State and Local Government (1970).

30. A. Breton & A. Scott, *supra* note 10, at 41-47.

31. *See id.*

32. Of course, in some forms of centralized decisionmaking—though none which would be used in a costless world—the task of the central authority is to coordinate decisions made at the departmental level. Coordination costs would therefore have to be incurred even in a system in which final authority resided at the center. It is hard to say how Breton and Scott would categorize such a governmental structure.

33. A. Breton & A. Scott, *supra* note 10.

34. As suggested above, Breton and Scott are not interested in this question but rather in the necessary conditions for determinateness—pure and simple.

and Lindahl prices consequently feasible?"[35]   In other words, all arguments about transactions costs reduce to the single proposition that the optimum governmental structure is the one that best solves the local public goods problem, taking into account the costs of coordination and administration. Breton and Scott's proxy for the ability of a governmental structure to solve the local public goods problem is the level of expenditure required to operate the structure, including the expenditures citizens make lobbying governments or moving from one jurisdiction to another.[36] Why this should be so is not clear, however. It is perfectly possible to imagine a governmental structure that gives rise to very few expenditures on signalling and mobility, not because citizens are happy with the level of public goods supplied, but because they are desperately unhappy yet believe that protest and/or mobility are futile. As a general rule, many different levels of dissatisfaction with the governmental structure can be associated with a single level of "organizational" expenditures.

In summary, Breton and Scott's model will justify the existence of a multilevel structure of government only if the increased costs of coordination are offset either by reduced administration costs or by the greater ease with which lower level governments can assess the true strength of consumer preferences. Since the problem of public choice posed by public goods is not simply one of collating responses to questionnaires or interviews, but also one of assessing the validity of these responses, it is not clear why one level of government should be expected to play the public goods game better than another. Nor is it clear how the ability of different governments to play games successfully could be tested. As suggested, the level of expenditure on signalling and mobility associated with each possible governmental structure seems an imperfect proxy for "solution" of the local public goods problem. If the assignment of responsibilities is indeterminate when the public goods problem is trivial, it must also be indeterminate when the problem is insoluble.

III

THE POSITIVE THEORY OF CONSTITUTION-MAKING

Perhaps by now it is evident that normative analysis of the problem of constitution-making may be of dubious value. In the first instance, the costs of signalling, mobility, administration, and coordination, while calculable in theory, are not likely to be calculable in practice. To state only the most obvious difficulty, the relevant data will be difficult to disentangle from general data on mobility, coordination, and signalling. Moreover, it will be hard to estimate data for other governmental structures than presently exist. Second, in a model in which participants seek out the least-cost solution to the assignment problem, but do this subject to several sets of constraints, there are likely to be many local optima. The nature of a local optimum is that any movement in the immediate neighborhood of the

---

35.   A. BRETON & A. SCOTT, *supra* note 10, at 46-47.
36.   *See id.*

optimum involves losses. How a society should grope its way from one of these local optima to the optimum optimorum is hard to say.

The most compelling argument against normative analysis, however, is simply that it may have little bearing on decisions actually taken in these matters.[37] It is now well established in the economics literature that what is best for a society is not necessarily best for the politicians who preside over that society.[38]

Breton and Scott's version of the normative argument is to imagine that a "constituent assembly" will attempt to find the least-cost allocation of responsibilities across the various levels of governments (if in fact it is decided to have different levels of government); that the members of this assembly will be perfectly indifferent as to who gets what powers; and that their only concern will be to minimize the total costs of making and acting on public decisions.[39] Of course, as Breton and Scott are the first to admit, their version is not a faithful depiction of how such decisions are actually made. Rather, once a governmental structure has been established in a country (or even before),[40] groups come into being whose interests probably are not best served by a least-cost solution to the constitutional question. Politicians and bureaucrats, for instance, are not likely to be indifferent to which level of government is responsible for which policies. In the case of bureaucrats, whose salaries are almost exclusively responsible for coordination and administration costs, this point is trivial. However, politicians may have their own view of the desirable constitution. Since their immediate aim is to win neither unanimous nor even potentially unanimous support for whatever they do, but only a majority or even a plurality of votes, they need not always give great weight to considerations of Pareto-efficiency in their deliberations. In addition, whether or not a governmental structure exists, ordinary citizens are not likely to be indifferent as to which level of government assumes responsibility for which policies. The desire of many English Quebecers that the federal government take a more prominent role in education arises from a belief, not that this will reduce the costs of government, but that it will better protect what they consider to be acquired rights.

A. What is Optimal Will Be?

Breton and Scott are fully aware that people have other constitutional objectives than minimization of the transactions costs involved in government. Indeed, they make a major contribution to the literature by setting up a model of self-interested constitutional revision. This "positive" model extends the economic

---

37. What can be construed as references to organizational costs can be found in the public debate on the British North America Act, although such costs can hardly be said to have preoccupied contemporary thinkers. *See* W. WHITE, R. WAGENBERG, R. NELSON & W. SODERLUND, CANADIAN CONFEDERATION: A DECISION-MAKING ANALYSIS (1979). John A. Macdonald argued at the Quebec Conference that "[w]ith one general government the expense would be very much less." CONFEDERATION 56 (J. Pope ed. 1895). On the question of signalling, he held that, "The people of every section must feel that they are protected, and by no overstraining of central authority should such guarantees be overridden." *Id.* at 55.

38. Breton himself has made a major contribution to this literature. *See* A. BRETON, THE ECONOMIC THEORY OF REPRESENTATIVE GOVERNMENT (1974).

39. *See* A. BRETON & A. SCOTT, *supra* note 10, at 68.

40. Or even before: disinterested constituent assemblies are seldom allowed a hand in the writing of a country's first constitution.

analysis of democracy not only to the process of governing, but also to the process of establishing the rules by which governments govern.[41] At times, however, it appears that Breton and Scott lose sight of the importance of this contribution to positive economics. They suggest, for instance, that in the long run the difference between a positive and a normative analysis of constitution-making may be insignificant—that, in effect, what is optimal (eventually) will be:

> [I]f the institutional structure is such that governing parties must, to remain in office, meet the preferences for public policies of a large number of citizens, then a representative government type constituent assembly will in the long run tend towards an assignment of powers identical to that produced by a least-cost assembly. This follows from the simple fact that politicians are elected by citizens and that citizens who ultimately must carry the burden of both their own and the governmental organizational costs will favor those parties which make these costs as small as possible.[42]

The premise is unobjectionable: in Canada, at least, governments do occasionally face the electorate. The conclusion to which this is held to lead, however, is not at all obvious. On the contrary, there are likely to be continuing, probably even permanent, differences between the assignment of functions that would minimize the transaction costs of government and the assignment that actually prevails.[43]

Perhaps this proposition can be elaborated with the help of a real-life example: the continuing constitutional conundrum presented by the persistence of a separate provincial government for Prince Edward Island. For the purposes of argument,[44] it will be asserted that any normative or least-cost model of federalism that is not tautological cannot justify the continued existence of three levels of government for an island whose population numbers only 125,000.

Before the consequences of this assertion are elaborated, it is important to make clear that in a least-cost model it is irrelevant whether or not the existence of a separate provincial government for the Island gives any special pleasure to Islanders, either in their role as citizens or in the role some of them play as bureaucrats or politicians. The only justification for a separate provincial jurisdiction must be that it reduces the costs of government, as might be the case if signalling and mobility costs were saved by allowing Islanders to make their own decisions regarding consumption of local public goods. The cost of lumping Islanders in with Nova Scotians, or with all Maritimers, would be perpetual dissatisfaction with Nova Scotia- or Maritime-wide decisions on various public questions. Therefore, higher signalling and mobility costs would be incurred as Islanders either petitioned the regional government for differential treatment or left the Island for jurisdictions whose policies were more to their liking. Thus, the assertion here is that doing away with the Island's government would bring about a net reduction in the transactions costs of government.

---

41. *See generally* A. BRETON & A. SCOTT, *supra* note 10.

42. *Id.* at 101.

43. This point is not inconsistent with the letter of what Breton and Scott say, though it does appear to conflict with their intent. The purpose of the following discussion is not mainly to criticize Breton and Scott, however.

44. Though, it is hoped, for other purposes as well—factual accuracy, for instance. Assertion is necessary, because, as suggested, it is the nature of such models that the data, if they exist in principle, are unknown in practice.

If this is true, then a positive theory of federalism which held—more or less—that what is optimal eventually will be done should predict that the separate jurisdiction of Prince Edward Island would be extinguished. The phrase itself would be less an affront to common sense if in Canadian history there ever had been a reduction in the number of jurisdictions, but this has not happened.[45] In Waite's phrase, provinces are "easy to create but difficult to get rid of."[46] By contrast, a positive theory of federalism that does not take this view has no trouble explaining the continued existence of a separate provincial government for the Island, even if abolition were in some sense "optimal." All that is required is the assumption that Island politicians and bureaucrats have strong interests in the continuation of a provincial government. This assumption is not unreasonable. Although more jobs might be opened up in the Nova Scotia bureaucracy, if abolition were truly an economizing step some people presumably would be left without jobs.[47] Moreover, citizens may attach value to an Island government per se on the grounds that they can expect to receive indulgences from a local government that might not be forthcoming from a differently located or a different order government. This is especially true when the costs of administration and coordination are paid partly by citizens of other jurisdictions. Finally, local politicians naturally will be biased in favor of the continued existence of their jurisdiction—having made such an effort to reach their present position in it. They also are likely to have an interest in winning the allegiance of bureaucrats, who have the power to make life miserable for them. If befriending their subordinates means departing from the strict constitutional optimum, their reaction is likely to be: "So be it."[48]

The practical difficulties of arranging abolition are therefore likely to be considerable: even if politicians overcame their natural antagonism to the idea, the ordinary complications of democratic processes would intrude. Politicians offer, and citizens respond to, bundles of attributes. Moreover, it often appears that citizens respond to these bundles lexicographically. Thus, the party with the "right" constitutional policy may have the "wrong" inflation, development, or social policy, or even the "wrong" leader. Because there are finite numbers of political parties, the "wrong" constitutional policy may persist for quite some time—perhaps forever—before the constitutional question reaches the top of the political agenda.[49]

Abolition of the separate jurisdiction of Prince Edward Island would require abolitionist agitation on the part of those citizens of the Island who do not owe their livelihood to the existence of a separate provincial government. Unfortu-

---

45. *See infra* p. 818.

46. P. WAITE, THE CHARLOTTETOWN CONFERENCE 4 (1963).

47. When British Columbia entered Confederation, several redundant officials were granted sinecures. *See* G. WOODCOCK, CONFEDERATION BETRAYED! 59 (1981).

48. The self-interest of Prince Edward Island politicians is not a purely hypothetical concern. It was the inability to accommodate the acquired rights of Island politicians that prevented Prince Edward Island from entering Confederation in 1867. The overriding difficulty was that of fitting five Parliamentary seats into three counties. Earlier, Islanders had ended hopes of a Maritime union by refusing to discuss any plan that did not provide for a capital at Charlottetown. P. WAITE, *supra* note 46, at 19.

49. This phenomenon would stem from the costliness of political organization—an idea that should appeal to Breton and Scott.

nately, the costs of organizing citizens into effective mass movements can be high, in part at least because of the "free-rider" problem.[50] The benefits of abolition would come in the form of reduced tax and private costs of government. These benefits are likely to be widely spread, however. As noted, part of the gain will accrue to citizens of other jurisdictions, which no longer would have to incur the costs of coordination with the Prince Edward Island government. While, in theory, out-of-province beneficiaries could bribe Islanders to submit to abolition, in practice, such bribes are hard to make.[51] The more important point, however, is that although each Islander might benefit by joining an abolitionist movement, he or she will benefit *more* if someone else does the political dirty work. This point illustrates the difficulty inherent in all collective action.[52]

Perhaps the point has been labored sufficiently. It is far from obvious that the equilibrium that emerges from real-world constitutional negotiations will coincide with the least-cost assignment of rights and responsibilities, even if that were calculable.

B.   What Is Is Optimal?

In brief, the previous argument is that departures from optimality in a governmental structure may persist because the political action necessary to eliminate such departures is costly. The obvious rejoinder is that if the problem is not eliminated because to do so would be costly, then the problem is not a problem in any operational sense. What is must therefore be optimal, or on its way to being optimal. If it is not optimal it will be changed. If it is not changed, this is because it is not worth changing. An argument very much like this has recently been presented by Becker, who suggests that the political system is likely to respond efficiently, not to the dictates of the economist's social welfare function, but to those of what he calls the "political influence function."[53] Groups' and individuals' weights in this function are determined by their media impact, their lobbying power, their voting strength, and like variables, all of which are subject to maximization by self-seeking groups and individuals. In a self-interested world, it is hard to see how the political influence function could be other than it is, and since the political system is held to respond efficiently to it, how policy could differ from what it is. If there are to be spontaneous, policy-induced improvements in social welfare, then it would seem, ironically, that the economist must place his faith in essentially altruistic behavior on the part of policymakers—which obviously rubs against the grain. If this is true, the economist's role becomes that of either poet laureate for the status quo, proselytizer for a new order, or seer. The job of seeking out unexploited exchanges, whether political or purely economic, presumably will already have been done by the parties concerned.

---

50. *See supra* note 12 and accompanying text.
51. Bribes are not impossible, however. The financial settlements made by the Dominion government at Confederation can be viewed as compensation of this sort. Of course, once it is known that bribes are available, Islanders will have every incentive to overstate their opposition to abolition.
52. *See generally* M. OLSON, THE LOGIC OF COLLECTIVE ACTION (1965).
53. G. Becker, A Theory of Political Behavior 3 (Oct. 22, 1981) (unpublished paper).

It may yet be possible, however, to find habitable territory between the twin deserts of "What is optimal will be" and "What is is optimal." As is well known, in a world in which transactions costs are the main impediment to the attainment of a theoretical optimum,[54] governments can do socially useful work by attempting to reduce such costs.[55] In the present instance, at least, this is not a negligible role. One aspect of that role involves reducing the costs of collective action by subsidizing public interest groups, polling, or simply by intuiting public opinion. There is also the possibility of propagandizing. Since knowledge is at least a partly public good, it is reasonable to suppose that information about constitutional inefficiencies may be underprovided. A second possibility is to aim, not at reducing transaction costs, but at altering the allocation of property rights. The main impediment to optimality in this case is that politicians and bureaucrats have special property rights. If these property rights are denied, one impediment to efficient constitutional change would be removed.

There is every reason to be skeptical on these two points, of course. In the first instance, self-interested politicians will not volunteer to subsidize citizens' groups that aim at reducing their privileges—even at challenging their very (political) existence. While it is true that if reductions in transaction costs were effected and/or the allocation of property rights altered, the world would move closer to the least-cost optimum, this is not likely to happen.

It is also possible that Becker overestimates the efficiency of the political system. In a recent paper, James Dean argues that because of strategic behavior by political actors, the political process may fail to carry through on many politically efficient deals.[56] In the end, however, the problem may be one of definitions. If the best that can be done deserves the adjective "optimal," then perhaps any constitutional equilibrium that persists should be called "optimal." However, this is not what Breton and Scott—or most economists—intend when they use the word.

IV
APPLICATION OF THE POSITIVE MODEL

Perhaps enough has been said about the relationship of equilibria to optima. A natural next question, and in many ways a more interesting one, is why any constitutional equilibrium that emerges from self-interested "higgling and bargaining" among provincial and federal politicians should not persist forever. In brief, why do constitutional deals continue to be made, and made, if Canadian experience is any guide, with great frequency?

A. Constitutional Prerogatives as Capital Assets

In what remains of this article, it will be useful to view constitutional preroga-

54. "Theoretical optimum" is awkward phrasing, but so long as transactions costs exist, any unattained optimum remains just that.
55. *See generally* Dahlman, *supra* note 20.
56. J. Dean, Interest Groups, Political Inefficiency and Negative Sum Regulations (Mar. 24, 1982) (unpublished paper).

tives as capital assets, and a particular jurisdiction's set of prerogatives as a port-folio of capital assets. While a country's first constitution gives rise to an initial allocation of portfolios, there is no reason to suppose that jurisdictions will be content with these portfolios indefinitely. In fact, as Alan Cairns has suggested, without much exaggeration, "The day after it is proclaimed, [a constitution's] evolution away from the agreement just reached will commence."[57] Just as the holders of more conventional capital assets will trade with one another when the actual and expected values of these assets change, jurisdictions can be expected to trade in constitutional prerogatives when their opinions of the actual and expected values of such prerogatives change. In addition, jurisdictions may attempt to seize assets, either by exercising new prerogatives or by challenging other jurisdictions' claims to ownership. As is true in the economic world, however, most transfers of constitutional assets seem to result from negotiated exchanges.[58] A positive analysis of constitutional evolution must therefore proceed by examination of the reasons why jurisdictions may be tempted to trade in constitutional prerogatives.

B.   The Return to Constitutional Capital

The return to ordinary capital takes the form of consumption services or cash accruing to the owner of the capital. The custodians, though perhaps not the "owners," of constitutional capital are the politicians who deal in it. While the return to constitutional capital may ultimately take the form of cash or consumption services accruing to these politicians, for this to occur it is necessary that the politician remain in office. As Douglas Hartle has put it, "A politician without elected office is like a fish out of water, gasping for the air of immediacy, involvement, risk taking, public attention, personal power, income and perquisites."[59]

It may be presumed, then, that politicians will try to deal in constitutional capital in a way that maximizes their chances for re-election. Opinions will differ about what accomplishes this maximization—whether it be doing good, being seen to do good, or merely presiding over good times. They will also differ about what is meant by "doing good." It may mean as little as maximizing the difference between taxes paid and public services and transfers received by forty to forty-five percent of the voting population, or it may actually mean attempting Benthamite or even Paretian improvements. The main point remains, however, that politicians will most prize the constitutional capital that most increases the possibility of their re-election.

C.   Changes in the Value of Constitutional Portfolios

An economic asset becomes more or less valuable to its owner as its ability to

---

57. Cairns, *supra* note 2, at 155.

58. This would also seem to be Richard Simeon's conclusion. R. SIMEON, FEDERAL DIPLOMACY: THE MAKING OF RECENT POLICY IN CANADA (1972). On the other hand, Donald Smiley, while possibly also concurring, has suggested that such "exchanges" have often been one-sided: "It can reasonably be argued that until the present decade Canadian federalism has been sustained because at every period either one level or the other has been relatively immobilist with respect to economic policy." D. SMILEY, CONSTITUTIONAL ADAPTATION AND CANADIAN FEDERALISM SINCE 1945, at 34 (1970).

59. D. HARTLE, PUBLIC POLICY DECISION MAKING AND REGULATION 34 (1979).

earn income changes. Such changes can occur either because tastes or technologies change, or because other peoples' opinions of the asset's value changes. This second factor is not unrelated to the first; other peoples' opinions of an asset may change because technology or tastes change in a way that makes it more valuable to them than to its owner. It is just such asymmetric changes in valuation that make trade in assets possible.

The same considerations enter into the valuation of constitutional prerogatives. Their worth to their custodians will change as tastes and/or technology change, or as other constitutional actors covet them more or less. In the constitutional domain, however, it is useful to define "technology" more broadly than is usual, so as to include the economic, social, and even the intellectual environment, as well as technology in the customary sense.[60] A series of examples will help to elaborate this point.

The privilege of imposing direct taxes is of slight advantage in an era in which the social and economic environment does not favor income taxation. Thus, Hector Langevin suggested during the Confederation debates in the Parliament of the Canadas that the provinces were to be granted the privilege of levying income taxes because it was not contemplated there would be any.[61] Since then, of course, times have changed and provincial income taxes now amount to seven percent of GNP.

The privilege of imposing taxes on resources is clearly of greater advantage when the resources in question are not timber harvested competitively, but petroleum whose world price is determined by a cartel.

Control over educational institutions means less when school attendance is rare and schools are largely private than when attendance is universal and publicly supplied. As is well known, the British North America Act (BNA Act) granted the provinces access to what were at the time the least important sources of public revenue. Smiley raises the less advertised but perhaps more important point that the provinces were also assigned what were then the least important public responsibilities.[62]

Control over property and civil rights is less valuable an asset in an era in which—perhaps because computers have not been invented—economy-wide control of wages and prices is prohibitively difficult.

Similarly, control over the money supply is more important—though perhaps not more valuable—an asset in an era in which monetary control is understood to be an instrument of economic stabilization.

D. Trade in Constitutional Capital

Perhaps it should be emphasized that the above changes in value do not necessarily justify the exchange of constitutional capital. That some forms of such capital grow more or less valuable as time passes can explain the enrichment or

---

60. This broadened definition does not suggest that "technology" will not influence the valuation of ordinary assets, though this often is overlooked in the economics literature.

61. *See* W. WHITE, R. WAGENBERG, R. NELSON & W. SODERLUND, *supra* note 37, at 71.

62. D. SMILEY, *supra* note 58, at 37.

impoverishment of different jurisdictions, but it will not explain why trade in such assets may occur. For example, if oil stocks go up and automobile stocks down, people holding oil stocks are better off and people holding automobile stocks worse off, though the two groups will not necessarily trade as a result. They will trade, however, if their relative valuation of each other's assets changes. If automobile stocks become more attractive to the person holding the oil stocks, and/or vice versa, an exchange may take place. The essence of the problem, then, is that changes may take place that make an asset less valuable to its owners than to others.

In fact, a couple of the examples cited above do provide clear illustrations of this possibility. In Canada, the legal power to control wages and prices resides with the provincial governments, yet controls—price controls, certainly—do not make much economic sense in a jurisdiction in which interjurisdictional trade is so important, since a large proportion of prices will be uncontrollable. Of course, the desire to control wages and prices on an economy-wide scale is a relatively recent phenomenon, arising from the combined influence of computerization (so that control is possible) and inflationary changes in the structure of the economy (so that it also appears desirable). Thus, as a result of technological change, broadly defined, the federal government is likely to be more jealous of the provinces' control over property and civil rights, without any corresponding increase in the provinces' valuation of this asset. In exchange for lease of the right to control wages and prices, the provinces can reasonably expect some form of indulgence from the federal government, either in the form of cash[63] or constitutional capital.

E. Predictions of a Positive Theory of Federalism

The proof of any theory is in its predictions. Unfortunately, in this area of analysis, as in many others in economics and the social sciences generally, prediction is made difficult by the absence of data on relevant costs and preferences. Thus, the speculations that follow cannot properly be called "hypotheses," for it is hard to know how they could be confirmed or refuted. Perhaps the accumulation of historical precedents may give some clue to their usefulness, though if this is the case, the task will have to be left to others more versed in the history of these matters.

1. *The Critical Importance of the Initial Endowment.* The original distribution of Canadian constitutional capital was made in the British North America Act of 1867.[64] The original distribution of endowments is bound to prove critical in the subsequent development of a country's constitutional practice. In fact, this usually is the intent of the framers of a constitution, although Jefferson, for one, believed that constitutions should be rewritten fairly frequently, while Alan Cairns argues that the Fathers of Confederation had no intentions for the future.[65] But even if

---

63. Breton and Scott are quite clear in suggesting that such trades can be on a cash basis. A. BRETON & A. SCOTT, *supra* note 10, at 97.

64. This Act reflected earlier constitutional practices.

65. Cairns, *supra* note 2, at 144.

unintended, some effect of the distribution must persist. The problem posed by an original endowment is that the framers of a constitution generally have little idea of what changes technology (broadly defined)[66] may effect in the values of the assets they distribute. A problem analogous to the one they face would be to try to reallocate the world's energy resources so as to assure a particular country's affluence two centuries from now.[67]

That the usefulness of different constitutional functions will change over time suggests at least two things. First, the framers of a constitution might do well not to try too hard to worry about the appropriateness of their decisions for future generations. They simply do not have the information to deal with this problem. Second, they should take care to leave means by which a constitution can be amended. Of course, Canadian experience suggests such mechanisms are likely to come into existence no matter what the original authors of a constitution intend. The BNA Act has been notoriously difficult to amend formally, yet in practice it has proved the cornerstone of "one of the most durable and successful constitutions in the world."[68] In fact, Corry argues that de facto amendment has provided "flexibility and an easy adaptability to the dominant winds of the country."[69] If the constitution will be amended anyway, a formal amending procedure might not be thought necessary. On the other hand, since some measure of inflexibility presumably is wanted in a constitution, it may be preferable, in the long run, to have the constitution altered formally and in the open.

A final point on the original endowment involves the composition of a constitutional convention. The view is widespread that citizens, rather than politicians, should devise a country's constitution.[70] The clear implication of the preceding argument is that this is likely to be futile. Once politicians come into the picture, the constitution will begin to change posthaste. In some cases, change has begun with almost embarrassing promptness. The process of constitutional renegotiation began in Canada in 1869—and in the United States in 1783—and it has not stopped in either country since. Unless a citizens' convention writes an airtight document, which would be unwise for other reasons, matters will soon be shaped according to politicians' liking.

2. *Ars Politica Non Facit Saltum.*   Alfred Marshall, the father of equilibrium theory in economics, argued that nature did not take leaps. The same is likely to be true of constitutional processes. When new opportunities for dealing in powers and responsibilities open up, deals presumably will be made between levels of government. But unless technology changes rapidly in ways that drastically alter relative valuations of prerogatives, constitutional change can be expected to proceed

---

66. *See supra* p. 101.
67. One way to accomplish this is to give all resources to that country. Many observers would argue that in constitutional terms the Fathers of Confederation tried to do this. It is well worth reflecting on the drastically centralized regime which the Fathers of Confederation envisaged. *See* Watson, *Confederation Then and Now,* POL'Y OPTIONS, Dec.-Jan. 1980-1981, at 61.
68. Cairns, *supra* note 2, at 143.
69. Corry, *Constitutional Trends and Federalism,* in A. LOWER, EVOLVING CANADIAN FEDERALISM 121-22, *quoted in* D. SMILEY, *supra* note 58, at 56.
70. *See* Grubel, *Reflections on a Canadian Bill of Economic Rights,* CAN. PUB. POL'Y 57 (1982).

gradually, regularly, and incrementally. This is not to say that rapid technological change will never induce precipitous constitutional change. The 1850's and 1860's clearly brought such changes. For example, the telegraph and the railway enabled much greater centralization in British North America than could be attained in the age of sail. The rapid industrialization of the Northeastern United States had a similar impact. On the other hand, despite Macdonald's intentions, pre-nineteenth century provincial demarcations proved extremely durable. Similarly, dramatic advances in present day communications and information processing may militate in favor of dramatic constitutional change. It is hard to tell, however, whether these advances will involve greater centralization, as might first be thought, or further decentralization, on the grounds that there now is too much information for any center to process.

Still, the emphasis on gradualism fostered by an economic approach to this problem suggests that the much heralded "second round" of constitutional negotiations dealing with division of powers will not take place. At most, what can be expected is a marginal adjustment in prerogatives and, possibly, a codification of existing constitutional practice. The reason is that if politicians are about their jobs, constitutional change will be their constant preoccupation. In Alan Cairns's phrase, the constitution will be a "continuous creation."[71] If an exchange of prerogatives can increase the chances that politicians at both (or the several) levels of government will be re-elected, it is hard to imagine it not being made at the first opportunity.

3. *A Ratchet Effect.* As already has been suggested at length, once a jurisdiction has been given constitutional sanction, it is unlikely to disappear. Responsibilities can be reallocated across jurisdictions, but the number of jurisdictions, if it changes, is likely only to increase. In this regard, the original surrender of "provincial" power in the 1860's to the new Dominion government is not an example of voluntary sacrifice. There is every evidence that the colonies were pushed reluctantly into Confederation by the Colonial Office, with Quebec acquiescing mainly because it felt federation preferable to legislative union.[72] Of course, the creation of an entirely new level of government held forth the promise of continued service for many provincial politicians and bureaucrats. In the present era, the atrophy of municipal powers can hardly be cited as self-sacrifice, since the municipal governments have never enjoyed explicit constitutional existence. Significantly, the national association of municipal officials was the one minority lobby of which the Parliamentary Committee on the Constitution made short shrift.

4. *No Trades Without Gains.* An obvious corollary of the proposition that self-interest will play a role in constitution-making is that jurisdictions can be expected to trade in prerogatives only if they expect to gain by this. Constitutional deals that might at first blush appear not to involve gains for one—or perhaps both—of

---

71. Cairns, *supra* note 2, at 146.
72. *See* D. CREIGHTON, THE ROAD TO CONFEDERATION (1964).

the trading parties may on closer inspection be seen to result from self-interested behavior.

To begin with, self-interest is not inconsistent with some jurisdictions becoming less "wealthy" over time. All trades a jurisdiction makes may involve gains, yet a jurisdiction's portfolio of powers may lose value for reasons beyond the powers of its politicians to control.[73] Moreover, what seems to be a giveaway of powers may actually be designed to gain electoral advantage. Powers that are not much use at one level of government may redound to all politicians' benefit, if their effective exercise at another level makes voters less irritable.

The payment of equalization grants by the federal to the provincial governments is an example of what may be self-interested charity. The federal government obviously would prefer to get direct credit for the expenditures equalization makes possible.[74] If this is not possible, however, a plausible second-best policy is to give the provinces funds to be spent where marginal utilities are high, rather than to add to the total of spending in federal jurisdictions where the marginal utility of funds spent may be low—perhaps even negative. This policy requires either that all incumbents benefit from good government, at whatever level it takes place, or that client provinces look with favor on federal proposals in other areas. Apparently, the latter consideration was of some practical importance in the early days of the equalization program. Dalton Camp describes a meeting between John Diefenbaker and the Conservative premier of New Brunswick during the 1957 federal election campaign, at which the national Conservative leader was persuaded, partly in exchange for electoral support, to endorse the "Atlantic Resolutions"—a set of proposals for greater federal aid to the Maritimes.[75] In early 1958, with Mr. Diefenbaker at the head of a minority Conservative government, the equalization program was revamped and expanded, and the ad hoc Atlantic Adjustment Grants program was introduced. *Post hoc ergo propter hoc* obviously is not the surest analytical guide, though perhaps it does not always lead the analyst astray.

During the last two years, the argument has been heard that governments, especially governments with lame-duck leaders, can afford to behave altruistically. Thus, Mr. Trudeau's concern with a charter of rights, which on the face of it will limit the powers of all governments and is therefore not something to be expected from a politician, may well reflect a genuine desire to serve the people.[76] On the other hand, Mr. Trudeau's intention may be to make the Liberals the party of the

---

73. This is essentially what happened to the Canadian provinces and the American states in the 1930's.

74. John Diefenbaker was characteristically bitter on the provincial reaction to federal transfers:

It is paradoxical but true that whatever assistance we gave to the provinces redounded to the political credit of the provinces. They forgot altogether the assistance that had come from my government. I know of no exception. This was true in Newfoundland. This was true in British Columbia. This was true even in Manitoba.

2 J. DIEFENBAKER, ONE CANADA: THE YEARS OF ACHIEVEMENT 1957-1962, at 294 (1976). The premier of Manitoba at the time was Duff Roblin, a staunch Conservative supporter.

75. *See* D. CAMP, GENTLEMEN, PLAYERS, AND POLITICIANS 337 (1970).

76. If so, this recent episode will have persuaded many observers that that government is worst which governs most altruistically.

Constitution, just as John A. Macdonald's Tories were the party of Confederation. If the "people's package" ultimately proves more popular than it initially appears to be, then this may be capital well spent. Of course, once spent it is gone; rights presumably can only be bestowed once.

5. *Force Majeure.*   In many negotiations, the rights of both parties to the assets they propose to trade are unchallenged. At other times, however, the question of ownership will be in doubt. In such cases—both for ordinary and constitutional assets—there can be appeal to binding arbitration. Ultimate authority on questions of constitutional ownership lies with the Supreme Court. Although the possibility of litigation suggests that the domain of negotiation may be limited, in many cases litigation will be more costly than negotiation.

In the first place, appeal to the courts is risky. The expected value of any outcome may be difficult to assess. In fact, a well respected school of Canadian constitutional law has it that the very nature of Confederation was transmogrified by a careless reading of the BNA Act by the Judicial Committee of the British Privy Council in the last decades of the last century.[77] Though Canadian judges presumably will not be casual in their interpretation, there may yet be considerable uncertainty concerning the outcome of adjudication. Better, perhaps, to negotiate a sure half loaf than to bet on winning a whole loaf in the courts.

The second major disadvantage of legal appeal is that it invariably takes time. Many of the politicians involved in constitutional negotiations are likely to be operating within a relatively short time horizon. Delay, especially if it threatens to take a decision past the next election, may be dangerous. There may be a temptation to split, say, disputed resource revenues, rather than wait for the courts to decide who rightfully owns the golden goose. Thus, it comes as no surprise that the recent agreement between the federal government and Nova Scotia on offshore energy resources says nothing about ultimate ownership of the resources, or that one of Mr. Peckford's demands in his negotiations with the federal government on the same question is that all claims to ownership be set aside for the duration of the talks. In fact, what is surprising is that Mr. Peckford chose to call an election on the question of oil revenues and, in effect, to run (successfully) against the federal government. From the perspective offered above, his decision to refer the question of ownership to the Supreme Court was also aberrant. In light of the federal government's prompt short-circuiting of the reference, and Mr. Peckford's subsequent request for further talks, it appears to have been a last ditch effort to use delay to make the best of what was a weak hand.

A final argument against constitutional confrontation is that force majeure on one front may spoil negotiations on several other fronts. This argument is the most compelling explanation for the senescence of the federal power of disallowance. As Smiley suggests, "[T]he use of disallowance in any but the most unusual circumstances would almost inevitably inhibit the kinds of federal-provincial collaboration that are necessary if the federal system is to operate in a tolerably effective

---

77. *See* F. SCOTT, ESSAYS ON THE CONSTITUTION (1977).

manner."[78] One clear message from Breton and Scott is that the different levels of government may need each other. Upper levels can provide finance and economies of large-scale operation, while lower levels may find it relatively inexpensive to gather information about citizens' preferences. Only when the stakes are large, presumably, will a government risk "linkage" of all outstanding issues.

Of course, like it or not, there may be times when politicians are forced into confrontation, especially legal confrontation. The usual occasion for involuntary confrontation is the third party suit, in which private interests raise the problem of jurisdiction in the courts. Professor Mallory has argued that with the advent of the welfare state and the growing congruence of official and corporate interests, business has been increasingly reluctant to take this route[79] (although there have been exceptions, of which the CIGOL case is perhaps the most notable example). The petroleum companies, for instance, are said to have "worked . . . long and hard to stay out of the dispute" between Newfoundland and the federal government on the question of offshore oil resources.[80] One consequence of this apparent decline in litigiousness is that the risk of going to the courts has increased; the predictability of the verdict presumably varies inversely with the interval since the last case. As Guy Favreau put it in the early 1960's: "Gone are the days when constant recourse to the courts was hurriedly made to obtain an interpretation that would . . . resolve jurisdictional conflicts . . . ."[81] Mallory argues that it remains to be seen whether the declaration of a charter of rights will prompt a new era of third party litigation.[82] If it does, the potentially arthritic effect on inter-jurisdictional relations may prove the sad fulfillment of Black and Cairns's dictum that hasty constitutional revision would be "an act of political immaturity for which succeeding generations would long curse their ancestors."[83]

6. *No Market for Albatrosses.* Popular wisdom notwithstanding, there are some powers and responsibilities whose exercise politicians probably do not relish: they have negative value, as it were. In such cases, governments may try to dispose quietly of these assets. If no takers are available, however, it may be necessary simply to deny ownership. Although past federal governments have not been reluctant to take credit for the conduct of macroeconomic policy when economic growth was rapid, employment high, and inflation low, in more recent times, when all three trends have been reversed, attempts have been made to deny responsibility. Nor are other levels of government likely to volunteer for such responsibilities. Were the provincial premiers' recent demands that they play a role in the conduct of macroeconomic policy heeded, no group in Canada would be more dismayed than the premiers themselves.

---

78. D. SMILEY, *supra* note 58, at 42.

79. *See* Mallory, *The Five Faces of Federalism,* in CANADIAN FEDERALISM: MYTH OR REALITY 55 (M. Meekison ed.) (2d ed. 1971).

80. The Financial Post, Feb. 27, 1982, at 6, col. 2.

81. Address given by Hon. Guy Favreau, Rebirth Through Reason: Cooperative Federalism, Chamber of Commerce, Matane, Quebec (Feb. 7, 1965) *quoted in* D. SMILEY, *supra* note 58, at 81.

82. Mallory, *The Politics of Constitutional Change*, LAW & CONTEMP. PROBS., Autumn 1982, at 53.

83. Black & Cairns, *A Different Perspective on Canadian Federalism,* in CANADIAN FEDERALISM: MYTH OR REALITY 83, 98 (J. Meekison ed.) (2d ed. 1971).

7. *No Man's Land.* The often observed tendency of governments to crowd into areas of policy where jurisdiction has not been properly defined is usually ascribed to the inherent rapaciousness of modern governments. From the perspective developed here, however, it is clear that such behavior need not be irrational. When property rights are ill-defined, it makes perfect sense to stake a claim, even if the property in question has no intrinsic value to the government laying claim to it. The reason is that it may have value in exchange. It is the height of economic rationality to attempt to appropriate assets merely for the purpose of trading them. A steady barrage of such claims may serve to keep other jurisdictions honest.

V

Conclusion

At the end of what obviously has been a speculative article, it seems appropriate to conclude with a word in support of speculation. Although the view of constitutional processes developed here may provide insights into phenomena that otherwise may seem explicable only as the result of irrational behavior, it is not likely to give rise to testable predictions. This, of course, is the classic difficulty of conducting science when the process studied is complicated, data are difficult to come by, and experiment is out of the question. If insight is all that is possible, however, insight obviously will have to suffice. On the other hand, insight may be all that is desirable. Even if verifiable predictions could be had, it is an open question whether the world could make use of a functional social calculus.

THE CONSTITUTION AND THE SHARING
OF WEALTH IN CANADA

Paul Davenport*

I
INTRODUCTION

The sharing of wealth among the provinces in Canada is one of the central parts of the country's federal system. Canada's provinces differ enormously in size, population, resource wealth, and income per capita, and some form of inter-provincial redistribution of revenues or income is essential to national unity. Moreover, the sharing of wealth has always been in part a constitutional issue in Canada. Sections 118 and 119 of the British North America (BNA) Act of 1867[1] included a specific statement of subsidies to be paid by the federal government to the provinces, with higher per capita subsidies to the Maritime provinces than to Central Canada.[2] In the forty years that followed, the subsidies were continually changed until a 1907 amendment to the BNA Act set down a new scale.[3] The BNA Act also gave the provinces jurisdiction over spending on health, education, and welfare.[4] As the importance of these areas of government spending expanded in the twentieth century, so too did the importance of revenue sharing, since the poorer provinces could fairly claim that their own revenue bases were insufficient to permit them to fulfill their constitutional responsibilities in social programs. Thus it is largely for constitutional reasons that the current system of wealth sharing through equalization payments is often called "the glue that holds Confederation together."[5]

There are two sections of the Constitution Act, 1982, which are of direct importance to the sharing of wealth: Part III, on equalization, and Part VI, on natural resources revenues.[6] The entrenchment of a specific equalization formula was suggested in 1968 by the Government of Nova Scotia,[7] which thought the move would reduce fiscal tensions in Canada. The 1982 Act stops short of specifying a

* Department of Economics; Chairman of Canadian Studies, McGill University. The support of a research grant from the Social Sciences and Humanities Research Council of Canada is gratefully acknowledged. I would also like to thank John Graham, James Dean, Derek Hum, and Robert Armstrong for helpful comments on an earlier draft of this paper.

1. British North America Act, 1867, 30 & 31 Vict., ch. 3 [hereinafter cited as the BNA Act, 1867].
2. At Confederation, the Maritime provinces were Nova Scotia and New Brunswick; Central Canada included Ontario and Quebec.
3. British North America Act, 1907, 7 Edw. 7, ch. 11.
4. BNA Act, 1867, §§ 92 and 93.
5. Task Force on Fiscal Arrangements, Fiscal Federalism in Canada 157 (1981).
6. Constitution Act, 1982, 1980-81-82 Can. Stat., [hereinafter cited as Constitution Act, 1982] Parts III & VI.
7. *Cf.* D. Smiley, Canada in Question: Federalism in the Seventies 115 (2d ed. 1976).

formula, for reasons which will become apparent below. Instead, the Act sets out the general principles which should guide equalization. Part III of the 1982 Act reads as follows:

> Equalization and Regional Disparities
> 36.(1) Without altering the legislative authority of Parliament or of the provincial legislatures, or the rights of any of them with respect to the exercise of their legislative authority, Parliament and the legislatures, together with the government of Canada and the provincial governments, are committed to
>> (a) promoting equal opportunities for the well-being of Canadians;
>> (b) furthering economic development to reduce disparity in opportunities; and
>> (c) providing essential public services of reasonable quality to all Canadians.
>
> (2) Parliament and the government of Canada are committed to the principle of making equalization payments to ensure that provincial governments have sufficient revenues to provide reasonably comparable levels of public services at reasonably comparable levels of taxation.[8]

Part VI of the 1982 Act[9] amends Section 92 of the BNA Act of 1867,[10] which sets out the exclusive powers of the provincial legislatures. The 1982 Amendment is concerned with the taxation and control of natural resources, a vital part of wealth sharing in Canada. This issue was of concern to the provinces because of two recent Supreme Court decisions[11] overturning legislation by the Government of Saskatchewan, which had sought to fix prices and control production in two major resource industries: potash and oil and gas. Part VI authorizes the provinces to enact laws regulating the export of natural resources to another part of Canada and to enact laws imposing any mode of taxation on natural resources, as long as such laws do not discriminate between production which is exported and production which is consumed in the province. The role of natural resources, and of this Amendment, in wealth sharing in Canada will be considered below.

While Parts III and VI of the Constitution Act, 1982, are important, neither one will change fundamentally the way wealth is shared in Canada. The process of redistributing revenues among the provinces will continue to be determined by federal-provincial negotiations, whose form and content will be little changed by the recent constitutional reform.[12] Yet the texts are significant, because they will be two elements in the complex combination of obvious self-interest and apparent feeling for national unity that underlies the unruly world of federal-provincial fiscal relations. The purpose of this paper is to explore the relationship between these texts and the current fiscal arrangements in Canada. For example, with

---

8. Constitution Act, 1982, Part III, §§ 36(1) & (2).
9. Constitution Act, 1982, Part VI.
10. BNA Act, 1867, § 92.
11. Canadian Indus. Gas & Oil Ltd. v. Government of Saskatchewan, 80 D.L.R.3d 449 (Can. 1977); Central Canada Potash Co. v. Government of Saskatchewan, 88 D.L.R.3d 604 (Can. 1978). For a discussion of the former case, see Paus-Jenssen, *Resource Taxation and the Supreme Court of Canada: The Cigol Case,* 5 CAN. PUB. POL'Y 45 (1979). For a discussion of the *Potash* case, see Bushnell, *The Control of Natural Resources through the Trade and Commerce Power and Proprietary Rights,* 6 CAN. PUB. POL'Y 313 (1980).
12. Thus while Part III entrenches the principle of equalization, and Part VI authorizes the provinces to levy both direct and indirect taxes on natural resources, the actual equalization formula and payments, and the overall federal-provincial distribution of resource rents will continue to be determined by federal-provincial negotiation and compromise. The mixing of political and economic concerns in such negotiations during the period 1964 to 1968 is described by R. SIMEON, FEDERAL-PROVINCIAL DIPLOMACY: THE MAKING OF RECENT POLICY IN CANADA, ch. 4. (1972).

regard to Part III, what is the relationship between "services of reasonable quality" and "reasonably comparable levels of taxation,"[13] and are both goals achievable with our current equalization formula? If not, what amendments to the current formula seem desirable?

The sections cited in the Constitution Act, 1982, will serve as a basis for reexamining our system of wealth sharing in Canada. While I have tried to keep the paper technically simple, it is still necessary to deal with many economic concepts not found in everyday language, and to examine the quantitative importance of variations in our equalization rules. The use of economic jargon and statistics in this area is the subject of the following scathing passage by Donald Smiley:

> Like prostitutes and golfers, those concerned with fiscal relations have developed their own argot, their own specialized vocabulary for communicating among themselves and mystifying outsiders. Thus we have "contracting out" and "tax room" and "fiscal equivalents" and "revenue equalization" and so on. In very recent years two new terms, "indexation" and "deconditionalization", have been added to this ghastly lexicon—certainly travesties of at least one of Canada's official languages if not of sound public policy. Nowhere more than in federal-provincial economic relationships is the threefold classification of falsehoods as "lies, damned lies and statistics" so applicable, and nowhere do Canadian politicians so embellish their pursuit of the crassest of purposes with appeals to the elegancies of economic analysis or what purport to be immutable principles. It is unlikely that in these matters the limits of chicanery have yet been reached.[14]

Whether the present paper reaches new levels of chicanery is for the reader to judge. This paper's purpose is to cut through the confusions and cross purposes which underlie our current equalization formula, and to show how it might be put on a more secure footing. A brief historical review of federal payments to the provinces designed to reduce disparities in provincial government per capita revenues is presented first. Two possible goals of equalization are then considered: tax equity and fiscal redistribution. The current representative tax system approach to equalization and a macroeconomic alternative are then reviewed. Two special problems with equalization are analyzed next: its impact on provincial incentives and its role in redistributing natural resource revenues. Finally, the importance of efficiency and national unity in the equalization program are considered.

II

THE HISTORICAL ROOTS OF EQUALIZATION

Today, as in 1867, federal-provincial fiscal relations involve two sorts of "balances." The concept of "federal-provincial fiscal balance" implies an appropriate distribution of revenues between the two levels of government, so that each level is able to finance its expenditure responsibilities; this notion of balance groups the provinces together as a whole. "Interprovincial fiscal balance," on the other hand, involves the reduction of disparities in revenue capacity and expenditure responsibilities among the provinces.

Concern with the federal-provincial balance could cause transfers of taxing powers or cash payments from one level of government to the other, while concern

---

13. Constitution Act, 1982, Part III, §§ 36(1)(c) & (2).
14. D. SMILEY, *supra* note 7, at 114.

with interprovincial balance is the basis of Canada's equalization program. Thus, in his presentation to the recent Task Force on Fiscal Arrangements, Minister of Finance Allan MacEachen called for a restraint in the growth of federal transfers to the provinces to correct a federal-provincial fiscal imbalance, evident in the growing federal budget deficit in the face of an overall provincial government surplus.[15] The overall provincial surplus, however, masked an increasing interprovincial imbalance, with surpluses in the three westernmost provinces and deficits elsewhere.[16]

The drafters of the BNA Act faced these same problems of federal-provincial balance and interprovincial balance;[17] they dealt more directly and successfully with the first than with the second.[18] The BNA Act effected a massive transfer of expenditure responsibilities from the provinces to the new federal government; to maintain the federal-provincial balance, an equally important transfer of revenues was enacted.[19] On the expenditure side, the parliament of Canada assumed responsibility for some $89 million in net debt which the provinces of Canada, Nova Scotia, and New Brunswick had accumulated,[20] largely in the construction of railroads and canals.[21] The corresponding physical assets were also transferred to the federal government, which henceforth would be responsible for large-scale investments in transportation facilities.[22]

On the revenue side, section 92 of the BNA Act of 1867[23] limited the provinces to direct taxation, reserving to the federal government customs and excise duties, which together accounted for nearly 60% of total revenue of $19.5 million in the three provinces in 1866.[24] Section 118[25] dealt directly with the issue of federal-provincial balance, establishing an annual transfer from the federal government to the provinces of about $2.7 million, presumably because the reduction in provin-

---

15. A. MacEachen, Federal-Provincial Fiscal Arrangements in the Eighties 8, 12 (1981).

16. *Id.* at 8, and Table II-6, at 39.

17. Report of the Royal Commission on Dominion-Provincial Relations, Book 1, at 36-46 (1940) [hereinafter cited as Report]. *See also* D. Creighton, British North America at Confederation, at 79-91 (1940).

18. My account of the fiscal aspects of Confederation to 1940 is taken mainly from the Report, *supra* note 17, especially Book 1, chapters 1 and 2; the classic study for the Commission, D. Creighton, British North America at Confederation (1940); the standard text, A. Moore, J. Perry & D. Beach, The Financing of Canadian Federation: The First Hundred Years (1966); two scholarly works by Maxwell, *A Flexible Portion of the British North America Act,* Can. Bar Rev. 11 (1933) [hereinafter cited as Maxwell (1933)], and Federal Subsidies to the Provincial Governments in Canada (1937) [hereinafter cited as J. Maxwell (1937)]; and a careful chronology of federal-provincial financial agreements from 1864 to 1927 in A. Boos, The Financial Arrangements Between the Provinces and the Dominion (1930).

19. BNA Act, 1867, §§ 91, 102-126; J. Maxwell (1937), *supra* note 18, at ch. 1; A. Boos, *supra* note 18, ch. 1.

20. Report, *supra* note 17, Book 1, Table 5A, at 42.

21. *Id.,* Book 1, at 37-39; D. Creighton, *supra* note 17, at 75-79.

22. Report, *supra* note 17, Book 1, at 41.

23. BNA Act, 1867, § 92.

24. Report, *supra* note 17, Book 1, Table 4, at 40.

25. BNA Act, 1867, § 118.

cial revenues otherwise enacted was felt to be greater than the reduction in provincial expenditure responsibilities.[26]

Behind the issue of federal-provincial balance, however, lurked some serious problems of interprovincial disparities. In a speech at Sherbrooke in late 1864, A.T. Galt, Finance Minister for the Province of Canada, presented estimates of provincial deficits after Confederation based on the planned transfers of revenues and expenditures to the federal government. As indicated in lines 1 to 3 of Table 1, he projected a deficit of 38 cents per capita in the Province of Canada, $1.70 in Nova Scotia, and $1.33 in New Brunswick.[27] The delegates to the Quebec Conference of 1864 were thus faced with the following problem: given that a federal subsidy to the provinces was required for federal-provincial fiscal balance, should the per capita subsidy vary among the provinces according to the projected deficits or some other measure of fiscal need? After a vigorous debate on the issue, Resolution 64 of the Conference proclaimed the principle of an equal per capita subsidy for each province, implying that a correction for interprovincial balance was unnecessary or undesirable.[28] But Resolution 65[29] allowed an exception to this principle: New Brunswick, because of its particular fiscal problems, might be allowed a special grant for a limited period.

These two Resolutions were embodied in Sections 118 and 119 of the BNA Act,[30] with the results indicated in lines 4 to 7 of Table 1. The principle of equal per capita grants resulted in a payment of 80¢ per person based on the 1861 population. This was well below Galt's estimate of the Maritime deficits, but well above the projected deficit for the provinces of Ontario and Quebec. Three concessions were made to interprovincial balance, however: a lump sum payment to each province (line 4 in Table 1), which amounted to about 6¢ per capita for Ontario and Quebec, but 18¢ to 20¢ per capita in the Maritimes; a ten-year special payment to New Brunswick of $63,000, or 25¢ per capita (line 6 in Table 1); and a difference of $2.85 in allowable debt per capita between New Brunswick and Ontario and Quebec (line 9 of Table 1). Since the federal government was to collect (or pay) interest at 5% on the difference between actual and allowable debt,[31] the $2.85 difference in allowable debt was worth 14¢ per capita to New Brunswick.

26. D. CREIGHTON, *supra* note 17, at 85, 86; J. MAXWELL (1937), *supra* note 18, at 6-14; REPORT, *supra* note 17, Book 1, at 44-46.

27. REPORT, *supra* note 17, Book 1, at 30-45. Galt's speech was printed in the Toronto *Globe* (November 28, 1864) and also published by Galt himself: SPEECH ON THE PROPOSED UNION OF THE BRITISH AMERICAN PROVINCES (Montreal, 1864).

28. *Cf.* A. BOOS, *supra* note 18, at 8, and the REPORT, *supra* note 17, Book 1, at 45, which states, "The prevailing individualism which enforced representation by population in the political sphere assumed without question that the first principle of equity in the financial settlement was per capita equity."

29. The Resolutions of the Quebec Conference are listed in PARLIAMENTARY DEBATES ON THE SUBJECT OF THE CONFEDERATION OF THE BRITISH NORTH AMERICAN PROVINCES 1-6 (1951); the debates were originally published by the Provincial Parliament of Canada (Quebec, 1865).

30. BNA Act, 1867, §§ 118, 119.

31. *Id.,* §§ 112-116.

Table 1

Provincial Finances at Confederation
(dollars per capita)

	Province of Canada[a]	Nova Scotia	New Brunswick	Total
Galt estimates, 1864				
1. Expenditures	.90	2.02	1.68	1.08
2. Revenues	.52	.32	.35	.48
3. Deficit	.38	1.70	1.33	.60
Federal Subsidies BNA Act				
4. Lump sum[b]	.06	.18	.20	.08
5. Grant in aid	.80	.80	.80	.80
6. Ten year payment	0	0	.25	.02
7. Total	.86	.98	1.25	.90
1859 Agreement				
8. Ten year payment	0	.25	0	.02
Allowable Debt				
9. BNA Act	24.92	24.17	27.77	25.07
10. 1869 Agreement	24.92	27.77	27.77	25.46
11. Value of differential	0	.14	.14	.03
12. Subsidies plus value of debt differential, 1869[c]	.86	1.37	1.39	.95
13. Population, 1861 (thousands)	2,508	331	252	3,091

[a]Ontario and Quebec after 1867.
[b]Paid as $80,000 to Ontario ($.057 per capita), $70,000 to Quebec ($.063 per capita), $60,000 to Nova Scotia, and $50,000 to New Brunswick.
[c]Line 12 is the sum of lines 7, 8, and 11.
Source: REPORT OF THE ROYAL COMMISSION ON DOMINION-PROVINCIAL RELATIONS, Book 1, at 45, 60; BNA Act, 1867, sections 118, 119; A. BOOS, THE FINANCIAL ARRANGEMENTS BETWEEN THE PROVINCES AND THE DOMINION 19 (1930); 1861 population is from HISTORICAL STATISTICS OF CANADA series A5-A8, at 14 (1965).

Section 118 says of the lump sum and per capita payments that "Such Grants shall be in full Settlement of all future Demands on Canada,"[32] a bold statement which held up for just two years. In 1868 Nova Scotia appealed to the Imperial government to repeal the Union, and then submitted a list of fiscal grievances to the new Dominion government.[33] In 1869, despite vigorous protests from Ontario, Nova Scotia was granted the same benefits as New Brunswick: a 25¢ per capita payment for ten years, and an allowable debt of $27.77 per capita.[34] Thus, as line 12 of Table 1 indicates, by 1869 the equal per capita subsidy principle had been

---

32. *Id.,* § 118.

33. A. BOOS, *supra* note 18, at 16.

34. Dominion Statutes, 1869-70, ch. 2; *cf.* J. MAXWELL (1937), *supra* note 18, at 28; A. BOOS, *supra* note 18, at 19.

bent to the point that the subsidy in the Maritimes was some 60% above that in Central Canada.

Interprovincial balance was thus an essential part of the political economy of Confederation right from the start, and has been so ever since. Indeed one could argue that the ad hoc arrangements with New Brunswick and Nova Scotia in the 1860's set the pattern for wealth and revenue sharing in Canada for the next ninety years, until the tax sharing arrangements of 1957 formally introduced the principle of revenue equalization based on tax yields. Canada's first-century grants to provinces in financial difficulty were made on an ad hoc basis in response to provincial political pressure. Just as Nova Scotia had threatened to leave the Union in 1868, so New Brunswick had threatened not to join in 1864.[35] In the words of George Brown, who believed in local taxation and was a critic of large federal subsidies: " 'New Brunswick imperatively demanded $63,000 per annum beyond her share, and we had either to find that sum for her or give up the hope of Union.' "[36]

In a similar manner, special arrangements were made to attract and then retain in the Confederation the provinces of Manitoba, Prince Edward Island, and British Columbia, all of which joined the Dominion between 1870 and 1873.[37] In 1907 an amendment to the BNA Act raised the grants to all nine provinces (including Alberta and Saskatchewan, which joined in 1905) according to a rather complicated schedule based on population, but there was also a special ten-year grant to British Columbia.[38] While the schedule is described as "a final and unalterable settlement,"[39] haggling over federal subsidies continued unabated in the twentieth century. The three Maritime provinces presented a continual problem because of their below average personal incomes and government revenues. The 1926 Duncan Commission recommended that the statutory payments to the three provinces be nearly doubled, with an increase of $875,000 to Nova Scotia, $600,000 to New Brunswick, and $125,000 to Prince Edward Island.[40] The federal government accepted this proposal, and then raised the Duncan grants by a total of $875,000 in 1934, on the recommendation of the White Commission.[41]

The depression of the thirties led to severe financial difficulties in all provinces, as revenues collapsed and expenditures soared for welfare and unemployment relief. The federal government responded with grants-in-aid and loans totalling about $500 million to provincial and municipal governments in all provinces.

---

35.   J. MAXWELL (1937), *supra* note 18, at 23-26.

36.   A. BOOS, *supra* note 18, at 10 (quoting G. BROWN, PROVINCE OF CANADA, CONFEDERATION DEBATES 93 (1865)).

37.   *Id.,* at chapter 3.

38.   BNA Act, 1907, 7 Edward 7, ch. 11.

39.   Maxwell (1933), *supra* note 18, at 155. Maxwell reviews the efforts to arrive at a "final" system of federal subsidies, beginning with the statement of section 118 of the BNA Act, 1867: "Such grants shall be in full settlement of all future demands on Canada . . . ." He shows that such declarations have in no way impeded an almost continuous tampering with the levels of the subsidies.

40.   J. MAXWELL (1937), *supra* note 18, at 144.

41.   *Id.* at 184.

Special grants were also made to the four western provinces.[42] The uneven regional incidence of the depression, which was particularly severe on the prairies, brought to the fore the lack of a coherent framework for maintaining interprovincial fiscal balance in Canada. In 1937 the Royal Commission on Dominion-Provincial Relations was appointed to study the issue of fiscal balance and recommended changes in Canada's fiscal arrangements.

In its report the Commission dealt directly with the problem of interprovincial balance, proposing a system of "National Adjustment Grants" rather similar to our current system of equalization payments. The Commission described the grant as follows: "[T]he adjustment grant proposed is designed to enable a province to provide adequate services (at the average Canadian standard) without excessive taxation (on the average Canadian basis) . . . ."[43] We will see below that the phrase "without excessive taxation" can be interpreted in two ways; one is compatible with the existing equalization formula based on government revenue, and another would imply a macroeconomic approach to equalization, based primarily on personal income.

An equalization scheme similar to the National Adjustment Grants approach was adopted by Canada in 1956 in the Federal-Provincial Tax-Sharing Arrangements Act.[44] Under this Act 10% of federal personal income tax, 9% of corporation profits, and 50% of federal succession duties were to be equalized among the provinces, using as a standard the average per capita yield for the two provinces with the highest yield. Provinces below the standard would receive an equalization payment to bring them up to the standard.[45] This formula, which is based on *government* revenue, was first proposed by Prime Minister St. Laurent at a federal-provincial conference in Ottawa in October 1955.[46] At the same conference the Province of New Brunswick tabled an equalization formula based on *personal income,* which would pay equalization to those provinces with per capita personal income less than 85% of the national average. The per capita payment would be a fraction of the difference between 85% of average personal income and personal income in the recipient province; the fraction would be equal to the ratio of total provincial and municipal government revenue in Canada to total personal

---

42. REPORT, *supra* note 17, Book 1, at 160-77, has an excellent account of provincial fiscal problems and federal responses during the thirties.

43. REPORT, *supra* note 17, Book 2, at 84.

44. Federal-Provincial Tax-Sharing Arrangements Act, 1956, 4 & 5 Eliz. 2, ch. 29, §§ 3, 4 [hereinafter cited as Tax-Sharing Act, 1956]. The description of equalization arrangements since 1957 is derived from A. MacEachen, *supra* note 15; J. Lynn, Federal-Provincial Fiscal Relations (1964); R. Simeon, Federal-Provincial Diplomacy: The Making of Recent Policy in Canada (1972); D. Smiley, *supra* note 7; P. Lewis, *The Tangled Tale of Taxes and Transfers,* in Canadian Confederation at the Crossroads (M. Walker ed. 1978); and various issues of Canadian Tax J. (published by the Canadian Tax Foundation), including an excellent article by Perry, *The Federal-Provincial Fiscal Arrangements Introduced in 1977,* 25 Can. Tax J. 429-40 (1977).

45. In fiscal 1957-58, Ontario and British Columbia had the highest per capita yields under the formula. In 1958, the federal government raised the equalized share of personal income tax from 10% to 13%; *see* A. Moore, J. Perry, & D. Beach, *supra* note 18, at 58, 60. J. Lynn, *supra* note 44, at 74-76, discusses both the tax-sharing and equalization provisions of the 1956 Act.

46. A. Moore, J. Perry, & D. Beach, *supra* note 18, at 49.

income.[47] New Brunswick's was a macroeconomic approach to equalization; a similar formula has recently been suggested by Milton Moore,[48] while the macroeconomic approach of the New Brunswick proposal has been supported by Paul Davenport.[49]

The equalization formula adopted in the 1956 Tax-Sharing Arrangements Act ignored natural resource revenue[50] in the calculation of equalization. This led to the bizarre result that the per capita payment in 1957-58 to Alberta ($10.32) was higher than the payment to Quebec ($9.74), even though per capita personal income and resource revenue were higher in Alberta than in Quebec by $169 and $106, respectively.[51] Pressure thus mounted to include natural resource revenue in the equalization formula. However, a problem arises here: if resource revenues were simply added to the 1956 formula, then Ontario would have become eligible for a payment, despite the fact that per capita personal income in Ontario was about 19% above the national average. This anomalous result occurs because the yields of the standard taxes (individual and corporate income taxes and succession duties) which were equalized amounted to only about 2.3% of personal income in 1962-63. Thus while the formula might count a dollar of resource revenue as a dollar, it counted a dollar of personal income as less than 3¢, precisely because the formula focused on *government* revenue alone. This problem of the uneven treatment of resource revenues and personal income became acute after 1972 with the sharp increase in energy prices, and still plagues the equalization program today.

To avoid a payment to Ontario, the federal government adopted an expedient which it has employed many times over the past two decades. To overcome the problems of an equalization formula based solely on government revenue, it simply changed the parameters of the formula in an ad hoc manner, while continuing to calculate the payments on the basis of government revenue alone. Thus in a statement to a federal-provincial conference in Ottawa in February 1961, Prime Minister Diefenbaker proposed two changes to the existing equalization formula: natural resource revenues would enter the formula, but only one-half of these revenues would be included, and the equalization standard would become average revenue in all provinces, rather than the average in the two provinces with highest revenue.[52] The Prime Minister said of this adjustment: "The reason only half of these revenues is provided is to make allowance for the variation in the rates of tax or charge imposed by various provinces, and to avoid discouraging the develop-

---

47. New Brunswick's proposal is reproduced in A. MOORE, J. PERRY, & D. BEACH, *supra* note 18, at 126.

48. M. Moore, The 1982 Renewal of the Tax Collection and Related Agreements: One Western View (paper presented to the Canadian Economics Ass'n Annual Meeting, Halifax, May 27, 1981).

49. P. Davenport, Equalization Payments and Regional Disparities (paper presented to the Canadian Economics Ass'n Annual Meeting, Saskatchewan, May 30, 1979).

50. Natural resource revenues are the royalties, rental payments, and lease payments collected by provincial governments from forestry operations, oil and gas production, other mineral production, and the use of water power; *see* Perry, *supra* note 44, at 430-32.

51. Data in this paragraph on tax yields and equalization payments for 1957-58 and 1962-63 are from A. MOORE, J. PERRY, & D. BEACH, *supra* note 18, at Tables 13, 16, and 18. Data on personal income and personal income per capita are from MINISTER OF FINANCE, ECONOMIC REVIEW 1982 (1982), Reference Tables 16 and 17.

52. *Reprinted in* A. MOORE, J. PERRY, & D. BEACH, *supra* note 18, at 130.

ment of these sources of revenue."[53] Neither of these reasons is convincing: the one-half ratio in no way corrects for provincial tax differences, and since equalization payments *for* resource revenues are not financed by taxes *on* resource revenues the payments can hardly discourage resource development. In my view, both the one-half ratio for resource revenues and the change in standard to the national average were designed to prevent a payment to Ontario. The one-half weight for resource revenue is in fact an implicit recognition of the uneven treatment of western resources and Ontario personal income in the standard equalization formula.[54]

Prime Minister Diefenbaker's proposal was put into effect for the 1962-63 fiscal year[55] but in 1964-65 the formula was changed again,[56] to fulfill a campaign promise of Prime Minister Lester Pearson that the equalization standard would be returned to average revenue in the two provinces with the highest revenue. To avoid making a large payment to Ontario, resource revenues were removed from the standard revenue yield, but then to avoid payments to Alberta and British Columbia, resource revenues in excess of the national average per capita were *deducted* from the grant otherwise payable. These ad hoc adjustments, like those of the Diefenbaker government, are additional evidence of the problems induced by a formula which focuses only on government revenue.

One of the losers from the inclusion of natural resource revenues in the 1962 formula, and their use as a deduction in 1964, was Saskatchewan, which had (and still has) below average personal income per capita but above average resource revenues.[57] Prime Minister Pearson announced the new fiscal arrangements for 1964-65 at a federal-provincial conference in Ottawa in November 1963.[58] Premier Lloyd of Saskatchewan promptly attacked the federal proposal as unfair to his province, particularly with regard to the treatment of resource revenues.[59] This paper will show that from a macroeconomic perspective the current equalization formula is indeed unfair to provinces with high resource revenues and low personal incomes.

In 1967-68, the current system of equalization was established.[60] The three standard taxes were replaced by a formula which included all provincial taxes, and has thus become known as the "Representative Tax System."[61] Although the

---

53. *Id.*
54. *Cf.* A. MOORE, J. PERRY, & D. BEACH, *supra* note 18, at 85.
55. The Federal-Provincial Fiscal Arrangements Act, 1962-63 Can. Stat., ch. 14.
56. The Federal-Provincial Fiscal Revision Act, 1964 Can. Stat., ch. 26; A. MOORE, J. PERRY & D. BEACH, *supra* note 18, at 74, 82-85.
57. *See* Tables 3 and 4 below.
58. A. MOORE, J. PERRY & D. BEACH, *supra* note 18, at 81-85.
59. *Id.* at 85. Ross Thatcher, who succeeded Lloyd as Premier in 1964, threatened to pull the Provincial Liberal Party out of the National Liberal Party if Prime Minister Pearson implemented the tax-indicator approach in 1966. The final settlement included a special transition payment to Saskatchewan—in 1965-66-67 Can. Stat., ch. 89, § 9(2)—but it is unclear whether the payment was directly related to Thatcher's protest; *see* R. SIMEON, *supra* note 44, at 75-76.
60. Federal-Provincial Fiscal Relations Act, 1967, 1965-66-67 Can. Stat., ch. 89.
61. The Representative Tax System was explained in masterful essays by James Lynn in COMPARING PROVINCIAL REVENUE YIELDS: THE TAX INDICATOR APPROACH (1968) and by Douglas Clark in FISCAL NEEDS AND REVENUE EQUALIZATION GRANTS (1969). Both Lynn and Clark became distinguished mem-

equalization standard reverted to the national average, total payments rose by 55% in the year the new system was introduced because of the inclusion of so many additional provincial revenue sources.[62] Provincial non-resource revenues were now great enough that all resource revenues could be included in the formula without a payment to Ontario. Provincial revenues were divided into 16 sources in 1967-68; the number rose to 19 in 1972-73, 20 in 1973-74, and 29 in 1977-78.[63]

The new equalization system remained unchanged during its first five years, but then ran into trouble when the rapid increase in the prices of oil and gas after 1973 led to a corresponding increase in resource revenues in the three westernmost provinces. These new revenues would have required large increases in equalization payments, and eventually a payment to Ontario; the Ontario payment would have been $660 million in 1977-78, and $1.7 billion in 1980-81.[64] The federal government adopted the same expedient as in 1962-63 when resource revenues were introduced into the formula system: it changed the parameters of the formula. In 1974-75 two-thirds of all new oil and gas revenues due to price increases after 1973 were removed from the formula;[65] this provision was replaced in 1977-78 by two new changes designed to limit payments on account of natural resources.[66] In 1982-83, the federal government simply removed Alberta from the calculation of the equalization standard,[67] thereby removing about 85% of

bers of the Federal-Provincial Relations Branch of the Department of Finance. Even those who, like the present author, believe that the Representative Tax System has serious flaws, must admire the skill with which this relatively complex fiscal formula was introduced and administered at the Department of Finance.

62. Total payments rose from $355 million in 1966-67 to $552 million in 1967-68; see A. MacEachen, supra note 15, Table V-1, at 63. The Representative Tax System was chosen in preference to an approach based on personal income, which had been suggested by New Brunswick in 1955 (see supra note 47). The two approaches were compared in papers presented by federal officials to a federal-provincial meeting on fiscal arrangements in February 1966. At subsequent meetings in July and September 1966, Nova Scotia strongly supported a macroeconomic approach based on total income, but the federal government's preference was for the Representative Tax System, which was ultimately adopted. See R. SIMEON, supra note 44, at 66-85, for an excellent account of federal-provincial fiscal negotiations during 1965 and 1966.

63. The original 16 revenue sources in 1967-68 are listed in D. CLARK, FISCAL NEEDS AND REVENUE EQUALIZATION GRANTS (1969), Table VI, at 39-40 [hereinafter cited as D. CLARK (1969)]. The growth in the number of revenue sources from 1967-68 to 1977-78 is described by A. MacEachen, supra note 15, at 68. The 29 sources in 1977-78, which are listed in Perry, supra note 44, at 431, include: personal and corporate income taxes; general sales taxes; taxes on tobacco and gasoline; alcohol revenues; natural resource revenues; and various other taxes and provincial government revenues.

64. Per capita figures are from Davenport, supra note 49, at Table 1 and from Table 3 below; these must be multiplied by the Ontario population to get the numbers in the text.

65. Federal-Provincial Fiscal Arrangements Act, 1972, 1972 Can. Stat., ch. 8, as amended by 1974-75 Can. Stat., ch. 65; section 1 of the latter statute describes the new treatment of resource revenues.

66. The Federal-Provincial Fiscal Arrangements and Established Programs Financing Act, 1977, 1976-77 Can. Stat., ch. 10. Sections 4(2) and 4(7) of the 1977 Act included only one-half of non-renewable resource revenues in the equalization formula, and put a limit of one-third on the share of total equalization payments which could be paid on account of natural resource revenues; § 4(2) lists the 29 revenue sources included in the formula. In 1981, equalization payments on account of natural resources were further reduced by the ad hoc removal of the revenues from the sale of leases on Crown oil and gas lands. 1980-81-82 Can. Stat., ch. 46, § 1(1); in 1980-81 the revenues involved were $952 million. As compared to including one-half of these revenues in the formula, removing them entirely reduced equalization payments by $172 million in 1980-81. See DEP'T OF FINANCE, PROVINCIAL FISCAL EQUALIZATION TABLES: FOURTH ESTIMATE, 1980-81, Summary Table 13 and Computation Table 20 (1981).

67. The 1982 amendments to The Federal-Provincial Fiscal Arrangements and Established Programs Financing Act, 1977, changed the standard of equalization payments from average provincial government

Canada's oil and gas revenues from the formula.[68]

This constant ad hoc reformulation of the program renders the incorporation of equalization in the Constitution of dubious significance: does it make sense to entrench a federal program whose payments are frequently changed and redistributed at the will of the federal government, on the pretense that the program is one of the fundamental principles on which the country is based? It is high time to rethink the equalization program, in order to put it in a more permanent framework.

Rethinking equalization requires a careful re-examination of the Representative Tax System. One of the recent changes to the equalization program denied a payment to any province with personal income per capita above the national average.[69] This personal income override was directed at Ontario, which otherwise would have been eligible for a payment in the late 1970's.[70] After objecting to this provision, the Task Force on Fiscal Arrangements notes that "This issue raises difficult problems of perception and may cast some doubts on the continued validity of the measures of fiscal capacity currently employed."[71] One of the themes of this paper is that the frequent ad hoc adjustments to the current program *should* cast doubts on the validity of the Representative Tax System as a framework for equalization. Indeed, the frequent changes remind one of the situation with regard to tax rentals in 1955,[72] before the 1956 equalization formula was introduced, as described by Moore, Perry, and Beach: "the formulae used for calculating payments under the rental agreements had become a disarray of improvisations and were badly in need of overhauling. The three bases had neither uniformity nor principle but had been designed to yield the amount of money each province would accept to enter an agreement."[73]

One source of the difficulties of the current equalization system is its concentration on government revenue and neglect of personal income. The recent Task Force on Fiscal Arrangements compares the current Representative Tax System approach to equalization, based on government revenue, with an alternative

---

revenue in all provinces (including Alberta), to the average revenue in five provinces—British Columbia, Manitoba, Ontario, Quebec, and Saskatchewan—thereby excluding Alberta's wealth from the equalization formula. 1980-81-82 Can. Stat., ch. 94, § 2.

68. The 85% figure is from ECONOMIC COUNCIL OF CANADA, FINANCING CONFEDERATION, Table B-1, at 147 (1982).

69. Federal-Provincial Fiscal Arrangements and Established Programs Financing Act, 1977, 1976-77 Can. Stat., ch. 10, as amended by 1980-81-82 Can. Stat., ch. 46, § 1(2).

70. On the relation between the override and Ontario's eligibility, see Courchene & Copplestone, *Alternative Equalization Programs: Two Tier Systems,* FISCAL DIMENSIONS OF CANADIAN FEDERALISM, at 15-16 (R. M. Bird ed. 1980), and TASK FORCE ON FISCAL ARRANGEMENTS, *supra* note 5, at 166-69. The override was passed by parliament in 1981, but was retroactive to 1977-78, when Ontario first became eligible for a payment.

71. TASK FORCE ON FISCAL ARRANGEMENTS, *supra* note 5, at 168.

72. The tax rental arrangements were begun in 1941 to aid the federal government in financing the war effort. Provincial and municipal income taxes were terminated, allowing the federal government to levy uniform income taxes throughout the country. In return, the federal government transferred part of the collected taxes to the provinces. These transfers were called "tax rental payments," to indicate that the federal government was "renting" the provincial income tax base. The rental agreements are analyzed in A. MOORE, J. PERRY & D. BEACH, *supra* note 18, at ch. 2.

73. A. MOORE, J. PERRY & D. BEACH, *supra* note 18, at 46.

macroeconomic approach based on an aggregate measure of income, including personal income.[74] While both the federal government[75] and the Task Force[76] prefer the Representative Tax System, the macroeconomic approach is not without supporters.[77] The theme of the present paper is that the choice between these two approaches should depend upon the goals of equalization, and in particular whether equalization is designed primarily to equalize tax rates among provinces or to redistribute income from high-income provinces to low-income provinces. In effect, we must determine the most sensible interpretation of the clause "reasonably comparable levels of public services at reasonably comparable levels of taxation" in Section 36(2) of the Constitution Act, 1982.

III

Tax Equity and Fiscal Redistribution

Fiscal equalization in Canada is a federal government program designed to promote equity among the residents of the various provinces. As applied to fiscal matters, however, "equity" is a slippery concept with at least two dimensions, horizontal and vertical. Horizontal equity consists of the equal treatment of equals— for example, insuring that people with a given income face similar tax rates across the country. Vertical equity involves the proper treatment of unequals, such as the issues of whether or not those with higher incomes should face higher tax rates, as they do with a progressive income tax. The interpretation of equity is particularly difficult in a federal country like Canada, where overall equity depends crucially upon the independent taxing and spending policies of the various levels of government.

The current equalization formula in Canada is based on the following approach to *tax equity*: each province in Canada should be able to achieve the average level of government spending while levying average tax rates.[78] In a truly federal country, however, it is both impossible and undesirable to impose identical systems of taxation and public services in all the provinces. Thus Canadian equalization grants are designed to give each province the *possibility* of achieving the average level of government spending while levying average tax rates; each province is then free to adjust its own levels of taxation and spending according to the desires of its citizens.

An alternative goal to tax equity is the redistribution of revenues from high-income provinces to low-income provinces, which we may call *fiscal redistribution*, with high and low income defined in terms not of government revenue, but of the total income available to provincial residents. The purpose of fiscal redistribution would be to reduce the sacrifice of private consumption necessary to achieve a

---

74. Task Force on Fiscal Arrangements, *supra* note 5, at 161-63.
75. A. MacEachen, Fiscal Arrangements in the Eighties: Proposals of the Government of Canada 12-16 (1981).
76. Task Force on Fiscal Arrangements, *supra* note 5.
77. P. Davenport, *supra* note 49; M. Moore, *supra* note 48; Moore, *Some Proposals for Adapting Federal-Provincial Financial Agreements to Current Conditions*, 24 Can. Pub. Ad. 232 (1981).
78. Courchene & Beavis, *Federal-Provincial Tax Equalization: An Evaluation*, 6 Can. J. Econ. 483 (1973).

given level of public services in poor provinces. Thus while tax equity is based on horizontal equity, fiscal redistribution is concerned with vertical equity. Equalization grants based on either tax equity or fiscal redistribution would allow recipient provinces to devote the grants either to increasing services or reducing taxes, so that the ultimate beneficiaries are the individuals in the recipient provinces. But equalization based on fiscal redistribution would be designed to increase the economic well-being of individuals in low-income provinces, rather than to equalize tax rates. Milton Moore argues strongly for a macroeconomic approach, with the objective of redistributing income "to reduce the inequality of welfare of persons."[79]

The problems evident in our current tax equity approach to equalization seem to arise from the fact that *when resource revenues are large and unequally distributed, tax equity may be inconsistent with fiscal redistribution.* In other words, tax equity could demand that we transfer revenue from a province with low total income to one with high total income. In such a case we would require a clear consensus as to whether the purpose of equalization is tax equity or fiscal redistribution. Our problem in Canada over the last decade has been that there is no such consensus. The federal government continues to use a formula largely based on tax equity, but then overrides it in an ad hoc manner when the results appear inconsistent with fiscal redistribution, as when Ontario became eligible for equalization payments.[80]

In a 1980 budget paper the Government of Ontario stated that "a thorough reform of the equalization program is required as part of the solution to Canada's problems of regional imbalance."[81] In my view the essential first step in such a reform is a consensus on the relative importance of tax equity and fiscal redistribution as goals of equalization. As will be shown below, giving priority to fiscal redistribution implies a preference for the macroeconomic approach to equalization, while the goal of tax equity would lead one to adopt a variant of the Representative Tax System (although perhaps not the one currently in use in Canada).

A.   The Representative Tax System

Equalization payments are currently distributed according to a Representative Tax System (RTS), based on the revenue each province would collect if it taxed its various revenue sources at the average provincial rates.[82] The current equalization formula is thus based solely on *government* revenue. In what follows we will consider an alternative macroeconomic formula based on total provincial incomes, including personal income and resource revenues.

Table 2 offers a hypothetical example to illustrate the operation of the current system and the macroeconomic alternative. Imagine a country with four provinces of equal population, so that country values of per capita variables are simple aver-

---

79.   Moore, *supra* note 48, at 246.
80.   *See supra* notes 69, 70.
81.   Government of Ontario, *Equalization and Fiscal Disparities in Canada,* in ONTARIO BUDGET 1980, at 16 (1980).
82.   J. LYNN, *supra* note 61, and D. CLARK (1969), *supra* note 63.

ages of the four provinces. Per capita personal income (Y) is 110 in region A, resource revenue (R) is 2, and their sum, total provincial income (TPI), is 112. Personal income tax at the average provincial rate (assumed to be 0.2) is $T^* = 22$. Revenue capacity (RC) in A is thus 24; RC measures the revenues collected by the provincial government at average provincial tax rates.[83] Regions B and C are poorer in personal income but rich in natural resources, and have higher government revenue than A. Region D is poorer than A by any standard. The RTS formula would rank the regions by RC as in line 5 and make payments to those with below average revenue to bring them up to the national average of 28. Thus A and D both receive $4 per capita in line 6. Since all regions pay central government taxes to finance the program, B and C are made worse off by the existence of equalization.

Table 2

An Equalization Example
(dollars per capita)

		Province				Average
		A	B	C	D	
1.	Y	110.0	95.5	72.0	82.5	90.0
2.	R	2.0	12.5	18.0	7.5	10.0
3.	TPI	112.0	108.0	90.0	90.0	100.0
4.	T^*	22.0	19.1	14.4	16.5	18.0
5.	RC	24.0	31.6	32.4	24.0	28.0
6.	E_1 (RC)	4.0	0	0	4.0	2.0
7.	E_2 (TPI)	0	0	4.0	4.0	2.0
8.	T	33.0	—	0	—	—
9.	T+R	35.0	—	18.0	—	—
10.	Y−T	77.0	—	72.0	—	—

Key	Y	personal income
	R	provincial government natural resource revenue
	TPI	Y+R, total provincial income
	T^*	0.2Y, provincial income tax at average tax rate of 0.2
	RC	T^*+R, revenue capacity
	E_1	equalization calculated as the difference between average RC and provincial RC
	E_2	equalization calculated as four-tenths of the difference between average TPI and provincial TPI
	T	hypothetical tax collections in A (0.3Y) and C.

RTS tax equity is here inconsistent with fiscal redistribution: tax equity requires that A, the region with the highest personal income before and after taxes,

---

83. We assume that resource revenue is collected by the same rules in all four provinces, so that no adjustment to actual revenue is required.

be a recipient of equalization. The payment to A is designed to enable A to reach the average level of government revenue ($28) while levying the average personal income tax rate (0.2). Note that without equalization, if the citizens of A wanted more government spending, they could raise provincial taxes above the average rate, as in lines 8 to 10, in which a tax rate of 0.3 gives the residents of A above average government revenue while retaining for A the highest after tax personal income (Y−T) in the country. Conversely, lines 8 to 10 show that C could eliminate income taxes altogether, suffer a lower level of government revenue than A, and still not achieve the level of Y−T in A. Nonetheless, the RTS goal of equal standardized tax rates demands that A receive a payment at the expense of C.

The macroeconomic alternative to government revenue as the basis for equalization would be some measure of the total income available to provincial residents. In Table 2 we add personal income and resource revenues to get total provincial income (TPI). The equalization payments in line 7 are an arbitrary fraction—in this case four-tenths—of the difference between provincial TPI and the national average of 100; total payments are the same as in line 6, but they are paid to the provinces poor in total income, C and D.

The macroeconomic approach to equalization is thus based explicitly on fiscal redistribution: by transferring income from rich provinces to poor, it seeks to increase government services and/or lower taxes in the poor provinces, and thereby reduce the overall disparity of real incomes in the country. Note that the RTS equalization may actually *increase* the disparities in government services among provinces by transferring revenue from low-income provinces to high-income ones. This will be the case, for example, if government spending is a fixed fraction (say 30% in our example) of TPI plus equalization in each province. Then before equalization, government spending is 33.6 in A and 27 in C, and this disparity will be increased by making an equalization payment to A through the RTS formula. The TPI formula, on the other hand, will reduce disparities in both government spending and private consumption by paying equalization to provinces poor in TPI.

From the point of view of fiscal redistribution, the problem with the RTS is that it ignores personal income not paid out in provincial taxes, and thereby violates elementary principles of equity, including the Carter Commission principle that "a buck is a buck is a buck."[84] Thus in our example, in the computation of RC a dollar of provincial resource revenue counts as a dollar, while a dollar of personal income counts for only twenty cents. As long as resource revenues were relatively unimportant, government revenue was a good proxy for personal income, and the RTS seemed to work well. The rapid rise of energy prices and revenues after 1973, however, created a growing divergence between personal income and government revenue, and revealed the flaw in the RTS.

Rather than scrapping the RTS, however, the federal government has attempted a series of modifications designed to reduce the importance of resource revenues (which were the source of the breakdown in the RTS) and to prevent

84. *Cf.* E. BENSON, MINISTER OF FINANCE, PROPOSALS FOR TAX REFORM 36 (1969).

Ontario from receiving payments (Ontario's eligibility was a graphic illustration of the dangers of ignoring personal income). In 1973-74 two-thirds of energy revenue increases due to price increases were removed from the formula;[85] in 1977-78 one-half of all non-renewable resource revenues were removed from the formula and equalization payments from all resources were limited to one-half the payments from all other sources;[86] and in 1981 revenues from the sale of Crown leases were removed from the formula.[87] Despite all this ad hoc tinkering, Ontario was still eligible for payments;[88] as a result, the 1981 amendments contained a provision removing Ontario's eligibility by declaring that provinces with above average per capita personal income were ineligible for payments. This personal income "override" was used to deny payments to Ontario in the five fiscal years from 1977-78 to 1981-82.[89]

All of these modifications have not solved the basic problem of the RTS, which is its omission of personal income not paid out in provincial taxes. The personal income override would effectively rule out a payment to region A in Table 2, but it would do the same to a region E (say), with above average personal income, little resource revenue, and below average TPI. Moreover, the RTS will continue to deny payments to a region like C, which is poor in personal income and TPI but rich in resource revenues. Nor are these idle examples. With oil and gas revenues, Newfoundland (or any other Atlantic Province) could soon look like region C and be denied equalization payments, while other provinces with higher TPI continue to receive them. Ontario, on the other hand, could one day approximate region E. Ontario's personal income per capita relative to the national average fell from 1.18 in 1970 to 1.07 in 1980;[90] the province may fall below average in TPI within the next decade.[91] The personal income override would have denied such a province an equalization payment.

In a document tabled with the budget on November 12, 1981, the federal government offered several proposals on equalization as part of the federal-provincial discussions on fiscal arrangements.[92] The government proposed to maintain the current RTS formula, but beginning in 1982-83 per capita government revenue in Ontario, and not the national average, would be the standard to which low revenue provinces would be equalized. Moreover, all natural resource revenues would be included in the RTS formula, there would be no limit on the proportion of the payments due to natural resources, the personal income override would be removed, and total equalization payments would be constrained to grow no more rapidly than the gross national product. Such changes do not in fact resolve the basic problems of the RTS formula illustrated in Table 2; the problems will persist

---

85. 1974-75 Can. Stat., ch. 65, § 1.
86. 1976-77 Can. Stat., ch. 10, §§ 4(2) and 4(7).
87. 1980-81-82 Can. Stat., ch. 46, § 1(1).
88. DEP'T OF FINANCE, PROVINCIAL FISCAL EQUALIZATION TABLES: FOURTH ESTIMATE, 1980-81 (Oct. 9, 1981), Summary Table 1.
89. 1980-81-82 Can. Stat., ch. 46, § 1(2).
90. MINISTER OF FINANCE, *supra* note 51, Reference Table 17, at 141.
91. As indicated in Table 3 below, Ontario's natural resource revenue per capita is only about 10% of the national average, so Ontario would fall below average in TPI before it did so in personal income.
92. A. MACEACHEN, *supra* note 15, at 36.

as long as the equalization formula is based solely on government revenue with a dollar of resource revenue treated differently from a dollar of personal income. Moreover, as we shall see below, using 100% of resource revenues rather than 50% in the RTS formula reduces by one-half the amount of new resource revenues a poor province can acquire before losing all equalization payments.

On April 5, 1982, exactly one week after the Canada Act was given royal assent in Britain, Canada's House of Commons passed Bill C-97 which amends the Fiscal Arrangements Act of 1977, and describes the arrangements for the next five years.[93] With regard to equalization, C-97 adopts the proposals of the November 1981 Budget Paper, mentioned above, with one exception: the new standard for equalization is not revenue in Ontario, but average revenue in five provinces: Quebec, Ontario, Manitoba, Saskatchewan, and British Columbia. Thus the government has found still another way to deal with the problems caused for the RTS formula by natural resources: in effect, Alberta has been removed from the equalization formula. Alberta's revenues will no longer have any bearing on the equalization program, as long as Alberta itself is not a recipient. For the purposes of equalization, Canada now consists of only nine provinces.[94] Thus, just as the equalization program was being entrenched in the Constitution as a cornerstone of national unity, the program itself was changed so that its scope is no longer national. In my view, this unfortunate situation was entirely induced by the anomalies in the RTS formula.

Column 7 of Table 3 shows preliminary figures for equalization payments in 1980-81, calculated using the RTS formula. If all resource revenues were counted, total payments would be about $6.6 billion including $1.7 billion to Ontario.[95] The modifications in place in 1980-81 remove over half of the resource revenue from the formula,[96] and reduce total payments by almost one-half to $3.5 billion. The actual per capita payment in column 7 is the difference in column 6 between average Canadian revenue of $1653, and the provincial revenue, e.g., the payment for Newfoundland is $641 = $1653 − $1012. Even with over half of resource revenue excluded, Ontario is below average in government revenue; it is denied a payment by the personal income override.

---

93. *An Act to Amend the Federal-Provincial Fiscal Arrangements and Established Programs Financing Act, 1977, and to Provide for Payments to Certain Provinces,* 1980-81-82 Can. Stat., ch. 94.

94. As indicated above, five provinces will enter into the calculation of the equalization standard, while four others (the Atlantic Provinces) will be involved in equalization as recipients. Alberta will not enter into either sort of calculation.

95. The $6.6 billion figure is the sum of the various hypothetical payments in column 4 of Table 3 multiplied by the provincial populations.

96. *See supra* notes 91, 92.

Table 3

Provincial Government Revenue from the Representative Tax System and RTS Equalization Payments, 1980-81
(dollars per capita)

	Natural Resource Revenue	Other Revenue	Total Revenue	Hypothetical Payment	Excluded Natural Resource Revenue	Revenue to be Equalized	Actual RTS Payment
	(1)	(2)	(3)	(4)	(5)	(6)	(7)
1. Nfld.	160	912	1072	738	60	1012	641
2. PEI	0	920	920	890	0	920	733
3. N.S.	19	1096	1115	695	8	1107	546
4. N.B.	61	1117	1178	632	18	1160	493
5. Que.	37	1333	1370	440	10	1361	292
6. Ont.	32	1578	1610	200	11	1599	(54)b
7. Man.	44	1290	1334	476	17	1317	336
8. Sask.	490	1368	1858	0	281	1577	76
9. Alta.	2391	2141	4532	0	1372	3160	0
10. B.C.	364	1763	2127	0	143	1984	0
11. Canada	298	1512	1810	275	157	1653	148
12. Totala	7118	36094	43212	6560	3741	39467	3544

aTotal value in millions of dollars; line 11 is line 12 divided by the population of the ten provinces in millions.

bOntario is denied a payment of $54 per capita because of the personal income override; see text.

Source: Calculated from data in DEPARTMENT OF FINANCE, PROVINCIAL FISCAL EQUALIZATION TABLES: FOURTH ESTIMATE, 1980-81 (1981).

B. The Macroeconomic Approach to Equalization

The suggested macroeconomic alternative to the Representative Tax System as a basis for equalization is Total Provincial Income (TPI), defined as the total income available to provincial residents before taxes. The Task Force on Fiscal Arrangements considers the use of a macroeconomic approach to equalization, but recommends that the RTS formula be maintained.[97] The Task Force finds that among the disadvantages of the macroeconomic approach are that it requires a calculation of Gross Domestic Product (GDP) by province, which we may be unable to do with sufficient accuracy, and that total equalization would be reduced with a macroeconomic formula.[98] Neither of these objections is correct; we will consider the second objection in the next section of the paper.

With regard to the calculation of provincial GDP, those familiar with the difficulty of estimating revenue from twenty-nine tax sources in the RTS[99] would hesitate to claim that our current measures of GDP in the Provincial Economic Accounts[100] are clearly inferior to the RTS numbers. Indeed the Task Force itself lists as one of the advantages of the macroeconomic approach its elimination of the

97. TASK FORCE ON FISCAL ARRANGEMENTS, supra note 5, at 162.
98. Id.
99. The complexity of the calculations is apparent in Computation Tables 1 to 30 in DEP'T OF FINANCE, PROVINCIAL FISCAL EQUALIZATION TABLES: FOURTH ESTIMATE, 1980-81 (Oct. 9, 1981).
100. Statistics Canada, PROVINCIAL ECONOMIC ACCOUNTS, Catalogue 13-213.

need to make what are often "arbitrary judgments" in the calculation of revenue sources and tax bases for the RTS.[101] Moreover, in my own view, provincial GDP is not the appropriate measure of income for the macroeconomic approach, because it includes incomes earned by non-residents. For the purposes of equalization we should measure TPI as the sum of three items: personal market income (personal income less transfers), federal transfers to individuals, and provincial government revenues at national tax rates from business incomes and natural resources. No new calculations are required: the first two items are standard parts of the national accounts,[102] while the third is part of the existing RTS calculation.

TPI so calculated is shown in column 4 of Table 4. While personal market income plus federal transfers alone give a fairly good indication of relative income levels among the provinces, they should be adjusted for certain kinds of government revenue from provincial sources. If two provinces were exactly the same, except that one had a great deal of natural resource royalty payments while the other had none, the first province would be better off, since it could offer its citizens more services and/or a lower level of taxation. The royalty payments may thus be seen as a net addition to personal income in the first province, precisely because they are not collected from personal income. This leads to a general rule: we adjust personal income by adding the revenue of those forms of government taxation whose incidence is not primarily upon personal income.

Thus, personal income in each province is *not* adjusted for tax receipts whose burden is primarily on provincial residents. For example, it would clearly be double counting to include provincial sales or personal income taxes in TPI, since their collection merely transfers income within the province from households to government. Natural resource revenues and taxes on corporations *are* included, however, on the grounds that they make a net contribution to provincial income. Taxes on corporations and royalties paid by resource corporations are reflected in either higher product price or lower corporate income. To the degree that the products are exported, or the corporations are owned outside the province, the incidence is on non-residents. Provinces with large accumulations of natural resources or corporate capital are thus seen as having higher provincial incomes, as reflected in the revenues collectable from these sources at average Canadian tax rates. This revenue can be used to increase government services or lower personal taxes for a given level of government services—in either case, provincial residents are better off. In a similar spirit, provincial transfer payments to individuals are not included in TPI, because for the most part they simply involve the redistribution of income within the province. If such transfers were included, a province could increase its equalization payment merely by cutting its own taxes and transfers. Federal transfers to individuals in each province are included in TPI, because they are financed by federal taxes in all provinces and they are not subject to provincial manipulation.

---

101. TASK FORCE ON FISCAL ARRANGEMENTS, *supra* note 5, at 162.
102. Statistics Canada, NATIONAL INCOME AND EXPENDITURE ACCOUNTS, Catalogue 13-201.

Table 4

Total Provincial Income and TPI Equalization Payments, 1980-81
(dollars per capita)

	Personal Income less Transfers	Federal Transfer Payments to Persons	Selected Government Revenue	Total Provincial Income	Income Gap Ratio	TPI Payment (α=0.3)	Relative Payment TPI/RTS
	(1)	(2)	(3)	(4)	(5)	(6)	(7)
1. Nfld.	4589	1018	228	5835	.410	717	1.12
2. PEI	5466	1182	56	6704	.322	647	.88
3. N.S.	6495	1023	98	7616	.230	524	.96
4. N.B.	5690	1040	179	6909	.301	624	1.27
5. Que.	7882	818	155	8856	.104	277	.95
6. Ont.	9493	756	183	10431	−.055	0	—
7. Man.	7743	874	160	8777	.112	295	.88
8. Sask.	7808	799	610	9218	.067	187	2.46
9. Alta.	9972	574	2690	13237	−.339	0	—
10. B.C.	9788	847	542	11176	−.131	0	—
11. Canada	8638	800	447	9885	0	152	1.02
12. Total[a]	206198	19094	10680	235972	0	3618	1.02

[a]Total value in millions of dollars; line 11 is line 12 divided by the population of the ten provinces in millions.

Source by column:

1. STATISTICS CANADA, MINISTRY OF SUPPLY AND SERVICES, NATIONAL INCOME AND EXPENDITURE ACCOUNTS 1966-1980 Catalogue 13-201, Tables 35 and 42 (1982).
2. STATISTICS CANADA, MINISTRY OF SUPPLY AND SERVICES, PROVINCIAL ECONOMIC ACCOUNTS, 1965-1980 Catalogue 13-213, Table 8, the sum of lines 12, 23, and 24 (1982).
3. DEP'T OF FINANCE, PROVINCIAL FISCAL EQUALIZATION TABLES, FOURTH ESTIMATE 1980-81 summary Tables 15 (for population), 16, and 18 (1981).
4. The sum of columns 1 to 3.
5. One minus column 4 divided by 9885.
6. Column 4 times column 5 times 0.3.
7. Column 6 of Table 4 divided by column 7 of Table 3.

Column 5 of Table 4 shows the "income gap ratio," the difference between the average Canadian TPI of $9885 and each province's TPI, expressed as a ratio to the Canadian TPI. Since we cannot wholly eliminate these gaps (as we do with the corresponding gaps in adjusted government revenue) because the resulting negative incentive effects would be too large, we require a rule which links equalization payments to the gaps. For purposes of illustration, we consider a rule which keeps the distribution of payments similar to what it is now: the per capita equalization payment is equal to a fraction α of provincial TPI multiplied by the income gap ratio. Writing Y for per capita TPI, e for the equalization payment, i for each province, and c for Canada, the rule is as follows:

$$e_i = \alpha Y_i[(Y_c - Y_i)/Y_c] \qquad (1)$$

Thus in recipient provinces, the ratio of equalization to TPI (e_i/Y_i) is a fraction α of the income gap ratio (shown in brackets in the equation).[103] Total equalization

---

103. Note that e_i falls (though e_i/Y_i continues to rise) as Y_i/Y_c declines below 0.5. If this were thought undesirable, a flat payment could be established for very low-income provinces: when $Y_i/Y_c <$

payments are proportional to α. Column 6 of Table 4 shows the TPI equalization payments when α = 0.3, which produces total payments of $3.6 billion, slightly more than the RTS payments of $3.5 billion.

The last column of Table 4 shows the ratio of TPI equalization payments to RTS payments. The importance of including personal income is apparent in the following three pairs of provinces: Prince Edward Island and Newfoundland, Nova Scotia and New Brunswick, and Manitoba and Saskatchewan. In each case the second province has more resource revenue per capita than the first, but personal income per capita is either greater in the first province or about equal in the two. Thus in all three cases the second province gains relative to the first when we switch from RTS to TPI payments, because the latter gives a heavy weight to personal income. Indeed, by neglecting personal income, the RTS system assigns a larger payment to Prince Edward Island than to Newfoundland, despite the fact that Newfoundland is a poorer province as measured by TPI or any other comprehensive measure of provincial income.

C. Comparisons of the RTS and TPI Formulas

Three of the most difficult problems which confront the equalization program in Canada are the instability of the size of the payments, the issue of resource revenues in poor provinces, and the treatment of Ontario. Comparing the RTS and TPI formulas, we may consider each of these in turn.

1. *Size of the payments.* As noted earlier, rising oil prices after 1972 led to large increases in equalization entitlements, inducing the federal government frequently to change the formula in order to keep the payments growing roughly in step with GNP. These changes would have been largely unnecessary with a TPI system in place, because resource revenues are only a small share of TPI (about 3.4% in 1980-81), and because TPI differences are only partly equalized. More generally, however, the issue of the size of equalization payments should be kept separate from the question of their distribution.

Having decided whether its primary goal is tax equity, fiscal redistribution, or something else, the federal government, in consultation with the provinces, should then choose a formula which distributes the payments in the desired manner. If the government has a constraint on the size of the payments—e.g., that they should grow at so many percent per year or at the same rate as the GNP[104]—the payments as distributed by the chosen formula can be uniformly scaled up or down so as to reach the desired size. Thus α in equation (1) can be adjusted each

---

0.5, e_i = $0.5\alpha Y_c$. This case does not currently arise in Canada: Newfoundland, the province with the lowest per capita TPI, has Y_i/Y_c = 0.6.

104. From 1972-73 to 1980-81, actual equalization payments rose from $1,070 million to $3,544 million, or from 1.02% of GNP to 1.22% of GNP. As line 12, column (4) of Table 3 indicates, however, without the modifications to the formula described in the text, payments in 1980-81 would have been $6,560 million, or 2.26% of GNP. The federal government changed the formula to avoid such a rapid rise in equalization as a share of GNP; *cf.* Courchene & Copplestone, *supra* note 70, at 11-15. The 1982 amendments to the equalization formula explicitly declared that the growth of payments could not exceed the growth of the GNP; *see* 1980-81-82 Can. Stat., ch. 94, § 2(9). The GNP constraint was originally proposed by Finance Minister Allan MacEachen in A. MACEACHEN, *supra* note 15, at 36.

year so that the payments grow at any desired rate, which could be decided at each five-year renegotiation. Such a procedure is surely preferable to the recent ad hoc efforts by the federal government to manipulate the formula which *distributes* the payments among the provinces so as to achieve a given *total* expenditure: e.g., reducing total payments after 1973 by progressively eliminating resource revenues,[105] then proposing Ontario as the base,[106] then seeking to increase the payments slightly by changing the proposed base from Ontario to the average of British Columbia, Saskatchewan, Manitoba, Ontario, and Quebec.[107] This confusion of equitable distribution with the appropriate or desired size of the payments makes agreement on either goal highly unlikely.

It was noted above that the Task Force on Fiscal Arrangements objected to a macroeconomic approach to equalization in part because total equalization payable "would . . . tend to be significantly less than that payable under the approach currently used."[108] This is only true if we constrain a parameter like α in (1) in some arbitrary manner, e.g., as equal to the share of provincial government spending in TPI. However, such a constraint is unwarranted; the macroeconomic approach is presumably based on the principle of fiscal redistribution, and there is no "right" amount of revenue to redistribute, any more than there is a "right" degree of progression to the tax system. Thus, if the federal government chooses the macroeconomic approach, by varying α it can adjust the payments to any desired total.[109]

2. *Resource revenues in poor provinces.* Under the RTS relatively small amounts of resource revenue can disqualify a low-income province from equalization, because the formula ignores its low level of personal income. Thus using the figures in column 7 of Table 3, with 50% of natural resource revenues included, an increase of just $762 million in resource revenues in Newfoundland ($1314 per capita) would eliminate equalization for that province, even though in terms of TPI it would remain poorer than Nova Scotia and Quebec. Using the new terms of the 1982 Fiscal Arrangements Act,[110] with 100% of resource revenues and equalization to the average provincial revenue in five provinces (Quebec, Ontario, Manitoba, Saskatchewan, and British Columbia), only about $360 million in new resource revenues ($621 per capita) is required in 1980-81 to deprive Newfoundland of equalization. With the TPI system, any new resource revenue in Newfoundland would be properly weighted against the low level of personal income

105. *See supra* notes 65-66 and accompanying text.
106. *See supra* note 92 and accompanying text.
107. The five-province proposal was made by Finance Minister MacEachen at the February 1982 Economic Summit in Ottawa, and was specifically designed to increase the total of equalization payments by $1 billion as compared to an Ontario standard, according to Deborah Dowling, *Fiscal Proposals Dismay Provinces,* Financial Post, Feb. 13, 1982, at 6. She cites a Saskatchewan official who claims that "the federal proposal was ill-developed and it fell apart in five minutes." Ill-developed or not, the five-province standard was incorporated in the Fiscal Arrangements Act for 1982.
108. TASK FORCE ON FISCAL ARRANGEMENTS, *supra* note 5, at 162.
109. To protect poor provinces from federal budget cutting, equalization could be constrained by agreement (or constitutional amendment) to be no less than some fixed fraction of GNP.
110. D. Clark, *Note on Equalization and Resource Rents,* in NATURAL RESOURCE REVENUES: A TEST OF FEDERALISM (A. Scott ed. 1976).

there. Using column 4 of Table 4, we can calculate that it would require $2295 million in resource revenue ($3954 per capita) to bring Newfoundland to the new average TPI, and hence eliminate its equalization payment.

The Newfoundland example brings out clearly the difference between the macroeconomic approach and those equalization systems which would treat separately the revenue from natural resources.[111] A separate equalization of natural resource revenue would mean that low-income provinces with natural resources would be expected to transfer funds to high-income provinces without resources, e.g., region C in Table 2 would transfer some of its resource revenue to region A, which has a higher per capita income. This transfer from a low-income province to a high-income province would make no sense to those in the low-income province and might in any case be politically impossible. From the macroeconomic perspective, to insure equity where resource revenue is unevenly distributed, it is essential to *integrate* resource revenue into the total income available to the residents of the various provinces. This is precisely what the TPI system does. Thus we disagree with Doug Clark who argues that equalization should not be expected to accommodate the large increases in resource rents of the past decade, and that if one wishes to equalize these rents a separate government program should be created.[112] In my view, resource rents can only be sensibly and equitably redistributed as part of a broader equalization scheme which includes personal income, precisely because low-income provinces should not be asked to transfer their rents to high-income provinces.

      3.   *The treatment of Ontario.*   One element of the current RTS which met with disapproval by the Task Force on Fiscal Arrangements was the personal income override which prevented Ontario from receiving an equalization payment, although it has been eligible for one by the RTS formula since 1977-78.[113] The Task Force recommended formally that "negotiations be directed toward an equalization formula that can apply uniformly to all provinces, without arbitrary or discriminatory special provisions."[114] The Task Force failed to point out that the personal income override is clear evidence that the federal government itself recognizes that personal income has a role to play in equalization. In fact, *discrimination among provinces is inherent in the RTS formula: one discriminates in order to correct the anomalies produced by ignoring personal incomes*. Changing to the TPI system would remove the need for discrimination and allow the uniform treatment of provinces that the Task Force recommends, with a dollar of personal income in Ontario given the same weight as a dollar of resource revenue in Alberta. With reference to the anomalies produced by the RTS system, Milton Moore writes: "The best way to avoid such anomalous results is to drop the use of fiscal capacities altogether and not to treat government resource revenues as though they enriched the residents of a province, dollar for dollar, by more than any other form of

---

111. *See* Courchene & Copplestone, *supra* note 70, and Task Force on Canadian Unity 73 (1979).
112. *See supra* note 93 and accompanying text.
113. Task Force on Fiscal Arrangements, *supra* note 5, at 166, 168, 169.
114. Task Force on Fiscal Arrangements, *supra* note 5, at 169.

income."[115]

IV

FEDERAL TRANSFERS AND PROVINCIAL GOVERNMENT INCENTIVES

In 1980 the federal government transferred $12.8 billion to provincial governments and $16.6 billion to individuals: total federal transfers were thus $29.4 billion, or 10% of gross national product.[116] Since many of these transfers are designed to help individuals or provincial governments in economic difficulty, they can create the classic insurance problem of moral hazard: if those experiencing economic difficulties are compensated, the compensation may induce behavior which increases the difficulties. Thomas Courchene argues that just such a problem currently exists with regard to the impact on provincial government employment policies of three federal transfer problems: equalization, cost-sharing in welfare expenditures, and unemployment insurance benefits to individuals.[117]

Following Courchene, we may assume that a provincial government pursues a policy which increases unemployment, such as raising the minimum wage or subsidizing business to create short-term jobs, in the expectation that when the jobs terminate those unemployed will be eligible for unemployment insurance benefits (UIB). The moral hazard problem exists because the federal government assumes many of the costs of the provincial policies, including all of the UIB and one-half of any welfare expenditures associated with long-term unemployment. In addition, since higher unemployment will generally lower revenue capacity, the federal government sweetens the pot for recipients of equalization by increasing the equalization payment when unemployment increases. Thus federal transfers may create an incentive for provinces to embark on policies which reduce employment.

A document of the Government of Quebec has recently deplored this same incentive system from a rather different point of view, by analyzing the very small return to the province from job creation programs.[118] The document offers the following example.[119] Suppose that in 1980 a Quebec government program succeeds in creating jobs at the average industrial wage of $16,500 for 6,060 workers, all of whom were on UIB before becoming employed. The resulting $100 million in wages is shared as follows: the workers have a net gain of $27 million after all taxes and after losing the $54.8 million in UIB which they received when they were unemployed; the Quebec government gets $10.2 million in new revenues but loses $5.5 million in federal transfers for a net gain of only $4.7 million; other provinces receive an increase in equalization of $1.2 million; the remaining $67.1 million is a net gain to the federal government, including tax revenues from the wage income of $8.0 million, a reduction in federal transfers to the provinces of

---

115. Moore, *supra* note 77, at 248.

116. MINISTER OF FINANCE, *supra* note 51, Reference Tables 3 and 52.

117. Courchene, *Avenues of Adjustment: The Transfer System and Regional Disparities,* in CANADIAN CONFEDERATION AT THE CROSSROADS 155, 161, 168 (M. Walker ed. 1978).

118. GOVERNMENT OF QUÉBEC, MINISTÈRE DES FINANCES, DIRECTION GÉNÉRALE DE LA POLITIQUE FISCALE, THE DYNAMICS OF FINANCES IN QUEBEC (1981).

119. *Id.* at 13-15; Table 2, at 14.

$4.3 million, and a reduction of unemployment insurance benefits of $54.8 million.[120]

After presenting this example, the Quebec document concludes that "most of the financial benefits of economic development in Quebec go to the federal government;" further, that the lack of a financial incentive for provincial governments to undertake development programs "is in itself a formidable, if not insurmountable, obstacle to reducing regional inequalities;" and finally, that these disincentives "have a greater impact on the provinces that receive equalization payments and on the provinces with a higher unemployment rate than the national average."[121] The reference to federal transfers as an "obstacle to reducing regional inequalities" is particularly significant in light of Part III of the Constitution Act, 1982, which commits the government of Canada to both equalization and the reduction of regional disparities in opportunities.[122] The Quebec government implies that equalization and other federal transfers may in fact retard the development of Canada's poorer regions, because of the tendency of the payments to contract as the economy of a region expands.[123]

One solution to the problem posed by Courchene and the Government of Quebec would be to have the provincial governments which receive equalization also share in the funding of unemployment insurance, so that total federal transfers to them would increase when their economies expand. This would give the provincial governments themselves an incentive both to avoid policies which increase unemployment (the Courchene problem), and to pursue policies which increase employment (the Quebec government problem). Table 5 illustrates one way of integrating UIB and equalization, using the TPI system. Column 1 of the table shows the initial TPI equalization payment calculated from equation (1) using $\alpha = 0.33$, chosen so that the total payment in column 4 is roughly the same as that in column 6 of Table 4. Column 2 of Table 5 shows UIB per capita in each of the provinces. The UIB adjustment in column 3 is one-half the difference between the national average UIB ($185 per capita) and UIB in each province. The total payment is then the initial payment plus the UIB adjustment, which is positive for Saskatchewan and Manitoba and negative for Quebec and the Atlantic provinces.

120.   These figures do not include an additional $4.2 million which is collected from employers, of which $2.4 million goes to the federal government, the remainder to the provincial government.
121.   GOVERNMENT OF QUEBEC, *supra* note 118, at 14, 16.
122.   *See* text accompanying notes 8-9.
123.   The idea that federal transfers may in fact increase regional disparities is also a major conclusion of the paper by Courchene, *supra* note 117.

Table 5

TPI Equalization Payments Adjusted for Unemployment Insurance Benefits, 1980-81
(dollars per capita)

		Initial Payment (α=0.33) (1)	UIB (2)	UIB Adjustment (3)	Total Payment (4)	Relative Payment TPI/RTS (5)
1.	Nfld.	789	461	−138	651	1.02
2.	PEI	712	370	− 93	619	0.84
3.	N.S.	578	247	− 31	547	1.00
4.	N.B.	686	358	− 87	599	1.22
5.	Que.	304	257	− 36	268	0.92
6.	Ont.	0	145	(+20)	0	—
7.	Man.	324	114	+ 35	359	1.07
8.	Sask.	204	82	+ 52	256	3.37
9.	Alta.	0	68	(+59)	0	—
10.	B.C.	0	163	(+11)	0	—
11.	Canada	167	185	14	153	1.03
12.	Total[a]	3980	4413	326	3654	1.03

[a]Total value in millions of dollars; line 11 is line 12 divided by the population of the ten provinces in millions.

Source by column:
1. From Table 4: column 4 times column 5 times 0.33.
2. Unemployment insurance benefits (UIB), from Statistics Canada, Ministry of Supply and Services Provincial Economic Accounts, 1965-1980 Catalogue 13-213, Table 8, line 4 (1982).
3. One-half the difference of column 2 and 185.
4. The sum of columns 1 and 3.
5. Column 4 in Table 5 divided by column 7 in Table 3.

The UIB adjustment is thus a modified form of cost-sharing: the adjustment is based on the difference between provincial UIB and the national average in order to reduce the cyclical variation in the adjustment. Thus if the economy goes into a recession and the UIB increases by $50 per capita in every province, there is no change in either the adjustment or the total equalization payment; if the UIB adjustment were simply one-half of UIB in each province, then equalization would fall by $25 per capita in each recipient province. Thus the adjustment is designed to reward those provinces which lower their demands on UIB relative to the national average, not to penalize all provinces simply because the national unemployment rate goes up.

Comparing column 4 of Table 5 with column 6 of Table 4 shows the effect of the UIB adjustment: while total payments are about the same, those provinces with relatively small UIB—Nova Scotia, Manitoba, and Saskatchewan—experience an increase in the total equalization payment, while the other four recipients experience a reduction. The purpose of the adjustment, however, is not this redistribution of equalization, but rather the change in provincial incentives. Consider the example given above from the government of Quebec, in which job creation reduces UIB in Quebec by $54.8 million. With the UIB adjustment of Table 5,

Quebec will now receive 36.8%[124] of the reduction in UIB payments as an increase in equalization; this amounts to $20.2 million which is added to Quebec's net gain and subtracted from the net gain of the federal government. Quebec now has a strong incentive to create jobs (or not to create unemployment) because both personal disposable income and federal transfers to the provincial government will rise (or will fall). Thus the provincial government will become more responsible for the result of its economic policies, as desired by Thomas Courchene[125] and the government of Quebec. If the principle behind the UIB adjustment is accepted, one may be tempted to extend it to the provinces which do not receive equalization. I propose a method of doing so in the next section.

V

Natural Resource Revenues and Equalization

Natural resource revenues represent the Achilles heel of the current equalization system, with regard to both payments and financing. On the payments side, the concentration of natural resource revenues in the three westernmost provinces demands large equalization payments to the other seven provinces, including Ontario. On the financing side, the traditionally small federal share of resource revenues meant that the federal government found itself taxing residents of Ontario in the 1970's to pay equalization to other provinces because of resource wealth in Alberta.[126] In what follows I consider first the sharing of resource revenues between producing provinces and the federal government, and then the interprovincial redistribution of resource revenues through the equalization system.

The federal share of resource revenues depends on the ability of the federal government to tax such revenues, an ability which has been limited by both constitutional and political considerations. Sections 92(5) and 109 of the BNA Act, 1867,[127] gave each province the ownership of Crown lands within its boundaries; these rights were extended to the Prairie provinces and British Columbia in the BNA Act, 1930.[128] Section 125 of the BNA Act, 1867, states that "No Lands or Property belonging to Canada or any Province shall be liable to Taxation."[129] The courts have interpreted this to mean that the property, including Crown corporations, of the federal government and the provinces may not be taxed by the other level of government; any government, however, may tax its own property.[130]

---

124. The 36.8% figure is equal to the UIB adjustment of one-half multiplied by one minus Quebec's share of the Canadian population (0.264): 0.368 = 0.5(1 − 0.264); the term in brackets is necessary to correct for the fact that when UIB payments fall in Quebec in our example, per capita UIB in the country as a whole also falls. In per capita terms, the fall is greater in Quebec, of course, because its population is much smaller than that of Canada.

125. Courchene, *supra* note 117.

126. *See* Courchene, *Equalization Payments and Energy Royalties,* in Natural Resource Revenues: A Test of Federalism 82 (A. Scott ed. 1976).

127. BNA Act, 1867, §§ 92(5) & 109.

128. BNA Act, 1930, 20 & 21 Geo. 5, ch. 26.

129. BNA Act, 1867, § 125.

130. *See* G. LaForest, Natural Resources and Public Property under the Canadian Constitution 162-63 (1969), and G. LaForest, The Allocation of Taxing Power under the Canadian Constitution, ch. 8 (1967).

Thus the federal government may tax resource revenues which accrue to a private company or individual, but not those which accrue to provincial governments or their Crown corporations. This state of affairs has been criticized by Gainer and Powrie,[131] and by Courchene and Melvin,[132] who suggest that both equity and interprovincial balance would be improved if all resource revenues were taxed in the same manner by the federal government, independent of the recipient.

If the sharing of natural resource revenue is desirable, and if Section 125 of the BNA Act is an obstacle to sharing, then an obvious solution is to remove the obstacle with a constitutional amendment. This remedy is offered by Anthony Scott, who suggests the creation by constitutional amendment of an independent agency responsible for the distribution of resource rents.[133] An alternative amendment would allow the federal government to tax provincial resource revenues and investment income in a manner consistent with its taxation of private corporate income.[134] In this context, then, what is striking about the Constitution Act, 1982, is the absence of any such amendment. Like the curious incident of the dog who did not bark in the nighttime in the Sherlock Holmes story "Silver Blaze,"[135] the absence of any reference to the sharing of resource revenues in the 1982 Act is clear evidence that our federal and provincial governments are not yet ready to remove the taxation anomaly created by Section 125 of the BNA Act.[136]

Instead of increasing federal powers with regard to resource taxation, Part VI of the Constitution Act, 1982, provides for an increase in provincial powers of taxation over natural resources. Part VI is an Amendment to Section 92 of the BNA Act, 1867, dealing with provincial powers. The Amendment did not appear in the 1980 version of the Act;[137] it was added to the 1981 text in the hopes of bringing some of the western provinces onside in the arduous battle during 1981 for provincial approval of the Act.[138] The Amendment authorizes the provinces to levy any taxes they wish on natural resources, and to regulate the development and management of natural resources and their export to other provinces, as long

---

131. *See* Gainer & Powrie, *Public Revenue from Canadian Crude Petroleum Production,* 1 CAN. PUB. POL'Y (1975), at 1-12.

132. *See* Courchene & Melvin, *Energy Revenues: Consequences for the Rest of Canada,* 6 CAN. PUB. POL'Y (1980), supplement at 192-204.

133. *See* Scott, *Comment,* 6 CANADIAN PUB. POL'Y (1980), supplement at 206-10.

134. Waverman, *The Visible Hand: The Pricing of Canadian Oil Resources,* in 1 ENERGY POLICIES FOR THE 1980's: AN ECONOMIC ANALYSIS 25-28 (1980), argues that federal (and indeed provincial) taxes on natural resources should be collected with net income taxes, rather than excise taxes, to avoid distorting production incentives, and to allow marginal oil to be produced.

135. A. CONAN DOYLE, THE COMPLETE SHERLOCK HOLMES (1930), Section IV, at 23. *Silver Blaze* was first published in *The Strand Magazine* in 1892.

136. On section 125 as an "anomaly," see Campbell, Gainer, & Scott, *Resources Rent: How Much and for Whom?* in NATURAL RESOURCE REVENUES: A TEST OF FEDERALISM 120 (A. Scott ed. 1976). This article is one of an excellent collection of papers on the sharing of resource revenues. The theoretical efficiency aspects of taxation and government spending in a federal country are treated in depth in several articles in a volume edited by J. Margolis, THE ANALYSIS OF PUBLIC OUTPUT (1970), and in a paper by Musgrave, *Approaches to a Fiscal Theory of Political Federalism,* in PUBLIC FINANCES: NEEDS, SOURCES, AND UTILIZATION (1961).

137. A draft of the Constitution Act, 1980, was announced by Prime Minister Trudeau in a Proposed Resolution for a Joint Address to the Queen respecting the Constitution of Canada. The text is reprinted in E. McWHINNEY, CANADA AND THE CONSTITUTION, 1979-1982, at 141-48 (1982).

138. E. McWHINNEY, *supra* note 137, at 63.

as provincial laws do not discriminate against production exported to other provinces. These issues had arisen in two recent Supreme Court decisions involving the Government of Saskatchewan. The Court had ruled in 1977 that a Saskatchewan tax and royalty surcharge on the oil industry was *ultra vires* Saskatchewan because it was an indirect tax and because it attempted to regulate trade outside the province's borders.[139] Then, in 1978, the Court ruled that a provincial government scheme for regulating production and prices in the potash industry was *ultra vires* Saskatchewan, again because it interfered with trade external to the province.[140] It is probable that both cases would now be decided in favor of Saskatchewan, given Part VI of the 1982 Act. In any case, Part VI will certainly strengthen the position of the provinces as owners and managers of their natural resources.

As already pointed out, however, Part VI does nothing to facilitate the sharing of resource revenues between the producing provinces and the federal government.[141] During the late 1970's the federal government's share of oil and gas revenues was only about 10%, as compared to 45% each for the producing provinces and corporations.[142] The small federal share of resource revenues meant that equalization and other transfers had to be financed almost entirely from non-resource taxes, which resulted in a heavy burden on Ontario relative to Alberta. Table 6 illustrates the financing of federal transfers to the provinces in 1980-81. Column 3 shows per capita payments for the three major transfer programs: equalization; Established Programs Financing (EPF) payments for health and post-secondary education; and payments for the Canada Assistance Plan (CAP), a cost-sharing program for welfare expenditures. These three programs account for about 90% of all federal transfers to provincial governments.[143]

Column 4 of Table 6 indicates the per capita tax payment from each province required to finance the $15.8 billion in transfers. The tax payments are distributed among the provinces according to the distribution of total federal revenues in the Provincial Economic Accounts;[144] this same procedure is used by the Economic Council.[145] The net transfer in column 5 shows how the tax-transfer system redistributes revenue from Ontario and the three westernmost provinces to the rest of the country. The provinces are listed in ascending order of per capita TPI. The net transfer is inversely related to TPI except in two cases: Prince Edward Island receives a larger net payment than Newfoundland because of the former's relatively large RTS equalization payment, an anomaly discussed above;[146] and Ontario makes a larger net contribution to the transfer system than British Columbia, although per capita TPI and government revenue are greater in British Columbia. Indeed, Ontario's net contribution per capita of $299 is only $73 less

139. Canadian Indus. Gas & Oil Ltd. v. Government of Saskatchewan, 80 D.L.R.3d 449 (Can. 1977); *see* Paus-Jenssen, *supra* note 11, at 45-48, 52, 53.
140. Central Canada Potash Co. v. Government of Saskatchewan, 88 D.L.R.3d 604 (Can. 1978); *see* Bushnell, *supra* note 11, at 313-24.
141. *See supra* text accompanying note 12.
142. MINISTER OF FINANCE, ECONOMIC REVIEW, 1980, at 44, Table 5.7.
143. A. MacEACHEN, *supra* note 15, at 32, Table II-2.
144. Statistics Canada, PROVINCIAL ECONOMIC ACCOUNTS, 1965-80, Table 3.
145. *See* ECONOMIC COUNCIL OF CANADA, FINANCING CONFEDERATION 19 (1982).
146. *See supra* text following note 103.

than Alberta's net contribution of $372, despite the fact that per capita TPI is $2806 higher in Alberta, and government revenue is $2922 higher.[147]

Table 6

Net Transfer Payments with RTS Equalization, 1980-81[a]
(dollars per capita)

		RTS Equalization Entitlement (1)	EPF and CAP Transfers[b] (2)	Total Transfer (3)	Tax Payment (4)	Net Transfer (5)
1.	Nfld.	641	515	1156	252	904
2.	PEI	733	522	1255	292	963
3.	N.B.	493	537	1030	414	616
4.	N.S.	546	500	1046	463	583
5.	Man.	336	493	829	506	323
6.	Que.	292	555	847	536	311
7.	Sask.	76	495	571	637	− 66
8.	Ont.	(54)	486	486	785	−299
9.	B.C.	(−331)	524	524	710	−186
10.	Alta.	(−1507)	499	499	871	−372
11.	Canada	148	514	662	662	0
12.	Total[c]	3544	12264	15808	15808	0

[a]Provinces are listed in ascending order of per capita TPI.
[b]Transfers for the Established Programs Financing (EPF) and Canada Assistance Plan (CAP) from the federal government to the provinces.
[c]Total value in millions of dollars; line 11 is line 12 divided by the population of the ten provinces in millions.

Source by column:
1. Column 7 of Table 3; the negative figures for Alberta and British Columbia are the difference between average revenue ($1653) and revenue in the two provinces.
2. DEPARTMENT OF FINANCE, BACKGROUND PAPER ON FEDERAL-PROVINCIAL FISCAL ARRANGEMENTS 39, 50 (1980). The Established Programs Financing (EPF) payment, including Extended Health Care payments, is $427 per capita for each province. The Canada Assistance Plan (CAP) payment per capita is thus the difference of column 2 and 427; the CAP figure for Quebec includes the value of the province's contracting-out tax transfer of 5.0 personal income tax points.
3. The sum of columns 1 and 2.
4. The tax payment is distributed among provinces according to the distribution of total federal revenue in STATISTICS CANADA, PROVINCIAL ECONOMIC ACCOUNTS, 1965-1980 Catalogue 13-213, Table 3, line 35 (1982).
5. Column 3 minus column 4.

There are two reasons why Ontario's net contribution in Table 6 is high relative to those in British Columbia and Alberta. The first is that while Ontario is lower in total income than the other two provinces,[148] all three receive the same equalization payment: zero. The second is that the small federal share of resource revenues leads to the result that per capita federal revenues from all sources in Ontario are greater than in British Columbia, and fully 90% of those in Alberta.

147. *See supra* Table 4, col. 4, and Table 3, col. 3.
148. *See supra* Table 4, col. 4.

This second problem will be alleviated by the energy agreements reached in the fall of 1981 between the three westernmost provinces and the federal government.[149] Helliwell and McRae estimate that with the new agreements about 35% of oil and gas revenues over the period 1981-86 will accrue to the federal government, whose share will be nearly as great as that of the provinces.[150] This will produce a substantial increase in the per capita federal revenues from Alberta over the coming years.

However, the 1981 energy agreements also exacerbate the first problem: by moving Canada toward world oil prices, the agreements will produce large revenue increases in Alberta and other producing provinces, but Alberta and Ontario will continue to receive the same zero equalization payment. The Fiscal Arrangements Act, 1982, adds local property taxes to the RTS, and equalizes to average revenue in Quebec, Ontario, Manitoba, Saskatchewan, and British Columbia.[151] By excluding from the revenue standard the province of Alberta, which has 70% of the country's resource revenue,[152] the RTS formula will deny a significant payment, and perhaps any payment at all, to Ontario over the next five years. Presumably, the federal government believes that it simply cannot afford an equalization payment to Ontario, given recent large federal deficits.[153] Thus the problem of federal-provincial balance (i.e., the effort to reduce the federal deficit) takes priority over the problem of interprovincial balance between Ontario and Alberta.

One way to describe the Ontario problem in equalization is that while the equalization formula distinguishes among low-income provinces—the lower the province's income, the larger the payment—it does not distinguish among the high-income provinces, all of whom receive a zero payment. Distinguishing among high-income provinces suggests the possibility of "negative" equalization, in which the greater the province's income, the greater its negative payment. The problem, of course, is in collecting the negative payments from the high-income "donor" provinces.[154] Four possibilities might be suggested: the federal government could raise its direct tax rates on corporations and individuals in the donor provinces, as suggested by Buchanan;[155] the donor provinces might voluntarily agree to give the payments to the federal government; a constitutional amendment could allow the federal government to tax the provincial governments of donor provinces; and the

149. Memoranda of agreement on energy pricing and taxation were signed during the fall of 1981 by the Government of Canada and the Governments of Alberta (Sept. 1), British Columbia (Sept. 24) and Saskatchewan (Oct. 26); see Helliwell & McRae, infra note 150.

150. See Helliwell & McRae, *Resolving the Energy Conflict: From the National Energy Program to the Energy Agreements,* 8 CAN. PUB. POL'Y, Table 2, at 20 (1982).

151. See supra note 93 and accompanying text.

152. See supra Table 3, col. 1.

153. A. MacEACHEN, supra note 15, at 12, 13, 39, cites projected federal deficits of $7 billion to $8 billion in 1977-78 to 1979-80, in calling for restraint in federal transfers to the provinces. With the worsening recession in the early 1980's, the federal deficit rose to about $26 billion in 1982-83, with projections of over $30 billion for 1983-84. See Hyman Solomon, *It's Now Down to the Wire on What's in the Budget,* Financial Post, Mar. 26, 1983, at 1, 2.

154. This problem is considered in Davenport, supra note 49.

155. See Buchanan, *Federalism and Fiscal Equity,* AMER. ECON. REV. 595, 596 (1950).

payments could be subtracted from federal transfers other than equalization to the donor provinces.

Table 7

Net Transfers with TPI Equalization, Including UIB Adjustment and "Negative" Equalization, 1980-81[a]
(dollars per capita)

		Income Gap (1)	Equalization Basic (2)	Equalization Total (3)	Total Transfers Amount (4)	Total Transfers TPI/RTS (5)	Net Transfer (6)	Net Transfer + Income Gap (7)
1.	Nfld.	4050	675	685	1200	1.04	948	.234
2.	P.E.I.	3181	530	585	1107	.88	815	.256
3.	N.B.	2976	496	557	1094	1.06	680	.228
4.	N.S.	2269	378	495	995	.95	532	.234
5.	Man.	1108	185	368	861	1.04	355	.320
6.	Que.	1029	172	284	839	.99	303	.294
7.	Sask.	667	111	311	806	1.41	169	.253
8.	Ont.	−546	− 91	77	563	1.16	−222	.407
9.	B.C.	−1291	−215	−56	468	.89	−242	.187
10.	Alta.	−3352	−559	−352	147	.29	−724	.216
11.	Canada	0	0	148	662	1.00	0	—
12.	Total[b]	0	0	3544	15808	1.00	0	—

[a]Provinces are in ascending order of per capita TPI
[b]Total value in millions of dollars; line 11 is line 12 divided by the population of the ten provinces in millions.

Source by column:
1. Column 4 of Table 4: the difference between 9885 and provincial TPI.
2. Column 1 times one-sixth.
3. Column 2 plus 148 plus the UIB adjustment in column 3 of Table 5.
4. Column 3 plus the EPF and CAP transfers in column 2 of Table 6.
5. Column 4 divided by column 3 of Table 6.
6. Column 4 minus the tax payment in column 4 of Table 6.
7. Column 6 divided by column 1.

A scheme implementing this last possibility is illustrated in Table 7, using the TPI system with an adjustment for UIB, now applied to all provinces. Equation (1) on page 129 above is replaced by

$$e_i = \alpha(Y_c - Y_i) + e_c - 0.5(UIB_i - UIB_c) \qquad (2)$$

The first term is a fraction of the "income gap" between average TPI in Canada (Y_c) and provincial TPI (Y_i); a value of one-sixth was chosen for α to produce a distribution of payments among the eastern provinces similar to the current one.[156] The first term of the equation is called "basic" equalization and is displayed in column 2 of Table 7. The other two terms are a fixed per capita payment (e_c) and the UIB adjustment discussed in the previous section. The total per capita cost of the payments is simply e_c, because the first and third terms of the equation must sum to zero, since they are deviations from the mean. The fixed payment is set at

---

156. *See* Table 3, col. 7.

$148 per capita, to keep the cost of the program at its current level.[157] In a dynamic setting e_c could be linked to GNP per capita or any other desired escalator.

Total equalization in column 3 is now positive in Ontario and negative in British Columbia and Alberta. The payment to Ontario is financed from British Columbia and Alberta, with no reduction in total equalization payments to the other seven provinces. Total transfers in column 4 are the sum of equalization and current EPF and CAP transfers; the negative equalization to British Columbia and Alberta is subtracted from the EPF and CAP transfers otherwise payable to those provinces. The message of this subtraction should be clear: in a world of scarce federal government revenue, British Columbia and Alberta simply do not require the same degree of federal assistance as the other provinces, in order to maintain an adequate level of social services. Despite its positive equalization payment, Ontario's tax contribution is still greater than the transfers it receives, so that its net transfer remains negative. Now, however, the British Columbia net contribution is slightly greater than Ontario's, and the Alberta contribution is far greater. Alberta's net contribution of $724 per capita represents about 22% of the $3,352 of income gap between the province and the country as a whole, as column 7 shows. All provinces are now subject to the UIB adjustment, so that all have an interest in avoiding policies which increase unemployment.

Figure 1 illustrates the redistribution of revenues produced by equation (2) and the EPF and CAP transfers, with net transfers (on the vertical axis) a negative function of TPI (in thousands on the horizontal axis). The negatively sloped dashed lines show the redistribution affected by basic equalization alone. The lengths of the solid lines show the *additional* redistribution produced by the zero-sum UIB adjustment, the payment of the equal per capita sum (e_c), the EPF and CAP transfers, and the taxes necessary to finance these transfers. For example, Newfoundland (province number 1) has a TPI of $5,835 on the horizontal axis, with a basic payment of $675 and a net transfer of $948 on the vertical axis. The negative relation between the net transfer and TPI extends to all provinces, including Ontario, British Columbia, and Alberta. The TPI system with negative equalization thus succeeds in distinguishing among the three richest provinces, something which the current equalization formula is unable to do. The significant redistribution of revenues evident in Figure 1 would certainly reduce the disparities in public services in Canada,[158] which is the intent of the equalization program, but would they unduly impede the efficient operation of the economy? It is to the question of efficiency that I now turn.

157. *Id.*
158. The relation between revenue transfers and public services is complex because part of any change in transfers may lead to a compensating change in provincial tax rates, and because the same service may have different costs in different provinces; *see* D. CLARK, FISCAL NEEDS AND REVENUE EQUALIZATION GRANTS 2-6, 18-26 (1969).

Figure 1
Net Transfer Payments with TPI Equalization
(dollars per capita)

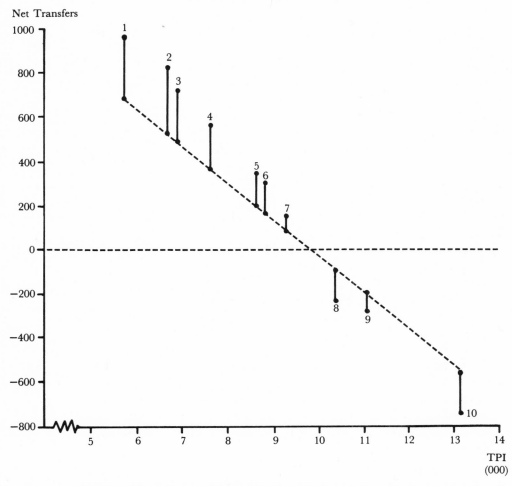

Source: Points on the negatively sloped dashed line show basic equalization from column 2 of Table 6. Numbered points at the top (provinces 1 to 7) or bottom (provinces 8 to 10) of the vertical solid lines show the total net transfers, including EPF and CAP, from column 6 of Table 6. TPI per capita is from column 4 of Table 3.

Key: Numbers refer to provinces in ascending order of TPI per capita:

1. Nfld.	2. PEI	3. N.B.	4. N.S.	5. Man.
6. Que.	7. Sask.	8. Ont.	9. B.C.	10. Alta.

VI

EFFICIENCY AND NATIONAL UNITY

Central government grants to the poor provinces or states of a federal country have often been justified with reference to the principle of *fiscal equity*. Fiscal equity requires that similar individuals in different provinces should receive an equal *net fiscal benefit*, or *fiscal residuum*, defined as the difference for an individual between government services received and taxes paid.[159] Fiscal equity is thought to promote efficiency, since if the principle were violated employees might move to jurisdictions where their real productivity was lower simply to obtain greater fiscal benefits (i.e., a lower level of taxation and/or a higher level of government services), thereby reducing total output in the country. Much recent work on federal transfers to the provinces has centered on the efficiency aspects of the transfers. Thomas Courchene has stressed the inefficient impediments to labor mobility which transfers to low-income regions may create.[160] Robin Boadway and Frank Flatters,[161] and Lorraine Eden[162] have shown that under certain conditions equalization payments may increase efficiency by reducing inefficient migration induced by resource rent differentials.

One reason for preferring the RTS to the macroeconomic approach would be the belief that the RTS satisfies the principle of fiscal equity, and therefore is more efficient than other systems. This seems to be the position of the Economic Council of Canada.[163] In fact, however, the current RTS formula bears little relation to the kind of system one would design on fiscal equity principles. With regard to resource revenues, fiscal equity would demand a rigorous full equalization financed from the resource-rich provinces, so that after equalization Alberta and Ontario would have the same per capita resource revenues. The current formula equalizes less than half the revenues, and finances the payments with general taxes on all provinces.[164] The Economic Council appears to favor an approach in which about 17.5% of resource revenues would be included in the RTS formula, but this is quite inconsistent with fiscal equity as it is usually defined.[165]

With regard to non-resource taxes on provincial residents (income, sales, etc.), it is not clear that fiscal equity requires that *any* equalization be paid. It is for this

159. *Cf.* Buchanan, *supra* note 155, at 588-91; Graham, *Fiscal Adjustment in a Federal Country,* 10-11, in INTERGOVERNMENTAL FISCAL RELATIONSHIPS (1964); and Buchanan & Wagner, *An Efficiency Basis for Federal Fiscal Equalization,* in THE ANALYSIS OF PUBLIC OUTPUT (1970). Buchanan and Wagner analyze fiscal equity in formal models of public goods and migration in a federal country.

160. *See* Courchene, *supra* note 117, at 159-68.

161. *See* Boadway & Flatters, *Efficiency and Equalization Payments in a Federal System of Government: A Synthesis and Extension of Recent Results,* 15 CAN. J. ECON. (1982).

162. *See* Eden, Fiscal Equity and Equalization Payments (paper presented to the Canadian Economics Ass'n Annual Meeting, Halifax, May 27, 1981).

163. *See* ECONOMIC COUNCIL OF CANADA, *supra* note 145.

164. ECONOMIC COUNCIL OF CANADA, *supra* note 145, estimates that net of taxes paid to finance equalization, Manitoba, Quebec, and the Atlantic Provinces received $767 million in equalization with respect to natural resource revenues, of which $431 million was financed with taxes paid in Ontario. The remaining $336 million in financing was contributed by the three westernmost provinces, which is about 5% of the $6660 million in total resource revenues in those provinces.

165. *Id.* at 46-47, 122.

reason that the term *tax equity* was used above to describe the goal of the RTS. Allowing governments to raise average revenue with average tax rates is in fact different from the fiscal equity goal of equal net fiscal benefits. Indeed, if provincial programs were fiscally neutral (each person receives in benefits just what he pays in taxes), then fiscal equity would require that equalization *not* be paid with regard to residence-based taxes, so that people in poor provinces would have inferior government services which accurately reflect their inferior market income.

Thus, if strict fiscal equity is the goal of equalization, the equalization of taxes on provincial residents requires non-neutrality of net fiscal benefits. The present system of fully equalizing such taxes is correct only in the very special case in which taxes are proportional to market income and benefits are equal in absolute amount for each taxpayer.[166] The Council describes this special case, and then, astonishingly, concludes that the "present Equalization Program would, therefore, seem adequate to achieve fiscal equity with respect to residence-based taxes,"[167] without any attempt to demonstrate that Canada satisfies the conditions of the special case. In fact, provincial and local taxes are not proportional to market income but regressive; benefits are progressive, but not nearly so much as being equal per capita;[168] hence net benefits are much less progressive than in the special case, and the amount of equalization of taxes on residents which is consistent with fiscal equity is considerably less than in the special case.[169]

One can still argue, of course, that even the current RTS is closer to the principle of fiscal equity than is a macroeconomic approach; but like all second best arguments this would be difficult to sustain as a general proposition, and in any case is a much weaker position than one that claims that RTS is consistent with fiscal equity. In my view, equalization should be justified not in terms of efficiency, but as a redistributive program which reduces the disparities in public and private services among the provinces. The federal government should pursue efficiency in other ways: by working to restore a fully free common market within Canada, reducing barriers to international trade, creating an effective competition policy, and linking our energy prices to world levels, for example. Such policies will favor some regions and penalize others—equalization is then the glue that holds the country together in the face of the uneven incidence of federal policies and the uneven distribution of resources. Equalization may thus contribute to efficiency to the degree that it makes federal economic policies based on efficiency considerations politically possible. Conversely, the decline or abolition of equalization might well lead to a less efficient Canadian economy by undermining the

---

166. *See* Davenport, Equalization and Fiscal Equity (manuscript 1982).

167. *See* ECONOMIC COUNCIL OF CANADA, *supra* note 145, at 30.

168. *See* Gillespie, *On the Redistribution of Income in Canada,* 24 CAN. TAX J. 417-50, Tables 2, A-6, and A-7 (1976).

169. Gillespie, *supra* note 168, finds that the sum of provincial and local taxes is in fact proportional *not* to market income, but to market income plus transfers and the benefits from government spending on goods and services (Gillespie, Table A-7). The benefits from provincial and local government spending, on the other hand, seem to be distributed about half in lump-sum form, and half in proportion to market income (Gillespie, Tables 2 and A-6). Under these conditions strict fiscal equity probably requires that less than one-half of provincial revenues from residence-based taxes be equalized. *See* Davenport, *supra* note 166, for a preliminary analysis, which parallels that of Boadway and Flatters, *supra* note 161, at 628-30.

power of the federal government, and the will of the provinces, to pursue policies consistent with a more open and competitive economy.

In this context we may consider a 1966 statement on the purpose of equalization by Mitchell Sharp, then Minister of Finance:

> They [equalization payments] represent one of the dividends of Canadian unity, designed as they are to enable all Canadians to enjoy an adequate level of provincial public services. Where circumstances—whether natural or man-made—have channelled a larger than average share of the nation's wealth into certain sections of the country, there should be a *redistribution* of that wealth so that all provinces are able to provide to their citizens a reasonably comparable level of basic services, without resorting to unduly burdensome levels of taxation.[170]

This statement contains elements of both fiscal redistribution and of tax equity. If we interpret the last clause to mean "with equal tax rates," then Sharp is thinking in terms of tax equity, and the RTS formula is appropriate. But "burdensome" could also be interpreted in terms of the relative level of per capita income in a province: thus comparing A and C in Table 2, the 20% tax rate might be seen as reasonable in A but unduly burdensome in C, because it pushes after-tax income in C to a very low level. If this interpretation were used, we could justify an equalization payment from A to C in a manner consistent with fiscal redistribution.

Alternatively, "burdensome" might be defined in terms of a specific progressive tax formula, such as

$$T_m = 0.6(Y - 60) \qquad (3)$$

where an actual tax T greater than T_m is "unduly burdensome." Thus equalization would allow each province to collect T_m in taxes and still acquire the average revenue. In the example in Table 2, T_m is 7.2 for C, and C should receive an equalization payment of 2.8, which added to T_m and the resource revenues of 18 allow it to reach the average revenue of 28. Thus C receives a payment while A does not, a result consistent with the TPI calculation in Table 2, but in conflict with the RTS result. In any case it seems highly unlikely that when Sharp spoke of enabling "all Canadians to enjoy an adequate level of provincial public services," he envisaged a situation in which revenues would be transferred from a high-income province to a low-income province to maintain an equality in hypothetical tax rates—for the low-income province involved, this transfer would not appear as "one dividend of Canadian unity."

VII

CONCLUSION

The entrenchment of the principle of equalization in the Canadian Constitution leaves unresolved the uncertainties about the purposes of equalization, and particularly whether the program's primary goal is fiscal equity, tax equity, or fiscal redistribution. The frequent ad hoc changes to the Representative Tax System formula over the last decade imply that the RTS is not adequately fulfilling the purposes of equalization as these are interpreted by federal officials and politicians. The problems with the RTS will become even more apparent if one of

---

170. *Proceedings of the Federal-Provincial Tax Structure Committee*, Ottawa, Sept. 14 and 15, 1966, at 15.

the Atlantic Provinces should begin to receive significant oil and gas revenues, because of the heavy weight given to such revenues in the current formula.

My own preference is for an equalization system based on fiscal redistribution, with a macroeconomic formula using total provincial income. Moreover, the integration of some form of cost-sharing for unemployment insurance benefits into the equalization program would greatly reduce the incentives for inefficient provincial economic policy induced by UIB and other federal transfers. Rising resource prices and rents will presumably increase interprovincial disparities over the next five to ten years, which in turn will induce an increased political and academic interest in the equalization program. Thus the entrenchment of equalization in the constitution heralds the beginning, rather than the end, of a vigorous debate over the proper extent and form of wealth sharing in the Canadian federation.

IMPLICATIONS FOR FEDERALISM OF THE REFORMED CONSTITUTION OF CANADA

RICHARD H. LEACH*

The reform of the Canadian Constitution in 1982 has profound implications for the functioning not only of the national government but of those of the provinces as well. In some respects the new constitution breaks new ground, so that it will be some time before the full impact of constitutional change in the provinces can be assayed.

Even though the necessity of central authority has always been begrudgingly acknowledged, the theme of local rights has been played over the years as stridently as it has been south of the Canadian border—and with much greater effect. In recent years especially, the Canadian governmental piper has been increasingly harkening to the tune of that theme. The purpose of this paper is to examine how the reformed Canadian Constitution may affect the federal-provincial dance in the future.

That dance must first be understood in historical terms, for the past was very much a factor in the negotiations leading to agreement on the terms of the reformed constitution. If anything stands out in Canadian history since 1867, it is the power of the provincial presence on the Canadian governmental stage. Even at the outset, the script for the confederation drama was written by provinces. Indeed, the patriated constitution of Canada continues the long tradition of a compact among the provinces as the basis of the Canadian state.

The development of that tradition need not be traced at any great length. Historians generally agree that the resolutions which were essentially enacted by the British Parliament and together served as Canada's first Constitution as the British North America Act of 1867[1] ("BNA Act") were regarded by the representatives from Canada East and Canada West as a treaty, a compact between the two founding peoples of Canada, and that the original idea of a "racial compact" was later transformed into a geopolitical compact. As G.F.G. Stanley summed it up: "the meeting of the maritime [sic] delegates with those of Canada at Charlottetown and at Quebec introduced a new interpretation which has had mighty impact upon the course of our later history, namely, the idea of a compact between the politico-geographic areas which go to make up Canada."[2] Stanley concluded that the "Compromise of Quebec became a compact between the provinces which

---

* Department of Political Science and Canadian Studies Center, Duke University.
1. British North America Act, 1867, 30 & 31 Vict., ch. 3 [hereinafter cited as BNA Act].
2. Stanley, *Act or Pact? Another Look at Confederation*, in CANADIAN HISTORICAL READINGS 94, 106 (1967).

participated in the conference,"[3] and the London Resolutions, which incorporated those made in Quebec with little substantive change and were submitted to Parliament, did nothing to alter "the contractual nature of the pact."[4]

For their part, members of the British Parliament also accepted the idea of a provincial compact. Charles Adderley, M.P., who introduced what was to become the BNA Act to the House of Commons, told the House that federation had "in this case . . . been a matter of most delicate mutual treaty and compact between the provinces."[5] Lord Carnavon said almost the same thing to the House of Lords.[6]

In other words, the immediate predecessor of the patriated constitution was the product of provinces negotiating as provinces. It accepted as basic the idea of provinces as the contracting parties. Though after the BNA Act went into effect differences of opinion arose among the provinces over the pact concept, it "has always been the principal buttress of provincial autonomy"[7] and is relied on particularly by Quebec in its insistence on a special place in confederation.

How important the idea of a compact of contracting provinces as the basis of a state is to the *amour propre* of those provinces can be understood more clearly when Canada is compared to the United States. The Federalists, who carried the day at the Constitutional Convention of 1787, rooted the American Constitution in the consent of the people, a concept whose challenge to the states was immediately obvious to the Antifederalists. The Convention, Patrick Henry noted, spoke "the language of, *We, the people,* instead of, *We, the states.* "[8] Indeed, that is precisely what the Constitution accomplished, Alexander Hamilton rejoiced in *The Federalist* No. 22.[9] Though Jefferson and others were later to insist on referring to the Constitution as a compact to which the states had acceded as states,[10] the idea never won wide acceptance and was finally laid to rest in 1869 by the U.S. Supreme Court in the landmark case *Texas v. White*.[11] The Court noted that the act "which consummated [Texas'] admission into the Union was something more than a compact; it was the incorporation of a new member into the political body."[12] What the Constitution had wrought was a complete and indissoluble union.[13] Thus, the Americans opted for something quite different from the Canadians. The American Constitution is founded on popular sovereignty, the BNA Act on provincial power.

In addition to being the midwives at Canada's birth in 1867, the provinces became increasingly influential in charting the course of Canada's growth into

---

3. *Id.* at 107.
4. *Id.* at 108.
5. *Id.*
6. *Id.* at 108-09.
7. *Id.*
8. 3 THE DEBATES IN THE SEVERAL STATE CONVENTIONS ON THE ADOPTION OF THE FEDERAL CONSTITUTION 22 (J. Elliot 1901).
9. THE FEDERALIST No. 22, at 146 (A. Hamilton) (J. Cooke ed. 1961).
10. Jefferson's clearest statement of the idea is in the Kentucky Resolutions of 1798, which he drafted.
11. Texas v. White, 74 U.S. (7 Wall.) 700 (1868).
12. *Id.* at 726.
13. *Id.* at 725.

adulthood. The provinces, for their own self-protection and advancement, chose in 1867 to devise a system in which the central government would have considerable power. Thus not only did the BNA Act vest in the national government a great many important legislative powers in section 91, it also lodged power in the central government to appoint provincial lieutenant governors, judges of the higher provincial courts, and members of the Senate from the provinces; gave the central government power to reserve or disallow any provincial legislation within a year of its passage; and enabled Parliament, under certain circumstances, to enact remedial legislation affecting the status of separate schools in a province. As Norman Ward concluded, "the British North America Act certainly intended to establish . . . a . . . system . . . in which the Dominion government was to be paramount."[14] And in fact a period of nation-building was entered into after 1867 on the basis of section 91, which brought the national government for a while into paramountcy among Canadian governments. In the process, the foundation for modern Canada was laid.

Even so, time was on the side of provincial power. To draw from Norman Ward on the point, the eventual development of responsible government in ten provinces "inevitably led to centralism within each province, and hence to rivalry with the Dominion." Moreover, the addition between 1870 and 1949 of only a few large provinces rather than of many smaller ones "minimized the Dominion government's opportunities either to dominate the provinces, or to play them off against each other . . . ." And the "mere problem of space" in so large a territory as Canada inevitably made Ottawa remote from much of the country and enhanced "the importance of provincial capitals . . . ." Perhaps the final blow to central dominance was the discovery and exploitation of natural resources in the provinces "and the rise of powerful industries based on them," the regulation and control of which were not among the powers bestowed on the national government in section 91. "And to these comprehensible economic and political elements must be added the mysteries of judicial decision," which steadily reduced Parliament's power, "while the powers of the provinces were at the same time steadily extended," generally under the property and civil rights clause in section 92 of the BNA Act itself.[15]

In short, as the conditions which led the four founding provinces to demote their own power in 1867 changed, as new political and economic conditions which

---

14. Ward, *The Structure of Government,* in THE CANADIANS 1867-1967, at 29 (J. Carclass and R. Brown eds. 1967).

15. *Id.* at 29-30. As Henry Albinski put the same point:

For nearly a generation the Privy Council followed the intentions of the Canadian founders, allowing the central authorities considerable latitude. A generous definition was accorded to the BNA Act clause that invested Ottawa with responsibilities over the "Peace, Order, and good Government of Canada." Then the Privy Council shifted its attention to Section 92 of the BNA Act, in which "Property and Civil Rights in the Provinces" were listed as among the areas of exclusive provincial jurisdiction. It came to insist that the jurisdictional domain of any particular enactment be construed according to whether in "pith and substance" its actual effect was to trench upon "property and civil rights." Thus "property and civil rights" were given very wide application, and generally superseded the "peace, order, and good government" entitlement of the federal government.

H. ALBINSKI, CANADIAN AND AUSTRALIAN POLITICS IN COMPARATIVE PERSPECTIVE 362 (1973).

called for exertions of provincial power developed, and as judges, over time, began to read the BNA Act differently, the coin of the Canadian state was flipped. As Cole Harris has summed it up:

> [T]he growing role and visibility of the provinces and of provincial governments . . . [took] place while governments were assuming a larger role in Canadian life and while the evolution of the Canadian economy was changing the significance of some of the terms of the British North America Act. In an age of water power and steam, control of natural resources did not mean what it does today. Provincial governments . . . assum[ed] a growing role in the economy, and the province a growing role in Canadian feeling. A host of activities that once were organized at many [local] scales [came to be] organized provincially. At the same time federal power . . . also increased, as Ottawa, too . . . expanded its services and its economic presence. In short, provincial and federal governments [grew] simultaneously at the expense of a multitude of other scales of Canadian interaction. This [was] a recipe for conflict. It reduce[d] a whole gamut of different relationships at different scales to a polarized struggle between two levels of government.[16]

Through the years the provinces more often than not were the victors in that struggle, while the power of the central government was diminished. War and depression in the twentieth century temporarily halted—and even reversed—the movement, but after World War II, it resumed with even more vigor.

Thus as the provinces approached the table to negotiate the patriated constitution with the federal government in 1980, they did so with a long tradition of provincial power behind them. They could hardly be expected to abandon that position as the negotiations proceeded.

The provinces had even more at stake at the bargaining table than preservation of the compact notion and continuation of their eminence in the exercise of governmental power, for they also had a vested interest in the process of intergovernmental consultation to defend. The federal-provincial conference had become, especially after World War II, the standard way of dealing with most important domestic policy questions which arose for governmental action. Whether it is a first ministers' (the Prime Minister and the provincial premiers) conference, a conference at the ministerial or departmental level, or one of a variety of special ad hoc intergovernmental conferences, Canadian domestic policymaking remains by and large the product of conference negotiation.

With increasing frequency in recent years, the provinces have taken the initiative in setting the agenda for federal-provincial meetings. Very often the end product is a bilateral agreement between Ottawa and a single province, though multi-governmental agreements are not uncommon. The provinces favor the process since each of the bargaining sessions is sui generis, often providing opportunities for particular provincial interests to be advanced.[17] Indeed, as Gordon

---

16. Harris, *The Emotional Structure of Canadian Regionalism,* in The Challenges of Canada's Regional Diversity 28 (1981).

17. Roger Gibbins points out, however, that while federal-provincial conferences do provide, undoubtedly, a badly needed forum for the representation of provincial interests . . . there are many definitions of "the provincial interest," depending on who is consulted: provincial voters, provincial governments or provincial representatives in the federal cabinet . . . . Within any single province definitions will differ among voters, interest groups, provincial parties, federal MPs and federal cabinet representatives. Thus it would be a mistake to accept uncritically the rhetoric of the provincial governments and to assume that they speak in the provincial interest. R. Gibbins, Regionalism, Territorial Politics in Canada and the United States 96 (1982).

Robertson, speaking out of his long intimate personal experience as a federal bureaucrat involved in the intergovernmental consultation process, put it recently, federal-provincial meetings have tended to become occasions "for the articulation of distinct provincial interests and for provincial intrusion into wholly federal areas of concern."[18] His observation was underscored by Michael Kirby, who was once secretary to the cabinet for federal-provincial relations: "Provinces, like individual citizens, are . . . tending to take an individualistic rather than a collective view of the country . . . on a scale that is unprecedented in Canadian history."[19] Alberta's protracted quarrel with Ottawa over an oil-pricing agreement is a specific example of Kirby's point. But a number of the other provinces approach bargaining with the federal government from a similarly self-centered position; even a "have-not" province like Newfoundland, under its feisty premier Brian Peckford, is learning how to get the most for itself out of negotiations with Ottawa.

The importance of the federal-provincial conference to the provinces, however, is not only that it provides a mechanism for provincial governments to be effectively involved in the handling of the important public policy issues, but also that it "has facilitated the adaptation of parliamentary procedures to a federal system . . . ." Each conference aims at reaching "mutual agreement." These agreements, numbering in the thousands, enable the Canadian system of government to work. They permit the partial acceptance of both centralist and regional viewpoints and reject "the idea that either one embodies the whole truth."[20] As such, the federal-provincial conference has been an admirable way over the years to settle most of the division of power issues that have arisen between Ottawa and the provinces.

Thus the provinces in Canada have come to occupy a powerful position in Canada's governmental matrix, both in fundamental power within confederation and in the procedure for developing public policy to convert that power into programs. It was from this position that they approached the challenge Prime Minister Trudeau gave them when he presented the *fait accompli* of a reformed constitution.

This is not the place to chronicle the events of the constitutional battle of 1980-81.[21] Suffice it to say here that on a number of crucial points the provincial premiers forced Prime Minister Trudeau to yield to their demands. Thus the draft finally sent off to London could rightly be considered as representing provincial interests—or at least those of the governments in power in nine of the ten provinces (Quebec never accepted the draft Constitution). Now that the patriation process is over, those nine provincial governments might be expected to be looking forward to living with the product of their labors happily ever after.

That expectation, however, is probably ill-founded. The acceptance of the

18. Gordon Robertson, *quoted in* CONFRONTATION AND COLLABORATION—INTERGOVERNMENTAL RELATIONS IN CANADA TODAY 82-83 (R. Simeon ed. 1979).
19. Lecture by Michael Kirby, Carleton University, Ottawa (April 1980), *quoted in* The Financial Post, May 3, 1980, at 7, col. 1, 4.
20. Elton, *Placing Constitutional Reform in Perspective,* 2 SPECTRUM 6 (1981).
21. See the contribution to this volume of Mallory, *The Politics of Constitutional Change,* LAW & CONTEMP. PROBS., Autumn 1982, at 53.

reformed constitution by the provinces will vary from province to province. Quebec provides the extreme case. She stands adamant on her rejection of the reformed constitution. Quebec's leaders oppose it, first of all, on general grounds as an improperly drawn up document that violates Canadian "constitutional conventions." The provincial government brought an action in the Quebec courts contending that the province has a right to veto a major constitutional change affecting provincial jurisdiction. The Quebec Court of Appeal ruled early in April 1982 that the province had no such right.[22] Quebec immediately appealed to the Supreme Court of Canada. The Court dismissed the appeal.[23]

In arguing its case before the Supreme Court, Quebec predictably contended that Canada is the product of a political compact between its two founding language groups and that no changes in the existing constitution (the BNA Act) can be made without Quebec's agreement in behalf of the Francophone group. The province also objected to several of the particulars of the 1982 Constitution: the elimination of financial compensation to provinces which choose to opt out of federal programs, the asserted right of mobility for workers across Canada, and the protection of language rights for the Anglophone minority within Quebec. In short, Quebec is concerned that it will lose its special status in confederation. Quebecers see this status as having been ravaged, especially by the Charter of Rights, which Premier René Lévesque refers to as "the contraption that's called the bill of rights."[24]

Ottawa has maintained a standing offer to resume constitutional negotiations with Quebec on the points of contention, but provincial leaders have not so far indicated any willingness to accept the offer. Far from manifesting a conciliatory attitude, Quebec's stance has become increasingly strident. Not only did Lévesque and leaders of the Parti Québécois boycott the formal promulgation ceremonies in Ottawa and stage a counter-demonstration at home, but Premier Lévesque "refused to rule out the possibility of individual acts of civil disobedience on the part of members of his government" after the constitution came into effect "and admitted that withholding tax transfers to the federal government" was not out of the question.[25] At the very least, Premier Lévesque promised that his government will make maximum use of the constitution's notwithstanding clause (section 33).[26] Bill 62, enacted by the Quebec National Assembly in early summer 1982, asserts that Quebecers' fundamental freedoms and rights are subject only to the provincial charter of rights, not to the constitution's Charter of Rights, and that the education provisions of Quebec's Charter of the French Language (Bill 101) will continue to be applied in the province rather than the parallel but different provision in the new constitution. By taking such actions, Quebec made sure that in Premier Lévesque's words, there will be "a lot of judicial muddling." In any case, the Premier promised, "we're working like mad at whatever can be done to

---

22. Re Attorney Gen. Que. & Attorney Gen. Can., 134 D.L.R.3d 719 (1982).
23. Re Attorney Gen. Que. & Attorney Gen. Can., 140 D.L.R.3d 385 (1983).
24. *Quoted in* Globe & Mail, Mar. 30, 1982, at 1, col. 1, 3.
25. *Id*.
26. For an explanation of the notwithstanding clause, *see infra* note 35 and accompanying text.

counter the bloody thing."[27]

Thus Quebec's future within confederation remains unclear. The ruling Parti Québécois has pledged to make sovereignty for Quebec the main issue in the next provincial election, which is not likely to take place for another two or three years. Premier Lévesque let himself be quoted in early June 1982 as saying that "with another push" Quebec would become independent by the end of the decade.[28] In the interim, Quebec, Canada's second largest province, is in constitutional limbo.

Not to belabor the point of different provincial reactions to the reformed constitution, it need only be said that the energy-rich provinces of Alberta and British Columbia can be expected to regard the reformed constitution from a different perspective than the other provinces because of section 50, which amends section 92 of the BNA Act with regard to power over non-renewable resources by shifting responsibility therefor to the national government. Similarly, the perspective of the Atlantic provinces will be skewed by the long dependence of that area on federal payments from Ottawa. And with provincial governments likely to remain of different political persuasions from the federal government—seven of the provinces in 1982 were under Progressive Conservative governments, one was under a NDP government, one under a Social Credit government, and Quebec, of course, under the Parti Québécois—a variety of perspectives toward the reformed constitution is to be expected.

The expectation of the continuation of a strong provincial presence in Canadian governmental affairs under the reformed constitution is further brought into doubt when the nature of the document itself is considered. One "disturbing aspect" of the whole process by which constitutional reform was achieved, Terrence G. Carroll concluded, "was the bargaining and horse-trading which took place" in the course of negotiations. "Proponents of a system of elite accommodation will properly point out that all of [the changes which resulted from the bargaining] represented a willingness to compromise and a real commitment to reach an agreement on the side of the political leaders of the country." But the other side of the coin was perhaps, Carroll thought, a weakening of public support for the constitution. The public was forced to witness a "conference at which the 'fundamental rights' of Canadians, and the 'fundamental rule' of the Canadian political system, changed hour by hour."

> If a constitution is to be effective it must be widely believed to embody the highest form of human law. It must be thought to represent the best interests and the best instincts of the society. It is unlikely that the Canadian constitution can quickly regain this status as a result of a complicated compromise arranged entirely by the political elite.[29]

Not only is the reformed constitution thus perhaps weakly rooted in popular acceptance, but much of its contents seem tentative or transitional in nature. In fact, perhaps one ought not to use the word constitution without quotation marks around it to indicate that it is not really a full-blown constitutional document, any more than was the BNA Act of 1867. Indeed, the BNA Act (now to be called

---

27. *Quoted in* Globe & Mail, Mar. 30, 1982, at 1, col. 1, 3.
28. Globe & Mail, June 10, 1982, at 4, col. 4.
29. T. CARROLL, POLITICAL PARTICIPATION 88 (1982).

Constitution Act, 1867) is fully incorporated into the patriated constitution, to be sure with some important new provisions. Not only is the new constitution also "merely a British statute," presented to Parliament after "little public debate, and [with no] endorsement by the electorate,"[30] but by its very terms it is incomplete and open-ended. It not only assumes that a great many amendments will be made in its text in forthcoming years—indeed, the nature of the amending process was one of the stickiest points in the negotiations leading up to the final agreement— but it calls in section 37 for a constitutional conference, "composed of the Prime Minister and the first ministers of the provinces," to be convened by the Prime Minister within one year after the Canada Act comes into force. Though the intention of the section seems to have been to provide a way to settle the rights of Canada's native peoples, an issue left unresolved in the negotiations process, the terms of section 37 require only that the conference "shall have included on its agenda an item" concerning native rights. The conference agenda, which presumably will be drawn up conjointly by the two levels of government, may be much longer—section 37 also speaks of "discussions on any items on the agenda."

The first "section 37" conference was held on March 15-16, 1983. It dealt with the narrow question of native peoples' claims that they were never properly compensated for the lands taken from them by the French and English settlers. No consensus was reached on the matter by the ten provincial premiers and Prime Minister Trudeau attending the sessions, and other agenda items were disallowed. Presumably other constitutional conferences on native rights will be held in the future.

The reformed constitution was also left open-ended by section 49, which provides that another "constitutional conference" is to be called by the Prime Minister within fifteen years, at which he and the provincial premiers will "review the provisions" of Part V, which is concerned with procedure for amending the constitution. The lack of agreement on an amending formula undoubtedly prevented earlier patriation of the constitution to Canada. The question is whether the 1981 version will turn out to be any more satisfactory than the earlier rejected formulae.[31] As Alexander Brady wrote years ago: "In a liberal federation . . . the devising of a satisfactory procedure for amendment is rarely easy and seldom gives satisfaction."[32]

Other parts of the reformed constitution threaten to diminish provincial power by shifting responsibility to the national government. These include the guarantee in sections 25 and 35 of the rights of aboriginal peoples, and the provisions in sections 50 and 51 amending section 92 of the BNA Act with regard to power over non-renewable natural resources, forestry resources, and electrical energy.

Special mention must be made of section 36, which commits both the provinces and the national government to the principle of equalization, specifically to

(a) promoting equal opportunities for the wellbeing of Canadians; (b) furthering economic

---

30. R. GIBBINS, *supra* note 17, at 28-29.
31. See the contribution to this volume by Dellinger, *The Amending Process in Canada and the United States: A Comparative Perspective*, LAW & CONTEMP. PROBS., Autumn 1982, at 283.
32. Brady, *Constitutional Amendment and the Federation*, 29 CAN. J. ECON. & POL. SCI. 486 (1963).

development to reduce disparity in opportunities; and (c) providing essential public services of reasonable quality to all Canadians.

The national government is further committed under section 36 to "the principle of making equalization payments to ensure that provincial governments have sufficient revenues to provide reasonably comparable levels of public services at reasonably comparable levels of taxation." Only time will tell what becomes of these principles in application. The wording of the first part of the section raises doubts in some minds as to its justiciability. "Without altering the legislative authority of Parliament or of the provincial legislatures, or the rights of any of them with respect to the exercise of their legislative authority," reads that section, "Parliament and the legislatures, together with the government of Canada, are committed" to equalization. That wording alone supports the judgment of Professor Thomas Courchene that the Canadian courts will ultimately have to become "the final arbiter" of what actions qualify as constitutional steps toward fulfilling that commitment, as indeed the courts will also become in determining what would be a "reasonable" equalization formula under the second part of section 36.[33] How the provinces will fare under judicial rulings is a matter of conjecture.

Similarly, the impact on the provinces of the centerpiece of the reformed constitution, its Charter of Rights, is a matter of conjecture. As with the equalization provision, Charles Campbell has concluded, "the main effect of the Charter will be to strengthen the role of the courts as a procedural policeman."[34] Already a spate of challenges to the Charter has been made in provincial courts. If Canadian experience follows that of the United States, judicial interpretations of federal versus provincial power over rights will be inconsistent. The Canadian experience will be complicated by the terms of the compromise that had to be included in the Charter in the form of the "notwithstanding" clause, which was intended to accommodate provincial uneasiness. This clause provides that provincial legislatures may override for five years (and longer if the override legislation is renewed) the Charter's provisions in the areas of fundamental freedoms (such as freedom of assembly, press and belief), legal rights (such as the prohibition of the use of illegally obtained evidence in court), and anti-discrimination guarantees. On the one hand, different reactions by individual provinces may be expected—the NDP government of Manitoba early said that it would not use the override provision—thus making any unified provincial position on rights highly unlikely. On the other hand, a Canada-wide statement of rights may in the long run be a strong force for nationalization. As the eminent Canadian political scientist, Donald Smiley, concludes, there will inevitably be "a disposition to change the Canadian political system and political culture in a fairly fundamental way by inducing Canadians to identify themselves and to frame their allegiances in terms of their rights as protected by national institutions, and thus the ongoing provincialization which has become so pervasive will be weakened."[35]

33. *Quoted in More Storm Clouds,* Alberta Report, April 10, 1981, at 3.
34. Campbell, *Charter of Rights Could Lead Courts into a Political Role,* Globe & Mail, Feb. 18, 1982, at 7, col. 1, 5.
35. Smiley, *A Report to the Ontario Economic Council,* quoted in Globe & Mail, Nov. 2, 1981, at 7.

Attention should also be paid to section 42, which alters the BNA Act's provision for admitting new provinces. Whereas the BNA Act left it up to negotiation between a territory and Ottawa, the patriated constitution allows a province to be created or to expand only by gaining the approval of the federal government and of at least six provinces containing in the aggregate half of Canada's total population. The effect of that provision may soon be tested. Even prior to the proclamation of the constitution, a plebescite was held in the Northwest Territories in which fifty-six percent of those voting approved splitting the territories into two parts, roughly corresponding to the Inuit and Dene populated areas there. Although it is not binding, the plebescite is widely regarded in the North as "the first step in the creation of at least two new northern provinces."[36] There are questions, the *Globe and Mail* observed editorially, "about whether the division would make Ottawa more reluctant to grant provincial status to the Northwest Territories. Anything that would postpone this political maturity would be unfortunate,"[37] particularly in light of the possibility that if the territories are not given self-government, "chunks of land could be swallowed by [provinces to] the south. . . . But it should be remembered that Nunavit [the name given to the Inuit portion of the area] is almost twice as populous as Manitoba was when it gained provincehood in 1870."[38] The impact of new provinces on the existing provinces and on the balance of power between the provinces and Ottawa is hard to assay. They would very likely add weight to the provincial side.

Finally, municipal governments, long at the bottom of the totem pole of governmental power and recognition in Canada, have in recent years increasingly asserted their desire to obtain formal constitutional status. As the details of the patriated constitution were being worked out in 1980 and 1981, municipalities repeatedly attempted to achieve that goal. They did not succeed, but they remain determined, even though they were chastised by Governor-General Edward Schreyer for taking that stand. In an address to the 1982 conference of the Federation of Canadian Municipalities in Ottawa, the governor-general, himself a former provincial premier, decried the idea as unduly complicating the formal order and structure of the nation. In any case, he doubted if anything like a consensus among provinces could be obtained to support the objective of municipal government. There is the possibility that municipalities would settle for a constitutional statement of the national government's responsibility for achieving balanced urban growth and development, but that too promises difficulties. Either answer to the municipalities' prayers would cause a shift in provincial power.

Thus by conference, amendment, interpretation, and legislative action over time, the position of the provinces under the 1982 constitution may be altered. A different balance may also be struck as the provinces, with the national government, explore ways of settling a wide variety of issues that have eluded resolution in recent years. The real test of the new constitution, indeed, may be in how well it serves the nation in making resolution of those issues possible. Certainly at first

---

36. Johnson, *First Step on the Road to Two New Provinces?*, Globe & Mail, Apr. 7, 1982, at 7, col. 2.
37. Globe & Mail, Apr. 8, 1982, at 6, col. 5.
38. *Id.* at col. 6.

glance the 1982 constitution does not seem to change the context within which resolution will occur. Among the issues the provinces wish to see resolved by some combination of governmental action are the pricing of oil, about which Alberta is still unhappy; control of telecommunications, in particular of cable and pay television; revision of anti-combines legislation; jurisdiction over offshore seabed resources and fisheries, an unresolved issue since at least 1949 and currently the major squeak point in the relations between Newfoundland and Ottawa; the propriety of national versus provincial lotteries; the establishment of uniform education standards across Canada; the removal of economic barriers to the free movement of goods, labor, and production factors across provincial boundaries; provincial versus national responsibility for energy policy; and the abandonment of the Crow's Nest Pass Agreement of 1897, under which western grain producers have been guaranteed cheap transportation by rail of their products to market.

While these issues are important, they pale in significance beside the settlement of the basic fiscal arrangements between the national government and the provinces, including arrangements both for collecting income taxes and for transferring funds from Ottawa to the provinces. Negotiations on these matters between the provinces and Ottawa for the five year period 1982-87 broke down in the winter of 1982, and Ottawa unilaterally enacted a set of arrangements. Although the arrangements will likely stand, and although the provinces will fare somewhat better over the period than they had expected, the provinces were unhappy with Ottawa's action, especially the dependent-on-Ottawa Atlantic provinces. In the next round of discussions the provinces will probably exert themselves more strongly than ever upon the resolution of these basic fiscal arrangements.

In the long run, it may appear that the reformed constitution itself is not cast so as to provide Canada with the kind of underpinning required for future national development. Except for the resource changes mentioned above, sections 91 and 92 stand in the reformed constitution even as they stood in the BNA Act, still food for negotiation and eventually, for parts of them, grain for the judicial grist mill, with no sure provincial or national advantage. As Eugene Forsey summed it up, "This is not a new constitution. It's the old constitution with some very important additions. There will be the same questions. Does this come under section 91 or 92? Does section 93 apply?"[39] In short, the new constitution does not get at the heart of the matter, the existing division of power between the national government and those of the provinces. In particular, it does not address the constitutional distinction made in the BNA Act between direct and indirect taxes, nor does it deal with the harmonization of national and provincial taxes in general. More broadly, the reformed constitution does not take into account "the economic imperatives" of the modern technological state which "require unified if not uniform economic policies throughout the entire territory [of a state] and do not brook that kind of economic fragmentation" so characteristic of Canadian federalism in the past.[40]

39. *Quoted in* Graham, *Happy and Glorious,* SAT. NIGHT, June 1982, at 30.
40. Lowenstein, *Reflections on the Value of Constitutions in Our Revolutionary Age,* in CONSTITUTIONS AND CONSTITUTIONAL TRENDS SINCE WORLD WAR II 191, 211 (A. Zurcher ed. 1951).

Indeed, the economic power of Alberta, and to a lesser extent, the other resource-rich provinces, challenges the efficiency of policy making by the national government and even of national leadership itself. At the very least, the interests and objectives of those provinces clash with those of the other provinces. It is unclear, in any event, how the new constitution will address the need for a new balance between those provinces and Ottawa and between them and their sister provinces. Nor is it clear how the new constitution speaks to the solution of any of the problems alluded to earlier.

All that can be done at this juncture is to wait and see. Canada's new constitution, like that of the United States in the early days, will only be a paper contrivance until time and experience have filled out its meaning.

Even more important than the impact of unsolved problems on constitutional development is the necessity many feel for fundamental reform in Canada's political institutions, changes which were avoided in the constitutional negotiations of 1980-81. Some proposed basic constitutional changes might increase provincial power. One proposed change would provide for an elected rather than an appointed Senate, a Senate which would not be "irrelevant," but which would perform the important function of providing a place where regional voices might be heard at the center:

> [W]here other federations have an elected second chamber to provide regional voices for their constituents, our Constitution has provided, effectively, nothing but a vacuum. It is a vacuum that has, of necessity, been filled extra-constitutionally . . . [by] provincial Premiers . . . step[ping] forward as spokesmen for their provinces on national issues. [But] provincial premiers are elected on provincial issues, to run provincial governments . . . . They are not elected for their views on national issues.[41]

The members of a reformed Senate would perhaps be elected by proportional representation. Quebec could possibly be given a set percentage of seats to protect its special status in confederation, and the smaller provinces could have delegations disproportionately larger than their populations, to compensate for their smaller representation in the House of Commons. A reformed Senate would probably be accorded only limited legislative authority, not the full equality with the House which the American Senate enjoys with the House of Representatives, out of respect for the parliamentary system's reliance on confidence in the House of Commons for responsible government. The Senate's role would be to increase the weight of regional considerations in parliamentary deliberations. In particular, Gordon Robertson believes, an elected Senate in place of the present one might reduce "the sense of alienation and frustration in the West toward the federal government."[42]

A second proposed basic structural change, not incorporated into the reformed constitution, is some sort of proportional representation scheme for elections to the House of Commons. The "first-past-the-post" electoral system traditionally

---

41. Kent, *How to Enjoy Regional Diversities,* in THE CHALLENGES OF CANADA'S REGIONAL DIVERSITY 40 (1981).

42. *Quoted in The Institute,* vol. 4, no. 2, Feb. 22, 1982, at 1. *But see* Fisher, *Personal Viewpoint: Senate Reform,* EXECUTIVE, Mar. 1982, at 81-82, who argues against any immediate change in the composition of the Senate.

employed in Canada has resulted in recent years in exclusion of "even the major parties from representation in certain regions of the country. As the [1979 and 1980] federal elections have shown, it is becoming increasingly difficult for any party to form a government with representation from all regions of the country."[43] Thus there is no surety that regional interests will be weighed as they should be in "the determination of programs, policies and priorities" in the House. Only if the method of representation is revised, it is argued, will parties be enabled to participate in a process of national consensus-building "which is not a sham but an active process in which regional diversities are acknowledged, assessed, in reason reconciled and for the successful party, integrated into policies that earn national confidence."[44]

In any case, the 1981 census will result in a realignment of the House of Commons. The membership of the House will rise to 310 at the first federal election after 1984. Added to that chamber then will be additional representatives from disaffected Quebec (6) and Alberta (6), as well as from Ontario (10) and British Columbia (5). This may improve regional representation in the House to some degree; even so, because of the constitutional necessity of overrepresenting the smaller provinces,[45] those four provinces, which contain 82.3% of the 1982 population, will even then have only 78.7% of the seats in the House.

A third suggestion for basic constitutional change, also not incorporated into the reformed constitution, would affect the well established pattern of intergovernmental consultation already referred to in this paper.[46] As the government of British Columbia pointed out in its 1978 series of *Constitutional Proposals*, the overall intergovernmental negotiation process is a piecemeal one, "with little regard for long-term objectives and priorities," consisting as it does of a "rather nebulous clutter of committees . . . often without consistent objectives or formal organization . . . [; too] little attention [has been] paid to coordinating the activities of [this] vast network of . . . meetings and conferences" across the wide range of policy areas involved.[47] Moreover, one set of participants in that process

> has been elected on issues in federal jurisdiction, the other ten on issues in the jurisdiction of [the] province[s]. They meet to argue, negotiate and, desirably, co-operate in the many matters that involve both jurisdictions. [But] they must . . . be true to their watching constituents on issues for which they were elected. . . . None of the participants has legitimacy as a spokesman for regional or provincial viewpoints on federal issues.[48]

In the view of some, a reformed Senate might take the place of some of the intergovernmental consultation process; or it could be regularized and brought into

---

43. Notes for Remarks by the Prime Minister [Pierre E. Trudeau] at the Tenth Anniversary of the Council of Maritime Premiers, Fredericton, New Brunswick, June 1, 1981, at 23. (Photocopy supplied to the author by the Canadian Embassy in Washington.)

44. Kent, *supra* note 41, at 46.

45. Prince Edward Island with four representatives for its roughly 120,000 people is the example par excellence of overrepresentation.

46. *See supra* notes 17-20 and accompanying text.

47. Province of British Columbia, *British Columbia's Constitutional Proposals,* Paper No. 5, "Improved Instruments for Federal-Provincial Relations," Sept. 1978, at 7-11.

48. Kent, *supra* note 41, at 41.

some semblance of order through specific constitutional provisions governing its conduct. However, David Elton argues,

> this type of reform should not be confused with, or substituted for, increasing the ability of national institutions to cope with regional diversity; intergovernmental mechanisms are not sufficient for this purpose. The institutionalization of federal-provincial conferences, without the reform of central government institutions in the direction of more effective regional representation, could further erode the credibility and capacity of the national government.[49]

Other proposed reforms include changing the basis of appointment of Supreme Court justices and improving regional representation on regulatory agencies of the national government, so that they too would better reflect provincial interests.

Finally, a set of issues put on the constitutional agenda as long ago as October 1976 by the provincial premiers remains unresolved. These issues include the national government's declaratory and spending powers, its moribund but still extant power to reserve or disallow provincial legislation, its power to implement treaties, and its residual power in general. Also left unaddressed are the issues put forward by the First Ministers' conference of February 1979: empowering governments adequately to fight inflation and unemployment; dealing with non-tariff barriers to interprovincial and international trade; providing for the regulation of the Canadian securities market; and dealing with the role of commodity marketing boards.

Whether any of these issues will win a place on the agenda of future constitutional conferences seems unlikely. One point, however, which is not arguable is the necessity of eventually facing most of these issues.

CONCLUSION

In their national political institutions, Canadians have tried to combine parliamentary and federal forms of government. But, as Roger Gibbins so effectively put it, parliamentarianism has "dominated and, as a consequence, national institutions have become too majoritarian in character, too insensitive to the diverse and pluralistic interests of a federal society." In particular, the traditional institutions of the national government, which remain unchanged in the 1982 version of the constitution, "have not facilitated the effective representation of territorial interests . . . . Parliamentary norms and the tightly disciplined party system they [engender bottle] up territorial conflict and [deny] it an effective outlet through the institutions of the national government. . . ." The Senate has never been a useful "forum for the protection and promotion of territorial interests," and in the House of Commons, the "less populated sections of the country [have been] outgunned and overrun in national politics when regional MPs found themselves on the wrong side of the party fence." Such ineffectual "territorial representation within the national government," Gibbins concluded, "has led to constitutional turmoil and uncertainty . . . ."[50]

In the constitutional negotiations leading up to the constitution of 1982, the

49. Elton, *supra* note 20, at 11.
50. R. GIBBINS, *supra* note 17, at 78.

issue of the lack of adequate regional representation within the institutions of the national government was sidestepped in favor of what were thought then to be even more important problems—securing a constitutional basis for Canadians' rights and a workable amendment process. Thus the new constitution, like the BNA Act it incorporates, leaves territorial conflict to be resolved almost exclusively by provincial governments. "The inability of the Canadian political system to handle territorial conflict effectively has in turn weakened its ability to handle other issues, as the contemporary energy and budget disputes between Ottawa [and the provinces] so clearly illustrates."[51] Change in these institutions will not be easy. Yet, the argument for change is a valid one, and the need to act on it is impelling.

The reformed constitution, in fine, as embodied in the Canada Act of 1982, should be regarded as the product of only the first phase of constitution-making in Canada. The struggle for power between Ottawa and the provinces has not been ended by its proclamation. Open-ended as the reformed constitution is, the balance of power is very likely to change considerably in the years ahead. Whether the change will favor the provinces or Ottawa depends on a number of variables which will be brought into play over time by the federal cabinet and Parliament, provincial premiers and legislatures, judges of courts of appeal and the Supreme Court of Canada, and federal and provincial bureaucrats. It is even possible that the Canadian people might eventually insist on having an input. And in the longer run, if constitution-making goes on to include some or all of the basic institutional changes just discussed, the final balance may be different still. As Roger Gibbins reasoned: "The creation of more effective means of regional representation in Ottawa would . . . weaken the power of the provincial governments," at the same time weakening "the power of the federal cabinet over national institutions." As he sees it,

> At heart, the traditional degree of cabinet control and effective territorial representation are incompatible . . . [I]f the federal cabinet is weakened by institutional reform while the control of provincial cabinets over their own legislature is not similarly reduced, if majoritarianism is reduced within the national government but not within the provincial governments, then in the short run the federal system may be further destabilized in the direction of greater devolution and provincial strength . . . [O]ver the long run, more effective regional representation will strengthen the position of Ottawa vis-a-vis the provinces, even though the federal cabinet's power within Ottawa would be diminished.[52]

Thus the new constitution's impact on Canadian federalism will be long in being felt. But that was to have been expected. As David Elton reminds us,

> [I]t should not be thought that an end to the debate on patriation, amending formulae and a charter of rights and freedoms will [have] conclude[d] the debate on constitutional reform in this country. Quite the contrary. Constitutional issues will continue to force themselves onto the public agenda and take precedence over other issues until such time as the structural framework of Canadian federalism has been adjusted to reflect the regional realities of Canada.[53]

What adjustments in the federal-provincial balance may finally result cannot

---

51. *Id*. at 194.
52. *Id*.
53. Elton, *supra* note 20, at 3.

be predicted with any surety. One thing, however, is sure: the flexibility and durability of the Canadian federal system will be put to the test in the years ahead. The likelihood is great that it will survive that test and be with us into the indefinite future.

LES CALCULS STRATEGIQUES DERRIERE LE "CANADA BILL"

Daniel Latouche*

The author views the 1982 Canada Bill as yet another attempt to "normalize" Quebec. He analyzes the forms of this political normalization and reflects upon the fact that the Constitutional Conference was actually a negotiation between Quebec and English Canada. He then moves on to the three other objectives of the Constitutional Conference, which were the repatriation of the constitution, a constitutional reform, and the political defeat of the "Parti Québécois." The author concludes that Quebec will have to use other avenues to achieve the political equality it still aspires to. Up until now Quebec thought equality could be achieved within Canada through renewed federalism, or with Canada through sovereignty-association. Now Quebec may consider that equality will be achieved against Canada through independence.

I

Introduction

Ce n'est pas faire accroc au discours scientifique que d'affirmer qu'on assiste depuis mai 1980 à une tentative de normalisation politique du Québec dont le *Canada Bill* de 1982 n'est qu'une étape. A cause d'une association avec la Tchécoslovaquie de 1968 ou la Pologne de 1983 une telle affirmation en choquera plusieurs. Pourtant les effets attendus sont les mêmes. Il s'agit, pour Ottawa et les autres gouvernements provinciaux, de mettre un terme une fois pour toutes aux velléités d'autonomie d'une société québécoise qui dérange passablement ce qui est devenu le projet politique canadien par excellence, soit la dépendance économique tranquille du Canada envers les Etats-Unis.

Elles furent rares au Québec français les manifestations, que ce soit sous forme de colloques universitaires ou de parades royales, organisées pour marquer la proclamation de ce *Canada Bill*. Que ce sentiment de dépit soit partagé à la fois par les partisans de la souveraineté et ceux du fédéralisme témoigne de la profondeur avec laquelle est ressenti ce sentiment d'échec. Pour les deux groupes, cet accord constitutionnel marque la fin du rêve qu'ils partageaient: celui de reconstruire le Canada afin d'assurer au Québec l'égalité politique qui le ferait sortir une fois pour toutes de son statut de collectivité minoritaire. Pour les souverainistes, l'accord constitutionnel, non pas tant par son contenu que par le rapport de forces et le processus qui l'a engendré, marque l'échec de l'idée même de souveraineté-association. Pour les fédéralistes, c'est la fin du projet d'un fédéralisme renouvelé

---

* Department of Political Science and French Canada Studies Program, McGill University.

en profondeur. A brève échéance, Claude Ryan, le chef du Parti Libéral du Québec, qui incarnait cette vision, en sera la victime.

Le Québec avait beaucoup à gagner et beaucoup à perdre dans cette négociation avec le reste du pays. Plusieurs stratégies auront été employées et toutes auront échoué. Jusqu'en 1976, c'est la stratégie des accommodements qui a prévalu. On a tenté d'aller chercher le plus grand nombre de pouvoirs législatifs, de responsabilités administratives et de ressources fiscales, bref, tout ce qui pouvait représenter un acquis pour le Québec. En 1976, le gouvernement du Parti Québécois effectua un virage de 180°. Fini la stratégie minimale des accommodements, la stratégie maximale allait réussir là où celle des "petits pas" avait échoué.

Cette stratégie, elle aussi, a échoué et, avant de songer à remettre le navire à flot, il faut évaluer correctement les dommages. Pour l'instant, ces dommages ont nom: normalisation politique, déstabilisation sociale et étranglement économique. Les grèves dans le secteur de l'éducation, des affaires sociales et de la fonction publique qui ont déchiré le Québec à l'hiver 1982 ne sont qu'un signe avant-coureur d'une situation qui risque fort de se généraliser. N'étant plus un bien de pouvoir, la scène québécoise va devenir le terrain privilégié de ces affrontements stériles.

La normalisation politique touche trois aspects de l'échiquier québécois: le déplacement vers Ottawa de centres de décision qui auparavant appartenaient en exclusivité à l'Assemblée nationale, la volonté d'éliminer électoralement le Parti Québécois et la vassalisation définitive du Parti Libéral du Québec.

Le texte qui suit est une évaluation des formes que prend cette normalisation ainsi qu'une réflexion sur ce qui fût sans aucun doute la principale erreur des élites québécoises, à savoir que la négociation constitutionnelle était en fait une négociation entre le Québec et le Canada anglais.

II

L'OBJECTIF STRATÉGIQUE: LA NORMALISATION POLITIQUE DU QUÉBEC

Ainsi donc, il n'y aura pas de véritable nouvelle entente politique au Canada. Que cette possibilité ait pu miroiter si longtemps aux yeux des élites politiques québécoises est certes le signe d'un espoir largement partagé, mais aussi d'une erreur d'appréciation.

Dans une unanimité touchante, les élus canadiens-français en poste à Ottawa et les "observateurs-canadiens-anglais-sympathiques-à-la-cause-québécoise" affirment maintenant que rien n'est terminé, que le rapatriement et l'accord sur la formule d'amendement rendent maintenant possible une véritable réforme constitutionnelle, etc.[1] Doit-on considérer ces propos comme les manifestations d'une

---

1. De telles opinions sont fréquemment exprimées dans plusieurs revues canadiennes anglaises dont *The Magazine, Canada Dimension, Options,* et *Canadian Forum*. En février 1983 le solliciteur général de l'Ontario, M. Roy McMurty, déclarait devant les étudiants de l'Université Laval qu'il fallait peut-être envisager de modifier la constitution pour accorder au Québec un droit de veto sur les questions culturelles. Robert Stanfield, l'ancien chef du Parti Conservateur du Canada, a très bien resumé cette "nouvelle" attitude dans *What to Do about Quebec's Isolation,* 3 POLICY OPTIONS 6 (1982).

bonne foi culpabilisée ou d'un paternalisme éhonté? Difficile à dire. Chose certaine, c'est considérer les Québécois comme une quantité politique bien négligeable que de les noyer ainsi sous ces propos faussement réconfortants. Cette incapacité du reste due Canada d'admettre ouvertement que le *Canada Bill* constitue ni plus ni moins qu'une "raclée constitutionnelle" infligée au Québec, témoigne à sa façon du manque de maturité politique qui ne veut même pas reconnaître ses victoires.

Pourtant une défaite est une défaite. Si un jour, elle doit être suivie d'une victoire pour le Québec, cela dépend davantage d'une évaluation sérieuse des erreurs passées que de bons mots des adversaires. En politique, comme au cinéma d'ailleurs, les "bons" ne gagnent pas toujours.

Que le gouvernement fédéral, les élites politiques canadiennes-anglaises, l'opinion publique et les intellectuels considèrent le *Canada Bill* comme une grande victoire, une manifestation du génie canadien ou simplement une étape importante dans le développement politique du pays, illustre mieux que tous les propos du plus biaisé des séparatistes la faillite du fédéralisme canadien.

Avec les Iles Tonga et la République Centre-africaine de l'empereur Bokassa, le Canada est le seul pays qui a cru bon réaffirmer récemment le caractère monarchique de ses institutions centrales. Que cette réaffirmation soit le fait de Sa Majesté elle-même dans le cadre d'un spectacle digne d'un Disneyland politique, fait ressortir pleinement la naiveté de tous ces Québécois, qui pendant des années ont pris pour acquis que le Canada se donnerait un nouveau cadre politique.

Il ne reste plus qu'à espérer que la réforme constitutionnelle n'ira pas plus loin. Le ridicule risquerait alors d'achever ce que ce pays conserve encore de dignité. Espérons aussi qu'un peu de "self-respect" bien placé fera réaliser au reste du pays que maintenant que le Québec a été normalisé, ce serait ajouter l'injure à l'insulte de lui offrir, comme on l'a fait pour les handicapés et qu'on s'apprête à le faire pour les autochtones, des garanties de protection pour sa culture et sa langue. A défaut de l'égalité politique, mieux vaut tout de même être une province comme les autres qu'une réserve culturelle qui viendrait témoigner de ce que le Canada aurait pu être.

D'ailleurs s'il fallait qu'une telle négociation reprenne, il est à prévoir que le Québec y perdrait encore quelques plumes. A-t-on dejâ vu un négociateur réussir à obtenir davantage lorsqu'il est en position d'extrême faiblesse. Que l'on discute depuis quelque temps à Ottawa de la possibilité d'accorder au Québec un droit de veto partiel avec compensation financière pour ce qui est des questions de culture, de langue, de droit civil et d'éducation vient confirmer que contrairement à l'esprit et à la lettre de l'entente de 1867, il est maintenant possible à la majorité politique du pays de modifier les équilibres régissant ces secteurs sans que le gouvernement de la province de Québec ne puisse y faire quoi que ce soit. Si tel n'était pas le cas, on ne parlerait pas ainsi des garanties constitutionnelles, dont on conditionne d'ailleurs le don à une bonne conduite des Québécois et de leur gouvernement. Le mépris a toujours plus d'un temps.

Chez ceux-là même qui ont imaginé et imposé ce *Canada Bill*, on ne fait plus confiance au jeu naturel des institutions politiques qui ont toujours été au coeur du fédéralisme canadien et qui ont su protéger adéquatement la plus importante minorité culturelle du pays. Après s'être assuré que cette minorité demeurerait une minorité, voilà qu'on s'inquiète de ce que la majorité purrait lui imposer. Ne dirait-on pas que la majorité anglophone du pays cherche à s'empêcher constitutionnellement de poser des gestes qu'elle pourrait être tentée de poser politiquement. Par la façon dont il a été imposé et par son contenu, ce *Canada Bill* vient confirmer ce que d'aucuns soupçonnaient et d'autres espéraient: le gouvernement et les institutions politiques du Québec ne sont plus des gardiens très solides de la spécificité française du Québec. Celle-ci est devenue maintenant l'affaire de tout le Canada. Même pour ce qui est de la culture, de la langue et de l'éducation, on cherche à faire du gouvernement québécois l'agent d'exécution de politiques décidées à Ottawa. La culture si importante, que tous les gouvernements du Canada, ceux de l'Alberta, du Yukon et d'Ottawa y compris, veulent maintenant s'en mêler. Jamais on aura tant "aimé" les Québécois.[2] Leur culture est même jugée trop essentielle pour leur en accorder la gestion exclusive.

S'étant rendu compte que l'affirmation culturelle et linguistique transcendait au Québec les lignes partisanes traditionnelles, on a voulu et on a réussi à les soustraire à l'exercice du champ politique québécois. Même les liberaux de Claude Ryan sont suspects. Ne sont-ils pas en danger eux aussi de succomber à la tyrannie d'une majorité électorale très satisfaite des lois linguistiques actuelles? C'est à des tribunaux dont les juges sont entièrement nommés par le gouvernement central, qu'il appartiendra maintenant de corriger les erreurs de parcours de la démocratie électorale québécoise. Il ne manque plus que la nomination par Ottawa d'un gauleiter en charge du Québec et la normalisation serait complète. Ce n'est pas une coïncidence si cette normalisation politique du Québec survient au moment même où la première génération québécoise née après 1960 fait son irruption sur la scène économique et politique.[3] Certes on se dit très content de voir cette génération manifester le sens et le goût des affaires, ainsi qu'une volonté de ne pas se contenter du Québec et des institutions canadiennes-françaises traditionnelles. On veut que cette génération se lance à l'assaut du Canada, mais pas à partir d'une situation d'égalité politique. C'est le propre de toute majorité d'aimer que ses minorités soient dynamiques et pittoresques, mais qu'elles demeurent avant tout des minorités.

A partir de la perspective peu suspecte de collectivisme et qui n'est pas sans rappeler les nouveaux économistes du "supply side," J.-L. Migué a montré com-

---

2. De nombreuses provinces (Alberta, Ontario, Saskatchewan, Manitoba, Nouveau-Brunswick) ont récemment mis sur pied des programmes culturels spéciaux pour leur minorités francophones, motivés en bonne partie par une volonté de faire échec à la prétention du gouvernement fédéral que c'était là l'une des responsabilités particulières du gouvernement "national." Nul doute que les tentatives anterieures du gouvernement du Québec, notamment au moment du référendum de 1980, d'obtenir l'appui de ces communautés, a aussi été un facteur déterminant dans ce renversement d'attitude face à la culture française hors-Québec.

3. Le groupe des 30-40 (en 1983) n'a été que faiblement marqué par la période Duplessiste. Très nationaliste, mais d'un nationalisme davantage politique et économique que culturel, ce groupe constitue ce qu'il est convenu d'appeler la nouvelle élite. Voir à ce sujet D. CLIFT, LE DECLIN DU NATIONALISME AU QUÉBEC (1981); Crete & Landry, *Vieillesse québécoise et changement politique 1960 à 1980,* 6 ANTHROPOLOGIE ET SOCIÉTÉS 45 (1982).

ment la langue, les réseaux culturels et même le nationalisme pouvaient être des instruments fort rentables de promotion économique pour les élites managérielles québécoises. Parlant de la survie de la société québécoise, il écrit à propos de la politique d'accommodement de Robert Bourassa:

> La politique libérale mène tout droit à l'effritement progressif des institutions québécoises et à l'intégration certaine, sinon lucide, des Québécois au réseau d'institutions le plus reluisant. Enfin la survie d'une société québécoise n'est compatible qu'avec le renforcement de ses propres institutions, c'est-à-dire avec l'institutionnalisation de ses relations avec la firme plurinationale. A son tour le processus ne peut s'implanter qu'avec la francisation de tous les échelons de la hiérarchie technique et administrative de la firme.[4]

C'est cette rentabilisation du nationalisme québécois que le *Canada Bill* veut à tout prix rompre, afin que même au Québec les jeunes managers francophones soit désavantagés par leur appartenance culturelle. Les tentatives de l'automne 1982 du gouvernement fédéral d'éliminer de la carte du ciel la compagnie Québecair, celle encore plus visible de limiter l'expansion de la *Caisse de dépôts et de placements du Québec* par le projet de loi C-31 en sont les exemples les plus récents.[5]

Encore une fois, on les aime tellement ces Québécois qu'on voudrait qu'ils se distribuent partout au Canada. A chaque province, ses petits immigrants québécois, mais des Québécois pour qui le Québec n'est qu'une province d'origine et non pas leur espace politique privilégié. Ce qu'on veut surtout préserver c'est une culture canadienne-française minoritaire, après tout n'est-il pas vrai que ce sont les minorités culturelles qui ont les cultures les plus dynamiques. Il faut donc protéger les Québécois contre la stérilité qui découlerait de leur statut de majoritaires. Nous l'avons échappé belle.

Les plus forts applaudissements au *Canada Bill* proviennent de la minorité anglophone du Québec. Cela aussi est fort significatif. Que sur une question qui a fait l'unanimité de toutes les fractions politiques du Québec français, il n'est pas trouvé un seul groupe de Québécois anglophones pour s'opposer à un *Canada Bill* qui réduit les pouvoirs de la communauté politique à laquelle ils ne cessent de proclamer leur appartenance, met en évidence toute l'hypocrisie de ces hauts cris.

L'appartenance des Canadiens anglais du Québec à la communauté politique du Québec n'est possible à leurs yeux que si le cadre politique fédéral impose au Québec un statut de minorité permanente à l'intèrieur du Canada. Pour les anglophones du Québec, l'existence d'un Canada français encadré et protégé légitimise leur participation à ce qu'ils considèrent être la véritable majorité du pays, la majorité anglophone, tout en leur permettant d'échapper au statut de minorité culturelle que l'actuel gouvernement du Québec voudrait leur imposer. Si les anglophones du Québec sont pour être une minorité au Québec, alors les Québécois vont aussi l'être à l'échelle du pays. A minorité, minorité et demie.

L'intégration des anglophones du Québec à la vie collective est un mythe qu'il

---

4. Migué, *La nationalisme québécois, le développement économique et la théorie économique de l'information,* dans LE SYSTÈME POLITIQUE QUÉBÉCOIS 449 (E. Cloutier et D. Latouche eds. 1979).

5. Ce projet de loi non encore adopté par le Parlement fédéral prévoit qu'une institution étatique provinciale ne pourra plus désormais détenir plus de 10% des intérêts d'une entreprise impliquée dans le transport inter-provincial. Cette mesure vise essentiellement à empêcher la *Caisse des dépôts* d'acquérir une participation trop importante dans la multinationale *Canadian Pacific*.

est temps de dénoncer. Certes, lorsqu'on leur demande s'ils sont bilingues, les anglophones du Québec ont de plus en plus tendance à répondre par l'affirmative[6] mais une majorité absolue de ceux-ci refuse encore de reconnaître que le français doit être la langue majoritaire au Québec.[7] Les récentes côtes d'écoute des stations de radio et de télévision montréalaises ont montré que l'écoute des médias francophones par les anglophones est tellement insignifiante qu'elle ne peut être comptabilisée.[8] Il suffit de travailler dans un milieu anglophone comme l'Université McGill pour mesurer le peu d'intégration des jeunes anglophones à la vie culturelle française qui les entoure. A ce sujet, le contraste avec les jeunes francophones est étonnant.[9]

D'ailleurs l'étude récente de T.R. Balakrishnan vient de confirmer que c'est à Montreal que la ségrégation ethnique residentielle est la plus élevée de toutes les villes canadiennes, surtout pour ce qui est de l'opposition entre d'un côté le groupe ethnique français et de l'autre tous les autres groupes (les taux de ségrégation residentielle entre les groupes ethniques non-français sont beaucoup plus faibles). De plus, cette ségrégation a augmenté entre 1961 et 1971 et demeure relativement insensible à la distribution du statut socio-économique.[10]

Quelques questions posées lors de différents sondages révèlent que cette faible intégration des anglophones du Québec est aussi le fait des nouvelles générations. (Voir Tableau 1.) A peine 5% s'identifient à la Fête nationale québécoise du 24 juin ou se definissent comme des Québécois. Moins de 20% d'entre eux s'identifient prioritairement au gouvernement du Québec plutôt qu'a celui d'Ottawa.

Tableau 1
Identification Nationale des Québécois Anglophones et Francophones
(1979)

		Total	18-24	25-34	35-44	45 et plus
Identification prioritaire	anglo	19%	21%	18%	21%	17%
au gouvernement du	franco	53%	70%	63%	50%	40%
Québec						
Identification au 24	anglo	5%	0%	8%	0%	8%
juin plutôt qu'au 1er	franco	55%	60%	62%	47%	32%
juillet						
Identification comme	anglo	5%	13%	8%	1%	1%
Québécois	franco	38%	55%	49%	31%	25%

Source: Compilations spéciales, *Sondages sur la perception des problèmes constitutionnels Québec-Canada,* Québec, Ministère des affaires intergouvernementales.

6. Sondage CROP-CBC, février 1982.

7. D'ailleurs on peut s'interroger sur la validité scientifique de demander directement, sans aucun contrôle ou définition préalable, à des gens s'ils sont bilingues ou non, alors qu'on sait que la très grande majorité de ceux-ci estiment qu'ils devraient l'être.

8. Sauf pour ces soirées ou un match de hockey est présenté en exclusivité à une station de télévision francophone.

9. Voir à ce sujet, P. Georgeault, Conscience Linguistique des Jeunes Québécois (1981).

10. Balakrishnan, *Changing Residential Segregation in Metropolitan Areas of Canada,* 19 Can. Rev. of Sociology and Anthropology 92 (1982).

Ces chiffres ne trompent pas. Depuis peu, les anglophones du Québec se sont donnés une association, *Alliance Québec*, dont on a vanté l'ouverture d'esprit et la modération parce qu'elle reconnaissait que les anglophones du Québec veulent vivre au Québec. Mais lorsque vient le temps de discuter des modalités de ce vouloir vivre, on se rend compte qu'ils veulent vivre exclusivement dans *leur* langue, dans *leurs* institutions, avec *leurs* structures. Certes, on admet le droit des 80% de francophones de vivre en français mais c'est une admission du bout-des-lèvres dictée par l'évidence de la situation. Ce qu'on espère obtenir, c'est le retour au bilinguisme d'antan, c'est-à-dire des francophones bilingues et des anglophones qu'on va cesser d'inquiéter à cause de leur unilinguisme.

Cet appui massif du groupe anglophone québécois au *Canada Bill* est une erreur qui risque rapidement de se retourner contre cette communauté. Plus grande est l'insécurité dans laquelle on place la culture française, plus grandes sont les menaces dirigées contre l'autonomie des institutions politiques québécoises, plus contraignantes risquent d'être les politiques linguistiques du gouvernement québécois. A court terme, il peut se révéler fort rentable pour ce groupe de devenir le pupille du gouvernement fédéral mais en se faisant ainsi l'allié objectif de ceux qui veulent normaliser le Québec, ces anglophones risquent de se placer eux-mêmes dans la situation peu enviable de devenir rapidement "expandable" politiquement. C'est ce qui est survenu aux communautés françaises hors Québec que le gouvernement central utilise maintenant comme autant de parcs d'exhibition pour sa politique linguistique. La décision prise à l'hiver 1981 par six Secrétariats d'Etat de remplacer ses subventions directes à l'Association canadienne-française d'Ontario par des subventions particulières à chaque organisme est un avant goût de cette nouvelle situation.

Cette volonté stratégique de remettre le Québec à sa place politiquement apres vingt ans de grignotage et de menaces a connu depuis le référendum de mai 1980 une accélération sans précédent. Ce fut d'abord la course contre la montre pour terminer l'opération avant l'arrivée au pouvoir du Parti Libéral du Québec dont les propositions de révision constitutionelle étaient jugées inacceptables par le gouvernement fédéral. Cette dernière manoeuvre a echoué à moitié. La conférence constitutionnelle de septembre 1980 n'a certes pas abouti mais le Parti Libéral de Claude Ryan a quant à lui été rejeté électoralement. Une toute nouvelle situation stratégique s'ouvrait alors aux négociateurs fédéraux et à ceux des provinces anglophones. C'est ce que nous voudrions montrer dans la section suivante.

III
Les Opérations sur le Terrain la Conférence et le Canada Bill

Probablement parce qu'ils sont aussi habitués aux conférences constitutionnelles qu'au retour de l'hiver, peu d'observateurs ont compris que la conférence de novembre 1981 ne pouvait pas aboutir de la même façon que les autres. Certes tous les ingrédients d'une conférence-comme-les-autres étaient présents: Front Commun de certaines provinces, menaces de dissension dans le Front Commun, dévoilement dans les journaux de documents hautement confidentiels, déclarations à l'effet qu'il s'agit de la conférence de la dernière chance, cynisme de la part du Québec, couverture exagérée par les médias. Ce qui était différent, c'est que pour la première fois, le Canada-anglais par la voix de ses premiers ministres, ainsi que le gouvernement fédéral avaient enfin la possibilité d'atteindre conjointement quatre objectifs qu'ils chérissaient individuellement depuis longtemps: (1) faire subir un échec politique de première importance au gouvernement du Parti Québécois, (2) isoler le Québec et mettre un terme à toute velléité de particularisation politique de cette province, que ce soit sous la forme de statut particulier, de fédéralisme asymetrique, d'états-associés ou de souveraineté-association, (3) rapatrier le document constitutionnel et ainsi satisfaire P.E. Trudeau et (4) réaliser une réforme constitutionnelle optimale, c'est-à-dire obtenir un accord sur le *maximum* de points qui mettraient en cause le *minimum* de changement des équilibres fondamentaux régissant la fédération.

On aura remarqué que cette façon d'envisager le processus de négociation constitutionnelle s'apparente au modèle III de G.T. Allison dans *Essence of Decision*.[11] Certes, l'étude Allison porte sur un sujet, la crise des missiles cubains de 1962, qui est fort éloigné de la question constitutionnelle canadienne, mais le cadre théorique demeure fort éclairant. Allison propose trois modèles pour expliquer une décision politique.

Le modèle rationnel privilégie l'existence d'un acteur unique qui déplace ses pions au gré des stratégies et tactiques qu'il aura élaborées. L'approche organisationnelle présume plutôt que le décideur n'est pas une entité unique, mais une alliance flottante entre des organisations semi-autonomes, chacune avançant ses pièces selon un code opérationnel précis. Quant au troisième modèle, il implique l'existence d'un nombre distinct de joueurs, chacun avec ses objectifs particuliers, mais qui partagent—certains étant plus importants que d'autres—la décision sur l'ensemble du jeu. Alors que dans le modèle I la décision politique est la résultante d'une évaluation coûts-bénéfices, le modèle II suppose au contraire la primauté d'une sorte de code de procédures dérivé d'un processus d'apprentissage organisationnel, tandis que le dernier modèle privilégie les relations de négociations et d'échanges entre les acteurs d'un même camp. Dans une métaphore devenue célèbre Allison caractérise ainsi ces trois modèles:

> A central metaphor illuminates the differences among these models. Foreign policy has often been compared to moves and sequences of moves in the game of chess. Imagine a chess game in which the observer could see only a screen upon which moves in the game were projected, with no information about how the pieces came to be moved. Initially, most observers would assume—as Model I does—that an individual chess player was moving the pieces with reference to plans and tactics toward the goal of winning the game. But a pattern of moves can be imagined that would lead some observers, after watching several games, to consider a Model II assumption: the chess player might not be a single individual but rather a loose alliance of semi-independent organizations, each of which moved its set of pieces according to standard operating procedures. For example, movement of separate sets of pieces might proceed in turn, each according to a routine, the king's rook, bishop, and their pawns repeatedly attacking the opponent according to a fixed plan. It is conceivable, furthermore, that the pattern of play might suggest to an observer a Model III assumption: a number of distinct players, with distinct objectives but shared

---

11. G. Allison, Essence of Decision (1971).

power over the pieces, could be determining the moves as the resultant of collegial bar-gaining. For example, the black rook's move might contribute to the loss of a black knight with no comparable gains for the black team, but with the black rook becoming the prin-cipal guardian of the palace on that side of the board.[12]

Mais revenons à notre constitution. Chacun des quatre objectifs identifiés plus haut peut être considéré comme l'objectif principal des quatre principaux acteurs qui formaient ce que nous appellerons le camp "canadien" (par opposition au camp québécois).

- rapatriement de la constitution: c'est l'objectif personnel prioritaire de Pierre E. Trudeau
- réforme constitutionnelle optimale: c'est l'objectif des neuf premiers ministres des provinces anglophones
- normalisation politique du Québec: l'objectif de l'appareil politique bureaucratique du gouvernement central
- défaite sérieuse du Parti Québécois: l'objectif de la députation canadienne-française à Ottawa

Nous faisons l'hypothèse que l'accord constitutionnel de novembre 1981 a été rendu possible parce qu'il rencontrait ces quatre objectifs. Il a certes fallu une bonne dose de négociations, de coordination forcée, de simple hasard et d'erreurs de l'adversaire québécois pour arriver à une entente, mais ce qu'il importe de con-stater c'est que pour la première fois ces quatre acteurs ont réussi à en arriver à un accord dont les principaux perdants—et là-dessus les deux camps sont d'accord— sont les antithèses québécoises des acteurs mentionnés plus haut, soit René Lévesque (P.E. Trudeau), la communauté politique du Québec (Canada anglais), le gouvernement et l'appareil étatique québécois (gouvernement central), le Parti Québécois (Parti Libéral fédéral).

Quatre acteurs, avons-nous dit, mais aussi deux camps. En effet, jamais une conférence constitutionnelle n'aura si ouvertement mis en présence deux adver-saires. Alors que la conférence s'est officiellement ouverte avec d'un côté, le camp du gouvernement central et ses deux alliés provinciaux et de l'autre, celui des huit provinces récalcitrantes, elle est rapidement devenue, au niveau de la pratique des négociations tout au moins, un affrontement entre le Québec et le reste du pays. Les représentants des autres provinces et ceux du gouvernement central auront beau proclamer leur innocence à ce sujet, les commentateurs et observateurs canadiens-anglais insister sur le jeu normal du "give-and-take" constitutionnel, ce n'est pas ainsi que les choses se sont passées. On peut certes reprocher aux négociateurs québécois de s'être fait joués comme autant de lapins mais si c'est le cas, il faut admettre aussi la contrepartie: ils avaient en face d'eux un groupe décidé de renards et de loups pour qui des accords signés et des paroles données ne voulaient rien dire. Si effectivement les Canadiens anglais sont fiers de la façon dont cette conférence s'est déroulée—rencontres secrètes dans la nuit où le Québec n'était pas invité, manoeuvres et chantages—cela en dit beaucoup sur le genre de pays auquel ils aspirent.

---

12. *Id.* at 7.

Il faudrait aussi rejeter une fois pour toutes l'explication qui veut que l'actuel gouvernement du Québec ait été décidé et surtout incapable de signer le moindre accord constitutionnel avec ses partenaires canadiens. D'ou son isolement à la conférence de novembre 1981. On reste bouche bée devant le mélange d'incompréhension du jeu politique et de mépris anti-québécois qu'un tel jugement suppose.

On mesure mieux aujourd'hui comment le gouvernement du Parti Québécois avait besoin d'un accord constitutionnel qui aurait englobé un rapatriement, une formule d'amendement, une charte des droits et une liste de grands principes. Il n'y a qu'à voir la dégringolade que ce gouvernement a subie dans l'opinion publique, les démissions qui l'affligent, les dissensions qui le déchirent, les défaites aux elections partielles et son état général de désarroi pour comprendre comment un accord aurait pu lui être bénéfique. Depuis sa ré-élection en avril 1981 le gouvernement du Parti Québécois a vu quatre de ses ministres démissionner: Claude Morin, Denis de Belleval, Claude Charron et Lucien Lessard, sans compter le président de l'Assemblée nationale, Claude Vaillancourt. Aujourd'hui, si un accord acceptable au Québec avait pu être signé, plus personne ne parlerait de cet accord et le débat aurait repris de plus belle sur le seul terrain où le gouvernement du Parti Québécois pouvait espérer jouer gagnant: celui du partage des pouvoirs.

Il faut accorder à l'actuel gouvernement du Québec un minimum d'intelligence politique. Toutes ces choses étaient connues. Certes, elles n'étaient pas appréciées par tous, mais les sondages internes menés par le Parti Québécois avaient facilement eu raison des récalcitrants: un accord constitutionnel était un objectif majeur du gouvernement québécois. Depuis 1975 le Parti Québécois effectue régulièrement des sondages d'opinion dont les résultats sont confidentiels mais auxquels l'auteur a pu avoir accès en tant qu'ancien membre du Bureau du premier ministre. L'un des derniers sondages publics et qui illustre bien la baisse de popularité du Parti Québécois est celui d'octobre 1982 du Centre de sondage de l'Université de Montréal (rapporté dans *la Presse*, 16 décembre 1982, p. B.7) et qui donne 42% des intentions de vote au Parti Québécois contre 51% au Parti Libéral et 7% aux autres partis. Parmi les autres sondages publics qui traitent des mêmes questions, mentionnons celui de la firme SORECOM (*Le Devoir,* 5 octobre 1981) et du Centre de sondage de l'Université de Montréal (*Le Devoir*, 20 janvier 1982). Ce calcul stratégique était tellement évident—trop peut-être—que le gouvernement québécois a accepté avant même que ne débute la conférence, davantage de compromis que l'ensemble des gouvernements québécois ne l'avaient fait avant lui. La liste de ces compromis "historiques" acceptés par le gouvernement Lévesque a probablement du faire frémir les Lesage, Johnson, Bertrand et Bourassa.

- accord sur le principe et les modalités du rapatriement
- accord sur une formule d'amendement
- accord sur la possibilité de rapatrier la constitution avant tout accord sur le partage des pouvoirs
- accord sur une Charte des droits y compris les droits linguistiques
- accord sur les principes directeurs de la fédération canadienne

- accord sur la place et la définition officielle du Québec dans un nouvel accord constitutionnel
- accord sur un calendrier de négociations futures.

Affirmer, à partir de ces faits et de l'entente signée entre le Québec et sept autres provinces, que le gouvernement du Québec n'aurait pas signé une entente constitutionnelle, revient à dire que l'actuel gouvernement du Québec est illégitime et qu'il ne respecte pas ses ententes parce que son objectif à long terme est la souveraineté du Québec. C'est là une insulte dont le caractère raciste n'aura pas échappé à tous les "Frenchies" du Québec: les 50% qui ont voté oui au référendum, ceux qui ont voté non en pensant que cela équivalait à une nouvelle constitution, les 60% qui ont appuyé le Parti Québécois lors du scrutin d'avril 1981 et tous ceux qui ont voté pour Claude Ryan en pensant que le Parti Libéral était en meilleure position pour négocier un accord qui reconnaisse les droits légitimes du Québec.

Le plus étonnant, ce n'est peut-être pas qu'on retrouve un tel argument dans la bouche des négociateurs fédéraux et chez ceux des provinces anglophones, mais qu'aujourd'hui bon nombre d'intellectuels canadiens-anglais acceptent de se prêter à cette entreprise de destabilisation politique.

C'est parce qu'ils avaient fait sensiblement la même analyse que les négociateurs québécois—a savoir qu'un accord constitutionnel favoriserait plutôt qu'il ne nuirait au gouvernement péquiste—que les négociateurs fédéraux et ceux des autres provinces ont jugé préférable de proposer un accord inacceptable au Québec. C'est le jeu normal des négociations: des que vous avez trouvé l'objectif minimal de l'adversaire, il faut tout mettre en oeuvre pour l'empêcher d'y arriver. La signature d'une entente aurait representé une victoire stratégique importante pour le Québec, car elle aurait effacé le stigma d'un gouvernement peu intéressé à la réforme constitutionnelle, alors qu'elle aurait placé le Parti Libéral de Claude Ryan dans une situation intenable: celle de s'opposer à un accord négocié par le P.Q. sous prétexte qu'il est fondé sur trop de compromis! La constitution rapatriée, la formule d'amendement adoptée et la charte des droits enchassée, toutes ces manoeuvres qu'on avait si souvent utilisées pour retarder la négociation véritable, auraient finalement été reglées.

Si on envisage maintenant la situation du point de vue du gouvernement fédéral et de celui des neuf autres gouvernements provinciaux, le renversement d'intérêts stratégiques est évident. Si le Québec signait un accord, la légitimité du gouvernement péquiste s'en serait trouvée renforcée et le débat politique relancé sur une base favorable au gouvernement québécois. Pour les élites politiques du Canada anglais cette situation devait être évitée a tout prix. Quand on examine de près le *Canada Bill* et le ridicule de certaines de ses provisions et l'absence de plusieurs autres, on doit conclure que le prix à payer a effectivement été très élevé. C'est donc dire que la determination des acteurs devait être très grande.

Pour le gouvernement Trudeau et le Parti Libéral fédéral, un accord signé aussi par le Québec aurait representé une véritable catastrophe. Au Québec, les succés électoraux de ce parti reposent en bonne partie sur la théorie des contrepoids. Avec un gouvernement péquiste ayant signé l'accord constitutionnel, il aurait été difficile au Parti Libéral fédéral de continuer à prétendre qu'il est la seule barrière efficace contre le séparatisme péquiste. Une analyse des calculs stratégiques des acteurs montre donc qu'au delà de la rhétorique, c'est le reste du Canada qui n'avait pas d'intérêt à s'entendre avec le Québec, et non l'inverse.

Ce n'est pas faire preuve de manichéisme que de croire que les négociateurs canadiens-anglais ont agi selon leurs intérêts. Le contraire aurait été surprenant. Pour l'instant, on ne peut qu'en prendre note. Il faudra donc que les Québécois envisagent d'autres routes pour parvenir à l'égalité politique à laquelle ils continuent d'aspirer. Jusqu'à présent, ils avaient espéré que cette reconnaissance s'obtiendrait *dans* le Canada (fédéralisme renouvelé) ou *avec* le Canada (souveraineté-association). Il faut maintenant envisager qu'elle se fasse *contre* le Canada (indépendance). A court terme, cela veut peut-être dire faire élire une nouvelle génération de députés à Ottawa afin de fausser encore un peu plus le jeu politique canadien ou empêcher la mise en place d'un plan canadien pour sortir le pays de la crise économique. Les Québécois et Canadiens paieront sans doute un prix élevé pour ces stratégies du pire, mais c'est la voie que semble avoir déjà choisi le reste du pays. Il ne reste plus qu'à lui emboiter le pas.

Real politik, quand tu nous tiens!

LANGUAGE AND EDUCATION RIGHTS IN QUEBEC AND CANADA (A LEGISLATIVE HISTORY AND PERSONAL POLITICAL DIARY)†

WILLIAM TETLEY, Q.C.*

I INTRODUCTION

It was Maurice Duplessis, Premier of Quebec from 1936 to 1939 and again from 1944 to 1959, who presumably said that governments should never legislate on language or education. Carefully following his own precept, he left Catholic education to Quebec's Roman Catholic bishops and Protestant education to Protestant school boards comprised of Protestant middleclass businessmen. Indeed, language was not the subject of any legislation in Duplessis's time.

The death of Duplessis, however, brought change. In 1964, the Lesage Liberal government took the necessary and courageous step of creating a Ministry of Education,[1] and in 1968, the Bertrand Union Nationale government presented Bill 85,[2] which provided for what is commonly called "freedom of choice"—that is the right of parents to choose the language of education for their children. In 1974, the Bourassa Liberal government adopted Bill 22,[3] which dealt with both language and education. In 1977, the Parti Québécois government adopted Bill 101,[4] and finally, the Trudeau government in December 1981 adopted a Resolution to Amend the Constitution of Canada.[5] Within that Constitutional Amendment is the Canadian Charter of Rights and Freedoms which specifically concerns language and education rights, among other matters. This article is intended to present a politician's view of the foregoing changes in the law and to reveal how the public reacted to such changes.

---

† The author is especially appreciative of the assistance of Allan A. Garber, B.A., M.A., LL.B.III of McGill Law Faculty.

* Professor, Faculty of Law, McGill University.

1. An Act to Establish the Department of Education and the Superior Council of Education, ch. 15, 1964 Que. Stat. 89.

2. Loi modifiant la Loi du Ministere de l'Education, la Loi du Conseil Supérieur de l'Education et la Loi de l'Instruction Publique. The bill, however, never became law. It was withdrawn under fire from within and without the government.

3. The Official Language Act, ch. 6, 1974 Que. Stat. 53.

4. La Charte de la langue française, ch. 5, 1977 Que. Stat. 55 (current version at QUE. REV. STAT. ch. c-11 (1977)).

5. Adopted in the House of Commons on December 2, 1981, and by the Senate on December 8, 1981. After adoption in the U.K. House of Commons and House of Lords, the Canada Act 1982, received Royal Assent on March 29, 1982. On April 17, 1982, Her Majesty the Queen signed the proclamation in Ottawa which brought into force the Constitution Act, 1982, which is Schedule B of the Canada Act 1982, 1982, ch. 11 (U.K.).

II THE CONSTITUTION IN RESPECT TO EDUCATION AND TO LANGUAGE—
CANADA

A. *The BNA Act, 1867 (The Constitution Act, 1867)*

1. *Section 93.* Under section 93 of the British North America Act, 1867 (BNA Act),[6] the provincial legislatures have exclusive jurisdiction to make laws in relation to education, subject to the restriction that such laws shall not prejudicially affect the rights or privileges of the Protestant and Roman Catholic denominational schools. Section 93 is silent as to whether the language of education is protected. The resolution of this issue turns on whether, at the time of Confederation, the denominational schools enjoyed the legal right to determine the language of instruction. It has been decided in the provinces of Ontario and Quebec that no such right existed.[7] Since the language of education is not protected, it appears that the provincial legislatures must, as ancillary to their exclusive jurisdiction over education, have the power to prescribe the language of instruction in the schools.[8]

2. *Section 133.* The only express protection of language rights in the BNA Act, 1867, is found in section 133.[9] The use of either French or English is *permitted* in "any pleading or process" in the courts of Canada and Quebec, in debates of the Parliament of Canada, and the Quebec Legislature.[10] The use of both English and French is *required* in the published statutes, records, and journals of the federal Parliament and Quebec Legislature.[11] These statutory guarantees are entrenched and are not subject to "modification by unilateral action of Parliament or of the Quebec Legislature" in as much as they are "part of the Constitution of Canada and Quebec in an indivisible sense."[12]

3.*Section 92(13).* It should also be noted that section 92(13) of the BNA Act, 1867, provides that the legislatures of each province have exclusive legislative authority in respect to property and civil rights.[13]

B. *Canadian Bill of Rights*

The Canadian Bill of Rights[14] was enacted by Parliament in 1960 and has been described by Chief Justice Laskin as a "quasi-constitutional instrument."[15] It is not entrenched, and can be amended, overridden, or repealed by an ordinary act of Parliament. Moreover, it applies only to federal statutes and to "matters

---

6. CAN. REV. STAT. app. II No. 5 (1970)(since April 17, 1982, called the Constitution Act, 1867)[hereinafter cited as BNA Act, 1867].

7. Trustees of the Roman Catholic Separate Schools of Ottawa v. MacKell, [1917] A.C. 62 (P.C.); Protestant School Bd. v. Minister of Educ., 83 D.L.R.3d 645 (1978)(Quebec Super. Ct.).

8. *See* Hogg, *Constitutional Power Over Language,* in THE CONSTITUTION AND THE FUTURE OF CANADA 229, 230-32 (Law Society of Upper Canada Special Lectures 1978). This right is now subject to section 23 of the Canadian Charter of Rights and Freedoms.

9. CAN. REV. STAT. app. II No. 5 (1970).

10. *Id.*

11. *Id.*

12. Attorney General of Quebec v. Blaikie, 101 D.L.R.3d 394, 400-01 (1980).

13. CAN. REV. STAT. app. II No. 5 (1970).

14. CAN. REV. STAT. app. III (1970).

15. Hogan v. The Queen, [1975] 2 S.C.R. 574, 597.

coming within the legislative authority of the Parliament of Canada."[16] The Canadian Bill of Rights does not protect language rights, except that section 2(g) guarantees a person "the right to the assistance of an interpreter in any proceedings in which he is involved . . . if he does not understand or speak the language in which such proceedings are conducted."[17] The right to an interpreter is available only in proceedings before federal courts, commissions, boards, or tribunals.

C. *Official Languages Act*

Even though the issue of language rights has been a persistent source of controversy in Canadian history, only recently has the concept of an "official language" received legal recognition. Nowhere is the term "official language" used in the BNA Act, 1867, nor is language one of the classes of subjects enumerated in the distribution of legislative powers in sections 91 and 92. In 1969, the Parliament of Canada enacted the Official Languages Act,[18] which guarantees the equal status of English and French "in all the institutions of the Parliament and Government of Canada."[19] Under section 2 of the Act, the English and French languages are declared the official languages of Canada for all purposes of the Parliament and Government of Canada, with each enjoying equality of status.[20] The remainder of the Act gives effect to the declaration in section 2 by indicating how and when the official languages are to be used by the departments and agencies of the federal government, judicial, quasi-judicial, administrative bodies, and Crown corporations established by Acts of Parliament.

The competence of Parliament to enact the Official Languages Act was upheld by a unanimous judgment of the Supreme Court of Canada in *Jones v. Attorney General of New Brunswick.*[21] The Court held that, although section 133 of the BNA Act, 1867, sets a minimum standard as to the use of languages which "may not be diminished by the Parliament of Canada,"[22] the section does not preclude "the conferring of additional rights or privileges or the imposing of additional obligations respecting the use of English and French, if done in relation to matters within the competence of the enacting Legislature."[23] The Official Languages Act was justified by the Court as within the ambit of federal power over criminal procedure at section 91(27), federal courts at section 101, and federal institutions, on the basis of the peace, order, and good government power of section 91.[24]

The Court also declared that section 91(1),[25] which conferred on Parliament the right to amend the Constitution of Canada except "as regards the use of the

---

16. CAN. REV. STAT. app. III, § 5(3) (1970).
17. *Id.* at § 2(g).
18. CAN. REV. STAT. ch. 0-2 (1970).
19. *Id.* at § 2.
20. *Id.*
21. [1975] 2 S.C.R. 182.
22. *Id.* at 192.
23. *Id.* at 192-93. Attorney Gen. of Quebec v. Blaikie, 101 D.L.R.3d 394 (1980), decided that the Quebec legislature could not diminish the language rights in section 133 of the BNA Act.
24. *Jones,* [1975] 2 S.C.R. at 191-92.
25. Repealed by Item 1 of the Schedule to the Constitution Act, 1982, ch. 11.

English or French language,"[26] was designed to maintain the language guarantees of section 133. It was not, however, a "general substantive limitation" which would prevent Parliament from extending the use of English and French beyond that which section 133 prescribed.[27]

III MANITOBA AND LANGUAGE

A. *Language of the Courts and of Government*

Since 1738, when the explorer La Vérendrye reached the site of what is now Winnipeg, there has been a French presence in the Province of Manitoba. Indeed, when Manitoba entered Confederation in 1870, there were more French- than English-speaking citizens.[28] Fearing a massive influx of English settlers from Ontario, delegates sent by the Riel provisional government to Ottawa carried with them a mandate to negotiate a constitutional guarantee of language rights for French-speaking Manitobans. These negotiations resulted in the inclusion of section 23 in the Manitoba Act, 1870.[29] This section is virtually identical to section 133 of the BNA Act.[30]

Due to uncertainty about the legislative competence of Parliament to enact the Manitoba Act, it was subsequently ratified by the Imperial Parliament of the United Kingdom in 1871.[31] Accordingly, as then supposed, the language rights secured by section 23 became constitutionally protected, and neither the Manitoba Legislature nor the Canadian Parliament could nullify or alter them.

In 1890, when the English-speaking citizens of Manitoba were in the majority, the Manitoba legislature adopted The Official Language Act[32] which abrogated section 23 of The Manitoba Act, 1870.[33] The Official Language Act provided that "the English language only shall be used in the records and journals of the Legislative Assembly of Manitoba, and in any pleading or process in or issuing from any court in the Province of Manitoba . . . [and] [t]he Acts of the Legislature of Manitoba need be printed and published only in the English Language."[34]

The Official Language Act was not contested until 1909, when the St. Boniface County Court[35] ruled the Act *ultra vires*. Nevertheless, the decision was unreported and ignored. In 1976, in *Regina v. Forest,*[36] the same Court again declared the Official Language Act unconstitutional. In response to Crown counsel's request that the Court pay heed to the serious consequences of such a finding, Judge Dureault quoted Lord Mansfield: "The constitution does not allow reasons of

26. *Jones,* [1975] 2 S.C.R. at 196.
27. *Id.*
28. W. MORTON, MANITOBA: A HISTORY 145 (1961).
29. CAN. REV. STAT. app. II No. 8 (1970).
30. *Compare* section 23 of the Manitoba Act, 1870, CAN. REV. STAT. app. II No. 8 (1970), *with* section 133 of the BNA Act, CAN. REV. STAT. app. II No. 5 (1970).
31. BNA Act, 1871, 34 & 35 Vict., ch. 28, § 5 (U.K.); CAN. REV. STAT. app. II No. 11 (1970).
32. MAN. REV. STAT. ch. 0-10 (1970).
33. Manitoba Act, CAN. REV. STAT. app. II No. 8 (1970).
34. MAN. REV. STAT. ch. 0-10 (1970).
35. Bertrand v. Dussault & Lavoie, 1909, at last reported in Re Forest & Registrar of Court of Appeal of Manitoba, 77 D.L.R.3d 445, 458 (1977).
36. 74 D.L.R.3d 704 (1977).

State to influence our judgments: God forbid it should! We must not regard political consequences, how formidable soever they might be: if rebellion was the certain consequence, we are bound to say 'fiat justitia, ruat caelum'. [Let justice be done even though the Heavens may fall] . . . ."[37]

This decision was also ignored. In what Mr. Justice Monnin of the Manitoba Court of Appeal called an "arrogant abuse of authority," the Attorney-General of Manitoba announced that "the Crown [would] not accept the ruling of the Court with respect to the constitutionality of the *Official Language Act* . . . ."[38]

On appeal, the Manitoba Court of Appeal ruled that the Legislature of Manitoba could not unilaterally amend section 23 of the Manitoba Act. In support of the holding, Chief Justice Freidman, speaking for the court stated:

> To say that Manitoba could on its own diminish rights conferred by s.23 would be to negate the very reason for the enactment of that section in the first place. History supports the view that s.23, like s.22 on denominational school rights, was intended to be a protection for minorities in Manitoba against the possible ill will of the majority. The French-speaking citizens of Manitoba, including not only the famous Louis Riel but all the representatives of the French-speaking parishes . . . were induced to put an end to the Red River Insurrection and to support the creation of a Province and its union with Canada only on the basis that their rights would be ensured for the future. The enactment of the *Official Language Act* deprived them of the linguistic rights which were safeguarded, or thought to be safeguarded, under s.23.[39]

Although the Chief Justice spoke of linguistic rights secured by section 23, he was unwilling to give effect to all of them, particularly the requirements that the records, journals, and statutes of the legislature be in both languages. Accordingly, the Chief Justice stated that he was not prepared "to declare that all of the statutes of Manitoba since 1890 . . . [were] constitutionally invalid."[40]

The Court was reluctant to declare all of the statutes of Manitoba unconstitutional for two reasons. First, since the Court itself "was established by a statute enacted wholly in English after 1890, it could hardly be that we could make any declaration at all if the statute providing for our existence were not valid."[41] In effect, such a declaration would require the Court to create its own jurisdictional mandate. Second, the Court refused to countenance the proposition that a failure to comply with the provisions of section 23 "has the effect of rendering the statutes invalid."[42] The Court noted that "British law draws a clear distinction between directory and mandatory statutes, and a further distinction between those mandatory statutes that result in nullities and those mandatory statutes that result in irregularities."[43]

Even though unwilling to declare the whole of the Official Language Act *ultra vires,* the Court did make a declaration that "the *Official Language Act* is inoperative in so far as it abrogates the right to use the French language in the Courts of

37. *Id.* at 717.
38. *Re Forest,* 77 D.L.R.3d at 458.
39. Forest v. Attorney Gen. of Manitoba, 98 D.L.R.3d 405, 421 (1980).
40. *Id.* at 423.
41. *Id.*
42. *Id.*
43. *Id.*

Manitoba, as conferred by s.23 of the *Manitoba Act, 1870,* confirmed by the *British North America Act, 1871.* "[44]

On appeal to the Supreme Court of Canada, the issue was fixed by order of the Chief Justice which may be paraphrased as follows: "Are the provisions of the [Official Language Act] . . . or any of those provisions, *ultra vires* or inoperative in so far as they abrogate the provisions of s.23 of the *Manitoba Act, 1870? . . .*"[45]

Once again, a narrow ruling was given. The Court did not answer the question directly, but dismissed the appeal, noting that Manitoba has no more power to amend section 23 of the Manitoba Act than Quebec has to amend section 133 of the BNA Act.[46]

Thus, the validity of Manitoba's post-1890 statute law remained uncertain. In *Regina v. Bilodeau,* [47] the defendant was charged with speeding under the Highway Traffic Act, and was issued a summons to appear in court pursuant to the Summary Convictions Act. The accused brought a motion for dismissal of the proceedings on the grounds that the statutes under which he was charged were invalid or inoperative because they had been printed in the English language only, contrary to section 23 of the Manitoba Act, 1870. The motion was dismissed by the Manitoba Provincial Court, and the accused was subsequently convicted of the charge.

An appeal from the conviction was dismissed by the Manitoba Court of Appeal. The Court, after commenting on the widespread chaos and social disorder that would result from a declaration that Manitoba's statutes were invalid, held that "the language requirements of section 23 are directory only, and not mandatory."[48] The Court also noted that if indeed the statutes were invalid, it would lack the authority to make such a declaration.[49]

The dissent, however, argued that language rights secured by section 23 were constitutionally entrenched, and could not be challenged "by the application of the principles of directory versus mandatory legislation."[50] In dissenting in part, Justice Monnin persuasively argued that,

> [E]ntrenched linguistic rights are by nature mandatory and never directory. If they were directory only, the risk is that they would never be enjoyed or be of any use to those to whom they were addressed. If it were merely directory it would fly in the fact of entrenchment, which by its very nature, is mandatory. The authorities submitted by counsel on the mandatory or directory nature of legislation has [sic] no application to entrenched rights. Violence to the constitution cannot be tolerated.[51]

An appeal to the Supreme Court, which was to have been heard in May of 1983, was withdrawn due to a momentous agreement announced on May 16, 1983

---

44. *Id.* at 424.

45. [1979] 2 S.C.R. 1032, 1035.

46. *Id.* at 1039. As a result of this decision the Official Language Act, 1890, MAN. REV. STAT. ch. 0-10 (1970), was repealed by An Act Respecting the Operation of Section 23 of the Manitoba Act in Regard to Statutes, chs. 3 & 7, 1980 Man. Stat. 11.

47. [1981] 1 W.W.R. 474.

48. Bilodeau v. Attorney General of Manitoba, [1981] 5 W.W.R. 393, 402.

49. *Id.* at 401.

50. *Id.* at 407.

51. *Id.* at 406-07.

by Prime Minister Trudeau.[52] The accord, involving Manitoba, Ottawa and the Société franco-manitobaine, was reached after a year of closed meetings, and is in the form of a proposed constitutional amendment whereby Manitoba will join New Brunswick in giving official recognition to the French language.[53] As of January 1, 1987, French and English will be the official languages of the courts and the Legislature in Manitoba, just as they were in 1870 when Manitoba joined Confederation. In addition, services in French will be available at the head offices of all government departments, agencies, and Crown corporations. As of January 1, 1986, all new regulations will be in both languages. All new laws will be adopted and published in both languages after January 1, 1987. The Manitoba government will have ten years to translate all of the statutes passed since 1890, when the use of French was abolished. Thus, it appears that the rights of the Franco-Manitobans after having been denied for so many years, will at last be vindicated.

B. *Language of Education—Manitoba*

In 1890, the School Acts[54] were passed in Manitoba which replaced the existing system of separate denominational schools with a unitary public school system supported by public taxes. This jeopardized the use of French as a language of instruction since French schools had been Roman Catholic. This legislation generated much controversy and was, therefore, immediately challenged in the courts. In *City of Winnipeg v. Barrett,*[55] the plaintiffs maintained that the new legislation contravened section 22 of the Manitoba Act, 1870, which is similar to section 93 of the BNA Act, 1867, and provides that "the . . . legislature may exclusively make laws in relation to education . . . [so long as] [n]othing in any such law shall prejudicially affect any right or privilege with respect to denominational schools which any class of persons have by law or practice in the province at the Union."[56]

The plaintiffs argued that they were in a less favorable position than those who could take advantage of free public education in that, although taxed to support public schools, the plaintiffs also bore the additional burden of supporting their own separate religious schools. The Privy Council upheld the constitutional validity of the School Acts. In addition, the Court emphasized the existence and consequences of freedom of choice in attending a sectarian or nonsectarian school, when it remarked that,

> Roman Catholics and members of every other religious body in Manitoba are free to establish schools throughout the province; they are free to maintain their schools by school fees or voluntary subscriptions . . . . No child is compelled to attend a public school. No special advantage other than the advantage of a free education in schools conducted under public management is held out to those who do attend . . . [w]hat right or privilege is violated or prejudicially affected by the law? . . . It is owing to religious convictions which

---

52. *Manitoba Saved from Illegal Laws, Pawley Confirms,* Toronto Globe & Mail, May 19, 1983, at 5.
53. *After 93 Years, a Reason to Cheer,* Toronto Globe & Mail, May 26, 1983, at 2.
54. An Act Respecting the Department of Education, ch. 37, 1890 Man. Stat. 175; The Public Schools Act, ch. 38, 1890 Man. Stat. 179.
55. [1892] A.C. 445.
56. CAN. REV. STAT. app. II No. 5, § 93 (1970).

everybody must respect, and to the teaching of their Church, that Roman Catholics and members of the Church of England find themselves unable to partake of advantages which the law offers to all alike.[57]

The harshness of this decision was tempered in *Brophy v. Attorney General of Manitoba*,[58] where the Privy Council continued to uphold the validity of the Acts, but ruled that the legislation adversely affected the rights and privileges of the Roman Catholic minority in relation to education, specifically the right to have their schools maintained out of the general taxation of the province. Consonant with section 22(2) of the Manitoba Act, the Privy Council decided that the plaintiffs were entitled to appeal to the Governor-General in Council for remedial orders.[59]

In 1896, the historic Greenway-Laurier[60] compromise was reached on the school question. An amendment to the Public Schools Act[61] provided that in any school in towns and cities where the average attendance of Roman Catholics was forty or more (in rural districts twenty-five and more), the trustees, when petitioned by the parents of such children, were required to employ at least one Roman Catholic teacher in such a school. The amendment also permitted Francophones of Manitoba to receive their school instruction in French: "[w]hen ten of the pupils in any school speak the French language, or any language other than English, as their native language, the teaching of such pupils shall be conducted in French, or such other language, and English upon the bi-lingual system."[62]

In 1916, however, the Francophones of Manitoba were dealt a stinging blow when the right to instruction in the French language was abolished.[63] The absence of the French language in the school system remained the status quo until 1966, when an amendment to the Public Schools Act[64] re-established French as a language of instruction for a period not to exceed fifty percent of the teaching day.

In 1970, the Public Schools Act was amended once again, and French language education was accorded a status it had not enjoyed since before 1916. In fact, for the first time in Manitoba's legislative history, both French and English were expressly declared to be "the languages of instruction in public schools."[65] A school board is required by section 258(8) to provide instruction in French if the parents of twenty-eight or more pupils in an elementary grade or twenty-three or more pupils in a secondary grade so request. According to section 258(9), however, the Minister of Education may, at his discretion, require a school board to set up classes for fewer students.

It is noteworthy that "mother tongue" is not a criterion for French language instruction in Manitoba; rather, the criterion is the *number* of students whose parents request instruction in French. This has had the effect of creating a heavy

57. *City of Winnipeg*, [1892] A.C. at 457-58.
58. [1895] A.C. 202.
59. *Id.* at 228.
60. R. BROWN & R. COOK, CANADA 1896-1921, at 12-17 (1974).
61. An Act to Amend the Public Schools Act, ch. 26 § 4, 1897 Man. Stat. 99.
62. *Id.* at § 10.
63. An Act to Further Amend the Public Schools Act, ch. 88, 1916 Man. Stat. 193.
64. An Act to Amend the Public Schools Act (2), ch. 49, 1966-67 Man. Stat. 247.
65. An Act to Amend the Public Schools Act (2), ch. 60 § 258, 1970 Man. Stat. 597.

demand for French second-language immersion programs for Anglophone students. In the years between 1976 and 1981, the number of students enrolled in French immersion programs in Manitoba more than tripled.[66]

IV NEW BRUNSWICK

A. *The Population*

The province of New Brunswick joined the Canadian Confederation in 1867 and soon developed a large French-speaking population. As is well known, New Brunswick now has a higher percentage of people belonging to a linguistic minority than any other Canadian province. In 1976, thirty-three percent of the population claimed French as their mother tongue.[67] The magnitude of this minority has been a distinctive feature of New Brunswick's political climate.

B. *Official Languages of New Brunswick Act*

No particular protection was given to the French language until 1969 when the provincial legislature, following the lead of the federal government, enacted the Official Languages of New Brunswick Act.[68] Few of the new Act's provisions were put into effect, however, until the late 1970's.

Section 2 of the Act declares the equality of status of French and English as follows: "[T]he English and French languages are the official languages of New Brunswick for all purposes to which the authority of the Legislature of New Brunswick extends, and possess and enjoy equality of status and enjoy equal rights and privileges as to their use for such purposes."[69] The remaining sections prescribe the specific ways in which language rights are to be protected. In any proceeding of the legislature or its committees, either of the official languages may be used.[70] In the printing of legislative records, reports,[71] bills,[72] and statutes[73] use of both official languages is mandatory. All notices and documents published by the government, its agencies, and Crown corporations are to be printed in both languages, subject to regulation.[74]

Individuals have the right, subject to regulation, to communicate with and obtain services from the government in either of the official languages.[75] Also, subject to regulation, individuals have the right to be heard in court proceedings in the official language of their choice.[76] Under the sound discretion of the court, the judicial proceedings may be conducted totally or partially in one of the official

---

66. 1981 COMM'R OF OFFICIAL LANGUAGES ANN. REP. 199.

67. COUNCIL OF MINISTERS OF EDUCATION, THE STATE OF MINORITY LANGUAGE EDUCATION IN THE TEN PROVINCES OF CANADA 176 (1978) [hereinafter MINORITY LANGUAGE EDUCATION REPORT].

68. N.B. REV. STAT. CH. 0-1 (1973).

69. *Id.* at § 2.

70. *Id.* at § 3.

71. *Id.* at § 4.

72. *Id.* at § 5.

73. *Id.* at §§ 6 & 7.

74. *Id.* at § 8.

75. *Id.* at § 10.

76. *Id.* at § 13(1).

languages if so requested by any party.[77]

As to the language of education, section 12 specifically provides:

> In any public, trade or technical school
> (a)   where the mother tongue of the pupils is English, the chief language of instruction is to be English and the second language is to be French;
> (b)   where the mother tongue of the pupils is French, the chief language of instruction is to be French and the second language is to be English;
> (c)   subject to paragraph (d), where the mother tongue of the pupils is in some cases English and in some cases French, classes are to be so arranged that the chief language of instruction is the mother tongue of each group with the other official language the second language for those groups; and
> (d)   where the Minister of Education decides that it is not feasible by reason of numbers to abide by the terms of paragraph (c), he may make alternative arrangements to carry out the spirit of this Act.[78]

The Act, nevertheless, fails to determine the language of instruction for immigrants whose mother tongue is neither French nor English. There may be situations where immigrants may not have the right to choose the language of instruction. For example, if Italian pupils were living in an area where the mother tongue of other pupils was exclusively French, then section 12(c) would not apply, and according to section 12(b) French would be the chief language of instruction.[79]

C.   *Equality of Two Linguistic Communities Act*

In 1981, the Equality of Two Linguistic Communities Act[80] was adopted by the Legislative Assembly of New Brunswick. The Act officially recognizes the existence and equality of the French and English linguistic communities within New Brunswick.[81] The Act also encourages the development of the two linguistic communities by providing that "[t]he Government of New Brunswick shall ensure protection of the equality of status and the equal rights and privileges of the official linguistic communities and . . . their right to distinct institutions within which cultural, educational and social activities may be carried on."[82] To this end, the Act requires the Government of New Brunswick to "take positive actions to promote the cultural, economic, educational and social development of the official linguistic communities."[83]

D.   *Canadian Charter of Rights and Freedoms*

In 1981, New Brunswick was the only Canadian province to agree to the enshrinement of language rights in respect to government and the courts in the new Canadian Charter of Rights and Freedoms.[84] These rights are identical to

---

77.   *Id.* at § 13(2).
78.   *Id.* at § 12.
79.   *Id.*
80.   Ch. 0-1.1, 1981 N.B. Stat. 1.
81.   *Id.* at § 1.
82.   *Id.* at § 2.
83.   *Id.* at § 3.
84.   Part I of the Constitution Act, 1982, which is Schedule B of the Canada Act 1982, 1982, ch. 11 (U.K.).

those imposed on the federal government and federal courts by the Charter. The Charter establishes that (1) English and French are the official languages of New Brunswick and each has equal status, rights, and privileges in respect to all institutions of the government of New Brunswick,[85] (2) each individual has the right to use either English or French in any debates or other proceedings of the legislature of New Brunswick,[86] (3) the statutes, records, and journals of the legislature of New Brunswick shall be published in English and French with each version having equal authority,[87] (4) English or French may be used in any pleading or process issuing from a New Brunswick court,[88] and (5) any member of the public has the right to communicate with, or receive available services from, the government or legislature of New Brunswick in English or French.[89] The foregoing rights are similar to those provided by the Official Languages of New Brunswick Act,[90] except that the guarantees provided by sections 19(2) and 20(2) of the Charter are now absolute and no longer subject to regulation.

IV ONTARIO

A. *Language of the Courts and of Government*

Ontario has a larger Francophone minority in terms of numbers than any other Canadian province. In 1976, over 460,000 residents of Ontario claimed French as their mother tongue, more than double the number of Francophones in the next closest province—New Brunswick.[91] Ontario's Francophones, however, represent only 5.6% of its total population, compared to 33% in New Brunswick.[92] Unlike Quebec, Ontario was not bound by section 133 of the BNA Act, 1867. Accordingly, its legislative and judicial institutions have remained unilingually English until recently.

In 1897, legislation was passed which formally recognized the existing practice regarding the language of the courts. Section 1 of An Act Respecting the Administration of Justice[93] made English the exclusive language of the courts by stipulating that "[a]ll writs, pleadings and proceedings in any court of justice within Ontario, shall be in the English language only." This provision was consolidated as part of the Judicature Act in 1914,[94] and it is still in force. It is now, however, subject to a modification. In 1978, the Judicature Act was amended to give the French language legal recognition in designated courts in certain counties and districts of Ontario.[95] Under section 130(4) of the Act, such courts, upon application of a party who speaks French, *must* direct that "the hearing in the proceeding be

---

85. *Id.* at § 16(2).
86. *Id.* at § 17(2).
87. *Id.* at § 18(2).
88. *Id.* at § 19(2).
89. *Id.* at § 20(2).
90. N.B. REV. STAT. ch. 0-1 (1973).
91. MINORITY LANGUAGE EDUCATION REPORT, *supra* note 67, at 84.
92. *Id.* at 84, 176.
93. ONT. REV. STAT. ch. 324, § 1 (1897).
94. ONT. REV. STAT. ch. 56, § 122 (1914).
95. An Act to Amend the Judicature Act, ch. 26, 1978 Ont. Stat. 125.

conducted before a judge who speaks both the English and French languages or, where there is a jury, before a judge and jury who speak both the English and French languages."[96] Furthermore, where an application and direction has been made under section 130(4), the court *may* direct "that the hearing or any part of the hearing be in the French language if, in the opinion of the court, the hearing or part can be so conducted effectually."[97]

In accordance with section 130(7), evidence given in French "in a proceeding in respect of which a direction is made . . . shall be received and recorded in the French language and shall be transcribed in that language for all purposes."[98] Additionally, section 130(8) permits any document filed by a party in a proceeding in a small claims court in any of the designated counties or districts to be in French.

There are no statutory requirements in Ontario pertaining to the use of English or French in the debates and records of the legislature. Notwithstanding the almost exclusive use of English, resort to the English language is not mandatory according to the rules of the House. This option was recently mentioned by Ontario's Premier Davis in a letter to four Members of Parliament from Quebec.[99] Since Confederation, the statutes of Ontario have been enacted, printed, and published exclusively in the English language. At present, some 150 of the province's most important statutes have been translated into French, but they have no official legal status. They are, however, admissible in court as evidence "to prove the contents thereof but, in the event of a conflict between the version published under the *Statutes Act* . . . and the French language translation, the version published under the *Statutes Act* shall prevail."[100]

B. *Education*

At the time of Confederation, the primary issue in respect to education was religion, involving language only indirectly. The Roman Catholic minority of Ontario and the Protestant minority of Quebec wished to maintain separate denominational schools and to have the rights to the establishment and preservation of such schools guaranteed by the constitution. This was accomplished by section 93 of the BNA Act, 1867.

By the turn of the century, the primary issue in education shifted from religion to language. Denominational schools, which initially had been a matter of local responsibility, became increasingly subject to provincial supervision as education reforms were instituted to promote more centralized and uniform school systems. In Ontario, this led to attempts to regulate the use of French as a language of instruction in the Roman Catholic schools. Regulations were first introduced in

---

96. ONT. REV. STAT. ch. 223, § 130(4) (1980).
97. *Id.* at § 130(G)(a).
98. *Id.* at § 130(7).
99. "In accordance with the rules of the House, members of the Legislature may address the House in French or English and his or her remarks recorded in the Debates in the language they were delivered [sic]." Letter from Premier William Davis to Céline Hervieux-Payette, David Berger, Eva Côté and Jean-Claude Malepart (Jan. 16, 1981).
100. Evidence Act, ONT. REV. STAT. ch. 145, § 25(2) (1980).

1885, culminating in the infamous regulation 17 of 1913.[101] This regulation severely curtailed the use of French in Catholic schools and provoked bitter controversy among French Canadians. They denounced it as a "deliberate and obvious policy of assimilation."[102] The regulation was supported by Irish Catholics who feared that the continued use of French in the schools would jeopardize the status of the separate schools in the province. Regulation 17 was contested in several cases,[103] most notably *Trustees of the Roman Catholic Separate Schools of Ottawa v. MacKell,*[104] as being an infringement upon the rights and privileges guaranteed to the denominational schools by section 93 of the BNA Act, 1867. In *MacKell,* the regulation was upheld by the Privy Council, which ruled that "the class of persons to whom the right or privilege is reserved must . . . be a class of persons determined according to religious belief, and not according to race or language."[105]

The status of the French language in Ontario schools remained virtually unaltered for the next fifty years until ferment and change in Quebec stimulated Francophone Ontarians to become more cognizant of their rights and aspirations. Furthermore, certain government leaders in Ontario began to recognize the historic linguistic arrogance of the large English majority and consequent ill-treatment of Ontario's French population.

The year 1968 was a breakthrough period for French-language education in Ontario. Following the recommendations of the Beriault Commission, the government adopted legislation which transformed what had been toleration of clandestine French education into full-fledged legal recognition. An amendment[106] to the Schools Administration Act required a school board to "provide for the use of the French language in instruction" when requested by the parents of at least thirty French-speaking pupils at the elementary level. Non-Francophones were also permitted to enroll in French language classes or schools if "the principal is satisfied that the attendance of such pupils will not delay the progress of the French-speaking pupils."[107]

In 1968, and for the first time in Ontario's history, French was provided as a language of instruction in secondary schools. An amendment to the Secondary Schools and Boards of Education Act required a school board to "provide for the use of the French language in instruction" when twenty or more students elected to be taught in French, and could be assembled in classes of twenty or more.[108]

---

101. 32 Ont. L.R. 252-54 (1917).

102. 2 ROYAL COMMISSION ON BILINGUALISM AND BICULTURISM, REPORT 51.

103. *See e.g.,* McDonald v. Lancaster Separate School Trustees, 31 Ont. L.R. 360 (1914), *aff'd,* 24 D.L.R. 868 (1915); Trustees of the Roman Catholic Separate Schools for Ottawa v. Ottawa Corp., [1917] A.C. 76.

104. [1917] A.C. 62.

105. *Id.* at 69.

106. An Act to Amend the Secondary Schools Administration Act, ch. 121 § 9, 1968 Ont. Stat. 536 (amending Schools Administration Act, ONT. REV. STAT. ch. 361, § 35 (1960)).

107. *Id.*

108. An Act to Amend the Secondary Schools and Boards of Education Act, ch. 122, § 10, 1968 Ont. Stat. 547 (adding § 113(a)(2) to the Secondary Schools and Boards of Education Act, ONT. REV. STAT. ch. 362 (1960)).

In 1974, the 1968 provisions were carried forward and consolidated, with some modifications, into the Education Act.[109] The provisions with respect to language comprise part XI entitled "French Language Instruction." The important and relevant changes are that:

(1) It is no longer the parents, but the pupils themselves who must elect to have instruction in French. Classes wil be set up if as few as 25 pupils can be assembled for such purpose.[110]

(2) English-speaking pupils, at the request of a parent or guardian, may attend French schools if approved by a majority vote of an admissions committee.[111]

The response to Ontario's language legislation has been impressive. In the school year 1979-80, there were over 69,000 students enrolled in French-language elementary schols or instructional units, and over 29,000 at the secondary level.[112] Equally impressive, in 1980-81 over 17,000 were enrolled in French immersion programs.[113]

The future of French-language teaching in Ontario seems assured. The Education Act now permits French-speaking ratepayers to elect members of a French Language Advisory Committee to a school board. Since teaching in French is now guaranteed, the issue for the future is whether Francophones will obtain the right to have their own schools and their own school boards. Manifestly, Ontario has come a long way towards the recognition and toleration of its French minority's right to exercise their linguistic and educational preferences. Nonetheless, the road is long and difficult, and the battle continues.

VI PERSONAL DIARY—QUEBEC

A. *The Bye-Election in Notre-Dame-de-Grâce 1968, and Bill 85*

In the fall of 1968 I was the Liberal candidate for the Quebec National Assembly in the Montreal constituency of Notre-Dame-de-Grâce (N.D.G.). During the campaign, Premier Jean-Jacques Bertrand of the Union Nationale promised the electorate of N.D.G. that they would have the freedom to choose whether their children would be educated in English or French. This promise was intended to appease the Italian immigrants of St.-Léonard, who were bitter over a decision by the trustees of the St.-Léonard School Commission to substitute unilingual French classes for bilingual classes. As a result of this decision and concomitant linguistic fervor, the language crisis in St.-Léonard became the main issue in the bye-election.

Despite Bertrand's campaign promise I received eighty percent of the ballots cast. Following the election, Premier Bertrand fulfilled his campaign promise when he personally presented Bill 85[114] in the National Assembly on December 9, 1968. It was designed to "préciser le rôle de la langue française dans le domaine de

---

109. ONT. REV. STAT. ch. 129 (1980).
110. *Id.* at § 258(2).
111. *Id.* at § 258(6).
112. COMM'R OF OFFICIAL LANGUAGES, *supra* note 66.
113. *Id.*
114. An Act to Amend the Education Department Act, The Superior Council of Education Act and The Education Act.

l'éducation au Québec."[115] The Bill sought to protect minority language rights by giving parents freedom of choice with respect to the language of instruction for their children. At the same time, the proposed Bill aimed to secure the position of the majority by requiring all students to have a working knowledge of French.

When the Bill was sent to committee, it became the subject of impassioned public debate. In general, Anglophones were supportive of the Bill; however, many Francophone nationalists denounced the principle of freedom of choice on the grounds that it would further imperil the status of the French language in Quebec. Undoubtedly, the Francophone concern and opposition against the Bill were not completely unwarranted. A rapidly declining birth-rate among Francophones combined with an overwhelming tendency of immigrants to voluntarily undergo integration with the English minority posed a serious threat to the French community. Since English was the language of upward mobility, even many French Canadians sent their children to English schools. Although over eighty percent of Quebec's population was Francophone, English was largely the language of work and business—especially in Montreal. Francophones argued that this linguistic domination was the consequence of economic domination by the English minority. And undeniably, the upper echelons of business and management were disproportionately occupied by Anglophones.

Four months after the introduction of Bill 85, it was withdrawn, much to the embarrassment of the government. It was, Premier Bertrand announced, "un bébé que personne ne veut."[116] He remained, however, committed to the principle of freedom of choice. Throughout the summer of 1969, the St.-Léonard situation became progressively worse, culminating in the riots of September 10th when French unilingualists and Italian immigrants clashed. This violent confrontation underscored the need to define language rights across the province.

B. *Bill 63. An Act to Promote the French Language in Quebec*

In October of 1969, after winning a leadership campaign against Education Minister Jean-Guy Cardinal, Premier Bertrand forced Cardinal to present Bill 63. According to Cardinal, the purpose of the bill was:

> d'assurer que les enfants de langue anglaise du Québec acquièrent une connaissance d'usage de la langue française et que les personnes qui s'établissent au Québec acquièrent la connaissance de la langue française et fassent instruire leurs enfants dans cette langue. Il confirme en outre la possibilité pour les parents de choisir entre le français et l'anglais, la langue dans laquelle les cours seront donnés à leurs enfants.[117]

The principal provisions of Bill 63 included:

---

115. *Id.* (taken from the "Explanation Notes" to Bill 85) (Translation: "to define the role of the French language within the realm of education in Quebec.")

116. Le Devoir, Mar. 20, 1969 *cited by* Macdonald, *In Search of A Language Policy: Francophone Reactions to Bills 85 and 63,* in Quebec's Language Policies: Background and Response 227 (J. Mallea ed. 1977). (Translation: "a baby whom no one wanted.")

117. *Explanatory Notes to Bill 62.* (Translation: to ensure that the English-speaking children of Quebec acquire a working knowledge of the French language and that persons who settle in Quebec may acquire the knowledge of the French language and have their children instructed in such language. It also confirms the parents' option to choose either French or English as the language in which courses will be given to their children.)

1. Amending the *Education Department Act* . . . [by adding:] The Minister shall take the measures necessary to . . . ensure a working knowledge of the French language to children to whom instruction is given in the English language."[118]

2. Amending [section 203 of] the *Education Act*. . . . To take the measures necessary to have the courses of study . . . adopted or recognized for Catholic, Protestant or other public schools . . . given to all the children domiciled in the territory under their jurisdiction . . . . Such courses must be given in the French language. They shall be given in the English language to any child for whom his parents or the persons acting in their stead so request . . . . [T]he curricula and examinations must ensure a working knowledge of the French language to such children . . . .[119]

3. Amending [section 3 of] the *Immigration Department Act* [by adding:]
[t]ake the measures necessary so that the persons who settle in Quebec may acquire the knowledge of the French language . . . and may have their children instructed in educational institutions where courses are given in the French language.[120]

We Liberals added the proviso in section 1, *supra,* that all English-speaking children had to be properly instructed in the French language. It was this article that caused the Protestant School Board of Greater Montreal (P.S.B.G.M.) and the body which it controlled, the Quebec Association of Protestant School Boards, to oppose Bill 63. The P.S.B.G.M. maintained that it could not and should not be forced to teach French, and particularly to teach *in* French, because it contended that the right to determine the language of instruction was a prerogative of the School Board, and not the legislature. For this reason, the P.S.B.G.M. had not supported the Italians in St.-Léonard. The argument of the P.S.B.G.M. was that insofar as the legislature was clearly without legal authority to force it to teach in French, it necessarily followed that the School Board of St.-Léonard could not be compelled to give instruction in English to the Italian Canadians.

Francophone condemnation of Bill 63 was based primarily on the grounds that freedom of choice would facilitate the assimilation of new immigrants into the English minority. The ultra-nationalist Société Saint-Jean-Baptiste de Montréal called the bill a fundamental capitulation.[121] In words of remarkable foresight, René Levesque, who had resigned from the Quebec Liberal Party, called for legislation that would (1) proclaim official French unilingualism, and (2) compel future immigrants to send their children to French schools. After a lengthy filibuster and many noisy demonstrations and protests, the legislation was nevertheless adopted and then assented to on November 28, 1969.

C. *Consumer and Corporate Language Legislation*

On April 29, 1970, the Liberal government of Robert Bourassa gained election by replacing the Union Nationale government of Jean-Jacques Bertrand. Very soon thereafter I became Minister of Revenue for five months and then the Minister of Financial Institutions, Companies and Cooperatives. The English-speaking population was concerned with the rising nationalism of French Canadians and in particular their desire to protect the French language. Maintaining the priority of the French language was our general theme, but priority also meant recognizing

---

118. Ch. 9, §1, 1969 Que. Stat. 61 (amending QUE. REV. STAT. ch. 233, § 2 (1964)).
119. *Id.* at § 2 (amending QUE. REV. STAT. ch. 235, § 205 (1964)).
120. *Id.* at § 3 (amending QUE. REV. STAT. ch. 68, § 3 (1968)).
121. Macdonald, *supra* note 116, at 231.

the second language. In this respect, I was particularly aware of and concerned about the delicate dichotomy—protecting the French language in English-speaking North America and at the same time preserving the rights of English Quebecers.

In 1971, I had the opportunity to write the priority of the French language into a new consumer law. This was the first legislation in Quebec history to recognize such priority. The Consumer Protection Act required consumer contracts to be drawn up in French, unless the consumer chose to exercise his undiminished right to have the contract worded in English.[122] This priority of French brought severe criticism from the English electorate in Quebec despite its fairness. On the other hand, French Canadians and even the Parti Québécois Official Opposition were satisfied with the compromise. The formula of French language priority along with recognition of the English language became the basic guide for Bill 22,[123] and, in my view, is a reasonably equitable solution to Quebec's linguistic dilemma. The English of Quebec, probably fearing "the thin of the edge of the wedge," were nevertheless strongly opposed to it.

In 1973, I presented much the same formula in an amendment to the Companies Act, which stated that "[a] company shall be incorporated only under a French name or a name consisting of both a French and an English version."[124] It was further stipulated that the company could use its French name, its English name, or its bilingual name. This, nevertheless, caused protests from the English in Quebec.

Since the new law did not apply retroactively, an attempt was made to persuade the 60,000 active existing Quebec corporations with solely English names to adopt a bilingual name. To accomplish this, the government offered amendment of their letters patent without charge and provided special forms for the process. Notices were sent to all these companies, but less than twenty-five complied. Without much hope, I then wrote a personal letter to the presidents of the 500 leading companies which induced only a few to add a French name. Finally, these companies were surveyed to determine why they had not acted and the reply was in effect that compliance was not in their best interests.

D. *Bill 22—The Official Language Act*

In 1973, the Bourassa government was reelected by an overwhelming margin, gaining 102 of the 110 seats in the National Assembly. On July 31, 1974, Bill 22, entitled the Official Language Act, was adopted by the government, despite opposition from both English and French Québécois. The preamble to the Act declared the purpose of the legislation:

> the French language is a national heritage which the body politic is in duty to preserve, and it is incumbent upon the government of the province of Quebec to employ every means in its power to ensure the preeminence of that language and to promote its vigour and

---

122. Ch. 74, § 4, 1971 Que. Stat. 603.
123. The Official Language Act, ch. 6, 1974 Que. Stat. 53.
124. An Act to Amend the Companies Act, ch. 65, § 31, 1973 Que. Stat. 724.

quality.[125]

To that end, the Act declared French to be the official language of Quebec.[126] The remaining sections of the Act outlined the requirements for its use in public administration,[127] public utilities and professional bodies,[128] labour,[129] business,[130] and education.[131] Generally, however, Bill 22 imposed only bilingualism with some priority given to the French language.

The English of Quebec opposed Bill 22 because they feared that this was only the beginning of change and that resistance to any such change was preferable to the risk involved in attempting to reach a final solution of Quebec's dilemma. They were also urged on by the P.S.B.G.M. ("Board") which wished to protect its position that "Protestant" in section 93 of the BNA Act meant "English." The Board had a long history of protecting the status quo including the failure to support the Italians of St.-Léonard who wanted English schooling in 1968. The Board did not support Bill 85 and publicly opposed Bill 63,[132] because the Board feared that the Bill gave the government the right to insure that instruction to English students in French was possible.

The Board's essential position on education was enunciated in an opinion[133] written by four leading Quebec lawyers who argued that a pre-Confederation law of 1861[134] conferred on the Protestants and Roman Catholics of Montreal and Quebec City a legal right to determine whether their denominational schools would employ French or English as the language of instruction. Accordingly, they contended that this was a "right or privilege with respect to Denominational schools" that was protected by section 93 of the BNA Act. This opinion, based on what was at best a complicated and tenuous historical argument, was rejected in a decision handed down in April of 1976 by the Quebec Superior Court.[135] The Court held that: "the restrictions imposed by s.93(1) on the exclusive power of the Province in matters of education apply to the *denominational* aspect of schools, but not to the *language* in which they function . . .[136] Even if the opinion had been accepted by the court, the Board generated expectations that were destined to remain unfulfilled. The express language of section 93 of the BNA Act protects only "Denominational" and "Dissentient" schools. Majority (common) school boards, although they may be denominational in *fact* are not denominational in

125. Ch. 74, 1974 Que. Stat. 713.
126. *Id.* at § 1.
127. *Id.* at §§ 6-17.
128. *Id.* at §§ 18-23.
129. *Id.* at §§ 24-29.
130. *Id.* at §§ 30-39.
131. *Id.* at §§ 40-44.
132. An Act to Promote the French Language in Quebec, ch. 9, 1969 Que. Stat. 61.
133. L<small>EGAL</small> C<small>OMMITTEE ON</small> C<small>ONSTITUTIONAL</small> R<small>IGHTS IN THE</small> F<small>IELD OF</small> E<small>DUCATION IN</small> Q<small>UEBEC</small>, R<small>EPORT TO THE</small> P<small>ROTESTANT</small> S<small>CHOOL</small> B<small>OARD OF</small> G<small>REATER</small> M<small>ONTREAL</small> (Nov. 29, 1969) [hereinafter cited as Report to the P.S.B.G.M.].
134. Acte concernant l'allocation provinciale en faveur de l'éducation supérieure,—et les écoles normales et communes, Consolidated Statutes of Lower Canada, ch. 15 (1861).
135. Protestant School Bd. of Greater Montreal v. Minister of Educ. of Quebec, 83 D.L.R.3d 645 (1978).
136. *Id.* at 655 (emphasis added).

law and, therefore, are denied protection by section 93. As the four authors of the Board opinion concede, "the legislature has full power to fix the language of instruction" in regard to majority school boards.[137] This was never brought to the attention of the English Catholics of St.-Léonard nor the Protestants of Westmount, both of whom represented majority school boards and clamoured vigorously for the protection of "rights" which they did not in law possess.

The Board's position was misleading in another important respect. The opinion specifically stated "[i]t is obvious that an education system designed to protect the rights of Roman Catholics and Protestants provides little comfort for those that belong to neither denomination."[138] The foregoing was never brought to the attention of Jews, Greek Orthodox, and others mistakenly led by the Board to believe that they had rights in law. The limitations of the Board opinion were never made clear to the public, especially to Home and School Associations who collected large sums of money to defend their "rights." The Board glossed over the opinion rendered by claiming that, in effect, the guarantee of "Protestant" education in section 93 of the BNA Act meant that English language education was an indisputable right guaranteed for all citizens throughout Quebec. Moreover, the English-speaking public was led to believe that English language rights existed in respect to contracts, public signs, corporate names, all business matters, and dealings with the government.

Bill 22 was finally adopted on July 31, 1974, after a long Parti-Québécois filibuster. Tempers cooled until the fall of 1975, when the school year began and some Italian-speaking children who could not speak English were refused admission to English schools. This prompted Anglophones to agitate for the abolition of Bill 22, and the situation soon became tense again.

E. *CFCF Petition*

The peak of the frenzy was reached when a petition was signed by nearly 600,000 Quebecers who paid fifty cents each to send a telegram to Ottawa and to Quebec. A campaign promoted by the Montreal English-speaking radio station CFCF initiated this petition:

> We, the undersigned, Canadians in the Province of Quebec, urgently demand that you use the power vested in you by the electorate to abolish the (sic) Bill 22 and restore our fundamental rights as Canadians, to work and to educate our children in the language of our choice.
> We feel Bill 22 violates and is in direct contravention of the Federal Government's clear and emphatic official stand on bilingualism.

The petitioners, however, disregarded the absence of any "fundamental rights as Canadians to work and educate [their] children in the language of [their] choice." At that time, these rights did not exist in law or practice in any province. In fact, Quebec provided more minority education and language rights than any Canadian province, particularly under Bill 22. As evidence of Quebec's relatively greater recognition and establishment of minority language rights, a statement of

137. REPORT TO THE P.S.B.G.M., *supra* note 133, at 22.
138. *Id.* at 62.

the Canadian government revealed that "the educational rights of the English-speaking minority in the province of Quebec have been, and still are, better respected and served than the rights of French-speaking minorities of comparable importance in the other provinces of Canada."[139]

The second paragraph of the petition ignored the fact that the federal government's language law[140] only applied to federal agencies and institutions. Furthermore, the call for bilingualism in the second paragraph was not consistent with the first paragraph, which really was a call for double unilingualism.[141]

F. *Contestation of Bill 22* (P.S.B.G.M. v. Ministry of Education)

The validity of Bill 22 and the dispute over language rights with respect to education was finally resolved in Quebec Superior Court in April of 1976 in *P.S.B.G.M. v. Minister of Education of Quebec.*[142] The Court held that "[t]here is nothing against the validity of the Act in question,"[143] and that "the choice of the language in the field of education remains the prerogative of the Legislature."[144] The Court arrived at its decision by first discussing the text of the BNA Act, 1867. After considering in order sections 133, 93, and 91(1), the Court noted that:

> In the face of a constitutional text which
>
> (i)   only clearly guarantees the use of a language in its legislative and judicial aspect;
>
> (ii)   only clearly confines itself, regarding schools, to the criterion of denomination;
>
> (iii)   distinguishes, in its exceptions to the power of amendment of Parliament, between the recognized rights regarding schools and the recognized rights regarding the use of English and French;
>
> what can one conclude other than that the restrictions imposed by s.93(1) on the exclusive power of the Province in matters of education apply to the denominational aspect of schools, but not to the language in which they function?[145]

The same conclusion was reached by the Court after reviewing the case law under section 93, particularly *Ottawa Separate Schools Trustees v. MacKell.*[146] The situation was similar in *MacKell,* except that the position of the respective language groups was reversed. In 1913, the Ontario Ministry of Education had issued a regulation restricting the use of French as the language of instruction for all schools, both public and private. Declaring the contested regulation *intra vires,* it was held by the Privy Council that with respect to section 93 "the class of persons to whom the right or privilege is reserved must . . . be a class of persons determined according to religious belief, and not according to race or language."[147]

---

139. MINISTRY OF SUPPLY AND SERVICES, A NATIONAL UNDERSTANDING—STATEMENT OF THE GOVERNMENT OF CANADA ON THE OFFICIAL LANGUAGES POLICY 70 (1977).

140.   Official Languages Act, CAN. REV. STAT. ch. 2 (1970).

141.   Double unilingualism is a term coined after a voter in N.D.G. complained to me about a teller in her local bank who could not speak to her in English. She said that she believed in bilingualism. By that she meant that she expected all public and commercial offices to be bilingual and thus able to speak to her in English and to others in French. She could not speak French and did not intend to learn. To me, bilingualism is the desire and ability to speak and work in two languages.

142.   83 D.L.R.3d 645 (1978).

143.   *Id.* at 676.

144.   *Id.* at 657.

145.   *Id.* at 655.

146.   [1917] A.C. 62.

147.   *Id.* at 69.

In writing for the majority, Chief Justice Deschênes then reviewed the school legislation in force prior to Confederation in order to determine whether that legislation conferred on the denominational schools the legal right to determine the language of instruction. Even after conceding that section 65(2) of the 1861 Act[148] conferred on the commissioners and trustees the power "to regulate the course of studies to be followed in each school," the Court declared that the plaintiffs were "letting their imagination run away" in attempting to "read in it the implicit power to choose the language of education."[149]

Lastly, the Court considered the plaintiff's argument that the protection of the denomination of schools in section 93 carried with it the protection of the language of instruction:

> When the constitutional text was similar, did anyone think of serving the French culture of the Catholic minority of Manitoba, when the language question was underlying the religious conflict which was jeopardizing its right to denominational schools? And when the constitutional text was identical did anyone think of saving the French culture of the Catholic minority of Ontario, when the language question also jeopardized its system of denominational schools?
>
> At each of these solemn moments in our history the Courts have distinguished between language and faith, between culture and religion; they have recognized constitutional guarantees to the denomination of schools only and never did they interpret the *British North America Act, 1867,* as an instrument of the protection of the language or the culture of a particular group.[150]

An appeal from the decision was dismissed by the Quebec Court of Appeal on January 18, 1978, because the Official Language Act (Bill 22)[151] was no longer law, having been superseded by the Charter of the French Language (Bill 101).[152]

VII   THE PARTI QUEBECOIS—BILL 101

A.   Bill 101

On November 15, 1976, the Parti Québécois was elected and immediately took steps to draft a language bill which would provide for considerably more than the mere priority of the French language.[153] To that end, Dr. Camille Laurin (then Minister of State for Cultural Development) presented a white paper entitled *La Politique Québécoise de la Langue Française*[154] to the National Assembly in April of 1977. The paper outlined the principles upon which the government's new language policy would be based. First and foremost, it stated: "Au Québec, la langue

---

148.   Consolidated Statutes of Lower Canada, ch. 15 (1861).

149.   83 D.L.R.3d 645, 670 (1978).

150.   *Id.* at 672-73.

151.   The Official Language Act, ch. 6, 1974 Que. Stat. 53.

152.   Charte de la langue française, ch. 5, 1977 Que. Stat. 55 (current version at QUE. REV. STAT. ch. C-11 (1977)).

153.   In May 1976, I made arrangements to teach on the McGill Law Faculty and not to run again in the next election. I had planned to be a member of the Quebec National Assembly for at most six to eight years and for no more than three elections. I had also had a final falling out with Premier Robert Bourassa in September of 1976.

154.   C. LAURIN, LA POLITIQUE QUÉBÉCOISE DE LA LANGUE FRANÇAISE (deposited in the National Assembly on April 1, 1977).

française n'est pas un simple mode d'expression mais un milieu de vie."[155] As the white paper explained, "Les francophones du Québec n'ont jamais cru que leur langue puisse être dissociée du destin de la nation tout entière, de son économie comme de sa culture."[156]

The identification of the French language with a way of life in Quebec and, more particularly, with a distinct national culture, precluded acceptance of a policy of institutional bilingualism:

> Ce que les francophones réclament n'a rien à voir avec les procédés de "traduction de l'anglais" que veulent garantir des politiques de bilinguisme. Il s'agit de protéger et de développer dans sa plénitude une culture originale: un mode d'être, de penser, d'écrire, de créer, de se réunir, d'établir des relations entre les groupes et les personnes, et même de conduire les affaires.[157]

Accordingly, the aim of the new language policy was clear. Far more than ensuring the priority of the French language, it was to give Quebec's institutions and its society "un caractère foncièrement français."[158]

A second principle of the new language policy was to respect "les minorités, leurs langues, leurs cultures."[159] While Dr. Laurin insisted that French be the common language of Quebec (just as English is for the rest of North America), he nevertheless recognized the important contributions and essential vitality of the other cultures that constitute Quebec and the necessity of preserving them. This was particularly true for the English minority:

> L'anglais, tout particulièrement, aura toujours une place importante au Québec. Non pas seulement, comme on le répète souvent, parce qu'il est le moyen de communication le plus répandu en Amérique du Nord, mais parce qu'il tient aussi à l'héritge culturel des Québécois. Cependant, dans un Québec vivant en français, il sera normal que les Québécois, quelle que soit leur origine ethnique et culturelle, puissent s'éxprimer en français, participer de plein droit à une société française, admettre que le français est ici la langue commune à tous.[160]

That Anglophones living in Quebec should be capable of expressing themselves in French was, according to Laurin, something that good manners should have taken care of long ago.[161]

After heated public hearings and protracted debates, the Parti Québécois kept

155. *Id.* at 19. (Translation: "In Quebec, the French language is not simply a means of expression but a social environment.")

156. *Id.* at 1. (Translation: "French Quebecers have always held their language to be an inherent part of the destiny of the whole nation, of its economy as well as its culture.")

157. *Id.* at 21. (Translation: "What Francophones are demanding has nothing to do with the process of 'translating from English,' which the policies of bilingualism are meant to guarantee. The issue here is the protection and the full development of an original culture, a way of being, thinking, writing, creating, meeting, establishing relations with other groups or individuals, and even of conducting business.")

158. *Id.* at 17. (Translation: "a fundamentally French character.")

159. *Id.* at 22. (Translation: "the minorities, their languages, their cultures.")

160. *Id.* at 23. (Translation: "The English language, in particular, will always play an important role in Quebec. Not only, as is often said, because it is the most widely used means of communication in North America, but also because it is part of the cultural legacy of Quebecers. However, in a Quebec living in French, all Quebecers, regardless of their ethnic and cultural origin, will naturally express themselves in French, participate by right in a French society, and recognize that in this province French is a language common to all.")

161. *Id.* at 27.

its campaign promise when Bill 101,[162] the Charter of the French Language,[163] became law on August 16, 1977. It is a comprehensive linguistic plan designed to ensure the primacy of French in business, government, the professions, and education. The preamble to the charter sets out its main objectives:

> . . . the French language, the distinctive language of a people that is in the majority French-speaking, is the instrument by which that people has articulated its identity;
> . . . the Assémblee Nationale du Québec recognizes that Quebecers wish to see the quality and influence of the French language assured, and is resolved therefore to make of French the language of Gouvernement and the Law, as well as the normal and everyday language of work, instruction, communication, commerce and business;
> . . . the Assémblée Nationale du Quebec intends in this pursuit to deal fairly and openly with the ethnic minorities, whose valuable contribution to the development of Quebec it readily acknowledges; . . . .[164]

After declaring French to be "the official language of Quebec,"[165] the Charter then defines the following "fundamental language rights":

> 2.   Every person has a right to have the civil administration, the health services and social services, the public utility firms, the professional corporations, the associations of employees and all business firms doing business in Quebec communicate with him in French.
> 3.   In deliberative assembly, every person has a right to speak in French.
> 4.   Workers have a right to carry on their activities in French.
> 5.   Consumers of goods and services have a right to be informed and served in French.
> 6.   Every person eligible for instruction in Quebec has a right to receive that instruction in French.

B.   *A Comparison—Bill 22*[166] *and Bill 101*[167]

An exact comparison of Bill 22 and Bill 101 is difficult but reference to only a few articles contained in each law reveals the dramatic differences.

Section 40 of Bill 22 provided that "[t]he school boards, regional school boards and corporations of trustees shall continue to provide instruction in English."[168] This section applied to all school boards providing education in English in 1974 and thus actually guaranteed the right to English language instruction as opposed to section 93 of the BNA Act, which only guarantees Protestant education. The P.S.B.G.M. hypocritically failed to recognize this right in their protests and publicity. Bill 101 does not provide this most important guarantee to the English of

---

162.   Originally the law was presented with a flourish as Bill 1, but the government had procedural difficulties in the House. Thus, instead of waiting the prescribed delays, Bill 1 was withdrawn and Bill 101 substituted. This short cut around the National Assembly rules caused considerable outrage, much of which was justified.

163.   Charte de la langue française, ch. 5, 1977 Que. Stat. 55 (codified at QUE. REV. STAT. ch. C-11 (1977)).

164.   *Id.* (preamble).

165.   *Id.,* § 1. The Parti Québécois, when in the Opposition in 1974, had not wished to debate Bill 22 and had, therefore, filibustered for six weeks in committee and never progressed beyond section 1. They proposed that section 1 read *"only* official language" (emphasis added), but section 1 of their own Bill 101 did not contain the word "only" when adopted three years later in 1977. In respect to French being the official language of Quebec, it is noteworthy that the Commissioner of official languages in his ANNUAL REPORT OF 1977, MINISTRY OF SUPPLY AND SERVICES, (1978), stated that "[i]n fairness, we should have little to question about this development, for with the exception of New Brunswick, much the same situation—but in reverse—prevails across the breadth of English-speaking Canada." *Id.* at 25.

166.   Official Language Act, ch. 6, 1974 Que. Stat. 53.

167.   Charter of the French Language, ch. 5, 1977 Que. Stat. 103.

168.   Ch. 6, 1974 Que. Stat. § 40.

Quebec. By the fall of 1976, it was clear that the English school population was increasing at the expense of the French school population, and Bill 22 was therefore criticized for permitting too many students to enter the English system. Accordingly, Bill 101 is much more stringent in its requirements for French education. Sections 72 and 73 require:

> 72) Instruction in the kindergarten classes and in the elementary and secondary schools shall be in French, except where this chapter allows otherwise . . . .
>
> 73) In derogation of section 72, the following children, at the request of their father and mother, may receive their instruction in English:
>
> (a) a child whose father or mother received his or her elementary instruction in English, in Quebec;
>
> (b) a child whose father or mother, domiciled in Quebec on the date of the coming into force of this act, received his or her elementary instruction in English outside Quebec;
>
> (c) a child who, in his last year of school in Quebec before the coming into force of this act, was lawfully receiving his instruction in English, in a public kindergarten class or in an elementary or secondary school;
>
> (d) the younger brothers and sisters of a child described in paragraph c.[169]

Bill 101 has one major advantage over Bill 22 in respect to education in that the criterion for determining the right of access to English schools is much more clearly defined and applied—attendance in an English primary school in Quebec by one parent. Under Bill 22, pupils were required to demonstrate a sufficient knowledge of the language of instruction in order to receive their instruction in that language. Pupils who did not have a sufficient knowledge of either French or English were required to receive their instruction in French.[170] Some pupils, therefore, had to be tested in order to determine their ability to receive English language instruction. The testing provoked bitterness and resentment, although only about 1200 students were tested annually. Most of those tested were children of parents who themselves spoke little English. Anglophone parents merely provided sworn affidavits, but this opened the way to deceit and false declarations. Bill 101, by excluding persons on the basis of status rather than ability, may appear to be quite harsh;[171] but its simplicity and finality avoid many personal confrontations. Bill 22 required pupils instructed in English to obtain a knowledge of spoken and written French and French students a similar knowledge of English.[172] There is no such provision in Bill 101.

---

169. Ch. 5, 1977 Que. Stat. §§ 72 & 73.

170. Ch. 6, 1974 Que. Stat. 62 (§ 41).

171. In respect to to article 73 of Bill 101, the Commissioner of Official Languages stated:

> These provisions undoubtedly represent restrictions on parental freedom of choice, and as such we cannot support them. Nevertheless . . . [one] might wish to keep in mind the glass house that is French education in the English-speaking provinces. The fact is that Quebec's English school system is still far more complete than any French school system in the other nine provinces. Furthermore, although freedom of choice for immigrants may exist in theory in other parts of the country, in the sense that it is not prohibited by law, it would be an exceptional immigrant who would in fact choose a French-language education for his children in most parts of English-speaking Canada . . . .
>
> Thus, although the changes set out in the new law are distasteful to many, they do in fact entail very little, vis-a-vis immigrants from abroad, that is not already the case elsewhere in Canada . . . . The key to a resolution of the problem probably lies therefore in a reasonable compromise over the matter of free choice of language of instruction for persons moving from one province to another.

ANNUAL REPORT, *supra* note 165, at 27.

172. Ch. 6, 1974 Que. Stat. § 44.

Bill 22 also gave every person the right to address the public administration in either French or English. There is no similar provision in Bill 101 except in some cases under section 15.

Bill 22 unequivocally provided that public signs must be drawn up in both French and English or in French and another language. In contrast, Bill 101 provides: "Except as may be provided under this act or the regulations of the Office de la langue française, signs and posters and commercial advertising shall be *solely* in the official language."[173]

Bill 22 required corporations to have a French name, but it also permitted an English version of that name and business under such an English name. More restrictively, Bill 101 states that "[f]irm names must be in French"[174] and "[a] firm name may be accompanied with a version in another language for use outside Quebec. That version may be used together with the French version of the firm name in the inscriptions referred to in section 51, if the products in question are offered both in and outside Quebec."[175]

Bill 101 closely resembles Bill 22 in having as a primary objective the implementation of francization programs designed to generalize the use of French at all levels of businesses. There is, however, a notable difference. Under section 136 of Bill 101, firms with fifty or more employees must have a francization certificate by December 31, 1983.[176] Under section 28 of Bill 22 the francization certificate was mandatory only for firms wishing to do business with the government.[177]

It should be noted that section 29(b) of Bill 22 required "francophone presence in management"[178] and initially some persons took the word "francophone" to mean French Canadian. This was an indication of the hysteria at the time and the extent to which people would go in finding fault with a law that in general was very reasonable. The regulations (in the drafting of which I played a considerable part) made it clear that Francophone meant anyone who could speak French. To its credit, Bill 101 does not mention Francophones or Anglophones. Section 141(b) requires: "an increase at all levels of the business firm, including the board of directors, in the number of persons having a good knowledge of the French language so as to generalize its use."[179]

A comparison of the use of French and English in government, municipalities, school boards, universities, hospitals, and business illustrates the difference between the two laws. Biligualism under Bill 22 was replaced under Bill 101 with a form of French uniligualism whereby English was permitted only in certain circumstances.

---

173. Ch. 5, 1977 Que. Stat. § 58 (emphasis added).
174. *Id.* at § 63.
175. *Id.* at § 68.
176. *Id.* at § 136.
177. Ch. 6, 1974 Que. Stat. § 28.
178. *Id.* at § 29(b).
179. Ch. 5, 1977 Que. Stat. § 141(b).

C.   *Contestation of Bill 101*

Bill 101, like Bill 22, was challenged in the courts. In *Blaikie v. Attorney-General of Quebec*, [180] the Court declared that articles 7 to 13 of the Charter of the French Language were *ultra vires* the Legislature of Quebec. The articles, comprising chapter III of the Charter, made French the official language of the legislature and courts in Quebec.[181] More specifically, articles 7 to 13 of the Charter established the following: (1) only the French text of statutes is official; (2) an English version as well as the official French version of all bills, statutes, and regulations shall be printed and published by the government; (3) all procedural documents and pleadings before the courts must be in French unless otherwise agreed to by the parties; and (4) all judgments by Quebec courts must contain a French version and only the French version of the judgment is official.[182]

The Quebec Superior Court held that the contested articles were invalid in that they directly violated the language guarantees of section 133 of the BNA Act, 1867.[183] Furthermore, the Court declared that it was not within the legislative competence of the Quebec National Assembly to unilaterally amend section 133, inasmuch as the section forms part of the Constitution of Canada and of Quebec in an "indivisible" sense.[184]

This decision was upheld by the Quebec Court of Appeal, where that Court found the relevant sections to be "en contradiction flagrante."[185]   On further appeal to the Supreme Court of Canada, the Court, in "matters of detail and history, [was] . . . content to adopt the reasons of Deschênes, C.J. as fortified by the Quebec Court of Appeal."[186]

In *Devine v. Attorney-General of Quebec*, [187] the validity of articles 53 and 57 through 61 of the Charter of the French Language was challenged. The articles are part of Chapter VII and they require the following: (1) catalogues, brochures, and similar publications must be drawn up in French; (2) applications for employment, order forms, invoices, and similar items must be drawn up in French; (3) except as may be provided otherwise by regulation, signs, posters, and commercial advertising must be solely in French; (4) firms of fewer than four people may erect signs in both French and English so long as the French inscription is prominently displayed; and (5) signs of a particular ethnic group's cultural activities may be in both French and the language of that group.[188]

The plaintiffs sought a declaration that the contested articles were *ultra vires* the Quebec National Assembly, and alternatively, that the articles were incompatible

180.   85 D.L.R.3d 252 (1978).

181.   Ch. 5, 1977 Que. Stat. §§ 7-13.

182.   *Id.*

183.   85 D.L.R.3d 252, 270 (1978).

184.   *Id.* at 280-81.

185.   [1978] C.A. 351, 361. (Translation: "in flagrant contradiction.")

186.   101 D.L.R.3d 394, 401 (1980). In response to the judgment of the Supreme Court the Quebec Government adopted a special statute, ch. 61, 1979 Que. Stat.

187.   [1982] Que. C.S. 355.

188.   Ch. 5, 1977 Que. Stat. §§ 53, 57-62.

with the Quebec Charter of Human Rights and Freedoms,[189] and thus void and inoperative.

With regard to the *ultra vires* issue, the plaintiffs first contended that the restrictions on the use of the English language caused them "prejudice dans leurs activités commerciales," and as such, the instant articles were an encroachment on the exclusive federal jurisdiction over the "regulation of trade and commerce."[190] The Quebec Superior Court rejected this argument in short order. It noted that the courts have long upheld the competence of provincial legislatures to enact legislation in the area of trade and commerce so long as the legislation concerned matters of a purely local nature. In this regard, the Court cited with approval a portion of the opinion in *Shannon v. Lower Mainland Dairy Products Board*:[191]

> It is now well settled that the enumeration in s.91 of "the regulation of trade and commerce" as a class of subject over which the Dominion has exclusive legislative powers does not give the power to regulate for legitimate Provincial purposes particular trades or businesses so far as the trade or business is confined to the Province . . . . And it follows that to the extent that the Dominion is forbidden to regulate within the Province, the Province itself has the right under its legislative powers over property and civil rights within the Province.[192]

The plaintiffs then maintained that the prohibition of English signs in section 58 was an encroachment on the federal power over criminal law under section 91(27) of the BNA Act, 1867. This argument was also rejected by the Court. In light of section 92(15) of the BNA Act, 1867, the Court stated that "une province a le droit d'utiliser le moyen de la prohibition pour atteindre une fin qui découle de sa compétence."[193] After deciding that the Province has "le droit . . . de légiférer sur la langue du commerce et des affaires," the Court determined that "la prohibition de l'art. 58 est un moyen d'atteindre le but de la loi qui est 'd'assurer la qualité et le rayonnement de la langue française' et de 'faire du français . . . la langue normale et habituelle du travail, . . . du commerce et des affaires.' "[194] In addition, the Court declared that,

> On peut dire que le moyen est radical, qu'il est sans mesure avec le besoin, la prohibition de l'article 58 ne cesse pas d'être un moyen légitimement choisi d'atteindre l'objectif légitime de la loi . . . . Si la Province a droit de se donner un visage français, l'article 58 est certes un moyen efficace d'y parvenir . . . Il n'appartient pas à la Cour de se prononcer sur les motifs ou les objectifs du législateur. Je comprends la déception des demandeurs. Ce fut celle des francophones lors de l'ârret *MacKell* et j'ai appris à partager la déception dé mes professeurs d'histoire. Mais au point de vue du droit public anglais, *MacKell* est inattaquable. *MacKell* a fait la oi du pays. Il pèse de tout son pieds dans ce débat. Il me lie.[195]

---

189. Ch. 6, 1975 Que. Stat. 51 (current version at QUE. REV. STAT. ch. C-12 (1977)).

190. [1982] Que. C.S. at 360. (Translation: "prejudice in their commercial activities.")

191. [1938] A.C. 708.

192. [1982] Que. C.S. at 361.

193. *Id.* at 370. (Translation: "a province has the right to use the means of prohibition to attain an end which arises from its competence.")

194. *Id.* at 370-71. (Translation: "the right . . . to legislate concerning the language of commerce and business.")

195. *Id.* at 371. (Translation:

It can be said that the method is a radical one, that it is out of all proportion to the need, the prohibition contained in section 58 is nevertheless a legitimately chosen means of fulfilling the legitimate purpose of the law . . . . If the Province has the right to take on a French character, section 58 is undoubtedly an effective way of reaching that goal. It is not part of the Court's function to rule on the

The Court next considered the plaintiff's submission that article 58 was incompatible with articles 3 and 10 of the Quebec Charter of Human Rights and Freedoms.

> 3. Every person is the possessor of the fundamental freedoms, including freedom of conscience, freedom of religion, freedom of opinion, freedom of expression, freedom of peaceful assembly and freedom of association.
>
> 10. Every person has a right to full and equal recognition and exercise of his human rights and freedoms, without distinction, exclusion or preference based on race, colour, sex, sexual orientation, civil status, religion, political convictions, language, ethnic or national origin, or social condition.
>
> Discrimination exists where such a distinction, exclusion or preference has the effect of nullifying or impairing such right.[196]

The plaintiffs submitted that the requirement imposed by article 58 of the Charter to use only French signs discriminated against them by reason of language. Furthermore, they argued that this restriction denied them freedom of expression. With regard to the first argument, the Court held that there was no discrimination by reason of language in that the sign law applied equally to all, regardless of language:

> . . . la loi s'applique aussi bien aux francophones qu'aux anglophones, aux italiens qu'aux grecs, à la majorité qu'à la minorité. Il est évidemment plus facile aux francophones d'y obéir, mais cela ne dépend pas de la loi, cela dépend de la familiarité des francophones avec la langue obligatoire de l'affichage . . . . Les anglophones subissent plus que les autres ethnies l'obligation qui leur est faite de n'utiliser que la langue française dans l'affichage parce que, plus que les autres, ils ont utilisé leur langue à cette fin. Mais l'obligation de n'utiliser que le français s'impose également à tous et en ce sens, il n'y a pas de discrimination contre eux en raison de leur langue.[197]

The plaintiff's submission that the requirement to use French signs denied them freedom of expression was also rejected when the Court held that "La liberté d'expression ne comprend pas la liberté de choisir la langue d'expression."[198] Freedom of expression, along with freedom of opinion, are "deux facettes d'une même liberté, la liberté de discussion."[199] The Charter of the French Language is not concerned with those matters, but only with "le code qui traduit la pensée—la langue, le dessin, l'image."[200] In this regard, the Court noted the distinction that

---

motives or objectives of the legislation. I understand the plaintiffs' disappointment. This is the disappointment that Francophones felt after the *MacKell* decision, and I have learned to share the disappointment of my history professors. But from the standpoint of English public law, *MacKell* is indisputable. It has set the law of this country. It bears heavily upon this debate. I am bound by it.)

196. Ch. 6, 1975 Que. Stat. §§ 3, 10 (current version at QUE. REV. STAT. ch. C-12 (1977)).

197. [1982] Que. C.S. at 374-75. (Translation:

The law applies equally to Francophones and Anglophones, to Greeks and Italians, to the majority and the minority. Naturally, it is easier for Francophones to obey it, but this has less to do with the law itself than with the fact that Francophones are more familiar with the compulsory language for signs and posters. More than other ethnic groups, Anglophones suffer under the obligation imposed upon them to use only French for signs and posters because, more than others, they have been accustomed to using their own language for that purpose. But the obligation to use French applies equally to all, and in this sense they are not being discriminated against because of their language.)

198. *Id.* at 379. (Translation: "Freedom of expression does not include the freedom of choosing the language of expression.")

199. *Id.* at 376. (Translation: "two facets of the same freedom, the freedom of discussion.")

200. *Id.* at 375. (Translation: "the medium that transmits thought—language, drawing, picture.")

exists in law between the message (beliefs, thoughts, opinions) and the medium of transmission ("le code").

During the course of its opinion, the Court engaged in a long discussion of a proposition put forward by the plaintiffs that the right to use a particular language is a "fundamental right." This proposition, according to the Court, had no basis in Canadian constitutional law. The Court noted that the *MacKell*[201] case determined that there are no substantive language "rights." The presumed legal right by the Francophones of Ontario to have their children educated in French was in reality a "privilege of a voluntary character."[202]

> L'ârret *MacKell* si douloureusement ressenti par les francophones Ontariens, était malheureusement conforme au droit public anglais qui tient que l'étendue de nos libertes est la somme de ce qui n'est pas défendu.[203]

That language is not a "fundamental right" is confirmed by English constitutional law. The preamble to the BNA Act, 1867, states that the Canadian Constitution is to be "similar in principle to that of the United Kingdom."[204] As far back as 1362, during the reign of Edward III, the use of French was forbidden in the courts of England.[205] In 1535, Parliament prohibited the inhabitants of Wales from using their language in a court of justice.[206]

In 1733 the use of any language in the courts other than English was prohibited by statute.[207] In 1840, the Parliament of the United Kingdom enacted the Act of Union[208] which reunited the provinces of Upper and Lower Canada. Following the recommendations of the Durham Report,[209] the statute sought to anglicize French Canadians. To that end, the Act abolished the use of French in the statutes and records of the Legislative Assembly. Henceforth, all such documents were to be "in the English language only."[210] In light of the foregoing statutes the Court in *Devine v. Attorney-General of Quebec* concluded: "Le droit constitutionnel anglais ne reconnaît pas a une minorité linguistique le droit de s'exprimer dans la langue de son choix."[211]

If the decision in *Devine* is disconcerting to some Anglophones, it is, nevertheless, a logical, reasonable, and just result achieved by carefully balancing the terms of contemporary law with its historical evolution.

D. *Regulations under Bill 101*

Title IV of Quebec's Language Charter (Bill 101) establishes a Conseil de la

---

201. [1917] A.C. 62.
202. [1982] Que. C.S. at 365.
203. *Id.* at 362. (Translation: "The *MacKell* decision, which was so painful to the Francophones of Ontario, was unfortunately in accordance with English public law, which holds that the extent of our freedom is the sum of what is not forbidden under the law.")
204. BNA Act, *supra* note 6.
205. 1362, 35 Edw. 3, ch. 15, § 15.
206. 1535, 7 Hen. 8, ch. 26, §20 (cited by Dugas, J., [1982] Que. C.S. at 363).
207. 1731, 4 Geo. 2, ch. 26, § 1 (cited by Dugas, J., [1982] Que. C.S. at 363).
208. The Union Act, 1840, 3 & 4 Vict., ch. 35 (U.K.); CAN. REV. STAT. app. II, No. 4 (1970).
209. LORD DURHAM'S REPORT ON THE AFFAIRS OF BRITISH NORTH AMERICA (1912).
210. CAN. REV. STAT. app. II, No. 4, § 41 (1970).
211. [1982] Que. C.S. at 363. (Translation: "English constitutional law does not recognize the right of a linguistic minority to the language of its choice.")

langue française to advise the government on questions relating to the interpretation and application of the Charter.[212] In March of 1982, Yves Ouellette, Dean of
Law at the University of Montreal, submitted a confidential report[213] to the Conseil indicating that many of Quebec's language regulations were either clearly *ultra
vires* the authority conferred by the Charter, or else of such questionable validity as
to encourage challenges in the courts. Ouellette argued that the problems with
respect to the regulations arise from the fact that many of the articles of the
Charter are poorly drafted. Unfortunately, attempts were made to remedy the
deficiencies and errors in the Charter by passing questionable regulations rather
than by amending the law itself. In support of this criticism Ouellette concluded:

> A vrai dire cependant, le malaise est infiniment plus profond; il découle de la Charte
> elle-même. D'un point de vue strictement technique, cette loi ne saurait être considérée
> comme un modèle de rigueur et de bonne rédaction. On a donc tenté d'en corriger les
> déficiences et les lacunes par voie réglementaire et c'est là que se situe le fond du
> problème.[214]

The regulations governing language tests prepared by the Office de la langue
française and administered to members of professional corporations are now being
contested in the courts. The Charter requires that all professionals practicing in
Quebec have a knowledge of French "appropriate to the practice of their profes-
sion."[215] According to Ouellette, the language of the Charter is too general to be
interpreted as conferring on a governmental agency the extraordinary power of
control over the right to earn a living.[216] To this end Ouellette noted: "ni l'article
35 ni les autres dispositions de la loi n'attribuent à l'Office la juridiction en cette
matière. Les [règlements] pretendent corriger cette lacune importante de la
loi."[217]

VIII THE AMENDMENT TO THE CONSTITUTION—1982

A. *The Canada Act, 1982*

Prior to 1981, attempts to patriate the Canadian Constitution were unsuccessful because of the inability of the federal and provincial governments to unanimously agree on an amending formula. The defeat of the Quebec referendum on
sovereignty-association in May of 1980 prompted renewed efforts by the federal
government to bring about constitutional reform. A first ministers' conference
four months later ended with the two levels of government still at an impasse; as a
consequence, the federal government announced it would act unilaterally to break

---

212. QUE. REV. STAT. ch. C-11 (1977).
213. Y. OUELLETTE, ETUDE DE LA VALIDITÉ DES RÉGLEMENTS ADOPTÉS EN VERTU DE LA CHARTE
DE LA LANGUE FRANÇAISE (submitted to the Conseil de la Langue Française March 15, 1982).
214. *Id.* at 41. (Translation: "In effect, however, the malaise goes infinitely deeper; it derives from
the Charter itself. From a purely technical standpoint, this law cannot be considered a model for clarity
and good writing. An attempt has been made to correct its deficiencies by way of regulations, and therein
lies the root of the problem.")
215. Ch. 5, 1977 Que. Stat. 108.
216. Ouellette, *supra* note 213, at 16.
217. *Id.* at 17. (Translation: " . . . neither section 35 nor the other provisions of the law give the
Office jurisdiction over this matter. The [regulations] are intended to correct this major deficiency of the
law.")

the deadlock. It proposed sending a Resolution to Westminster requesting the United Kingdom Parliament to adopt the Canada Act, 1982.

The Resolution was to accomplish three things. First, it would patriate the constitution, thereby giving Canada full sovereign independence; no longer would the U.K. Parliament have the power to legislate for Canada. Second, a domestic amending formula would be included in order to permit future constitutional reform. Third, a charter of human rights and freedoms, including language rights, was to be entrenched as part of Canada's constitution.

Eight of the provinces, including Quebec, formed an alliance opposing the plan. After a lengthy filibuster in Parliament, the issue as to whether provincial consent was required was referred to the Supreme Court of Canada.[218] On September 28, 1981, the Court ruled that as a matter of law, the federal government could send the Resolution to Westminster without provincial consent.[219] The Court also held, however, that a constitutional convention requires "substantial" provincial agreement in order to permit constitutional change.[220] Following the Supreme Court's decision, negotiations between the two levels of government resumed. Another first ministers' conference was held, and on November 5, 1981, all of the provinces except Quebec gave their consent to the historic Resolution. Four days later, in a speech before Quebec's National Assembly, Premier René Levesque voiced his contempt for the new agreement:

> Il est donc clair que nos ne pouvions absolument pas accepter cette nouvelle constitution fabriqueé en une nuit de fourberies. D'abord, parce qu'elle nous aurait forcés à accepter une limitation importante des pouvoirs exclusifs de l'Assemblée nationale en ce qui concerne la langue d'enseignement dans nos écoles. Je l'ai dit et je le répète: Aucun gouvernement québécois qui se respecte ne pourra jamais abandonner la moindre parcelle de ce droit absolument fondamental pour la protection du seul îlot français dans la mer anglophone du continent nord-américain.[221]

Notwithstanding Quebec's dissent,[222] the Resolution was adopted by the House of Commons on December 2, 1981, and by the Senate on December 8, 1981. The Canada Act 1982 was in turn adopted by the United Kingdom House of Commons and House of Lords, and received royal assent on March 29, 1982. The Constitution Act, 1982, being schedule B of the Canada Act 1982, was brought into force by a proclamation signed by Her Majesty the Queen in Ottawa on April

---

218. Reference re Amendment of the Constitution of Canada, 125 D.L.R.3d 1 (1982).

219. *Id.* at 7-9.

220. *Id.* at 3-6.

221. 26 JOURNAL DES DÉBATS 4 (Nov. 9, 1981)(Translation:

It is therefore clear that we absolutely cannot accept this new constitution created in a night of double dealing. First of all, because it would force us to accept a significant limitation to the exclusive powers of the Assemblée Nationale with respect to the language of instruction in our schools. I have said it before and I repeat: No self-respecting Quebec government could ever abandon the smallest fraction of this absolutely fundamental right to protect the only French island in the English-speaking sea of the North American continent.)

222. It is now settled that Quebec's consent is not essential for constitutional reform. In a recent reference to the Quebec Court of Appeal [1982] Que. C.A. 33; 134 D.L.R.3d 719 (1982), Quebec maintained that as one of the founding nations of Canada, it enjoyed a veto power over proposed constitutional changes. This argument was rejected by the Court. 134 D.L.R.3d at 720. Furthermore, the Court declared that Quebec's consent to the Resolution was not necessary because only substantial agreement was required. *Id.* at 726.

17, 1982.[223] The Canadian Charter of Rights and Freedoms comprises Part I of the Constitution Act, 1982.

B. *Official Languages of Canada*

The provisions respecting the official languages of Canada comprise sections 16 to 22 of the Canadian Charter of Rights and Freedoms. These provisions create no new language rights.[224] Several of the sections maintain existing constitutional guarantees, while the others constitutionally entrench existing statutory provisions.

Sections 17(1), 18(1), and 19(1) reproduce the language rights binding on the federal government under section 133 of the BNA Act, 1867, by establishing that (1) everyone has the right to use either English or French in Parliament, (2) legislative materials and statutes of Parliament shall be published in English and French with each given equal authority, and (3) either English or French may be used in any judicial pleadings or process in any court established by Parliament.[225] Sections 17(2), 18(2), and 19(2) of the Act entrench identical provisions for New Brunswick.[226] These provisions were originally conferred by provincial legislation in 1969.[227]

Section 16 declares French and English to be the official languages of Canada and New Brunswick, and gives each language equality of status in all institutions of both governments. The Act entrenches statutory provisions enacted over a dozen years ago by the federal government[228] and the legislature of New Brunswick.[229]

Section 16(3) confirms that legislation in respect to language is a matter of concurrent jurisdiction divided between the two levels of government. Although it is clear that Parliament and the provincial legislatures are free to advance "the equality of status or use of English and French"[230] beyond the minimum standards established by the Charter, it is not certain whether the legislatures must *exclusively* pursue that objective. There are many ways in which Parliament or the provincial legislatures might diminish the status or use of one of the two languages, and still

223. Canada Act 1982, 1982, ch. 11 (U.K.).

224. It has been argued that the equality rights secured by section 15(1) of the Canadian Charter of Rights and Freedoms prohibit discrimination based on language. This argument is at best tenuous. It is not easy to disregard the fact that language is specifically omitted from the prohibited forms of discrimination listed in section 15(1), which only includes "race, national or ethnic origin, colour, religion, sex, age, or mental or physical disability." Canada Act 1982, 1982, ch. 11 (U.K.), Part I, § 15(1). Admittedly, the prohibited forms of discrimination are not exhaustive, but rather are only particular ways in which equality before the law is not to be denied. Nevertheless, given the crucial importance of the language issue in Canada, the failure to include language among the prohibited forms of discrimination cannot be summarily dismissed as a mere oversight on the part of the legislators. If they had intended the section to apply to language, it is clear that they would have included it in the list.

225. Canada Act 1982, 1982, ch. 11 (U.K.), Part I, §§ 17(1), 18(1) & 19(1).

226. *Id.* at §§ 17(2), 18(2) & 19(2).

227. Official Languages of New Brunswick, N.B. REV. STAT. §§ 3, 4, 6, 7, 13 (1973). *See supra* text accompanying note 84.

228. Official Languages Act, CAN. REV. STAT. ch. 0-2, § 2 (1970). *See supra* text accompanying note 18.

229. N.B. REV. STAT. ch. 0-1, § 2 (1973). *See supra* text accompanying note 69.

230. Canada Act 1982, 1982, ch. 11 (U.K.), Part I, § 16(1).

not violate any of the guarantees found in the Charter. Quebec's sign law[231] is an example of such provincial legislation.

Section 20 ensures that members of the public will be able to communicate with and receive services from the federal government and the government of New Brunswick in the official language of their choice.[232] Again, this section entrenches existing statutory provisions.[233] While Quebec's Charte de la langue française does not guarantee government services in English, it does permit the use of a language other than French in "correspondence between the civil administration and natural persons when the latter address it in a language other than French."[234]

Section 21 of the Canadian Charter preserves existing constitutional language rights by providing that "[n]othing in sections 16 to 20 abrogates or derogates from any right, privilege or obligation with respect to the English and French languages, or either of them, that exists or is continued by virtue of any other provision of the Constitution of Canada."[235]

C. *Minority Language Educational Rights*

French and English minority language education supported by public funds up to the university level is now constitutionally guaranteed (where numbers warrant) by section 23 of the Canadian Charter of Rights and Freedoms. Under section 23(1)(a), Canadian citizens (a) whose first language, learned and still understood is French or English, or (b) who have received their primary school instruction in Canada in French or English, are guaranteed the right to have their children receive primary and secondary school instruction in that language.[236] In addition, if any child has received or is receiving primary or secondary school instruction in English or French, the parents of such a child have the right to have all their children instructed in that language.[237] These rights are guaranteed so long as there are sufficient children to justify the use of public funds for minority language instruction.[238] Finally, the section also provides that where there are sufficient numbers requiring minority language instruction, educational facilities supported by public funds for minority language instruction will be made available.[239]

Section 23 is one of the most controversial provisions of the Canadian Charter. The Quebec government has argued that the section seriously encroaches upon provincial autonomy in the area of education and, by extension, presumably undermines Quebec's ability to preserve and protect its unique linguistic and cultural identity.[240] As a concession to Quebec, section 59 of the Constitution Act,

---

231. Charter of the French Language, ch. 5, § 58, 1977 Que. Stat. 111-12.
232. Canada Act 1982, 1982, ch. 11 (U.K.), Part I, § 20(1).
233. Official Languages Act, CAN. REV. STAT. ch. 0-2, § 9 (1970); Official Languages of New Brunswick Act, N.B. REV. STAT., ch. 0-1, § 10 (1973).
234. Charter of the French Language, ch. 5, § 15, 1977 Que. Stat. 105.
235. Canada Act 1982, 1982, ch. 11 (U.K.), Part I, § 21.
236. *Id.* at § 23(1).
237. *Id.*
238. *Id.* at § 23(2).
239. *Id.* at § 23(3)(a).
240. *See supra* text accompanying note 222 and *infra* text accompanying note 246.

1982, stipulates that section 23(1)(a) will come into force in respect to Quebec only when authorized by the legislative assembly or government of Quebec.[241]

Shortly after the Constitution Act, 1982, came into force the Quebec government adopted legislation to ensure that such authorization will be given only with the consent of the National Assembly. Section 4 of An Act Respecting the Constitution Act, 1982 (Bill 62) provides: "[t]he Government shall not authorize a proclamation under subsection 1 of section 59 of the Constitution Act, 1982, without obtaining the prior consent of the National Assembly of Quebec."[242]

A comparison of section 23(1)(b) of the Canadian Charter of Rights and Freedoms with article 73(a) of the Charte de la langue française brings into sharp relief the differences that exist between Ottawa and Quebec over minority language educational rights. Section 23(1)(b) of the Canadian Charter stipulates that any child whose parents were educated in English in *Canada* has the right to receive his or her school instruction in English.[243] In contrast, section 73(a) of the Quebec Charter provides that such a right is guaranteed only to children whose parents were educated in English in *Quebec.*

The clash between the two sections reveals the opposing objectives of the two pieces of legislation. Broadly speaking, the purpose of the Canadian Charter is to ensure that French and English-speaking citizens can move freely throughout the country, secure in the knowledge that at least with respect to educational and federal government institutions, certain language rights will be uniformly recognized. This view directly conflicts with Quebec's Charte de la langue française, which is designed to protect Quebec's distinctive French culture. The Quebec government has expressed a willingness to protect the status of English schools in Quebec, but this does not include the right of the English in Quebec to maintain their numbers through contributions from the rest of Canada.[244] As Laurin stated in the white paper:

> Par ailleurs, s'il y a lieu de garantir à la minorité anglaise du Québec l'accès à l'école anglaise, il est légitime de s'assurer que les personnes qui viendront s'installer au Québec dans l'avenir enverront leurs enfants à l'école française. En d'autres mots, l'école anglaise, qui constitue un système d'exception accordé à la minorité actuelle du Québec, doit cesser d'être assimilatrice et doit donc être réservée à ceux pour qui elle a été créée.[245]

Undoubtedly, Laurin's description of English schooling as "a special privilege granted to the present minority of Quebec" prompted the adoption of Bill 101's language of instruction provisions.

On May 5, 1982, several weeks after the Canadian Charter of Rights and Freedoms came into force, Camille Laurin issued an eight-page declaration in which

241.   Schedule B, Canada Act 1982, 1982, ch. 11 (U.K.).
242.   Ch. 21, 1982 Que. Stat.
243.   Canada Act 1982, 1982, ch. 11 (U.K.), Part I, § 23.
244.   Toronto Globe & Mail, Aug. 9, 1977 at 9, col. 2 *cited in* Note, *Language Rights and Quebec Bill 101,* 10 CASE W. RES. J. INT'L LAW 543, 552 (1978).
245.   Laurin, *supra* note 154, at 46. (Translation: "Moreover, if it is fitting to guarantee access to English schooling to Quebec's English minority, it is legitimate to ensure that, in the future, those who settle in Quebec will send their children to French schools. In other words, English schooling, which is a special privilege granted to the present minority of Quebec, must cease being an assimilating force and must be reserved to those for whom it was created.")

he announced on behalf of the Quebec government that section 73 of Bill 101 would continue to apply in full force:

> Cette loi de la langue française au Québec est enracinée dans la légitimité la plus authen-tique, je dirais même la plus sacrée, et aucun texte légal, émanant d'un autre pouvoir, ne saurait prévaloir contre elle.
>
> (. . .)
>
> En qualité de Ministre de l'Education et de Ministre responsable de l'application de la Charte de la langue française, je tiens à reaffirmér clairement, sereinement mais fermement, que la loi 101 continuera de s'appliquer intégralement, dans toutes ses parties, sous tous ses aspects et a l'echelle du Québec tout entier.[246]

As the next school year approached, the constitutional validity of section 73 was challenged in the courts. In *Quebec Association of Protestant School Boards v. Attorney-General of Quebec,*[247] a declaration was sought that the restrictions on access to English language education contained in section 73 of Bill 101 were inconsistent with section 23 of the Canadian Charter of Rights and Freedoms, and therefore of no force or effect.

The Quebec Superior Court found that section 73 and section 23 are incompatible, and that by virtue of section 52 of the Constitution Act, 1982, "the Canada clause (section 23) must prevail.[248] However, the Court noted that section 52 must be read with section 1 of the Charter, which stipulates that the rights and freedoms guaranteed by the Charter are "subject only to such reasonable limits prescribed by law as can be demonstrably justified in a free and democratic society."[249]

The Attorney-General for Quebec put forward an argument that section 73 of Bill 101 did not involve a denial of a right, but only a limitation, since the right to English education secured by section 23 was a collective right established for the benefit of the English-speaking minority as a group. "The limitation on this collective right," so the argument ran, might "well involve the loss of the right by certain members of the collectivity, but the right is not denied to the group as a whole: it is simply limited."[250]

This argument is susceptible to the kind of criticism that has often been levelled against utilitarianism: it would justify sacrificing the interests of the few in order to promote the interests of the many, thus violating the principle that each and every human being has equal intrinsic worth. With justifiable indignation, the Court denounced the "collective rights" argument:

---

246. Declaration of the Minister of Education and Minister responsible for the application of the Charte de la langue française, M. Camille Laurin, in conjunction with the tabling of Bill 62, An Act respecting the Constitution Act, 1982, May 5, 1982, p. 2. (Translation:

> This law concerning the French language in Quebec has its roots in the most authentic, I would even say the most sacred, legitimacy and no legal text emanating from any other power, can prevail over it.
>
> * * *
>
> In my capacity as Minister of Education and Minister responsible for the application of the Charte de la langue française, I wish to reaffirm, clearly, calmly, but firmly, that Bill 101 will continue to apply as written in all its parts, in all aspects and throughout the whole of Quebec.).

247. 140 D.L.R.3d 33 (1982). For the French judgment, *see* [1982] Que. C.S. 673.
248. 140 D.L.R.3d, at 48.
249. *Id.*
250. *Id.* at 64.

Quebec's argument is based on a totalitarian conception of society to which the court does not subscribe. Human beings are, to us, of paramount importance and nothing should be allowed to diminish the respect due to them. Other societies place the collectivity above the individual. They use the Kolkhoze steamroller and see merit only in the collective result even if some individuals are left by the wayside in the process.

This concept of society has never taken root here—even if certain political initiatives seem at times to come dangerously close to it—and this court will not honour it with its approval. Every individual in Canada should enjoy his rights to the full when in Quebec, whether alone or as a member of a group; and if the group numbers 100 persons, the one hundredth has as much right to benefit from all the privileges of citizens as the other ninety-nine.[251]

Even if section 73 of Bill 101 constituted a "limit" within the meaning of section 1 of the Charter, the Court ruled that Quebec failed to satisfy all of the conditions stipulated in section 1. In particular, the Court held that section 73 exceeded "reasonable limits" in that it was disproportionate to the admittedly legitimate objective of "solidifying the French fact in America."[252] The Court found that the operation of section 23 would not "have a negative effect in the area of the language of instruction which is still, as a rule, French," and that "the influx of new students into the English language school system because of section 23 of the Charter would be negligible."[253]

The decision of the Superior Court was upheld by the Quebec Court of Appeals on June 9, 1983 (as yet unreported),[254] and it is expected there will be an appeal to the Supreme Court.

Since the Canadian Charter of Rights and Freedoms has come into force, the rancour between Ottawa and Quebec has continued unabated. Indeed, Premier Levesque has threatened to make independence the theme of the next general election in Quebec.[255] Thus, it is clear that far from resolving the "language problem," the new Constitution has exacerbated the division between Ottawa and Quebec.

It should be pointed out that unlike the fundamental freedoms enumerated in section 2 or the legal and equality rights set out in sections 7 to 15 of the Canadian Charter, the language rights are not subject to the notorious "notwithstanding" clause of section 33 whereby: "Parliament or the legislature of the province may expressly declare in an Act of Parliament or of the legislature, as the case may be, that the Act or a provision thereof shall operate notwithstanding a provision included in section 2 or sections 7 to 15 of this Charter."[256] The language guarantees are binding on both the federal and provincial governments in respect to all matters falling within the authority of each legislature.

The constitution may be amended in respect to the use of the English or the French language in one of two ways. First, section 41 prescribes the normal procedure: "by proclamation issued by the Governor General under the Great Seal of Canada only where authorized by resolutions of the Senate and House of Com-

251. *Id.*
252. *Id.* at 70.
253. *Id.* at 89.
254. *Levesque Vows Language Fight,* Toronto Globe & Mail, June 11, 1983, at 11.
255. *P.Q. Returns to Independence Hard Line,* Toronto Globe & Mail, June 13, 1983, at 8.
256. Canada Act 1982, 1982, ch. 11 (U.K.), Part I, § 33.

mons and of the legislative assembly of each province."[257] Second, section 43 prescribes the procedure to amend any provision that relates to the use of the English or the French language *within a province*: "by proclamation issued by the Governor General under the Great Seal of Canada only where so authorized by resolution of the Senate and House of Commons and of the legislative assembly of each province to which the amendment applies."[258] An amendment to section 133 of the BNA Act, 1867, insofar as it applies to Quebec, and similarly the proposed amendment[259] to the language provisions of the Manitoba Act, 1870, would be accomplished according to the latter formula.

X SCHOOLING IN QUEBEC

A. *Private Schools—Bill 56*

Private education in Quebec began over three centuries ago when, in the early part of the seventeenth century, Quebec was colonized by Roman Catholic settlers from France. At that time, the idea of a public school system was foreign to the French regime and responsibility for education was left to the Roman Catholic Church. The subsequent years witnessed a gradual growth of government involvement in public education, but the tradition of private education remained strong and continues to this day. Currently, private schools are far more numerous in Quebec than in any other Canadian province. Even more important, they receive a level of public financial support that is virtually unprecedented in the western world.

Until the 1960's the public and private sectors operated quite independently of each other; rapid changes in Quebec's social, political, and economic milieu, however, created pressure for educational reform. The Parent Commission on Education,[260] organized in 1961, recommended that a more unified educational system be established. To that end, it proposed that legislation be adopted to bring about "collaboration, integration and coordination" between the two school systems.[261]

The Commission made additional recommendations. Indeed, because of concern about the quality of education in the private sector and possible abuses, the Commission recommended that the state exercise a degree of supervision and inspection over all private schools.[262] This was to ensure that certain uniform standards relating to curricula and teaching qualifications were satisfied. The state was required to assume such duties, according to the Commission, as "a consequence of the responsibility it bears with regard to everything which affects the public interest and the welfare of the people."[263] The Commission also proposed that the system of government grants to private schools should be made commensurate with the schools' ability to serve the public and to contribute to educational

---

257. *Id.* at Part V, § 41.2.
258. *Id.* at § 43.
259. *See, supra* text accompanying notes 52 and 53.
260. 1966 REPORT OF THE ROYAL COMMISSION OF INQUIRY ON EDUCATION IN THE PROVINCE OF QUEBEC 115. [hereinafter cited as REPORT OF THE ROYAL COMMISSION].
261. *Id.* at 207.
262. *Id.* at 219.
263. *Id.*

progress in Quebec.[264]

Many of the recommendations of the Parent Commission were incorporated into Bill 56, Private Education Act,[265] introduced by the Union Nationale Government in December of 1968. When presenting the Bill, Jean-Marie Morin, then Minister of Education, recognized the special status of private schools in Quebec: "Nous devons dire que la liberté de l'enseignement n'a jamais été contestée au Québec, et que les institutions privées ont pu naître et se developper librément sous l'oeil bienveillant et souvent même avec l'aide de l'État qui n'exerçait qu'un controle minimal, parfois même insuffisant."[266] While acknowledging that the private schools have made a valuable contribution to education in Quebec, Morin nevertheless pointed out that the private schools all too often functioned at the fringe of the school system, thereby undermining efforts to create a unified and coordinated school system. In addition, Morin noted the difficulties caused by the precarious financial position of many private schools.

To ensure that the private schools would have "les moyens de continuer leur oeuvre bénéfique,"[267] Bill 56 provided that private schools declared to be "of public interest" and which satisfied certain regulations designed to ensure teaching quality and the advancement of education in Quebec would receive a government grant "equal to eighty percent of the average cost per pupil, as computed for the preceding school year for public establishments of the same class. . . ."[268]

The Bill also authorized the Minister of Education to recognize "for the purposes of grants" private schools not declared to be "of public interest."[269] These schools were to receive sixty percent of the average cost per pupil in comparable public institutions so long as they satisfied certain regulations.[270] Bill 56 was unanimously adopted by the National Assembly in December of 1968 and it remains law today, although modified somewhat by Bill 101 in section 72.[271]

Camille Laurin's 1982 white paper[272] on educational reform reiterates the state's "responsibility for monitoring the quality of services"[273] provided by private institutions. Laurin, however, also cautions, as did the Parent Commission,[274] that "[t]he right to private education does not, in itself, confer any inherent right to receive public funds for this purpose."[275]

The reasons for the popularity of private schools today include the high quality of education, the greater discipline, the personal attention, and the extra-curric-

---

264. *Id.*
265. Ch. 67, 1967-68 Que. Stat. 445 (codified at QUE. REV. STAT. ch. E-9 (1977)).
266. 1968 JOURNAL DES DÉBATS 5015. (Translation: "It must be said that freedom of education has never been contested in Quebec, and that private schools were created—and developed freely—with the blessing and even the help of the state, whose control was minimal and sometimes insufficient.")
267. *Id.* (Translation: "the means to continue their useful work.")
268. QUE. REV. STAT. ch. E-9, § 14 (1977).
269. *Id.* at § 15.
270. *Id.* at § 16.
271. Ch. 67, 1967-68 Que. Stat. 445.
272. C. LAURIN, THE QUEBEC SCHOOL: A RESPONSIBLE FORCE IN THE COMMUNITY (deposited in the National Assembly on June 21, 1982). *See infra* text accompanying notes 292-94.
273. *Id.* at 82.
274. REPORT OF THE ROYAL COMMISSION, *supra* note 260.
275. C. LAURIN, *supra* note 272, at 82.

ular activities which are not always found in public schools. Children otherwise ineligible for English instruction because of Bill 101 are able to attend English private schools, but such children do not qualify for the appropriate government grants to the private schools as provided by section 72 of Bill 101. Section 72 is an ambiguous provision untested in the courts and its total effect on the entire grant to a school at which an unqualified student attends is far from clear.

B. *Public Schools and the Laurin White Paper*

Since before Confederation, the public school system in Quebec has been organized along Roman Catholic and Protestant denominational lines. Generally, this has run parallel to a division between French- and English-speaking pupils. In 1978, ninety-two percent of the students enrolled in Catholic schools in Quebec were taught in French, while ninety-eight percent of the students enrolled in Protestant schools were educated in English.[276]

Various attempts to reform the denominational and linguistic dualism of Quebec's schools date back to the Parent Commission. In 1966, the Commission recommended in its report that the denominational character of Quebec's school boards be abolished and replaced by unified school boards responsible for "Roman Catholic, Protestant and non-confessional education, insofar as the requirements for quality in education can be satisfied in each instance."[277] The Commission further recommended that the new unified school system "be made up, by law, of both French and English schools."[278] Thus, at least in theory if not in practice, the possibility existed that a school board might administer no fewer than six types of schools.

By the summer of 1967, the key recommendations of the Parent Commission gained the support of the Conseil supérieur de l'éducation and the Catholic Committee of the Council. The Protestant Committee, however, strongly opposed the creation of unified school boards. In the fall of 1967, the Union Nationale government established a Council to examine more closely the problem of restructuring more than forty school boards on the Island of Montreal. The Page Report of 1968[279] rejected the idea of unified school boards, and favoured instead the creation of school boards organized along linguistic lines. It recommended that nine French-language and four English-language boards should be established on the Island of Montreal, with the former responsible for Catholic and pluralist (non-denominational) schools, and the latter responsible for Catholic, Protestant and pluralist schools.[280] Moreover, several minority opinions were submitted with the Page Report, one of which favored retention of confessional division, while another proposed unification of the school boards.[281]

On November 4, 1969, Jean-Guy Cardinal, then Education Minister for the

---

276. MINORITY LANGUAGE EDUCATION REPORT, *supra* note 67, at 137.
277. REPORT OF THE ROYAL COMMISSION, *supra* note 260, at 85.
278. *Id.* at 115.
279. C. LAURIN, *supra* note 272, at 8 (reviewing the recommendations made by the Conseil de restructuration scolaire de l'île de Montréal in the Rapport Page).
280. *Id.*
281. *Id.*

Union Nationale Government, presented Bill 62, An Act Respecting School Organization on the Island of Montreal. The Bill proposed replacing the existing Protestant and Catholic school boards on Montreal Island with eleven unified school boards, each responsible to administer "l'enseignement catholique, l'enseignement protestant et l'enseignement autre que catholique ou protestant aux enfants de leur territoire."[282] The Bill also provided for the formation of school committees "compose de parents des éleves et chargé de veiller à la qualité de l'enseignement"[283] and an overall Montreal Island School Council responsible for financing and co-ordinating the activities of the eleven school boards.

Bill 62 made no mention of minority-language schooling, and this provoked criticism from the English-language community. According to Cardinal, the reason for the absence of language provisions in Bill 62 was simply that Bill 62 was conceived as companion legislation to Bill 63.[284] Unlike Bill 63, however, Bill 62 was never passed. The proposed legislation died on the National Assembly's order paper amidst the controversy and uproar generated by Bill 63.

Following the defeat of the Union Nationale in the next general election, the Liberal government continued to pursue the objective of educational reform. Bill 27,[285] dealing with the regroupment and integration of school boards along denominational lines *off* the Island of Montreal, was adopted on July 11, 1971. Unlike Bill 27, however, Bill 28,[286] introduced by the then Education Minister, Guy Saint-Pierre, was never adopted.

Bill 28 was an improved version of the controversial Bill 62. Similar to Bill 62, it provided for the replacement of Montreal Island's forty-three Catholic and Protestant school boards with eleven unified boards under a central Council. Each school board was to be responsible for Catholic, Protestant, and non-denominational schooling in both English and French. Bill 28 also proposed the creation of parent-student advisory committees for each school to assess the quality of education.

Unlike Bill 62, which made no provision for minority-language schooling, Bill 28 required each school board to offer its multidenominational services "également adaptés aux réalités linguistiques de chaque secteur de l'île."[287] Bill 28 required English and French-speaking personnel to be appointed to senior administrative positions on each school board. Moreover, the bill provided for the hiring of the necessary administrative staff in the academic, student, and personnel services of each school district for the English- or French-speaking minority, depending upon which linguistic sector was in that position. An additional protection for minority-language groups was found in a clause permitting appointment by the government

---

282. 1969 Journal des Débats 3509. (Translation: "the Catholic education, Protestant education and education other than Catholic and Protestant of children under their jurisdiction.")

283. *Id.* (Translation: "composed of the parents of students and charged with watching over the quality of instruction.")

284. *See supra* text accompanying notes 118-21.

285. An Act Respecting the Regrouping and Management of School Boards, ch. 67, 1971 Que. Stat. 493.

286. An Act Respecting the Reorganization of School Boards, 1971 Journal des Débats 3059.

287. *Id.* (Translation: "equally adapted to the linguistic realities of each sector of the island.")

of two additional school commissioners in any district where the minority-language group was insufficiently represented. Thus, examined from the point of view of minority language rights, Bill 28 was an equitable document.

The P.S.B.G.M. reacted to Bill 28 with characteristic concern and hostility. The P.S.B.G.M. chairman, A. Reid Tilley, said the proposed legislation threatened "the whole web and woof of the English and North American culture."[288] In a letter directed to parents, Tilley stated:

> [i]t is the considered opinion of the Protestant School Board of Greater Montreal that unifying at the school board level offers few advantages, needlessly duplicates and complicates the administrative and pedagogical processes in each Board and *will so fragment the English-language minority that they will in due course lose their individual identity and cultural values.*[289]

Not surprisingly, the Parti Québécois felt Bill 28 did not contain enough guarantees for the *French* language. The P.Q. staged a lengthy filibuster on the language issue shortly before Christmas in 1971 and as a consequence Bill 28 was subsequently dropped. As a compromise, Bill 71,[290] adopted in December of 1972, regrouped the existing Montreal Island school boards into six Catholic and two Protestant school boards. Bill 71 also established an Island School Council responsible for financing and co-ordinating common services of the school boards. The problem of restructuring, however, was far from resolved.

In 1976, an ad hoc committee of the School Council proposed that the government create French-Catholic, French-neutral, English-Catholic, and English-Protestant school boards. This recommendation was rejected by the Council, which in turn submitted a recommendation to the Minister of Education proposing that the status quo be maintained, but with two improvements—the creation of a non-confessional sector in Catholic school boards, and better means of representation for linguistic minorities.[291]

Little action was taken regarding the matter of restructuring the school boards on Montreal for another five years. In June 21, 1982, however, Camille Laurin, Minister of Education for the P.Q. government, deposited in the National Assembly a white paper on educational reform.[292] In accordance with recommendations dating as far back as the Parent Commission[293] of the 1960's, the white paper proposes abolishing the existing denominational school boards, and replacing them with unified regional boards drawn up along geographical lines. Each school will then decide whether it wishes to operate as a Protestant, Catholic, or non-denominational institution. On the Island of Montreal, the white paper recommends that school boards should be drawn up along linguistic lines with eight French-speaking and five English-speaking school boards. This is precisely what the P.S.B.G.M. suggested over a decade ago during the debate over Bill

---

288. Montreal Star, Sept. 8, 1971, at 3.
289. Letter from P.S.B.G.M. to parents (Sept. 17, 1971)(emphasis added).
290. An Act to Promote School Development on the Island of Montreal, ch. 60, 1972 Que. Stat. 1127 (now Part 9 of the Education Act, QUE. REV. STAT. ch. I-14 (1977)).
291. C. LAURIN, *supra* note 272, at 10.
292. *Id.*
293. REPORT OF THE ROYAL COMMISSION, *supra* note 260.

28.[294] The white paper also recommends that linguistic committees be established off the Island of Montreal where a school district has at least three English schools whose students represent at least ten percent of the total student population. The responsibility of these linguistic committees includes administration over most of the affairs of the English schools.

Already, the proposed reforms, particularly the creation of linguistic committees, have proved to be very debatable. Alliance Quebec, recently formed to represent the interests of English-speaking Quebecers, has denounced the committees as "totally inadequate" and has threatened court action.[295] Whether this reaction is justified remains to be seen. Nonetheless, it appears that all too often in the past, the fear of losing privileges has motivated the English in Quebec to resort to impassioned rhetoric and little real study of proposals with the net result that reasoned negotiation has been nearly impossible. Compromise this time requires a more calm, careful appraisal of the proposed reforms, and a genuine effort to reach a fair and proper solution.[296]

X CONCLUSION

It is clear that the Canadian Constitution has done very little to promote or even protect Canada's two great languages which should have been—and should be today—a great national asset. The British North America Act, 1867, failed to protect the French language and culture which were violated in such judgments as *Ottawa Separate Schools Trustees v. MacKell* or such legislative action as Manitoba's Official Language Act, 1890, and Regulation 17 of Ontario.

The constitution as interpreted by the courts should have provided a high standard of conduct, a spirit of natural justice, and a tradition of fair play. Instead, there was often harshness and no apparent legal recourse. It was only in the 1960's that political action in Quebec, beginning with the quiet revolution, brought about change. This occurred not only in Quebec but in the rest of Canada as well, where in varying degrees the enormity of the situation was finally acknowledged. But change in Quebec was too quick for the English and change in the rest of Canada was too slow for the French. Understandably, change of any kind causes animosity and mistrust because most individuals are naturally conservative and usually content with the status quo unless one's own personal interests clearly dictate otherwise.

The result has been a loss of Canadian unity. This is particularly unfortunate

---

294. Letter, *supra* note 289.
295. Montreal Gazette, June 23, 1982, at 2, col. 2.
296. Bill 40, An Act Respecting Public Elementary and Secondary Education, was tabled in the Quebec National Assembly on June 20, 1983. There are some changes from the White Paper. The Bill calls for five French and three English school commissions for Montreal Island, with 143 French and 10 English commissions covering the rest of the province. To forestall a constitutional challenge, Quebec's four original Protestant and Catholic school boards will be permitted, if they so choose, to retain their denominational status as provided by section 93 of the BNA Act, 1867. However, in such a case, they would revert to their original boundaries of 1867. The original boundaries of the Protestant School Board of Greater Montreal encompass an area now known as "Old Montreal." There are no schools in "Old Montreal." A court challenge can certainly be expected.

because bilingualism unquestionably is a great personal and national asset. Indeed, it has been said that one does not know one's own language completely and properly until a second is learned. Canada is amply blessed with two major languages—English and French—both of which are leading languages in the world of culture and commerce. It is significant and more than a little ironic that the only other major source of conflict and disunity in Canada is geographic disparity in our other great blessing—abundant natural resources; this latter conflict, incidentally, closely resembles our linguistic problems.

Although our two linguistic cultures have not aided unity or national understanding or even provided a large body of bilingual Canadians, quite clearly the imbalance towards the French language has been largely rectified. This has been, however, greatly outweighed by antipathy towards manifestations of French linguistic culture by certain English Canadians and an aversion by some Quebecers towards English Canadians.

Perhaps the most unfortunate consequence of the animosity has been its contribution towards the exodus of English-speaking Montrealers and business from Montreal. The great metropolis of the past which should have been a world center of commerce because of its bilingualism is now becoming a branch office community. Will the new constitution of 1982 rectify the situation? It is unlikely to remedy the situation in the short run and, in fact, its creation has only caused even greater estrangement and exacerbated already present linguistic animosity. The new constitution includes the Canadian Charter of Rights and Freedoms, but it has been so tempered by special arrangements entered into with various provinces in order to gain their participation that the Charter is no longer a document of dignity, of refuge, of hope, or of justice. Rather, it sonorously presents balkanized human rights and optings out on a zig zag geographical plan.

Despite the present situation, I am optimistic for the future of Quebec and Canada. Most other bilingual Quebecers and I are content and at home in Quebec, a doubly and truly enriched culture. Furthermore, I also find that a major change has overtaken many (but not all) Quebecers—there is a spirit of understanding among some of the young, both French and English, who realize that one cannot be unilingual anymore. It is this growing spirit that makes me sanguine about the future of Canada. And if the youth of the rest of Canada are not and cannot be bilingual, they nevertheless seem to have an openness of mind and of the heart that their elders have not revealed. There is hope!

THE RIGHTS OF PERSONS ACCUSED OF CRIME UNDER THE CANADIAN CONSTITUTION: A COMPARATIVE PERSPECTIVE

A. KENNETH PYE*

The Canadian Charter of Rights and Freedoms provides significant constitutional protections to persons accused of crime.[1] The purpose of this article is to examine generally the nature of these rights and how they compare with the constitutional protections afforded to those accused of crimes in the United States. The breadth of the issues involved necessarily requires selectivity in this comparison.

I

THE STRUCTURE OF THE PROTECTIVE PROVISIONS

The Charter enumerates specific "Legal Rights," some of which belong to everyone,[2] and some of which belong only to "[a]ny person charged with an offence,"[3] "[a] witness,"[4] or "[a] party or witness."[5] These provisions are part of the Constitution of Canada which is declared to be "the supreme law of Canada."[6] Any law that is inconsistent with a provision "is, to the extent of the inconsistency, of no force or effect."[7] The Charter applies both "to the Parliament and government of Canada . . . and . . . to the legislature and government of each province . . . ."[8]

The Charter clearly reflects a rejection of the views of opponents of a written bill of rights who have argued that the good judgment of Parliament and provincial legislatures provides sounder assurances for fundamental rights than a written document subject to the vagaries of interpretation by activist or conservative justices.[9] The Charter places implicit faith in the courts to interpret and enforce the

---

* Samuel Fox Mordecai Professor of Law, Duke University.
1. Constitution Act, 1982, ch. 1, §§ 7-14, 24. *See also id.* § 15.
2. Constitution Act, 1982, ch. 1, §§ 7-10, 12.
3. *Id.* § 11.
4. *Id.* § 13.
5. *Id.* § 14.
6. *Id.* § 52.
7. *Id.*
8. *Id.* § 32(1)(a).
9. *See, e.g.,* Lord Lloyd of Hampstead, *Do We Need a Bill of Rights?*, 39 MOD. L. REV. 121 (1976); Russell, *A Democratic Approach to Civil Liberties,* 19 U. TORONTO L.J. 109 (1969); Schmeiser, *Disadvantages of an Entrenched Canadian Bill of Rights,* 33 SASK. L. REV. 249 (1968); Smiley, *The Case Against the Canadian Charter of Human Rights,* 2 CAN. J. POL. SCI. 277 (1969).

enumerated rights of the citizenry,[10] despite a less than auspicious record of judicial leadership in civil liberties during the last two decades.[11]

Absent from the Charter is language used in the Canadian Bill of Rights that has been interpreted to limit significantly the rights apparently enumerated in that document. No longer is there language such as "have existed and shall continue to exist" which has been interpreted to permit civil liberties to be "frozen."[12] The clear language of the Charter that inconsistent laws are "of no force or effect"[13] should avoid the problems caused by the ambiguous language of the Canadian Bill of Rights that laws should "be so construed and applied as not to abrogate, abridge or infringe" rights.[14] The application of the Charter to federal and pro-

---

10. *See, e.g.,* COMMITTEE ON THE CONSTITUTION, THE CANADIAN BAR ASSOCIATION, TOWARDS A NEW CANADA (1978) [hereinafter cited as TOWARDS A NEW CANADA]; W. TARNOPOLSKY, THE CANADIAN BILL OF RIGHTS (2d ed. 1975); TASK FORCE ON CANADIAN UNITY, A FUTURE TOGETHER (1979); Brewin, *The Canadian Constitution and a Bill of Rights,* 31 SASK. L. REV. 251 (1966); Gibson, *Charter or Chimera? A Comment on the Proposed Canadian Charter of Rights and Freedoms*, 9 MAN. L.J. 363 (1979); McConnell, *Some Comments on the* Constitutional Amendment Bill: *A Quasi-Presidential System for Canada?,* 4 QUEENS L.J. 290 (1979); Tarnopolsky, *A Bill of Rights and Future Constitutional Change,* 57 CAN. B. REV. 626 (1979); Tarnopolsky, *The Canadian Bill of Rights: From Diefenbaker to Drybones,* 17 McGILL L.J. 437 (1971); Tarnopolsky, *A Constitutionally Entrenched Charter of Human Rights—Why Now?,* 33 SASK. L. REV. 247 (1968); Tarnopolsky, *A New Bill of Rights in the Light of the Interpretation of the Present One by the Supreme Court of Canada,* 1978 L. SOC'Y OF UPPER CAN., SPECIAL LECTURES 161 [hereinafter cited as *Tarnopolsky Lecture*]; Tarnopolsky, *The Supreme Court and the Canadian Bill of Rights,* 53 CAN. B. REV. 649 (1975).

11. Some opponents as well as proponents of an "entrenched" Bill of Rights seem to agree on the record of the courts in interpreting the Bill of Rights. *See* Schmeiser, *The Role of the Court in Shaping the Relationship of the Individual to the State—The Canadian Supreme Court,* 3 CAN.-U.S. L.J. 67, 69 (1980) ("Subject to a few exceptions, the Supreme Court has had a very negative influence on the development of individual rights in criminal law."). The Tarnopolsky articles and book, *supra* note 10, echo the same refrain. *See Tarnopolsky Lecture, supra* note 10, at 166-84 (cases concisely summarized).

12. An Act for The Recognition and Protection of Human Rights and Fundamental Freedoms, *reprinted in* CAN. REV. STAT. app. III § 1 [hereinafter cited as CAN. BILL OF RIGHTS] ("It is hereby recognized and declared that in Canada there have existed and shall continue to exist without discrimination by reason of race, national origin, colour, religion or sex, the following human rights and fundamental freedoms . . . ."). This provision was interpreted by Ritchie, J., in Robertson and Rosetanni v. The Queen, 41 D.L.R.2d 485, 491 (Can. 1963) ("It is to be noted at the outset that the *Bill of Rights* is not concerned with 'human rights and fundamental freedoms' in any abstract sense, but rather with such 'rights and freedoms' as they existed in Canada immediately before the statute was enacted."). *See* P. HOGG, CONSTITUTIONAL LAW OF CANADA 437-38 (1977); Brandt, *The Constitutional Amendment Act (Bill C-60),* 17 U. W. ONT. L. REV. 267, 278 (1979); Gibson, *supra* note 10, at 368; *see also* Regina v. Miller, 70 D.L.R.3d 324 (Can. 1976); Regina v. Burnshine, 1975-1 S.C.R. 693 (Can. 1974); Attorney-General of Canada v. Lavell, 38 D.L.R.3d 481 (Can. 1973).

The Canadian Bill of Rights is, of course, a statute which does not limit the powers of the provinces.

13. Constitution Act, 1982, ch. 1, § 52.

14. CAN. BILL OF RIGHTS, *supra* note 12, § 2:

Every law of Canada shall, unless it is expressly declared by an Act of the Parliament of Canada that it shall operate notwithstanding the *Canadian Bill of Rights,* be so construed and applied as not to abrogate, abridge or infringe or to authorize the abrogation, abridgment or infringement of any of the rights or freedoms herein recognized and declared, and in particular, no law of Canada shall be construed or applied so as to . . . .

Both judges and commentators have attributed part of the reluctance of the Supreme Court to accord greater significance to the expressed rights in the Bill to this language. *See* Regina v. Drybones, 9 D.L.R.3d 473 (Can. 1969) (Cartwright, C.J.C., dissenting); Regina v. Gonzales, 32 D.L.R.2d 290, 292 (Can. 1962); Brandt, *supra* note 12, at 278; Tarnopolsky, *A Constitutionally Entrenched Charter of Human Rights—Why Now?, supra* note 10, at 247-48. Others have criticized the drafting of the Canadian Bill of Rights. *See, e.g.,* D. SCHMEISER, CIVIL LIBERTIES IN CANADA 52 (1964); Laskin, *An Inquiry Into the Diefenbaker Bill of Rights,* 37 CAN. B. REV. 77, 125 (1959).

vincial governments as well as to Parliament and provincial legislatures[15] should make it clear that citizens are protected from administrative action as well as from legislation.[16] Unlike the Canadian Bill of Rights, the Charter provides protection at the prearrest stages of a criminal prosecution.[17]

The Charter recognizes that most fundamental rights are not absolute, but guarantees the enumerated rights "subject only to such reasonable limits prescribed by law as can be demonstrably justified in a free and democratic society."[18] The inclusion of the requirement of "demonstrable justification" serves notice that the government has the burden of producing cogent cause if it seeks to limit rights in the interests of public safety, health, peace and security, morals, or other reasons.[19]

---

15. Constitution Act, 1982, ch. 1, § 32.

16. The matter is not free from doubt, however. While Constitution Act, 1982, ch. 1, § 52(1) provides that the Canadian Constitution is the supreme law of Canada, it provides only that any *law* not consistent with its provisions is, to the extent of the inconsistency, of no force or effect. There appears to be no provision similar to the 1978 Proposed Constitutional Amendment which said that certain rights should "be incapable of being alienated by the ordinary exercise of such legislative or *other authority* as may be conferred by law on its respective *institutions of government*." GOVERNMENT OF CANADA, THE CONSTITUTIONAL AMENDMENT BILL (1978) [hereinafter cited as 1978 PROPOSALS] (emphasis added). This language was clearly intended to overrule decisions such as that of Beetz, J., in Attorney-General of Canada v. Canard, 52 D.L.R.3d 548, 565 (Can. 1975). Beetz interpreted the Canadian Bill of Rights as not extending to matters of administration as distinguished from matters of legislation. *Id.* at 578; *see also* Brandt, *supra* note 12, at 280. The problem was concisely stated by Mr. David Copp, Vice-President, British Columbia Civil Liberties Association, in his testimony before the Parliamentary Committee:

> First, Section 25 reasonably provides that laws that are inconsistent with the Charter are, to the extent of their inconsistency, inoperative. This does not go far enough, because many official standards which are not laws may be objectionable. For instance, a rule within a penitentiary could authorize a cruel punishment. In this case, a court asked to protect inmates in light of Section 12 of the Charter should have the power to strike down the offending tule [sic] without having to interfere with any statutes.
>
> Accordingly, we suggest that Section 25 be amended to follow Section 26 of the discussion draft of August 22, which reads "that any law, order, regulation or rule that authorizes, forbids or regulates any activity in a manner inconsistent with the Charter may be declared inoperative."

22 SPEC. JOINT COMM. OF THE SENATE AND OF THE HOUSE OF COMMONS ON THE CONSTITUTION OF CANADA, MINUTES OF PROCEEDINGS AND EVIDENCE OF THE SPECIAL JOINT COMMITTEE OF THE SENATE AND OF THE HOUSE OF COMMONS ON THE CONSTITUTION OF CANADA, 2d Parl., 1st Sess. 107 (1980) [hereinafter cited as JOINT COMMITTEE PROCEEDINGS].

It is unfortunate that the Constitution does not include language similar to that suggested by Professor Tarnopolsky that would have made it crystal clear:

> To the end that the paramountcy of this Charter be recognized and that full effect be given to the rights and freedoms herein proclaimed, any law, whether enacted before or after the coming into the effect of this Charter, and any administrative act in enforcement thereof, which is inconsistent with any provision of the Charter, except as specifically provided for, shall be inoperative and of no effect to the extent of the inconsistency.

Tarnopolsky, *Bill of Rights and Future Constitutional Change, supra* note 10, at 639. The Supreme Court has applied the Canadian Bill of Rights to police action denying an arrestee access to counsel. Hogan v. The Queen, 48 D.L.R.3d 427 (Can. 1974).

17. *See, e.g.,* Constitution Act, 1982, ch. 1, § 8.

18. *Id.* § 1.

19. Laskin, *The Canadian Constitutional Proposals,* 1981 PUB. L. 340, 342. The 1980 PROPOSALS § 1 provided that the freedoms set out were subject to "such reasonable limits as are generally accepted in a free and democratic society with a parliamentary system of government." GOVERNMENT OF CANADA, THE CANADIAN CONSTITUTION: PROPOSED RESOLUTION (1980) [hereinafter cited as 1980 PROPOSALS]. The 1978 PROPOSALS provided that:

> Nothing in this Charter shall be held to prevent such limitations on the exercise or enjoyment of any of the individual rights and freedoms declared by this Charter as are justifiable in a free and demo-

Rights declared to be fundamental in a written constitution are usually not subject to legislative modifications except through the process of amendment. But nations with traditions of parliamentary supremacy usually do not have written bills of rights.[20] Canada has adopted a constitutional hybrid by which Parliament or the legislature of a province may "opt out" by expressly declaring in a law that it, or a provision thereof, shall operate notwithstanding any "Legal Rights" otherwise assured by the Charter.[21] An American lawyer would be appalled by the notion that a state or the federal government could pass a law abridging a citizen's constitutional rights simply by providing that the law should operate without regard to the Constitution. However, the tradition of Parliamentary supremacy, the need to achieve acceptance by provinces where consensus concerning some of the provisions of the Charter may not exist, the existence of a similar provision in the Canadian Bill of Rights for over two decades, and the belief of experienced observers that Parliament, at least, would be unlikely to enact such a law, provide some assurances that the power may not be as significant as it appears at first glance.[22] But because of the opt-out possibility, it is incorrect to say that the rights of an accused are "entrenched" by the Charter; "quasi-entrenchment" may be a more accurate description.

---

cratic society in the interests of public safety or health, the interests of the peace and security of the public, or the interests of the rights and freedoms of others, whether such limitations are imposed by law or by virtue of the construction or application of any law.
1978 PROPOSALS, *supra* note 16, § 25. The next year the Government of Canada proposed that all such limitations should be "prescribed by law" and that "national security" and "morals" were interests also justifying limitations. *Federal Draft Proposals Discussed by First Ministers, Federal-Provincial Conference of First Ministers on the Constitution*, Doc. No. 800-010/037, Ottawa, Feb. 5-6, 1979 [hereinafter cited as 1979 FEDERAL PROPOSALS], *discussed in* Gibson, *supra* note 10, at 385. Earlier proposals also contained limitations on governmental power less stringent than those in the new constitution. Article 3 of the 1971 VICTORIA CHARTER would have permitted such limitations on the exercise of the fundamental freedoms as are "reasonably justifiable" in a democratic society in the interests of public safety, order, health, or morals, of national security and freedoms of others. GOVERNMENT OF CANADA, CONSTITUTIONAL CONFERENCE PROCEEDINGS 52 (1971) [hereinafter cited as 1971 VICTORIA CHARTER]. The 1972 Joint Committee on the Constitution recommended that any limitations should be only such "as are reasonably justifiable in a democratic society." SPEC. JOINT COMM. OF THE SENATE AND OF THE HOUSE OF COMMONS ON THE CONSTITUTION OF CANADA, CONSTITUTION OF CANADA: FINAL REPORT, 28th Parl., 4th Sess. 21 (1972) [hereinafter cited as 1972 JOINT COMMITTEE REPORT]. In 1981, questions were raised concerning the meaning of "reasonable limits" and "demonstrably justified." 38 JOINT COMMITTEE PROCEEDINGS, *supra* note 16, at 41-42 (1981). The Minister of Justice indicated that the intent of the language was to meet the objections of Professor Tarnopolsky, Mr. Fairweather and others that such language was needed "to limit the scope of the legislature and Parliament in relation to the fundamental rights of Canadian citizens." *Id.* at 42.
    20. *See* McConnell, *supra* note 10, at 291.
    21. Constitution Act, 1982, ch. 1, § 33. Legislation is required renewing the decision to opt out at least every five years. *Id.* §§ 33(3)-(5).
    22. The Task Force on Canadian Unity proposed the power to opt out as one technique for achieving provincial acquiescence to the Charter. *See* TASK FORCE ON CANADIAN UNITY, *supra* note 10, at 108. Some commentators had urged such a provision as a compromise with the principle of legislative supremacy. *See, e.g.,* P. HOGG, *supra* note 12, at 434. Others have regarded such language in a statute to "seriously undermine any notion that a Charter is intended to have paramount effect." Brandt, *supra* note 12, at 278. No such provision was included in the 1980 PROPOSALS, *supra* note 19. A provision permitting the provinces, but not the federal government, to opt out appeared in the 1979 FEDERAL PROPOSALS, *supra* note 19. No such proposals appeared in the 1972 JOINT COMMITTEE REPORT, *supra* note 19, the 1971 VICTORIA CHARTER, *supra* note 19, or the amendments to the constitution proposed in 1969. GOVERNMENT OF CANADA, THE CONSTITUTION AND THE PEOPLE OF CANADA (1969) [hereinafter cited as 1969 PROPOSALS].

The division of powers between the federal and provincial governments and the power to opt out of observance of some of the rights guaranteed to those charged with a crime pose the possibility of significant confusion in the administration of criminal justice. The federal parliament has exclusive jurisdiction to enact legislation concerning criminal law and criminal procedure.[23] Experienced observers think it unlikely that Parliament will attempt to avoid the protections of the Charter by opting out amendments to such statutes[24] as the Criminal Code[25] and the Canada Evidence Act.[26] Likewise, it is reasonable to expect that the opting out provisions will be used sparingly, if at all, in the exercise of federal power to impose criminal penalties pursuant to its jurisdiction over matters such as trade and commerce, banking, national defense, and Indians. This should also be true for penalties imposed under the federal parliament's arguable "residual power" under section 91 of the British North America Act to make laws for the "peace, order, and good government of Canada" in areas not within the exclusive jurisdiction of the provinces.[27]

The provinces possess the power to enact legislation concerning "the administration of justice" and the "construction, maintenance, and organization of provincial courts." They may also pass laws under their "quasi-criminal" law jurisdiction[28] derived from their power to legislate and enforce through penal sanction a number of specific matters of local concern. The provinces may be more likely to exercise the power to "opt out" in this area.

In an area where jurisdictional lines are blurred, there may be difficulties if a province opts out in a law establishing the procedures governing, for example, the investigation and prosecution in provincial courts of "quasi-criminal" conduct,[29] and the federal parliament has not done so. Constitutional conflict may also arise between the provision providing protection against unreasonable search and seizure and the power of a province to enact legislation concerning "the administration of justice." The issue is posed whether a provincial statute can authorize a provincial law enforcement officer to conduct a search that would otherwise be

---

23. British North America Act, 1867, 30 & 31 Vict., ch.3, § 91 (27) [hereinafter cited as BNA].

24. *See Tarnopolsky Lecture, supra* note 10, at 165; Gibson, *supra* note 10, at 387 ("Because the inclusion of such a 'flag' in any piece of legislation would inevitably stir up a great debate and controversy both in and out of Parliament, no government would employ the device lightly.").

25. CAN. REV. STAT. ch. C-34 (1970).

26. CAN. REV. STAT. ch. E-10 (1970).

27. *See* C. GRIFFITHS, J. KLEIN & S. VENDIN-JONES, CRIMINAL JUSTICE IN CANADA 10 (1981).

28. BNA, *supra* note 23, § 92(14)(15).

29. Professor McConnell has discussed the impact upon provinces who do not opt out:

[I]t is very possible that the interpretation of such an amendment in Canada could have an impact on "searches" in certain civil areas under provincial jurisdiction, such as compliance by home owners with sanitary conditions or building codes; the entitlement of welfare recipient's [sic] to further social assistance and inspecting conditions under which their children are being kept, and possibly the ascertainment of whether school children were using marijuana, which would at least in part concern the administration of schools. The search power might also arise in relation to provincial quasi-criminal offences relating to a wide range of matters.

McConnell, *Unreasonable Searches and Seizures: A "Fourth Amendment" for Canada?,* 11 R.D.U.S. 155, 189 (1980); *see also* Regina v. Dignard, [1954] 2 D.L.R. 539 (Can.); Regina v. Millar, 10 W.W.R. (n.s.) 145 (Man. Ct. App. 1955).

deemed unreasonable.[30] Even if the lawfulness of such a search is determined to be governed by federal law enacted pursuant to the federal power to enact laws governing criminal procedure, an issue may be raised as to whether such an "unreasonable search," ostensibly authorized by the law of the province in which it took place and performed by an officer of that province, "would bring the administration of justice into disrepute"[31] when the evidence was obtained in accordance with the unconstitutional provincial law. The conflicts may be complicated if a province has contracted with the Royal Canadian Mounted Police (RCMP) to provide local policing,[32] or if the RCMP and local municipal forces are jointly investigating organized crime activities that may uncover violations of municipal, provincial, and federal law.

The narrow reach of federal preemption reflected in the "paramountcy" cases suggests an attitude of accommodation rather than confrontation in dealing with arguable conflict between federal and provincial differences in penal matters.[33] In those provinces which depend upon the RCMP for policing, for example, adherence to the constitutional design might be facilitated by federal limitations upon the RCMP to assure that their behavior is consistent with the constitutional mandate, thereby affording the provincial government the alternative of providing their own police at much greater cost or accepting the limitations on RCMP investigative powers imposed by the Government of Canada.

II

SPECIFIC RIGHTS

A.   With the Same Meaning as Those Provided by the Bill of Rights

The Bill of Rights and the Charter provide a broad panoply of rights to persons suspected or accused of a crime.[34] The Canadian Bill of Rights is clearly the model for the "Legal Rights" section of the Charter. In some instances the language of the Bill is simply incorporated into the Charter. In others a change in language appears to have been adopted for stylistic rather than substantive reasons:

> 9.   Everyone has the right not to be arbitrarily detained or imprisoned.[35]

---

30.   *See* McConnell, *supra* note 29, at 189.

31.   Constitution Act, 1982, ch. 1, § 24(2); *cf.* Michigan v. DeFillippo, 443 U.S. 31 (1979).

32.   *See* C. GRIFFITHS, J. KLEIN & S. VENDIN-JONES, *supra* note 27, at 12-13.

33.   *See, e.g.,* Ross v. Registrar of Motor Vehicles, 42 D.L.R.3d 68 (Can. 1974).

34.   Constitution Act, 1982, ch. 1, §§ 7-14.

35.   The Bill provides that no law of Canada shall be construed or applied so as "to authorize or effect the arbitrary detention, imprisonment or exile of any person." CAN. BILL OF RIGHTS, *supra* note 12, § 2(a). No similar provision was contained in the 1969 PROPOSALS, *supra* note 22. The 1971 VICTORIA CHARTER, *supra* note 19, made no provision for Legal Rights. The 1972 Joint Committee adopted the formulation of the 1969 PROPOSALS and hence had no similar provision. 1972 JOINT COMMITTEE REPORT, *supra* note 19. The 1978 PROPOSALS included the right "not to be arbitrarily detained, imprisoned or exiled." 1978 PROPOSALS, *supra* note 16, § 7. The Canadian Bar Association proposals did not include similar protection. TOWARDS A NEW CANADA, *supra* note 10. The 1979 FEDERAL PROPOSALS would have been diluted to read "the right against detention or imprisonment except in accordance with prescribed laws and procedures." Gibson, *supra* note 10, at 372. The 1980 PROPOSALS continued the weakened formulation: "Everyone has the right not to be detained or imprisoned except on grounds, and in accordance with

10. Everyone has the right on arrest or detention (a) to be informed promptly of the reasons therefor; . . .

. . .

(c) to have the validity of the detention determined by way of *habeas corpus* and to be released if the detention is not lawful.[36]

11. Any person charged with an offence has the right . . .

. . .

(d) to be presumed innocent until proven guilty according to law in a fair and public hearing by an independent and impartial tribunal;

(e) not to be denied reasonable bail without just cause;[37] . . . .

12. Everyone has the right not to be subjected to any cruel and unusual treatment or punishment.[38]

---

procedures established by law." 1980 PROPOSALS, *supra* note 19, § 9. The provision in this form would have greatly diluted the protection, and objections were voiced by the Premier of New Brunswick, the Canadian Civil Liberties Union, the Canadian Jewish Congress, the United Church, the Canadian Bar Association, and others. The government agreed to the present language reflecting its view that the language means that "the fact procedures are established by law will not be conclusive proof that . . . detention is legal. Such procedures and the laws on which they are based will have to meet the tests of being reasonable and not being arbitrary." 36 JOINT COMMITTEE PROCEEDINGS, *supra* note 16, at 11 (1981) (statement of Minister of Justice, Mr. Chretien).

36. The Bill of Rights provides that no law of Canada shall be construed or applied so as to deprive a person who has been arrested or detained (i) of the right to be informed promptly of the reason for his arrest or detention . . . (iii) of the remedy by way of *habeas corpus* for the determination of the validity of his detention and for his release if the detention is not lawful. CAN. BILL OF RIGHTS, *supra* note 12, §§ 2(c)(i) (iii). Similar language appears in the 1969 PROPOSALS, *supra* note 22, 2(b), the 1972 JOINT COMMITTEE REPORT, *supra* note 19, the Canadian Bar Association Proposals, TOWARDS A NEW CANADA, *supra* note 10, at 19, and the 1978 PROPOSALS, *supra* note 16, § 7. The language of the 1980 PROPOSALS is identical to that in the 1982 Charter. 1980 PROPOSALS, *supra* note 19, § 10(a), (c).

37. The Bill of Rights provides that no law of Canada shall be construed or applied so as to "deprive a person charged with a criminal offence of the right to be presumed innocent until proved guilty according to law in a fair and public hearing by an independent and impartial tribunal, or of the right to reasonable bail without just cause." CAN. BILL OF RIGHTS, *supra* note 12, § 2(f). The protections were endorsed in the 1969 PROPOSALS, *supra* note 22, § 2(e), the 1972 JOINT COMMITTEE REPORT, *supra* note 19, the Canadian Bar Association Proposals, TOWARDS A NEW CANADA, *supra* note 10, at 19, and the 1978 PROPOSALS, *supra* note 16, § 7. The language relating to the presumption of innocence in the 1982 Chapter is identical to that in the 1980 PROPOSALS, *supra* note 19, § 11(c). The bail provisions were weaker in the 1980 PROPOSALS: "Anyone charged with an offence has the right (d) not to be denied reasonable bail except on grounds, and in accordance with procedures, established by law." *Id.* § 11(d). The Government accepted the many objections to the weaker standard and reverted to language reflecting the wording of the Bill of Rights. 36 JOINT COMMITTEE PROCEEDINGS, *supra* note 16, at 13 (1981).

Mr. Justice McDonald raises the question whether the provision for the presumption of innocence will preclude transferring the burden of proof to a defendant in certain cases; whether the requirement for a "fair hearing" will permit convictions to be set aside on the ground of incompetent counsel; and whether the mandate of a public hearing will preclude closed courts in cases involving juveniles and national security. D. MCDONALD, LEGAL RIGHTS IN THE CANADIAN CHARTER OF RIGHTS AND FREEDOMS 92, 102, 104 (1982). All three of these grounds have caused substantial litigation in the United States. *See* Allen & DeGrazia, *The Constitutional Requirement of Proof Beyond Reasonable Doubt in Criminal Cases: A Comment Upon Incipient Chaos in the Lower Courts,* 20 AM. CRIM. L. REV. 1 (1982); Bazelon, *The Defective Assistance of Counsel,* 42 U. CIN. L. REV. 1 (1973); Cox, *Foreword: Freedom of Expression in the Burger Court,* 94 HARV. L. REV. 1, 19-26 (1980).

38. The Bill of Rights provides that no law of Canada shall be construed or applied so as to "impose or authorize the imposition of cruel and unusual treatment or punishment." CAN. BILL OF RIGHTS, *supra* note 12, § 2(b). Protection against cruel and unusual punishment was contained in the 1969 PROPOSALS, *supra* note 22, § 2(h), the 1972 JOINT COMMISSION REPORT, *supra* note 19, the Canadian Bar Association Proposals, TOWARDS A NEW CANADA, *supra* note 10, at 19, and the 1978 PROPOSALS, *supra* note 16, § 7. The 1979 FEDERAL PROPOSALS recommended "cruel or inhuman" in lieu of "cruel and unusual." *See* Gibson, *supra* note 10, at 372. The language of the 1980 PROPOSALS is identical to that in the 1982 Charter. 1980 PROPOSALS, *supra* note 19, § 12. The dispute over whether the language should be "and" or "or" apparently reflects the concern of some that, as the section was worded, punishment, no matter how

14.   A party or witness in any proceedings who does not understand or speak the language in which the proceedings are conducted or who is deaf has the right to the assistance of an interpreter.[39]

Similarly, a person accused of crimes in the United States is protected against arbitrary arrest and detention,[40] has access to habeas corpus to test the legality of a detention,[41] is presumed to be innocent,[42] has the right to a public trial by an impartial tribunal,[43] and is protected from the infliction of cruel and inhuman punishment.[44] The right to be informed promptly of the reason for a detention is not explicitly recognized in the U.S. Constitution but may be protected by the due process clause.[45] While a defendant is protected against excessive bail by the eighth amendment,[46] the United States Supreme Court has never held that it applies to the states,[47] or that the amendment guarantees a right to bail.[48]

The fact that both Canada and the United States recognize a constitutional right does not, of course, suggest that each interprets the dimensions of that right in the same manner. Thus, what constitutes cruel and inhuman punishment in the United States may not necessarily be so regarded in Canada.[49] In Canada, just cause to detain an arrested defendant pending trial may be predicated upon the need to protect the public from any substantial likelihood that the accused, if released, will commit a criminal offense involving serious harm or an interference

---

cruel, would be lawful so long as it was not unusual. 22 JOINT COMMITTEE PROCEEDINGS, *supra* note 16, at 110 (1980) (testimony of Mr. William Black, British Columbia Civil Liberties Association); *see also id.*, vol. 42, at 7-8 (1981).

39.   The 1982 Constitution adds protection for the first time to a party or witness who is deaf. The Bill of Rights provided that

no law of Canada shall be construed or applied so as to . . . deprive a person of the right to the assistance of an interpreter in any proceedings in which he is involved or in which he is a party or witness, before a court, commission, board or other tribunal, if he does not understand or speak the language in which such proceedings are conducted.

CAN. BILL OF RIGHTS, *supra* note 12, § 2(g). The 1969 PROPOSALS, and subsequent proposals, contained similar protections. 1969 PROPOSALS, *supra* note 22, § 2(f); 1972 JOINT COMMISSION REPORT, *supra* note 19; 1978 PROPOSALS, *supra* note 16, § 7; TOWARDS A NEW CANADA, *supra* note 10, at 19.

40.   An illegal arrest violates the fourth amendment. Terry v. Ohio, 392 U.S. 1 (1968); Henry v. United States, 361 U.S. 98 (1959).

41.   U.S. CONST. art. I, § 9, ch. 2.

42.   The presumption of innocence is constitutionally protected by the requirement that guilt be established beyond a reasonable doubt. *In re* Winship, 397 U.S. 358 (1970); *see also* Kentucky v. Whorton, 441 U.S. 786 (1979); Taylor v. Kentucky, 436 U.S. 478 (1978).

43.   U.S. CONST. amend. VI; Ward v. Village of Monroeville, 409 U.S. 57 (1972); *In re* Oliver, 333 U.S. 257 (1948); Tumey v. Ohio, 273 U.S. 510 (1927).

44.   Furman v. Georgia, 408 U.S. 238 (1972); Robinson v. California, 370 U.S. 660 (1962); U.S. CONST. amend. VIII.

45.   U.S. CONST. amends. V, XIV. Modern reformers regard the warning as necessary. *See, e.g.,* A MODEL CODE OF PRE-ARRAIGNMENT PROCEDURE § 130.1(2) (1975).

46.   U.S. CONST. amend. VIII.

47.   U.S. Courts of Appeals have held that the eighth amendment applies to the States. Sistrunk v. Lyons, 646 F.2d 64 (3d Cir. 1981); Hunt v. Roth, 648 F.2d 1148 (8th Cir. 1981), *vacated as moot,* 455 U.S. 478 (1982).

48.   A recent decision holds that it does not. United States v. Edwards, 430 A.2d 1321 (D.C. 1981) (en banc), *cert. denied,* 455 U.S. 1022 (1982).

49.   *Compare* Regina v. Miller, 70 D.L.R.3d 324 (Can. 1976), *with* Furman v. Georgia, 408 U.S. 238 (1972). Whipping was available as a punishment for certain offenses in Canada until 1972. R. SALHANY, CANADIAN CRIMINAL PROCEDURE 213 (2d ed. 1972). Such a punishment has been held in the United States to be "cruel and unusual punishment." Jackson v. Bishop, 404 F.2d 571 (8th Cir. 1968).

with the administration of justice.[50] Whether detention pending trial can be justified on any basis other than the necessity to ensure the attendance of the defendant at his trial is much more doubtful in the United States.[51]

B.   Due Process and Principles of Fundamental Justice

Some provisions of the Charter have their origin in the Bill of Rights, but are expressed in language that suggests an intent to modify the substance of the right protected. Thus the Charter provides that: "Everyone has the right to life, liberty, and security of the person and the right not to be deprived thereof except in accordance with the principles of fundamental justice."[52] In comparison, the Bill of Rights asserted the existence of "the right of the individual to life, liberty, security of the person and enjoyment of property, and the right not to be deprived thereof except by due process of law."[53]

The protection of property has been deleted from the guarantee of the Charter, and "principles of fundamental justice" has replaced "due process of law" as the criterion for justifying deprivation.[54] The phrase "principles of fundamental jus-

---

50.   R. SALHANY, *supra* note 49, at 63.
51.   *See* Stack v. Boyle, 342 U.S. 1 (1951); United States v. Edwards, 430 A.2d 1321 (D.C. 1981) (en banc), *cert. denied*, 455 U.S. 1022 (1982).
52.   Constitution Act, 1982, ch. 1, § 7.
53.   CAN. BILL OF RIGHTS, *supra* note 12, § 1(a).
54.   The constitutional protection of property rights was severed from the rights to life and liberty and security of the person in the 1969 PROPOSALS. Those proposals would have assured life, liberty, and security of the person against deprivation "except by due process of law;" an individual could not be denied the right to the enjoyment of property "except according to law." 1969 PROPOSALS, *supra* note 22, § 1(e)(f) at 52. The distinction was intended to indicate "that what should be required for the protection of property is procedural fairness, whereas 'due process' might be capable of a broader meaning which could unduly limit legislative action." *Id.* at 52. No similar provision was included in the 1971 VICTORIA CHARTER, *supra* note 19. The language of the 1972 JOINT COMMITTEE REPORT is identical to that of the 1982 Charter. 1972 JOINT COMMITTEE REPORT, *supra* note 19, at 19. The Parliamentary Committee explained its choice of language:

> We should like to avoid the use of the phrase "due process of law" entirely, because it is a phrase which has no tradition in our law, despite its incorporation in the 1960 Bill of Rights, and because of its unfortunate interpretation in the United States under substantive due process. At its worst this phrase gave judges leeway to substitute their socio-economic views for those of legislatures. In our view it is more desirable to use another phrase found in the Canadian Bill of Rights, "the principles of fundamental justice."

Id. It should be noted that the phrase "the principles of fundamental justice" is used only in an oblique fashion in the Bill of Rights provision that no law shall be construed or applied so as to "deprive a person of the right to a fair hearing in accordance with the principles of fundamental justice . . . ." CAN. BILL OF RIGHTS, *supra* note 12, § 2(e). The Parliamentary Committee in 1972 also proposed a separate provision to protect property rights: "The right of the individual person to the enjoyment of property, and the right not to be deprived thereof except in accordance with the public good and for just compensation." 1972 JOINT COMMITTEE REPORT, *supra* note 19, at 20.

The Canadian Bar Association Proposals approved the formula of the 1969 PROPOSALS, rejecting the 1972 proposal for explicit constitutional protection for property rights on the grounds that "the question whether the taking of property is for the public good is clearly one for the legislatures" and that "economic rights are not appropriate for protection in a Bill of Rights." TOWARDS A NEW CANADA, *supra* note 10, at 18-19. The 1978 PROPOSALS returned to the language of the 1969 PROPOSALS. 1978 PROPOSALS, *supra* note 16, at § 6. The 1979 FEDERAL PROPOSALS recommended that the right to use and enjoy property be extended to groups as well as individuals and provided that the right to enjoy property is subject to deprivation only "in accordance with law that is fair and just," while calling for specific provision for the right of legislatures to make laws "which control or restrict use of property in public interest." Gibson, *supra* note 10, at 368-69. The language of the 1980 PROPOSALS is identical to that of the 1982 Charter, the explana-

tice" is not defined in the constitution. Perhaps this phrase was used instead of the phrase "due process" in order to forestall the possibility of entrenching in Canadian jurisprudence a concept of "substantive due process," as exemplifed by the United States Supreme Court cases dealing with economic regulation in the 1930's. If so, the choice of language seems questionable.[55] The separation of property rights from personal rights would have been adequate protection against resurrection of an American doctrine which has been largely quiescent for almost half a century. Indeed, with the exception of a few areas, it is difficult to find examples in recent American history of the use of "substantive due process" in matters affecting life and liberty.[56]

The use of the phrase "principles of fundamental justice" may reflect concern that courts might hold that any procedure permitted by the law constitutes "due

---

tory notes indicating that the provision is derived from § 1 of the Canadian Bill of Rights. 1980 PROPOSALS, *supra* note 19, at 16. No explicit provision for the protection of property is included in the 1982 Constitution, allegedly out of respect for the provincial property and civil rights jurisdiction under § 92(13) of the BNA. Laskin, *supra* note 19, at 343 n.12.

The Joint Parliamentary Committee considered a number of phrases: "due process of law," 21 JOINT COMMITTEE PROCEEDINGS, *supra* note 16, at 21 (1980); "principles of natural justice," *id.*, vol. 41, at 98 (1981); and "principles of fundamental justice, including the principles of due process of law," *id.*, vol. 46, at 30-45. Views were expressed that "principles of fundamental justice" was a "more encompassing" phrase than "due process," *id.*, vol. 2, at 21 (1980) (statement of Mr. Edwin Webking, Canadian Federation of Civil Liberties and Human Rights Associations); that "fundamental principles of justice" might be "more restrictive," *id.*, vol. 46, at 35 (1981) (statement of Mr. John Fraser); that "due process" would not only include the concepts of procedural fairness covered by "principles of fundamental justice," but also might include "substantive fairness" permitting the courts to second guess Parliament or legislatures on the policy of law, *id.* at 36 (statement of Dr. B.L. Strayer); that "principles of natural justice" has been limited to the right to an impartial tribunal and a right to be heard, while "principles of fundamental justice" leaves the opportunity for courts to move into new fields of jurisprudence, *id.* at 36; *id.*, vol. 44, at 19 (statements of Mr. Robinson); and that the terms "fundamental justice" and "natural justice" are essentially the same, each referring to procedural fairness, *id.*, vol. 46, at 38 (statement of Dr. B.L. Strayer). The Minister of Justice tersely stated the government's objection to including "due process" as the standard: "In simple terms, you are giving more power to the courts over the substance of the legislation that a different legislature will pass in Canada." *Id.* at 41 (statement of Mr. Chrétien).

It has been argued alternatively that the section includes the other enumerated rights in addition to broader protection and may be "one and the same" as due process. D. MCDONALD, *supra* note 37, at 20, 23.

55. *See* Laskin, *supra* note 19, at 343.

56. The decision declaring certain abortion laws to be unconstitutional is an example. Roe v. Wade, 410 U.S. 113 (1973); *see also* Loving v. Virginia, 388 U.S. 1, 12 (1967); Kent v. Dulles, 357 U.S. 116 (1958); *but see* Morgentaler v. The Queen, 53 D.L.R.3d 161 (Can. 1975) (rejecting challenge to abortion law). It seems more likely that the intent of the government was to limit the powers of courts to invalidate legislation dealing with life and personal liberty. The examples used by the Minister of Justice in opposing "due process" as a standard were capital punishment and abortion:

The point, Mr. Crombie, that it is important to understand the difference is that we pass legislation here on abortion, criminal code, and we pass legislation on capital punishment; Parliament has the authority to do that, and the court at this moment, because we do not have the due process of law written there, cannot go and see whether we made the right decision or the wrong decision in Parliament.

If you write down the words, "due process of law" here, the advice I am receiving is the court could go behind our decision and say that their decision on abortion was not the right one, their decision on capital punishment was not the right one, and it is a danger, according to legal advice I am receiving, that it will very much limit the scope of the power of legislation by the Parliament and we do not want that; and it is why we do not want the words "due process of law". These are the two main examples that we should keep in mind.

46 JOINT COMMITTEE PROCEEDINGS, *supra* note 16, at 43 (1981) (statement of Mr. Chrétien).

process of law."[57] The concern that "procedural due process" might become a residuary source of judicial power to expand procedural rights of an accused beyond those originally intended by the constitution, as has arguably been the case in the United States,[58] has some justification; yet it is difficult to see how the phrase "principles of fundamental justice" provides less opportunity for expansion to a court so inclined. Arguably, if the phrase "due process of law" were used, Canadian justices might be unduly influenced by the interpretation of similar language by their American cousins, a proposition not sustained by their past behavior.[59]

C. Custodial Interrogation, Right to Counsel, and Self-Incrimination

1. *Custodial Interrogation.* The Canadian Bill of Rights provided that no law shall be construed or applied "so as to . . . deprive a person who has been arrested or detained . . . of the right to retain and instruct counsel without delay."[60] Section 10 of the Charter incorporates this protection but goes further and assures that an arrestee or detainee is informed of that right.[61] The right to counsel is obviously of little significance to an accused who is ignorant of the existence of such a right, and there is reason to believe that a high percentage of arrested persons are unaware that they have the right to retain counsel at this stage of a police investigation.[62]

The combination of the right to retain and instruct counsel with assurance that an accused will know he has such a right, the right to be informed promptly of the reasons for the arrest, and the right to test the legality of a detention, provides theoretically significant protections to an accused who has been taken into police custody. Whether they provide realistic protection to suspects who are most in need of counsel is more doubtful.

---

57. Brandt, *supra* note 12, at 284; Gibson, *supra* note 10, at 372.

58. The application of provisions of the U.S. Bill of Rights to the states by "incorporation" into the due process clause of the fourteenth amendment, perhaps the most far reaching "extension" of due process by the Supreme Court of the United States, would not appear to be a problem because the provisions of the 1982 Canadian Constitution apply to the provinces directly. Other themes in the American precedents, such as equality of treatment for the rich and the poor, reflected in the overtones of cases such as the right to counsel cases, *e.g.,* Gideon v. Wainwright, 372 U.S. 335 (1963); the willingness to ignore the long history of a practice when "changed circumstances suggest the wisdom of a different result," *e.g.,* Taylor v. Louisiana, 419 U.S. 522, 537 (1975); the occasional propensity to use a particular case to legislate a code of permissible practices, *e.g.,* North Carolina v. Pearce, 395 U.S. 711 (1969); and the cases that used the due process clause to create a constitutional standard of "voluntariness" governing the admission of confessions, *e.g.,* Haynes v. Washington, 373 U.S. 503 (1963), Rogers v. Richmond, 365 U.S. 534 (1961), may provide greater causes for concern.

59. Thus far there is little evidence of such an abdication of independent judgment. *Tarnopolsky Lecture, supra* note 10, at 177-81; *see also* Regina v. Miller, 70 D.L.R.3d 324 (Can. 1976); Smythe v. The Queen, 1971 S.C.R. 680 (Can.). One wonders if the Supreme Court of Canada would tolerate the use of a stomach pump as in Rochin v. California, 342 U.S. 165 (1952).

60. CAN. BILL OF RIGHTS, *supra* note 12, § 2(c)(ii).

61. Constitution Act, 1982, ch. 1, § 10(b). The right does not appear in the earlier proposals. The Supreme Court had stated that the police had no obligation to advise an accused of his rights. Brownridge v. The Queen, 28 D.L.R.3d 1 (Can. 1972). The government added the phrase at the suggestion of several witnesses. JOINT COMMITTEE PROCEEDINGS, *supra* note 16, at 12 (1981).

62. *See* Comment, *Due Process Safeguards and Canadian Criminal Justice—A Reply to a Critique,* 14 CRIM. L.Q. 276 (1972) (discussing CANADIAN CIVIL LIBERTIES EDUCATION TRUST, DUE PROCESS SAFEGUARDS AND CANADIAN CRIMINAL JUSTICE (1972)).

The period between arrest and presentment before the magistrate may give rise to several quite different situations: (1) a simple detention following arrest, during which no significant interaction occurs between the police and the accused; (2) a detention accompanied by police efforts to persuade the accused to cooperate with investigative efforts by measures short of interrogation, such as participating in a lineup or submitting to a breathalyzer; or (3) detention accompanied by efforts by interrogators to obtain incriminating statements from the arrestee. This period of time is frequently characterized by police conduct of the kind described in (2) and (3). It is a fair inference that an arrestee who is informed of his right to counsel and has retained counsel usually has reasonable protection in both (2) and (3). The same results may be true if the legal aid scheme of a province provides counsel for an indigent at the detention facility, or if the accused or his family is otherwise able to acquire the services of such counsel. Quite a different result may occur, however, when the person detained has no access to a lawyer. A suspect who does not know how to retain an attorney or who is unable to afford one and who is arrested in a place where Legal Aid Duty Counsel is unavailable may find that the constitutional right of counsel is illusory. The level of protection in such cases falls far short of the protection afforded a person subjected to a custodial police interrogation in the United States, if the suspect asserts his desire to consult counsel, no counsel is provided him, and a statement is elicited from him.[63]

The Charter does not expressly grant to an accused the right to remain silent, and, hence, he is not entitled to a warning that he possesses such a right. For the same reason, the Canadian arrestee is not entitled to a warning that anything said may be used against him in court, nor, apparently, is there any requirement that an interrogation must cease if the defendant indicates that he wishes to remain silent.

While he must be informed of his right "to retain and instruct counsel," it is not clear that the Canadian suspect must be told that he has the right to have the lawyer with him during his interrogation. Arguably, "the assertion by a defendant of his desire to consult an attorney without delay" would require that the interrogation cease until an attorney is present,[64] as is required in the United States. He is not entitled to be informed that he has a right to have a lawyer appointed for him if he is unable to afford one because he has no such constitutional right.

2. *Right to Counsel.*   The difference in approach stems from the narrower concepts of "right to counsel" and "self-incrimination" reflected in the Charter. The

---

63. *See* Edwards v. Arizona, 451 U.S. 477 (1981). The rights of a defendant in a custodial interrogation in the United States are set forth in Miranda v. Arizona, 384 U.S. 436 (1966). The procedural safeguards, while not themselves constitutional rights, are "measures to insure that the right against compulsory self-incrimination was protected." Michigan v. Tucker, 417 U.S. 433, 444 (1974). A number of witnesses urged that provision be made to supply counsel to an accused unable to afford a lawyer. *See, e.g.,* 37 JOINT COMMITTEE PROCEEDINGS, *supra* note 16, at 24 (1981); *id.*, vol. 29, at 26 (1980); *id.*, vol. 24, at 44; *id.*, vol. 26A, at 3. Efforts to include such a proposal failed. *Id.*, vol. 46, at 127-35 (1981). The government resisted such incorporation on the grounds that legal aid was presently a part of the legal system, was unlikely to be repealed, and that all rights could not be placed in the Constitution. *Id.*, vol. 36, at 25-26 (1981); *id.*, vol. 46, at 131 (statements of Mr. Chrétien, Minister of Justice).

64. It can cogently be argued that Hogan v. The Queen, 48 D.L.R.3d 427 (Can. 1974), requires such a result.

"right to counsel" provision is limited to the right to "retain and instruct" and does not require that counsel be appointed for an accused unable to afford one at trial, much less at a police interrogation. The 1972 Parliamentary Committee expressly rejected the wisdom of including a provision in the constitution assuring counsel to those unable to afford a lawyer on the understandable basis that the provinces were not yet willing to pay for the implementation of such a proposal, and on the less understandable ground that providing positive benefits are appropriately the subject of nonconstitutional legislation and not that of charters, which should have a primarily negative thrust.[65] The crucial significance of appointing counsel for a defendant to protect against the excesses of government power and the inherent unfairness of any contest in which only one side has a goalie was apparently as unpersuasive in 1981 as it had been in 1972.

Obviously, provisions for legal aid made by the provinces may greatly ameliorate the practical impact of the omission from the constitutional scheme of provision for counsel for the indigent. It is nevertheless surprising that more concern has not been expressed over the failure to provide such a right in the constitution. It seems unlikely that the "fair hearing" provision[66] will be interpreted to require the appointment of counsel for an indigent,[67] and arguments predicated upon the "equal protection clause" are not likely to be persuasive.[68]

---

65.   Just as important as these guarantees of fair legal process is the provision of legal advice and legal counsel to those who cannot otherwise afford them. Although there has been a growing awareness across the country of the acute need in this field, the majority of the Provinces still do not have publicly supported programs of legal aid which are generally available. It is our hope that the initiative which the Federal Government has recently taken in establishing a legal aid program in the Northwest Territories will be followed elsewhere and expanded everywhere. We would particularly stress that the disadvantaged in our society need counselling as well as counsel, and that an adequate program of legal assistance will ensure that this need is met, through the development of direct governmental services, if necessary. Nevertheless, since the provision of adequate legal service necessitates the development of a considerable program of implementation, we cannot recommend it for inclusion in a Bill of Rights: for a constitutional charter of liberties most needs have a primarily negative thrust, by way of protecting people against an excess of governmental power. The providing of positive benefits is rather the stuff of ordinary legislation. 1972 JOINT COMMITTEE REPORT, *supra* note 19, at 20-21.

66.   Constitution Act, 1982, ch. 1, § 11(d) ("Any person charged with an offence has the right . . . (d) to be presumed innocent until proven guilty according to law in a fair and public hearing . . . ."). Arguably, the protection is less clear than the provision of the Canadian Bill of Rights from which it was apparently derived. Section 2(e) of the Bill of Rights provided that no law should be so construed or applied so as to "deprive a person of the right to a fair hearing in accordance with the principles of fundamental justice for the determination of his rights and obligations." CAN. BILL OF RIGHTS, *supra* note 12. The language of the Bill of Rights was copied in the 1969 PROPOSALS, *supra* note 22, § 2(e), the 1972 JOINT COMMITTEE REPORT, *supra* note 19, the Canadian Bar Association Proposals, TOWARDS A NEW CANADA, *supra* note 10, at 19, and the 1978 PROPOSALS, *supra* note 16, § 7. The language of the 1982 Canadian Constitution first appeared in the 1980 PROPOSALS, with the explanatory note that it would "assure rights of accused in criminal and penal proceedings" at present found in paragraphs 2(e) and 2(f) of the Bill of Rights. 1980 PROPOSALS, *supra* note 19, at 18.

67.   See the arguments advanced in Black, *Right to Counsel at Trial,* 53 CAN. B. REV. 56 (1975).

68.   Constitution Act, 1982, ch. 1, § 15(1) provides that "[e]very individual is equal before and under the law and has the right to the equal protection and benefit of the law without discrimination and, in particular, without discrimination based on race, national or ethnic origin, colour, religion, sex, age or mental or physical disability." The provision is not included in the "Legal Rights" sections of the Charter, but might in appropriate cases have significance in criminal litigation, such as cases in which discriminatory enforcement of laws can be established. *Cf.* Oyler v. Boles, 368 U.S. 448 (1962) (reasonable selectivity in enforcing habitual criminal statute no violation of equal protection, if not based on arbitrary classification); Butler v. Cooper, 554 F.2d 645 (4th Cir. 1977) (allegations of racially selective enforcement of liquor laws not proven); United States v. Falk, 479 F.2d 616 (7th Cir. 1973) (en banc) (selectivity in enforcing law

3. *Self-Incrimination.*   Protection against self-incrimination is found in two sections of the Charter: section 11(c) provides that any person charged with an offense has the right "not to be compelled to be a witness in proceedings against that person in respect of that offence."[69] Additional protection is afforded by section 13, which states that a witness who testifies in any proceeding has the right "not to have any incriminating evidence so given used to incriminate that witness in any other proceedings, except in a prosecution for perjury or for the giving of contradictory evidence."[70] Each is different from the provision in the Bill of Rights that no law shall be construed or applied so as to "authorize a court, tribunal, commission, board or other authority to compel a person to give evidence if he is denied counsel, protection against self crimination or other constitutional safeguards."[71]

An accused is protected in two different ways by the constitutional provisions. He cannot be compelled to be a witness against himself in "proceedings against that person in respect of that offence."[72] Furthermore, if he does testify in such a

---

requiring possession of draft registration card may violate equal protection if based on conduct protected by first amendment). The history of the provision does not suggest that the purpose of the provision was to deal with the problem of low visibility disparities that exist between the rich and the poor in the criminal process. *Cf.* Mayer v. City of Chicago, 404 U.S. 189 (1971); Douglas v. California, 372 U.S. 353 (1963); Griffin v. Illinois, 351 U.S. 12 (1956).

69. Constitution Act, 1982, ch. 1, § 11(c).

70. *Id.* § 13.

71. CAN. BILL OF RIGHTS, *supra* note 12, § 2(d). The 1969 PROPOSALS recognized "the right of a person not to give evidence before any court, tribunal, commission, board or other authority if he is denied counsel, protection against self-crimination, or other constitutional safeguards." 1969 PROPOSALS, *supra* note 22, § 2(c). The 1972 JOINT COMMITTEE REPORT, *supra* note 19, the Canadian Bar Association Report, TOWARDS A NEW CANADA, *supra* note 10, at 19, and the 1978 PROPOSALS, *supra* note 16, § 7, contained the same provision. The 1979 FEDERAL PROPOSALS limited the right not to testify to circumstances when the individual was "compelled to testify." Gibson, *supra* note 10, at 372. The limitation was continued in the 1980 PROPOSALS: "A witness has the right when compelled to testify not to have any incriminating evidence so given used to incriminate him or her in any other proceedings, except a prosecution for perjury or for the giving of contradictory evidence." 1980 PROPOSALS, *supra* note 19, § 13. The explanatory note indicated that the provision was an "elaboration of the right now provided in paragraph 2(d) by the Bill of Rights." *Id.* at 18. Section 13 of the 1982 Canadian Constitution tracks the 1980 PROPOSALS except that it does not require that the testimony has been compelled. The Minister of Justice explained the reasons for the change in § 13:

> Section 13 of the proposed Charter as drafted does not protect an accused or other witness who voluntarily gives evidence from having the evidence so given used to incriminate him in subsequent proceedings.
>
> I would propose an amendment to ensure that this clearly recognized principle in the law of evidence be reflected in the constitutional protection against self-crimination.

36 JOINT COMMITTEE PROCEEDINGS, *supra* note 16, at 13 (1981) (statement of Mr. Chrétien).

Section 11(c) appears for the first time in the constitution. It was added in the Joint Committee on the motion of Mr. Irwin. *Id.*, vol. 47, at 43-44. The limited nature of the protection was made clear by the explanation provided by the Director of the Criminal Law Amendments Section of the Department of Justice, Mr. Ewaschuk: "What this means is only when he is being tried does he have the right not to testify against himself. So that is only when his liberty is at stake during that trial." *Id.* at 44.

72. The protection given to an accused not to testify is thus put on a constitutional footing, where previously it rested upon the common law principle that an accused was not compellable, a principle that was not changed when an accused was made competent to testify. *See* E. RATUSHNY, SELF-INCRIMINATION IN THE CANADIAN CRIMINAL PROCESS 67 (1979). It will be interesting to see whether the new constitutional status of "noncompellability" will put some teeth in the prohibition against commenting on the failure of a defendant to testify:

> It has been demonstrated that the rule in Section 4(5) of the Canadian Evidence Act, forbidding comment upon a failure to testify, has been greatly restricted in scope. It is operative only in jury

proceeding, or in any other proceeding, and provides evidence which proves incriminating, it may not be used against him except in a subsequent prosecution for lying.

In comparison, an individual in the United States cannot be called as a witness in a case where he is accused of a crime, and if he is called in a case in which he is not charged, civil or criminal, he can refuse to answer any questions that tend to incriminate him,[73] unless he is granted immunity from the subsequent use of that evidence against him.[74] A Canadian accused of a crime can be required in a civil proceeding to answer a question that tends to incriminate him.[75] If he is charged separately from other parties, he can be compelled to testify about the offense with which he is charged if called as a witness at their trial.[76] An individual already charged with a crime may be compelled to testify in an investigatory proceeding, the object of which is to explore the matter that gave rise to his prosecution.[77]

The Canadian accused who answers self-incriminating questions, even if he is not compelled so to testify, is apparently protected, however, against the use of such statements against him in a subsequent proceeding.[78] The language of the Charter would seem to indicate that if *A* is charged with a crime and *B* testifies on *A*'s behalf and in so doing *B* incriminates himself, the government is precluded from using those admissions in a subsequent trial of *B*.[79] In substance, the witness is given a limited form of "use" immunity whenever he testifies. Section 13 of the Charter does not expressly require that a witness be called by the prosecution or

---

trials. Moreover, it is clearly permissible in law for the trier of fact, including a jury, to draw adverse inferences against an accused because of his failure to testify.

Id. at 331. *Compare* Avon v. The Queen, 21 D.L.R.3d 442 (1972) (instructions by the court "stating" but not "commenting" upon the accused's failure to testify did not amount to reversible substantial wrong or miscarriage of justice), *with* Griffin v. California, 380 U.S. 609 (1965) (the fifth amendment privilege against self-incrimination forbids comment by prosecution on accused's silence and instructions by the court that such silence is evidence of guilt).

73. Lefkowitz v. Turkey, 414 U.S. 70 (1973).

74. Kastigar v. United States, 406 U.S. 441 (1972).

75. Canada Evidence Act, CAN. REV. STAT. ch. E-10, § 5(1) (1970).

76. *In re* Ragan, [1939] 2 D.L.R. 135 (Can.).

77. *See* Regina v. Quebec Mun. Comm'n, 11 D.L.R.3d 491 (Can. 1969). The Canadian Supreme Court has precluded calling a person to testify at a coroner's inquest when he already has been charged with murder. Batary v. Attorney Gen., 52 D.L.R.2d 125 (Can. 1965). *But see* Faber v. The Queen, 65 D.L.R.3d 423 (Can. 1975).

78. The language of the Canadian Constitution is much broader than the existing statutory language which reads as follows:

> Where with respect to any question a witness objects to answer upon the ground that his answer may tend to criminate him, or may tend to establish his liability to a civil proceeding at the instance of the Crown or of any person, and if but for this Act, or the Act of any provincial legislature, the witness would therefore have been excused from answering such question, then although the witness is by reason of this Act, or by reason of such provincial Act, compelled to answer, the answer so given shall not be used or receivable in evidence against him in any criminal trial, or other criminal proceeding against him thereafter taking place, other than a prosecution for perjury in the giving of such evidence.

Canada Evidence Act, CAN. REV. STAT. ch. E-10, § 5(2) (1970). The existing law requires the witness to claim the privilege if he wishes to preclude the use of his testimony against him in the future. Tass v. The King, [1947] 1 D.L.R. 497 (Can.).

79. It is, of course, possible that the constitutional protection may be limited to the existing statutory protection despite the breadth of the language. Such a holding would require some judicial ingenuity in view of the change of language between the 1980 PROPOSALS and the 1982 Canadian Constitution, *see supra* note 71, and the statement of the Minister of Justice, *supra* note 71.

that he assert the privilege when called.[80]

The prohibition against use of prior testimony of a witness to incriminate him in other proceedings does not go so far as to provide "transactional" immunity to that witness.[81] Nor does the prohibition go so far as to prohibit the use of "derivative evidence," obtained as a result of testimony of a witness[82] even if the testimony is compelled. An American defendant, on the other hand, is entitled to protection from the use of "derivative evidence" as the price for his compelled testimony.[83]

It is not clear why a privilege against self-incrimination should protect persons who voluntarily incriminate themselves. The spectacle of A obtaining an acquittal as a result of B's admission of guilt, and B then obtaining an acquittal on the basis of A's judicial confession of guilt, when his previous statement is inadmissible, will do little to raise public confidence in the criminal justice system. It is also not clear why a person should not be protected from any use of his testimony, including the use of evidence obtained as a result of it, if his testimony is compelled when he otherwise would have chosen to remain silent.

While providing for a privilege against self-incrimination, sections 11(c) and 13 both limit their applicability to statements made in "proceedings." There is nothing that suggests any intention to extend the protection against self-incrimination to a person arrested or detained but not yet charged with an offense, or to test the admissibility of a pretrial statement to the police by any standard other than voluntariness.[84]

D. Other Protections for Persons Charged with Offenses

The Charter contains several other provisions of importance to persons charged with an offense that were not included in the Bill of Rights. Sections 11(a) and 11(b) guarantee an accused the right "to be informed without unreasonable delay of the specific offence" and "to be tried within a reasonable time."[85] The meaning

---

80. "The Fifth Amendment does not protect an individual from every incriminating statement he might make. Barring all self-incriminating admissions from introduction at trial would immeasurably hinder the administration of criminal justice." C. WHITEBREAD, CRIMINAL PROCEDURE 264 (1980); see also United States v. Washington, 431 U.S. 181, 187 (1977).

81. "Transactional immunity" refers to a grant by the state of immunity from prosecution for the transaction to which the compelled testimony relates as distinguished from "use immunity" which only prohibits the use of the incriminating statements themselves, and evidence derived therefrom, in a future prosecution. Cf. C. LILLY, AN INTRODUCTION TO THE LAW OF EVIDENCE 341-42 (1978).

The American Constitution is satisfied if use immunity is given in exchange for the compelled testimony. Kastigar v. United States, 406 U.S. 442 (1972).

82. Thus, the QUIMET REPORT comments: "A searching examination may . . . elicit facts or clues which enable the case to be independently proved." REPORT OF THE CANADIAN COMMITTEE ON CORRECTIONS 68 (1969).

83. See Kastigar v. United States, 406 U.S. 441 (1972).

84. In Curr v. The Queen, 26 D.L.R.3d 603 (Can. 1972), § 2(d) of the Bill of Rights was interpreted to limit the privilege against self-incrimination to testimony before a court or like tribunal. See Rothman v. The Queen, 35 N.R. 485 (Can. 1981); see generally F. KAUFMAN, THE ADMISSIBILITY OF CONFESSIONS (1979); E. RATUSHNY, supra note 72, at 65; Schrager, Recent Developments in the Law Relating to Confessions: England, Canada and Australia, 26 McGILL L.J. 435, 503-05 (1981). A proposal to assure that any person charged with an offense would be entitled to protection against self-incrimination from the moment of arrest and the right to be informed of that right was defeated. 47 JOINT COMMITTEE PROCEEDINGS, supra note 16, at 28.

85. These rights were included in the 1979 FEDERAL PROPOSALS, Gibson, supra note 10, at 372, and

of the "speedy trial" provision is unclear, but it seems reasonable to infer that it is concerned with delay between charge and trial, and not with delay between commission or arrest and charge.[86]

Under Canadian law, a right to trial by jury in serious cases is assured by a constitutional provision granting the right to trial by jury where the maximum punishment for the offense is imprisonment for five years or more, except in cases coming under military law.[87] Presumably, a defendant will still be permitted to elect trial by the court where permitted to do so by statute.[88] It is unclear whether the jury must be composed of twelve persons.[89] There is no reason to infer that a less than unanimous verdict would suffice under the provision.[90] In the United States, on the other hand, a defendant in a civilian court has a right to jury trial in all criminal prosecutions[91] except those for "petty offenses,"[92] but neither a jury of twelve[93] nor a unanimous verdict[94] is required. A person may not be tried within the United States by court-martial for a "civilian type" offense.[95]

In a sense the most extraordinary provision of the Charter is the provision prohibiting ex post facto laws:

were contained in the 1980 PROPOSALS, which indicated that they were derived from similar provisions in the U.N. Covenant. 1980 PROPOSALS, *supra* note 19, at 18. There was extensive discussion of the use of "without unreasonable delay" instead of "promptly" in § 11(a), with the former preferred because of the greater flexibility implicit in the language. 47 JOINT COMMITTEE PROCEEDINGS, *supra* note 16, at 32-43. It has been suggested that the provision may give rise to the development of the concept of abuse of process. D. McDONALD, *supra* note 37, at 88.

86. The American cases have so interpreted the provision of the sixth amendment guaranteeing that "the *accused* shall enjoy the right to a speedy . . . trial." U.S. CONST. amend VI (emphasis added); *see also* United States v. MacDonald, 456 U.S. 1 (1982); United States v. Marion, 404 U.S. 307 (1971). *But see* United States v. Lovasco, 431 U.S. 783 (1977) (due process has limited role to play in protecting against preindictment delay). The American test balances a number of factors in determining if the defendant's right has been violated, including the length of the delay, the claimed justification, the prejudice caused to the defendant, and whether the defendant sought earlier trial. Barker v. Wingo, 407 U.S. 514 (1972).

87. Constitution Act, 1982, ch. 1, § 11(f): "Any person charged with an offence has the right . . . (f) except in the case of an offence under military law tried before a military tribunal, to the benefit of trial by jury where the maximum punishment for the offence is imprisonment for five years or a more severe punishment." The provision does not appear in earlier proposals. The absence of a provision for trial by jury was criticized by witnesses, 21 JOINT COMMITTEE PROCEEDINGS, *supra* note 16, at 8 (1980), and a proposal for trial by jury in all cases where the punishment imposable was two years or more was made by the New Democratic party. *Id.*, vol. 42, at 7 (1981), *id.*, vol. 47 at 54. The government proposed the provision, stressing that it was a minimal provision and that the Criminal Code would continue to provide jury trials in many cases where the maximum punishment is less than five years. *Id.*, vol. 36, at 12.

88. When the offense charged is punishable by less than five years in prison, the Attorney-General may require under existing law that the accused be tried by a court composed of judge and jury. Criminal Code, CAN. REV. STAT. ch. C-34, § 498 (1970).

89. At present in the Yukon and Northwest Territories, six persons instead of twelve may be sworn as a jury to try an indictment. R. SALHANY, *supra* note 49, at 145 n.40. A trial may continue with consent of the parties following the death or discharge of a juror if the number of jurors is not reduced below ten (five in the Yukon and Northwest Territories). *Id.* at 152-53.

90. *Cf.* R. SALHANY, *supra* note 49, at 167: "From the earliest times, the criminal law of England has recognized that the verdict of the jury must be unanimous either for conviction or acquittal of the accused."

91. U.S. CONST. amend. VI.

92. Baldwin v. New York, 399 U.S. 66 (1970); District of Columbia v. Clawans, 300 U.S. 617 (1937).

93. Williams v. Florida, 399 U.S. 78 (1970); *cf.* Ballew v. Georgia, 435 U.S. 223 (1978) (five persons are too few).

94. Apodaca v. Oregon, 406 U.S. 404 (1972). *But see* Burch v. Louisiana, 441 U.S. 130 (1979) (5-1 vote not sufficient).

95. O'Callahan v. Parker, 395 U.S. 258 (1969).

11.   Any person charged with an offence has the right . . .

(g) not to be found guilty on account of any act or omission unless, at the time of the act or omission, it constituted an offence under Canadian or international law or was criminal according to the general principles of law recognized by the community of nations;
. . .

(i) if found guilty of the offence and if the punishment for the offence has been varied between the time of commission and the time of sentencing, to the benefit of the lesser punishment.[96]

The presence of an ex post facto provision is less extraordinary than would be its absence in a charter of rights.[97] What is remarkable is the use of "international law" and the "general principles of law recognized by the community of nations" in addition to domestic law as the base point from which the lawfulness of retroactive legislation will be judged. The scope of what constitutes an offense under international law, much less what is criminal according to the general principles of law recognized by the community of nations, is less than clear. Even if certain conduct clearly constitutes an offense against such "law" or "principles," it is less than clear that a national sovereign should be authorized to retroactively make such conduct an offense against its domestic laws.[98] The Canadian Parliament clearly has the power to punish acts done outside Canada, at least acts committed by its own citizens, and the Parliament has exercised that power in punishing conduct such as the hijacking of an aircraft.[99] In the future, it could presumably enact a law creating an offense such as "torture" and apply it retroactively to the conduct of its citizens abroad if "torture" is found to be either an offense against international law or criminal conduct according to the principles of law recognized by the community of nations.[100] Thoughtful observers may differ as to the

96.   Constitution Act, 1982, ch. 1, § 11(g)(i). The 1969 PROPOSALS recommended protection of the right of a person not to be held guilty of an offence on account of any act or omission which at the time of its commission or omission did not constitute an offence, and the right of a person on being found guilty of an offence not to be subjected to a penalty heavier than the one applicable at the time the offence was committed.
1969 PROPOSALS, *supra* note 22, § 2(g), at 54. The 1972 JOINT COMMISSION REPORT, *supra* note 19, the Canadian Bar Association Proposals, TOWARDS A NEW CANADA, *supra* note 10, at 19, the 1978 PROPOSALS, *supra* note 16, § 7, the 1979 FEDERAL PROPOSALS, Gibson, *supra* note 10, and the 1980 PROPOSALS, *supra* note 19, § 11(e), (g) recommend the same or similar language.
97.   Limitations upon the power to enact retrospective legislation are a part of the U.S. Constitution. U.S. CONST. art. I, § 9, cl. 3, § 10, cl. 1.
98.   Incorporation of the standard referring to international law resulted from concerns voiced by the Canadian Jewish Congress, the North American Jewish Students Association, and others that the ex post facto provisions not preclude the possibility of prosecuting persons alleged to have committed crimes recognized under international law. The International Covenant on Civil and Political Rights recognizes the right of a country to prosecute a person for an offense that was, at the time of the commission, a crime under international law even if not so recognized under domestic law. The provision reflects such an approach. 36 JOINT COMMITTEE PROCEEDINGS, *supra* note 16, at 12-13. The language "general principles of law recognized by civilized nations" apparently refers to the general principles of law common to the major legal systems of the world. Recent commentators have argued that whether a general principle is appropriate for absorption by international law will change with the development of international law, suggesting that it is now plausible to consider whether a rule against torture is part of international law, derived from the fact that such a principle is common to all major legal systems. RESTATEMENT OF FOREIGN RELATIONS LAW OF THE UNITED STATES § 102, reporter's note 7 (Tent. Draft No. 1, 1980). Assuming that a rule against torture is common to all major legal systems, it is unclear to the author what the common penalty is supposed to be.
99.   Criminal Code, CAN. REV. STAT. ch. C-34, §§ 6, 46 (1970); P. HOGG, *supra* note 12, at 206-07.
100.   *See* Filartiga v. Pena-Irala, 630 F.2d 876 (2d Cir. 1980).

wisdom of such a power or its exercise, but implicit authorization of such conduct by governments in a charter of rights designed to provide enhanced protection to citizens seems somewhat strange.

The Charter also provides that any person charged with an offense has the right "if finally acquitted of the offence, not to be tried for it again and, if finally found guilty and punished for the offence, not to be tried or punished for it again."[101] It seems clear that the provision does not bar a second prosecution when the first prosecution was terminated prior to a final judgment.

Experience in the United States suggests that few prosecutors would consider trying a defendant again for the same offense after acquittal or conviction and punishment. There seems to be a greater tendency to seek a retrial where a mistrial has occurred. Where the mistrial was not caused by "manifest necessity" or the "ends of public justice," a retrial is prohibited under U.S. law, even if the first trial never concluded in a final judgment.[102] If the mistrial was caused by the prosecution and the defendant objects, "manifest necessity" is unlikely to be found,[103] and retrial is prohibited. In the absence of extraordinary circumstances, a prosecutor could not, for instance, withdraw the charges after a trial has commenced, even with permission of the court, and commence prosecution again at a later time.[104]

The language of the second clause of the provision may cause difficulty. It is difficult to conclude that a person has been "found guilty and punished" when he has been found guilty and absolutely discharged by the court, for example when the sentence is suspended or the defendant is put on probation. The defendant would, however, have a statutory right to plead *autrefois convict*,[105] if retried under such circumstances, despite the fact that he has not been technically "convicted."[106]

The Charter provision does not clearly state whether a person may be prosecuted and convicted under federal law and provincial law for the same conduct. There are good grounds for arguing that successive prosecutions should be barred

---

101. Constitution Act, 1982, ch. 1, § 11(h). The 1979 FEDERAL PROPOSALS recommended the inclusion of a double jeopardy provision. Gibson, *supra* note 10, at 372. Its absence from the Bill of Rights and earlier proposals had been criticized. *Id.* at 371. The 1980 PROPOSALS provided that anyone charged with an offense has the right "not to be tried or punished more than once for an offence of which he or she has been finally convicted or acquitted." 1980 PROPOSALS, *supra* note 19, § 11(f). A proposal to modify the language to prohibit retrial of anyone "found guilty of and punished for any act or omission constituting the offence," obviously designed to provide protection against prosecution for related offenses or for offenses substantially the same as the principal offense, failed. 47 JOINT COMMITTEE PROCEEDINGS, *supra* note 16, at 60.

102. Illinois v. Somerville, 410 U.S. 458 (1973). United States Supreme Court cases involving double jeopardy are discussed in Hudson v. Louisiana, 450 U.S. 40 (1981).

103. *See, e.g.,* Downum v. United States, 372 U.S. 734 (1963).

104. *Cf.* Crist v. Bretz, 437 U.S. 28 (1978); R. SALHANY, *supra* note 49, at 136-37.

105. The plea of "autrefois convict" is the legal counterpart at common law of "autrefois acquit," and the rule forbids a second trial for the same offense whether the accused at the former trial was acquitted or convicted. Johnson v. State, 62 A.2d 249, 250, 191 Md. 447, 450 (1948).

106. Criminal Code, CAN. REV. STAT. ch. C-34, § 535(5)(c) (1970);, R. SALHANY, *supra* note 49, at 223-24. *See generally* Gautier, *The Power of the Crown to Reinstitute Proceedings after the Withdrawal or Dismissal of Charges,* 22 CRIM. L.Q. 463 (1980).

when the criminal justice system in each province is "to a large extent unitary."[107] It would be unjust to sentence a defendant more than once for the same conduct or require him to defend more than once for the same charge. Successive prosecution is permitted by the Constitution in the United States.[108] Presumably, prosecution for different crimes arising out of the same transaction is not barred.

E. Unreasonable Search or Seizure

The Charter provides that "[e]veryone has the right to be secure against unreasonable search or seizure."[109] Its exact meaning is understandably unclear[110] since similar language in the U.S. Constitution remains uncertain after almost 200 years.[111] There is no reason to assume that Parliament intended to adopt the gloss placed upon the phrase "unreasonable searches and seizures" by the Supreme

---

107. P. HOGG, *supra* note 12, at 112. A unitary system is one that has one set of courts and prosecutors. *Cf.* 47 JOINT COMMITTEE PROCEEDINGS, *supra* note 16, at 62.

108. Abbate v. United States, 359 U.S. 187 (1959); Bartkus v. Illinois, 359 U.S. 121 (1959).

109. Constitution Act, 1982, ch. 1, § 8. The 1969 PROPOSALS recognized and guaranteed "the right of the individual to be secure against unreasonable searches and seizures." 1969 PROPOSALS, *supra* note 22, § 2(a), at 52. The language was endorsed in the 1972 JOINT COMMITTEE REPORT, *supra* note 19, and the Canadian Bar Association Proposals. The Bar Association went further and proposed a right to personal privacy, quoting with approval the Manitoba Law Reform Commission proposal:

   (1) No person shall be subjected to unreasonable interference with her or his privacy.

   (2) For the purpose of this section, a search, seizure or intentional interception of communication shall be deemed to be unreasonable interference unless lawfully made:

   a. in accordance with an order made by a court of competent jurisdiction;

   b. in accordance with a search warrant issued by a court of competent jurisdiction on reasonable grounds supported by adequate information describing the purpose of the search and who or what is to be searched.

   c. in response to circumstances of such seriousness and urgency as to require and justify immediate action without the authority of such an order or warrant.

and in any event, every search, seizure, or interception of communications shall be effected with no more force or interference with privacy than is necessary to carry out the provisions of the order or warrant or to meet the seriousness or urgency of the circumstances.
TOWARDS A NEW CANADA, *supra* note 10, at 19.

The 1978 PROPOSALS included "the right to be secure against unreasonable searches and seizures." 1978 PROPOSALS, *supra* note 16, § 7. The 1979 FEDERAL PROPOSALS added a "right against unreasonable interference with privacy." Gibson, *supra* note 10, at 372. The 1980 PROPOSALS were much narrower: "Everyone has the right not to be subjected to search or seizure except on grounds, and in accordance with procedures, established by law." 1980 PROPOSALS, *supra* note 19, § 8. The explanatory note indicates that the provision "derives in part from the U.N. Covenant." *Id.* at 16. Existing Canadian law is summarized in McConnell, *supra*, note 29. *See generally* Bracken, *Federal Law Relating to Search and Seizure,* 28 U.N.B.L.J. 53 (1974). In response to the recommendations of a number of witnesses, the government returned to the language of the earlier proposals. 36 JOINT COMMITTEE PROCEEDINGS, *supra* note 16, at 11 (1981).

110. For instance, it remains to be seen whether the courts will refuse to apply the exclusionary rule to the fruits of an illegal search. *See* Hogan v. The Queen, 48 D.L.R.3d 427 (1974), in which the Supreme Court of Canada refused to apply the exclusionary rule in a case arising under the CAN. BILL OF RIGHTS, *supra* note 12.

111. At first blush it would appear that the provision provides protection against searches of persons or places and against seizures of persons and things. But an amendment to alter the language to read "not to be subjected to unreasonable search and seizure of person or property" was unsuccessful. 46 JOINT COMMITTEE PROCEEDINGS, *supra* note 16, at 102, 108 (1981). In opposing the provision as unnecessary and possibly restrictive, the Deputy Minister of the Department of Justice argued that seizure of the person is covered by § 9, the right not to be arbitrarily detained or imprisoned. *Id.* at 104-05 (statement of Mr. Tasse). It was also argued by the government that the addition was unneeded and might preclude an interpretation that interceptions of aural communications are protected under the provision. *Id.* It would be difficult to argue that privacy itself is protected in view of the decision to reject the proposed amend-

Court of the United States, but the rich judicial history of the fourth amendment in the United States can certainly provide a guide to the kinds of issues which will face the Supreme Court of Canada in interpreting the enigmatic clause.[112] Presumably, a search or seizure can be unreasonable although permitted by statute. Otherwise, the change in language from the 1980 Proposals was meaningless.[113] Likewise, there may be some searches which violate statutes or regulations, but which are not "unreasonable."[114] A wide variety of other issues can also be anticipated: What interests are protected?[115] What constitutes a search?[116] What constitutes a seizure?[117] What constitutes justification for a search or seizure: must there be "probable cause" or will a lesser standard suffice for all or some searches or seizures?[118] Can a search or seizure otherwise reasonable become "unreasonable" because of the manner in which it is conducted?[119] Do different tests of "unreasonableness" apply to searches of homes,[120] cars,[121] and closely regulated businesses?[122] Are searches incident to an arrest per se reasonable,[123] and if so, what is the scope of such a search?[124]

There are a host of other questions that will require resolution. It may be going too far to say that "concern over limitations upon the police powers to conduct searches and seizures have never been critical issues in Canada."[125] But the absence of both protection against unreasonable searches and seizures and an exclusionary rule in the Bill of Rights has produced a jurisprudence of search and

---

ment to § 7 that would have expressly assured protection against arbitrary or unreasonable interference with privacy. *See id.* at 62, 70.

Mr. Justice McDonald points out that the French version speaks not only of searches and seizures, but also of rummaging ("*les touilles*"). He also notes that "unreasonable" appears in the French version as "abusives" in § 8, while "reasonable" in §§ 11(3) and 11(6) is expressed as "raisonnable" in the French, with no explanation for the difference in language. D. MCDONALD, *supra* note 37, at 29.

112.   U.S. CONST. amend. IV:

The right of the people to be secure in their persons, houses, papers, and effects, against unreasonable searches and seizures, shall not be violated, and no Warrants shall issue, but upon probable cause, supported by Oath or affirmation, and particularly describing the place to be searched, and the person or things to be seized.

For a comparison of the American experience under the fourth amendment with Canada's experience without such a constitutional provision, see McConnell, *supra* note 29, at 158.

113.   *See supra* note 109.

114.   *See* United States v. Caceres, 440 U.S. 741 (1979).

115.   For the U.S. interpretation, see Katz v. United States, 389 U.S 347 (1967); Abel v. United States, 362 U.S. 217 (1960).

116.   For the U.S. interpretation, see Smith v. Maryland, 442 U.S. 735 (1979); Cardwell v. Lewis, 417 U.S. 583 (1974); Hester v. United States, 265 U.S. 57 (1924).

117.   For the U.S. interpretation, see United States v. Mendenhall, 446 U.S. 544 (1980). In particular, the issue of the legality of "stops and frisks" may become significant. *See* D. MCDONALD, *supra* note 37, at 65.

118.   For the U.S. interpretation, see United States v. Brignoni-Ponce, 422 U.S. 873 (1975); Adams v. Williams, 407 U.S. 143 (1972).

119.   For the U.S. interpretation, see Payton v. New York, 445 U.S. 573 (1980); Ker v. California, 374 U.S. 23 (1963).

120.   For the U.S. interpretation, see Vale v. Louisiana, 399 U.S. 30 (1970).

121.   For the U.S. interpretation, see Chambers v. Maroney, 399 U.S. 42 (1970).

122.   For the U.S. interpretation, see United States v. Biswell, 406 U.S. 311 (1972).

123.   For the U.S. interpretation, see United States v. Robinson, 414 U.S. 218 (1973).

124.   For the U.S. interpretation, see Chimel v. California, 395 U.S. 752 (1969).

125.   Katz, *Reflections on Search and Seizure and Illegally Seized Evidence in Canada and the United States,* 3 CAN.-U.S. L.J. 103, 118 (1980).

seizure that provides little help in resolving the issues which will soon confront Canadian judges.[126]

A case such as the one involving the "Fort Erie" raid provides an example of Canadian jurisprudence under the Bill of Rights. In 1974, Canadian police officers conducted a drug raid in a Fort Erie hotel. In the course of their investigation, they searched virtually all of the 115 patrons on the premises, including 35 women patrons who were stripped and subjected to vaginal and rectal examinations.[127] The police had no warrant but had reason to suspect that there were drugs in the hotel. A special Royal Commission held that (1) the searches were lawful because police are entitled to enter forcibly and conduct a search of a place other than a dwelling house without a warrant if they have reasonable grounds to believe that the entered premises contain unlawful narcotics, and (2) the police can lawfully search everyone found on such premises, including those not reasonably suspected of possessing narcotics.[128] It is clear that entry into the premises without a warrant under such circumstances would be "unreasonable" under American precedents,[129] and even if a warrant authorized search of the hotel, search of its occupants would be unreasonable unless they were named in the warrant.[130] Whether the Canadian courts will reach a similar conclusion under the new Charter provision is less sure.

Certainly, careful scrutiny will be given to writs of assistance, general search warrants which can be obtained by designated officers of the RCMP and certain other federal agents charged with the enforcement of the Customs Act,[131] Excise Act,[132] Narcotic Control Act,[133] and Food and Drugs Act.[134] One of the primary reasons for the American fourth amendment was colonial opposition to writs of assistance, particularly those used to enforce customs laws.[135] In Canada, writs of assistance authorize the holders to enter homes whenever they have reasonable belief that a search will reveal evidence of drugs, customs violations, or excise violations; the writ need not relate to any specific offense, and it continues to be in force throughout the career of the officer to whom it is issued.[136] It is difficult to imagine how breaking into a home without prior judicial approval in the absence of exigency by an officer who holds a writ issued years earlier could be held to be

---

126.   See R. SALHANY, supra note 49, at 45-56. See generally Gibson, Illegally Obtained Evidence, 31 U. TOR. FAC. L. REV. 23 (1973); Spiotto, The Search and Seizure Problem—Two Approaches: The Canadian Tort Remedy and the U.S. Exclusionary Rule, 1 J. POLICE SCI. AND AD. 36 (1973).

127.   Borovoy, The Powers of the Police and the Freedoms of the Citizen, in THE PRACTICE OF FREEDOM 425 (1979).

128.   REPORT OF THE ROYAL COMMISSION ON THE CONDUCT OF POLICE FORCES AT FORT ERIE ON THE 11TH OF MAY, 1974 (1975); Borovoy, supra note 127, at 425.

129.   Agnello v. United States, 269 U.S. 20 (1925).

130.   Ybarra v. Illinois, 444 U.S. 85 (1979).

131.   Customs Act, CAN. REV. STAT., C-58, § 139 (1952).

132.   Excise Act, CAN. REV. STAT. C-99, §§ 78, 79 (1952).

133.   Narcotic Control Act, Can. Stat. C-35, § 10(3) (1960-61).

134.   Food and Drug Act, Can. Stat. C-38 (1952-53) amended by Can Stat. C-37, § 36(3) (1960-61).

135.   Katz, supra note 124, at 110, 125.

136.   R. SALHANY, supra note 49, at 56. See generally Katz, supra note 125, at 124; Parker, The Extraordinary Power to Search and Seize and the Writ of Assistance, 1 U. BRIT. COLUM. L. REV. 688 (1963); Trasewick, Search Warrants and Writs of Assistance, 5 CRIM. L.Q. 341 (1963); Comment, Writs of Assitance in Canada, 9 ALBERTA L. REV. 386 (1971).

"reasonable," even if the officer reasonably believes contraband will be found.[137]

III

THE EXCLUSIONARY RULE

The power granted to courts to enforce the guaranteed rights may be the most important provision of the Charter:

24. (1) Anyone whose rights or freedoms, as guaranteed by this Charter, have been infringed or denied may apply to a court of competent jurisdiction to obtain such remedy as the court considers appropriate and just in the circumstances.

(2) When, in proceedings under subsection (1), a court concludes that evidence was obtained in a manner that infringed or denied any rights or freedoms guaranteed by this Charter, the evidence shall be excluded if it is established that, having regard to all the circumstances, the admission of it in the proceedings would bring the administration of justice into disrepute.[138]

The provision responds to those who have urged that the most important problem in the protection of civil liberties is not the existence of generally accepted rights, but the existence of adequate remedies for their violation.[139]

The first subsection simply authorizes application to a court of competent jurisdiction and grants discretion to the court to provide an "appropriate and just" remedy under the circumstances. It is unclear which courts are "courts of competent jurisdiction." Furthermore, it is difficult to determine the meaning of an "appropriate remedy" as applied to criminal proceedings. Presumably, the authority to issue an extraordinary writ or an injunction might be appropriate in certain cases. It has been suggested that granting an acquittal or a new trial might

---

137. Two government officials, the Acting Minister of Justice, Mr. Kaplan, and the Senior Counsel, Public Law, Mr. Jordan, recognized that writs of assistance as they have been used in the past may be unreasonable under the provision. 41 JOINT COMMITTEE PROCEEDINGS, *supra* note 16, at 14 (statement of Mr. Kaplan); *id.*, vol. 46, at 108 (statement of Mr. Jordan).

138. Constitution Act, 1982, ch. 1, § 24. The 1978 PROPOSALS provided:

Where no other remedy is available or provided for by law, any individual may, in accordance with the applicable procedure of any court in Canada of competent jurisdiction, request the court to define or enforce any of the individual rights and freedoms declared by this Charter, as they extend or apply to him or her, by means of a declaration of the court or by means of an injunction or similar relief, accordingly as the circumstances require.

1978 PROPOSALS, *supra* note 16, § 24. The 1979 FEDERAL PROPOSALS provided that "where no other effective recourse or remedy exists, courts empowered to grant such relief or remedy for a violation of *Charter* rights as may be deemed appropriate and just in the cicumstances[sic]." Gibson, *supra* note 10, at 385. The 1980 PROPOSALS rejected such an approach: "No provision of this Charter, other than section 13, affects the laws respecting the admissibility of evidence in any proceeding or the authority of Parliament or a legislature to make laws in relation thereto." 1980 PROPOSALS, *supra* note 19, § 26. The explanatory note indicated that the section "would make it clear that no provision of the Charter other than the sections respecting self-incrimination (section 13) would affect existing or future laws respecting the admissibility of evidence." *Id.* at 24. Opposition to proposed § 26, voiced by the Canadian Bar Association, the Chief Commissioner of the Canadian Human Rights Commission, and others persuaded the government to drop the section. 36 JOINT COMMITTEE PROCEEDINGS, *supra* note 16, at 19 (1981). Assertions of the need for remedies for breach of Charter rights by the Canadian Civil Liberties Association, the Canadian Jewish Congress, and others persuaded the government to propose § 24(1). *Id.* The second clause, the exclusionary rule, was proposed later. As originally drafted, it provided that "evidence *may* be excluded . . . ." The government agreed to substitute "shall" for "may," and the provision was approved by the Committee in its present form. *Id.*, vol. 48, at 120-21 (1981) (emphasis added).

139. Mewitt, *Entrenching the Enforcement of Rights*, 23 CRIM. L. Q. 129, 129 (1981).

be the appropriate remedies to enforce rights in some circumstances.[140]

The most surprising innovation is the inclusion of a narrow exclusionary rule when only a year earlier the idea apparently had been rejected.[141] The Canadian Supreme Court decisions in *The Queen v. Wray*,[142] permitting the admission of a murder weapon found as a result of an involuntary confession, and *Hogan v. The Queen*,[143] in which breathalyzer test results obtained in violation of the defendant's right to the assistance of counsel were admitted, had effectively rejected the concept of a rule excluding evidence obtained illegally. The obvious purpose of section 24(2) is to introduce the concept of excluding tainted evidence in the limited circumstances where the admission of the evidence "would bring the administration of justice into disrepute." The provision clearly does not go as far as the American rule, which automatically excludes evidence obtained unlawfully, no matter how "mild," "technical," or "inadvertent" the police conduct.[144] Nor would exclusion hinge solely upon the "good faith" of the officials who violated the Charter[145] or on the "substantiality" of the violation,[146] although these might constitute factors relevant to the issue of the effect of admission on the reputation of the system for the administration of justice. Instead, the Charter provision focuses on the effect of the admission of the evidence upon the process of justice. The approach is one of ensuring the "imperative of judicial integrity."[147]

The test of whether admission of evidence would "bring the administration of justice into disrepute" is the same as that recommended by the 1977 Report of the Law Reform Commission. The Commission proposed that:

> [I]n determining whether evidence should be excluded under this section, all the circumstances surrounding the proceedings and the manner in which the evidence was obtained shall be considered, including the extent to which human dignity and social values were breached in obtaining the evidence, the seriousness of the case, the importance of the evidence, whether any harm to an accused or others was inflicted willfully or not, and whether there were circumstances justifying the action, such as a situation of urgency requiring action to prevent the destruction or loss of evidence.[148]

The Commission made it clear that its intent was to protect the integrity of the

---

140. Gibson, *supra* note 10, at 384. It was apparently understood within the Joint Committee that a court would clearly have jurisdiction to award compensation. 48 JOINT COMMITTEE PROCEEDINGS, *supra* note 16, at 121.

141. *See supra* note 138.

142. The Queen v. Wray, 11 D.L.R.3d 673 (Can. 1970).

143. Hogan v. The Queen, 48 D.L.R.3d 427 (Can. 1974).

144. *See, e.g.,* Whitely v. Warden, 401 U.S. 560 (1971); Spinelli v. United States, 393 U.S. 410 (1969). *See generally* Kamisar, *A Defense of the Exclusionary Rule,* 15 CRIM. L. BULL. 5 (1979). The United Kingdom has recently rejected such an automatic rule of exclusion. Report of the *Royal Commission on Criminal Procedure* 112-18 (1981). Some witnesses proposed an automatic rule of exclusion. *See, e.g.,* 22 JOINT COMMITTEE PROCEEDINGS, *supra* note 16, at 108 (1980). *Cf. id.* vol. 39, at 57 (1981).

145. *Cf.* Stone v. Powell, 428 U.S. 465, 499 (1976)(Burger, J., concurring); United States v. Williams, 622 F.2d 830 (5th Cir. 1980), *cert. denied,* 449 U.S. 1127 (1981).

146. Proposals for using "substantiality" of the violation as the criterion for exclusion have been proposed as a rule that would permit the balancing of several factors such as the extent of the deviation from the law; the good faith of the official; the impact on deterrence if the evidence was excluded or admitted. A MODEL CODE OF PRE-ARRAIGNMENT PROCEDURE, § 290.2 (1975).

147. *See* Mapp v. Ohio, 367 U.S. 643, 659 (1961). *But see* Stone v. Powell, 428 U.S. 465 (1976)(the imperative of judicial integrity has limited force as justification for the exclusion of highly probative evidence).

148. LAW REFORM COMMISSION OF CANADA, REPORT ON EVIDENCE, tit. IV, pt. I, § 15, at 22 (1977).

adjudicative process, not to control the police, and that it rejected an absolute exclusionary rule. Instead, it sought to give judges the right in "exceptional cases" to exclude evidence unfairly obtained.[149]

It seems unlikely that there will be many instances in which the "fruit of the poison tree doctrine"[150] will be applied, or where technical or inadvertent violations will result in exclusion. The obvious difficulty of balancing factors that are different in kind, and the judicial reluctance to exclude reliable evidence reflected in the existing case law, suggest that the operation of section 24(2) may not be significantly different from the discretion exercised in the courts of the United Kingdom.[151] It would not be surprising if exclusion were limited to cases of willful, gross violations.[152] The exclusion of evidence may occur infrequently, particularly in serious cases, but it may nevertheless occur more often than under a rule that excludes only evidence "the admissibility of which is tenuous and whose probative force in relation to the main issue before the Court is trifling."[153] The importance of the provision is indicated by the fact that neither Parliament nor provincial legislatures can opt out of its operation.[154]

IV

THE SUBSTANCE OF THE CONSTITUTIONAL PROTECTIONS

A.   Areas Left Unprotected

It is difficult to predict the degree to which the constitutional protections afforded by the Charter to persons accused of crime will provide realistic and significant safeguards against the dangers of government abuse of power. The Charter obviously provides important protections, but it simultaneously ignores some contemporary, crucial issues concerning the appropriate balance between the state and the individual in criminal prosecutions.

Obviously, no charter of rights should attempt to deal with all issues of criminal procedure, but the observer is struck by the high degree to which specific

---

149.   *Id.* at 61-62. The concept also is responsive to the position tersely stated by the President of the Vancouver People's Law School Society, Mrs. Diana Davidson: "It is particularly important that we not supply the police with a document which in effect says that they may violate the human rights with impunity." 32 JOINT COMMITTEE PROCEEDINGS, *supra* note 16, at 13.

150.   The doctrine of "fruit of the poisonous tree" was first enunciated in Silverthorne Lumber Co. v. United States, 251 U.S. 385, 392 (1920): "The essence of a provision forbidding the acquisition of evidence in a certain way is that not merely evidence so acquired shall not be used before the Court but that it shall not be used at all." The phrase was first used to describe the doctrine in Nardone v. United States, 308 U.S. 338 (1939).

151.   *See* Report of the *Royal Commission on Criminal Procedure, supra* note 144, at 63-64, 112-17 (1981).

152.   *See* A MODEL CODE OF PRE-ARRAIGNMENT PROCEDURE § 290.2(3) (1975): "A violation shall in all cases be substantial if it was gross, willful and prejudicial to the accused." It has been argued that § 8 prohibits unreasonable searches by private persons as well as by police. D. MCDONALD, *supra* note 37, at 45. If so, it is doubtful if many such seizures should warrant exclusion under the test of § 24(2).

153.   The Queen v. Wray, 11 D.L.R.3d 673, 689-90 (Can. 1970). The Charter might also form a "standard against which government performance may be evaluated in Parliament, the press and in political discussion generally," making government "more sensitive to civil libertarian values in framing new law and administering existing laws." P. HOGG, *supra* note 12, at 443. It also performs an educational value of inculcating into each new generation a perception of preferred values.

154.   Constitution Act, 1982, ch. 1, § 33.

protections are given to the citizen in areas where the danger of abuse by the state is relatively slight, such as the right to be presumed innnocent, the right to have a hearing before an impartial tribunal, the right to be tried within a reasonable time, the limited protection provided against double jeopardy, and protection against ex post facto laws. These are important rights, and deserve protection, but they are unlikely to be the focal point of confrontation between the individual and the state in the twenty-first century. Like the rights to confrontation and compulsory process, which are surprisingly absent from the Charter,[155] these rights are the stuff of an earlier history which fortunately are now accepted as fundamental. In a nation with a common law tradition, these rights would probably be respected even if not reflected in a written document. They are not likely to be regarded as the primary areas where government abuse of power is most likely to occur.

In contrast, in areas where the danger of government abuse is great, the constitution provides few protections. The document is silent on matters such as the rights of a recalcitrant suspect from whom the police are attempting to extract a confession and the rights of a suspect when asked to participate in pretrial identification procedures. Consider the protection against abuse needed by an indigent member of a minority group who is subjected to an incommunicado interrogation without access to counsel, while a mafia chieftain stands no such risk because of his financial ability to obtain counsel to protect himself. It is unclear whether the constitution makes provision for the rights of an individual to be free from electronic surveillance. The protection of papers from unreasonable search and seizure is less meaningful if one's privacy can be invaded by bugs and wiretaps.[156]

It is nice to know, too, that a person will be informed without unreasonable delay of the offense with which he is charged, and tried within a reasonable time. But such a right is unhelpful if the counsel provided for him by legal aid is unable to locate the witnesses he seeks, and the government is not prepared before trial to assist him by granting him access to favorable evidence. It is particularly discouraging to realize that the citizen's right to counsel at trial may depend upon the financial capacity of the province in which he resides rather than upon the Constitution of Canada.

The effect of the Constitution in these areas will depend, in part, on the interpretation of various provisions. Much will depend upon the manner in which the Supreme Court of Canada interprets section 7 of the Charter, providing that no one will be deprived of the right to liberty except in accordance with the principles of fundamental justice. This provision could be interpreted to assure that the protections accorded Canadians in criminal prosecutions are those that a society of the 1980's thinks are fundamental, not those which were the source of controversy two centuries ago. Thus, rights such as the right to counsel at trial might be protected as required by the "principles of fundamental justice." A broad interpretation of the protection against unreasonable search and seizure could provide protection for the privacy needs of our century as well as for the privacy needs that existed in an era in which telephones, parabolic microphones, and pen registers

---

155. A proposal to include such protections was defeated. 47 JOINT COMMITTEE PROCEEDINGS, *supra* note 16, at 69, 73.

156. Protection may be provided by § 8 of the Charter. *See supra* note 111.

were unknown. On the other hand, a narrow interpretation of the exclusionary rule could reduce the Charter to a noble statement of principles to which all pay lip service, but to which no court turns when the going gets rough.[157]

B.   The Charter As a Consensus

A foreign observer can hope that the courts will approach the Charter with more enthusiasm for civil liberties than has been evidenced in decisions interpreting the Bill of Rights.[158] Whether the courts will take this approach may depend in part on their perception of the inherent legitimacy of the document, that is, the extent to which it reflects a national consensus concerning basic values as distinguished from a political compromise effected by the party in power to accomplish other objectives.[159]

Unfortunately, the record is not clear on the extent to which the documents genuinely reflect a popular will to limit legislative and executive power in order to protect certain rights. The polls reported that the people wanted a charter; the polls were less clear, however, about whether the people knew what they were and were not receiving. There is a difference between a bill of rights hammered out in a constitutional convention or adopted after proposals are debated in state or provincial legislatures over a period of years, and a bill of rights drafted by the party in power in Parliament.

This difference is highlighted when the party in power presents a reasonably narrow statement of rights in one year, and is prepared to alter them significantly the following year, as occurred in Canada. In 1980, the Charter would have provided protection against searches and seizures, detentions, and denial of bail only when they were not carried out "on grounds, and in accordance with procedures established by law."[160] In 1981, the provisions were changed so that, even if authorized by law, a search and seizure is impermissible if "unreasonable";[161] a detention must not be "arbitrary";[162] and reasonable bail cannot be denied

---

157. *Cf.* Laskin, *supra* note 19, at 343-44.

158. Professor Tarnopolsky has admirably described the narrow interpretation of the last two decades. *See* sources cited *supra* note 10.

159. It seems reasonably clear that the 1980 PROPOSALS were subject to such criticism. The Minister of Justice stated:

> We were on the horns of a dilemma when we started and now we want to secure the support of as many provinces as possible. We have introduced a bill of rights to be entrenched in the constitution that was meeting a lot of the objection from the Ministers during the meeting I had with them during the summer.
>
> Despite a very conciliatory attitude on our part, the provinces who were opposed in the summer to the whole process did not offer any support to the Bill of Rights whatever, after we came in public, even if they had some great interest in the summer to have the Charter of Rights inscribed. I do think that the ones who were the most opposed in principle, I guess, it was Manitoba, Mr. Lyons who always said he did not want at all the Bill of Rights in the constitution entrenched.
>
> But most of the other provinces had kind of a sympathy to it and did not want to oppose it squarely.
>
> We introduced that watered down Bill of Rights in October but that did not change the attitude of those who were opposing.

37 JOINT COMMITTEE PROCEEDINGS, *supra* note 16, at 25-26 (1980); *see also id.* vol. 50, at 51, 70 (1981).

160. 1980 PROPOSALS, *supra* note 19, §§ 8, 9, 11(d).

161. Constitution Act, 1982, ch.1, § 8.

162. *Id.* § 9.

without "just cause."[163] In 1981, it was concluded that a person charged with an offense should not be compelled to be a witness in proceedings against him in respect to that offense;[164] that an accused has a right to be informed of his right to counsel;[165] and that an accused has a right to a jury trial where the maximum punishment for the offense is five years or more.[166] Such rights were apparently not regarded as fundamental a year earlier since they were not included in the proposals. In 1980, the proposals made it clear that no provision of the Charter would affect existing or future laws respecting the admissibility of evidence;[167] yet in the next year the Charter included an exclusionary rule.[168] Authority to opt out is given by the 1982 Charter, where a year earlier no similar provision was included in the document.[169] The legitimacy of the document as a fundamental expression of a social contract is not improved by the changes in "fundamental" rights, by recognition that several of the proposals in 1980 reflect retreats from proposals previously made, nor by charges that the process of enactment was "tainted by unilateralism."[170]

Understandably, the final draft of the Charter benefitted from extensive Parliamentary hearings in 1980 and 1981[171] and from wide public discussion. Some of the provisions that finally emerged, such as the protection from unreasonable searches and seizures, while not present in the same form in the 1980 proposals, had been proposed at least as early as 1969.[172] Few observers on the American side of the border would deny that the "Legal Rights" provisions of the 1982 Charter are a significant improvement over the 1980 Proposals. It can presumably be argued that the 1980 draft was a "law and order" document that retreated, for temporary political reasons, from earlier understandings concerning the degree to which the rights of the citizen deserved protection.[173] The 1981 document more accurately reflects the growing consensus concerning the proper balance between citizens and the state, a balance reflected in the proposals considered before 1980.

In addition to playing the role of arbiter of federalism, the Supreme Court of Canada has been presented with the challenge of assuming the constitutional role of protector of the rights of the citizenry. It should welcome this opportunity. The Charter itself is a significant step forward. As confidence in a written charter of rights develops, so may the desire to expand the constitutional protection of individual rights.

---

163. *Id.* § 11(e).

164. *Id.* § 11(c).

165. *Id.* § 10(b).

166. *Id.* § 11(f).

167. 1980 PROPOSALS, *supra* note 19, at § 26. An exception was made for the protection against self-incrimination in § 13.

168. Constitution Act, 1982, ch. 1, § 24(2).

169. *Compare id.* § 33 *with* 1980 PROPOSALS, *supra* note 19.

170. Laskin, *supra* note 19, at 347.

171. The Joint Committee, composed of 10 members from the Senate and 15 from the House of Commons, held 106 meetings on 56 sitting days for a total of 267 sitting hours, considering submissions from 914 individuals and 294 groups. 57 JOINT COMMITTEE PROCEEDINGS, *supra* note 16, at 5 (1981).

172. *See* 1969 PROPOSALS, *supra* note 22, at 52.

173. *See supra* note 159.

THE CANADIAN CONSTITUTIONAL
AMENDMENT PROCESS

STEPHEN A. SCOTT*

PROLOGUE

No one, as recently as two years ago, could have foreseen, even in general out-
line, the nature of the major Canadian constitutional reform now but ten days old.
One cannot but marvel at the hazards and vicissitudes which attend constitution-
making. Indeed, I note, with much relief, that, on August 20, 1787, the American
Constitutional Convention at Philadelphia, by a vote of eight states to three,
defeated a proposal to empower the "[l]egislature of the United States" to "make
sumptuary laws."[1] I count it my great good fortune that Congress cannot restrain
the otherwise limitless bounds of your hospitality. Mr. Mason of Virginia, indeed,
denounced as "a vulgar error" the objection that sumptuary laws "were contrary
to nature;" whilst Mr. Elseworth [sic] of Connecticut presciently replied that "[t]he
best remedy is to enforce taxes and debts. As far as the regulation of eating &
drinking can be reasonable, it is provided for in the power of taxation."[2]
Governeur [sic] Morris of Pennsylvania warned that "sump. laws were calculated
to continue great landed estates for ever in the same families—If men had no
temptation to dispose of their money they would not sell their estates."[3] North
Carolina, I am pleased to note, was amongst the states opposed to federal sumptuary laws.

While it would be churlish even to hint at liquidation of your endowments in
the interests of conviviality, I am sure that, as Mr. Ellsworth would doubtless have
done, we will all see in President Reagan's tax reductions the direction of American public policy, and, as good citizens, be moved accordingly.

I

INTRODUCTION

On April 17, 1982, Canada became, in terms of its own internal law, a sovereign state legally independent of the United Kingdom.[4] Legal reality was brought

---

* Of the Bar of the Province of Quebec and the Faculty of Law, McGill University. (The author,
critical of inaccuracies in the American style of citation, has requested specific identification of United
Kingdom statutes and statutes of Great Britain. Other deviations from American style are likewise used at
the author's request.)

1. 2 RECORDS OF THE FEDERAL CONVENTION OF 1787, at 337, 344 (M. Farrand 2d ed. 1937).

2. *Id.* at 344.

3. *Id.* at 351.

4. Canada Act 1982, 1982 ch. 11 (U.K.), §§ 1 and 2. By its terms, section 2 operates from the coming
into force of the Constitution Act, 1982 (which itself is Schedule B to the Canada Act 1982). Pursuant to
section 58 thereof, the Constitution Act 1982 was (subject to section 59) brought into force by proclamation
of Her Majesty the Queen at Ottawa in a mid-morning ceremony on that date. *See infra* note 21

into accord with an internationally-recognized political reality of at least fifty years' standing. The intervening decades had been marked by repeated, and unsuccessful, attempts[5] within Canada to devise legal processes to which the residual sovereignty of the United Kingdom Parliament might be transferred: in other words, to define a new sovereign or constituent authority for Canada.

Rehearsal of the history of these attempts—even a very summary rehearsal— would carry us much too far afield. Suffice it to begin at a rather recent date, and to recall that, on October 2, 1980, the Government of Canada presented to the House of Commons of Canada a draft constitutional text[6] having more or less the scope of (though very different provisions from) the reform which recently became law. The October 1980 text was proposed as the terms of a joint address by both Houses of the federal parliament to the Sovereign, praying for the enactment by the United Kingdom Parliament of a statute which would confer upon Canada legal independence with a series of constitutional amending processes and a Canadian Charter of Rights and Freedoms "entrenched" against both the federal parliament and the provincial legislatures. It was intended to proceed to Westminster without the consent of the provincial legislatures or governments.

This scheme immediately encountered opposition and resistance—in most cases, opposition and resistance of the most sustained and bitter character—from the opposition parties (the Progressive Conservatives especially) in the federal parliament, and from eight of the ten provincial governments: all, that is, save Ontario and New Brunswick.

A special Joint Committee of the Senate and the House of Commons of Canada was appointed to consider the draft. Its report,[7] tabled in the House of Commons on February 13, 1981, proposed a variety of changes. Although various compromises had succeeded in securing the (rather unenthusiastic) concurrence of the federal New Democratic Party, and of most of its M.P.'s, the revised draft was met with nearly the same obstruction in the House as its predecessor, and no less opposition from the provinces. Only on April 8, 1981—with no end to the debate in sight—was all-party agreement on procedure announced in the House of Commons.[8] Under this agreement a special order was unanimously adopted, fixing a timetable for the disposition of all amendments to the text reported from the Committee, and, ultimately, for the disposition of the final text as it might be amended. This agreement, however, committed the government to await the judgment of the Supreme Court of Canada on pending appeals from decisions of the Manitoba, the Newfoundland, and the Quebec Courts of Appeal on questions referred to them by the governments of these provinces, both as to the constitutional propriety and the

---

5. *See, e.g.,* the accounts in P. GÉRIN-LAJOIE, CONSTITUTIONAL AMENDMENT IN CANADA (1950), and *Editor's Diary,* introducing a symposium in 12 McGILL L.J. 337 (1966-67).

6. *Proposed Resolution for a Joint Address to Her Majesty the Queen respecting the Constitution of Canada* (October 2, 1980), Government of Canada, document number 25005-2-10-80.

7. Canada, House of Commons, VOTES AND PROCEEDINGS, Friday, February 13, 1981, being 32nd Parliament, 1st Session, No. 142, at 1244 ff.

8. Canada, House of Commons, VOTES AND PROCEEDINGS, Wednesday, April 8, 1981, being 32nd Parliament, 1st Session, No. 179, at 1677 ff. *See also* 8 HOUSE OF COMMONS DEBATES 9072 ff. (Apr. 8, 1981).

legal validity or consequences of the course of action upon which the federal Houses had embarked.

The Supreme Court of Canada's majority decision of September 28, 1981,[9] held that, *as a matter of law,* the authority of the United Kingdom Parliament survived intact and unimpaired; that is, it could validly and effectively legislate on the Canadian constitution, either on its own motion or in response to any request of its choosing. But the Court also held that (extra-legal) "conventions" existed rendering constitutionally *improper* a federal parliamentary approach to the Imperial Parliament without a sufficient provincial consensus; and that, whatever the "necessary" consensus might be, the two provinces of Ontario and New Brunswick did not suffice.[10]

Even if it had remained politically possible for federal parliamentary majorities to force the measure as it then stood (with amendments approved by the House of Commons on April 23, 1981,[11] and by the Senate on April 24, 1981[12]) through both Houses of the Canadian Parliament, it was doubtful that the Government of the United Kingdom would (even, perhaps, that it *could*) carry a bill in the terms requested through the Parliament at Westminster.

A negotiated solution became the only alternative. This was achieved on November 5, 1981,[13] the signatories being the governments of Canada and of all provinces save Quebec. The agreed scheme was based largely on an earlier interprovincial agreement of April 16, 1981 (the "April Accord") amongst the eight "opposing" provincial governments. In particular, the federal-provincial agreement of November 5, 1981, introduced the "legislative override" (reflected in section 33 of the Constitution Act, 1982)[14] allowing the Parliament of Canada and the provincial legislatures to override, by express statutory language, most of the guarantees of the Canadian Charter of Rights and Freedoms. It also adopted from the "April Accord" a scheme of constitutional amending formulae which Prime Minister Trudeau had repeatedly denounced as tending to create a "chequerboard Canada." These amending procedures had, and have, almost no resemblance on essential points to the federal proposals which they displaced.

The Minister of Justice of Canada, by notice of motion of November 18, 1981,

---

9. Reference re Amendment of the Constitution of Canada (Nos. 1, 2 & 3) 125 D.L.R.3d 1, 41 (Can. 1981).

10. *Id.* at 103.

11. Canada, House of Commons, VOTES AND PROCEEDINGS, Thursday, April 23, 1981, being 32nd Parliament, 1st Session, No. 187, at 1741 ff.

12. Canada, MINUTES OF PROCEEDINGS OF THE SENATE, Friday, April 24, 1981, being 32nd Parliament, 1st Session, No. 117, at 1150 ff. The proposals, as they then stood, are most conveniently read in a consolidation printed by the Department of Justice of Canada, TEXT OF PROPOSED CONSTITUTIONAL RESOLUTION FILED BY THE DEPUTY ATTORNEY GENERAL OF CANADA WITH THE SUPREME COURT OF CANADA ON APRIL 24, 1981, document number 25005-24-4-81.

13. The (unpublished) document recording the agreement was tabled by the Prime Minister in the House of Commons on November 5, 1981; *see* HOUSE OF COMMONS DEBATES for that date, at 12536 ff., and in particular the Prime Minister's statement.

14. The Constitution Act, 1982, is Schedule B of the Canada Act 1982, 1982 ch. 11, the United Kingdom statute enacted on March 29, 1982, to give effect to the request of the Senate and House of Commons of Canada that the provisions of the Constitution Act, 1982, be enacted. *See* text accompanying notes 21-28 *infra*.

accordingly introduced into the House of Commons a resolution[15] for a joint address to the Sovereign conforming to the federal-provincial agreement. Although changes had been made in order to accommodate positions adopted by the Government of Quebec, it proved impossible to secure the province's agreement to the project. Quebec has remained steadfastly and intransigently opposed to the ultimate Canada Act and has not accepted the issue as settled politically.

On December 2, 1981, the House of Commons of Canada,[16] and, on December 8, 1981, the Senate of Canada[17] adopted the final text of what has now become the Canada Act, 1982—the ultimate exercise of Imperial legislative authority for Canada.

II

"PATRIATION"

[T]he King's Majesty, by and with the Advice and Consent of the Lords Spiritual and Temporal, and Commons of *Great Britain* . . . had, hath, and of Right ought to have, full Power and Authority to make Laws . . . of sufficient Force and Validity to bind the Colonies and People of *America,* Subjects of the Crown of *Great Britain,* in all Cases whatsoever.[18]

He has combined with others to subject us to a jurisdiction foreign to our constitution, and unacknowledged by our laws, giving his Assent to their acts of pretended Legislation: . . . . For . . . declaring themselves invested with Power to legislate for us in all cases whatsoever.[19]

The British Parliament's statutory challenge in the "Declaratory Act" of 1766 drew from the inhabitants of the North American "thirteen colonies" their formal response in the Declaration of Independence ten years later. For them, Imperial legislative supremacy was ended by war: its end was consecrated by treaty[20] in 1783.

On April 17, 1982, Her Majesty Queen Elizabeth II, in a mid-morning ceremony at Ottawa, proclaimed[21] into force the Canada Act 1982[22] (with its sched-

---

15.   The text, standing in the name of the Minister of Justice and dated November 18, 1981, may be found under "Government Notices of Motions" at xiv ff. of the "Notice Paper" appended to Canadian House of Commons ORDER PAPER AND NOTICES, Thursday, November 19, 1981, being 32nd Parliament, 1st Session, No. 259.

16.   Canada, House of Commons, VOTES AND PROCEEDINGS, Wednesday, December 2, 1981, being 32nd Parliament, 1st Session, No. 268, at 4304 ff. The final text, incorporating amendments, appears at 4308 ff., and is separately printed under the title TEXT OF THE RESOLUTION RESPECTING THE CONSTITUTION OF CANADA ADOPTED BY THE HOUSE OF COMMONS ON DECEMBER 2, 1981, document number 25005-2-12-81.

17.   Canada, MINUTES OF PROCEEDINGS OF THE SENATE, Tuesday, December 8, 1981, being 32nd Parliament, 1st Session, No. 162, at 1722 ff. The final text, incorporating amendments, and approved on division, appears at 1759 ff.

18.   An Act for the better securing the Dependency of Her Majesty's Dominions in *America* upon the Crown and Parliament of *Great Britain* (American Colonies Act), 1766, 6 Geo. 3, ch. 12 (G.B.).

The American Colonies Act of 1766 long survived the particular historical circumstances which had induced its passage, standing on the British statute book until its repeal by the Statute Law Revision Act, 1964, 1964 ch. 79 (U.K.), which collectively declared a number of acts to be "obsolete, spent or unnecessary or . . . superseded by other enactments." *Id.* at § 1.

19.   The Declaration of Independence, paras. 15, 24 (U.S. 1776).

20.   Treaty of Versailles, Jan. 20, 1783, 8 Stat. 58, T.I.A.S. No. 103, at 6.

21.   Can. Gaz. Extra No. 20 (April 17, 1982), 116 Can. Gaz. Part I 2927-28 (1982); *see also* Canada Act 1982, 1982 ch. 11 (U.K.).

uled Constitution Act, 1982), to which Her Majesty had assented in the United Kingdom Parliament on March 29, 1982. With effect from the beginning of the day of Proclamation,[23] the overriding legislative sovereignty of the United Kingdom Parliament—declared for the Empire generally in the Colonial Laws Validity Act, 1865,[24] and effectually preserved for Canada by section 7 of the Statute of Westminster, 1931[25]— came to an end for us. The Canada Act 1982,[26] with its Schedule B, the Constitution Act, 1982,[27] substituted for the "Imperial" legislative authority of the United Kingdom Parliament (and for certain existing "domestic" constitutional amendment processes[28] of rather limited scope) the procedures which this paper will examine. These procedures are found in Part V of the Constitution Act, 1982, entitled "Procedure for Amending Constitution of Canada."

---

22. *Id.*

23. Interpretation Act, 1889, 52 & 53 Vict., ch. 63 (U.K.), § 36(2); *see also* Regina v. Logan, [1957] 2 Q.B. 589, 590-91.

As to the operation of section 58 of the Constitution Act, 1982, providing that for most purposes the Act would come into force on a day to be fixed by proclamation of the Queen or the Governor General under the Great Seal of Canada, *see* Interpretation Act, 1889, 52 & 53 Vict., ch. 63 (U.K.), § 37.

24. 28 & 29 Vict., ch. 63 (U.K.). Section 2 of the Act provides:

> Any Colonial Law which is or shall be in any respect repugnant to the Provisions of any Act of Parliament extending to the Colony to which such Law may relate, or repugnant to any Order or Regulation made under the Authority of such Act of Parliament, or having in the Colony the Force and Effect of such Act, shall be read subject to such Act, Order, or Regulation, and shall, to the extent of such Repugnancy, but not otherwise, be and remain absolutely void and inoperative.

Section 1 provides, "An Act of Parliament, or any Provision thereof, shall, in construing this Act, be said to extend to any Colony when it is made applicable to such Colony by the express Words or necessary Intendment of any Act of Parliament . . . ."

25. 22 Geo. 5, ch. 4 (U.K.). Sections 2 and 7(3) of the Statute empowered the Parliament of Canada, within the scope of its legislative authority, to enact laws repugnant to Imperial legislation extending to Canada. (Sections 7(2) and 7(3) of the Statute placed the provincial legislatures in the same position.)

Conversely, section 4 of the same Statute barred extension "to a Dominion" (defined by section 1 to include Canada) of any future United Kingdom statute "unless it is expressly declared in that Act that that Dominion has requested, and consented to, the enactment thereof."

The whole Statute, however, was subject to section 7(1), which provided that "[n]othing in this Act shall be deemed to apply to the repeal, amendment or alteration of the British North America Acts, 1867 to 1930, or any order, rule or regulation made thereunder." This clause effectively saved an unrestricted power to exercise lawmaking authority in Canada. It left Canadian constituent power in the hands of the United Kingdom Parliament. *See generally* Reference re Amendment of the Constitution of Canada (Nos. 1, 2 & 3), 125 D.L.R. 3d 1 (Can. 1981); Scott, Opinion Submitted to the Foreign Affairs Committee of the House of Commons of the United Kingdom on the Role of the United Kingdom Parliament in Relation to the [BNA] Acts, *reprinted in* 26 McGILL L.J. 614, 615-18 (1981).

26. 1982, ch. 11 (U.K.), §§ 1-2.

27. §§ 52, 53(1) and Schedule Items 1, 17, 22. Together, these provisions repeal sections 4 and 7(1) of the Statute of Westminster, 1931, 22 Geo. 5, ch. 4 (U.K.) (*see supra* note 25), as well as sections 91.1 and 92.1 of the British North America Act, 1867, 30 & 31 Vict., ch. 3 (U.K.), as amended by the British North America (No. 2) Act, 1949, 12, 13 & 14 Geo. 6, ch. 81 (U.K.). (The Schedule to the Constitution Act, 1982, also renames the British North America Act, 1867, as amended by the 1982 Act's Schedule, Item 1, the "Constitution Act, 1867." Hereinafter, the original name will be used unless the 1867 Act is being alluded to in its current form.)

28. British North America (No. 2) Act, 1949, 12, 13 & 14 Geo. 6, ch. 81 (U.K.) (amending §§ 91.1 and 92.1 of the British North America Act, 1867, 30 & 31 Vict., ch. 3 (U.K.)).

III

"THE CONSTITUTION OF CANADA" AND "THE CONSTITUTION OF THE PROVINCE"

Anglo-Canadian public law is deeply legitimist, placing a great weight on strict legal continuity. Law may be made according to law, and not otherwise: that is, by the persons, and according to the processes, prescribed by law. Failure to comply with conditions of manner and form of lawmaking, if these be not merely directory, results in the radical nullity of the purported enactment. This approach probably results from the notion that lawmaking power—indeed public authority generally—is to be derived from the law itself, rather than from the people. The Constitution Act, 1982, represents no departure from this legitimist tradition.

Part V of the Constitution Act, 1982, is entitled "Procedure for Amending Constitution of Canada." Section 52(3) of the Constitution Act, 1982 (not found in Part V at all, but rather in "Part VII General"), imposes a condition upon the validity of amendments by providing that "[a]mendments to the Constitution of Canada shall be made only in accordance with the authority contained in the Constitution of Canada." This, in a sense, is a corollary of section 52(1), which provides that "[t]he Constitution of Canada is the supreme law of Canada, and any law that is inconsistent with the provisions of the Constitution is, to the extent of the inconsistency, of no force or effect."

The terms "Constitution of Canada" and "constitution of the province" appear in the various formulae of Part V. If a proposed enactment would amend the one or the other "constitution," section 52(3) requires that its passage must be accomplished in virtue of "the Constitution of Canada." While this is, of course, true of the making of *all* laws, it is clear from the language of section 52(3) and Part V that, in most if not all cases, recourse to the procedures of Part V is necessary where an amendment to either "the Constitution of Canada" or "the constitution of the province" is involved.

Thus, definition of these two classes of amendment is pertinent to the identification of the subject-matter to which the various procedures of Part V are addressed, and therefore to the identification of the cases where a given procedure must be employed.

At the same time, the term "Constitution of Canada" is broader than merely "Part V of the Constitution Act, 1982." Section 52(3) leaves open the possibility that pre-existing rules of law admittedly forming part of the "Constitution of Canada" may be altered by processes outside the confines of Part V; and this is so, even though that Part gives the general appearance of an exhaustive scheme.[29]

---

29. For example, it may be that despite the provisions of sections 42(1)(e) and 43 of the Constitution Act, 1982, section 3 of the Constitution Act, 1871, retains at least a limited operation:

> The Parliament of Canada may from time to time, with the consent of the Legislature of any Province of the said Dominion, increase, diminish, or otherwise alter the limits of such Province, upon such terms and conditions as may be agreed to by the said Legislature, and may, with the like consent, make provision respecting the effect and operation of any such increase or diminution or alteration of territory in relation to any Province affected thereby.

What, then, is "the Constitution of Canada"? Section 52(2) (with which, for the sake of convenience, is reproduced section 53(1)) gives only partial guidance:

> (2) The Constitution of Canada includes
>   (a) the *Canada Act, 1982*, including this Act;
>   (b) the Acts and orders referred to in the schedule; and
>   (c) any amendment to any Act or order referred to in paragraph (a) or (b).
> 53. (1) The enactments referred to in Column I of the schedule are hereby repealed or amended to the extent indicated in Column II thereof and, unless repealed, shall continue as law in Canada under the names set out in Column III thereof.

Section 52(2) gives only partial guidance because, by employing the term "includes" in preference to the word "means," the definition does not purport to be exhaustive.

The list in the schedule to the Constitution Act, 1982, begins with The British North America Act, 1867, and continues with various direct and other amendments made by federal[30] and Imperial statutes. The Statute of Westminster, 1931, appears in the list, as do the Imperial Orders-in-Council and federal statutes creating new provinces. Many statutory enactments *not* enumerated in the schedule, and many common-law rules,[31] are, however, inherently quite as "constitutional" in nature as those instruments which *are* so enumerated.

For example, much of the "organic" law dealing with the constitution and structure of the federal parliament is to be found on the federal statute book.[32] Are these enactments parts of the "Constitution of Canada"? Consider, for instance, the existing rules making a seat in any house of a provincial legislature incompatible with a seat in the House of Commons. Putting aside provincial statutory provisions, few lawyers could, from memory, venture to say with confidence where these rules are to be found, just as few could indicate the source of the rule making a seat in the Senate of Canada incompatible with a seat in the House of Commons. The answer, of course, is that the former are to be found in the House of Commons Act,[33] whilst the latter is in the Act of 1867.[34] They seem equally "constitutional" in their nature; and, since 1949, they would seem to have stood on an equal footing as regards Parliament's power to amend them unilaterally.[35] Yet

---

Constitution Act, 1871, 34 & 35 Vict., ch. 28 (U.K.), § 3 (originally the British North America Act, 1871; renamed in Item 5 of the Schedule to the Constitution Act, 1982).

Section 42(1)(e) provides that an amendment to the Constitution of Canada extending existing provinces to the territories must be made in accordance with the "general procedure" of section 38(1). *See infra* Part V.

Section 43 furnishes a "special arrangements" procedure whereby certain amendments pertaining to one or more, but not all, provinces may be made. *See also infra* Part VII.

30. In virtue of section 91.1 of the Constitution Act, 1867, as amended (*see supra* note 27), and the Constitution Act, 1871, as amended (*see supra* note 29).

31. In Reference re Amendment of the Constitution of Canada Act (Nos. 1, 2 & 3), 125 D.L.R.3d 1 (Can. 1981), the majority held that "part of the Constitution of Canada consists of the rules of the common law." *Id.* at 81. Examples follow in their Lordships' reasons. *Id.* at 82.

32. *See, e.g.,* House of Commons Act, CAN. REV. STAT., ch. H-9 (1970); Senate and House of Commons Act, CAN. REV. STAT., ch. S-8 (1970); Speaker of the House of Commons Act, CAN. REV. STAT., ch. S-13 (1970); Speaker of the Senate Act, CAN. REV. STAT., ch. S-14 (1970).

33. CAN. REV. STAT., ch. H-9, §§ 2-5 (1970).

34. British North America Act, 1867, 30 & 31 Vict., ch. 3 (U.K.), § 39.

35. *See* British North America (No. 2) Act, 1949, 12, 13 & 14 Geo. 6, ch. 81 (U.K.), §§ 1-2; Constitution Act, 1982, 1982 ch. 11 (U.K.), Sch. B § 44.

the relevant provisions of the House of Commons Act long antedate Parliament's acquisition in 1949 of nominate powers to amend parts of the "Constitution of Canada."[36] It was doubtless (and, in my view, quite correctly) assumed that Parliament, from the birth of the federation in 1867, had legislative authority to enact such provisions, and this probably in virtue of its "residuary" authority (although section 41 of the 1867 Act[37] *may* confer a relevant power). Indeed, in upholding the constitutional validity of the federal Official Languages Act,[38] Chief Justice Laskin, speaking for the Supreme Court of Canada, held as follows in *Jones v. Attorney-General of Canada*:

> Apart from the effect of s. 133 and s. 91(1), to be considered later in these reasons, I am in no doubt that it was open to the Parliament of Canada to enact the *Official Languages Act* (limited as it is to the purposes of the Parliament and Government of Canada and to the institutions of that Parliament and Government) as being a law "for the peace, order and good Government of Canada in relation to [a matter] not coming within the Classes of Subjects . . . assigned exclusively to the Legislatures of the Provinces". The quoted words are in the opening paragraph of s. 91 of the *British North America Act, 1867;* and, in relying on them as constitutional support for the *Official Languages Act,* I do so on the basis of the purely residuary character of the legislative power thereby conferred. No authority need be cited for the exclusive power of the Parliament of Canada to legislate in relation to the operation and administration of the institutions and agencies of the Parliament and Government of Canada. Those institutions and agencies are clearly beyond provincial reach.[39]

Now, under section 52(2) of the Constitution Act, 1982, the rule making a seat in the Senate incompatible with a seat in the House of Commons is part of the "Constitution of Canada" since it is found in the Act of 1867, one of the enactments enumerated in the schedule. By contrast, the status of the federal statutory incompatibility of membership in a provincial legislative body with membership in the Commons of Canada cannot be determined with the same certainty.

Probably, in this particular instance, it does not much matter. For, if the relevant provisions of the House of Commons Act *do* form part of the "Constitution of Canada," they can be altered by simple federal statute in virtue of section 44 of the Constitution Act, 1982, and, possibly, also in virtue of the "residuary power" of Parliament. If they do *not* form part of the "Constitution of Canada," the federal "residuary" legislative power seems certainly available.

However, a decision that a proposed enactment would, or would not, if it became law, amend "the Constitution of Canada" (or "the constitution of the province") would, in some cases, have important consequences. Some rules of law dealing with the executive government, or the legislative institutions, of Canada or of a province may concern (for example) "the office of the Queen, the Governor General and the Lieutenant Governor of a province." If they form part of the "Constitution of Canada," these will, under section 41(a), be amendable only through a proclamation issued by the Governor General of Canada with the authorization of resolutions of the Senate and House of Commons (or of the Com-

---

36. *See* British North America (No. 2) Act, 1949, 12, 13 & 14 Geo. 6, ch. 81 (U.K.) (adding a sweeping new section 91.1 to the 1867 Act).

37. *See* Constitution Act, 1867, 30 & 31 Vict., ch. 3 (U.K.), § 41.

38. CAN. REV. STAT., ch. O-2 (1970).

39. Jones v. Attorney-Gen. of Canada, 45 D.L.R.3d 583, 588-89 (Can. 1981).

mons alone under section 47(1)) and of the legislative assembly of *every* province. The common law, "received English" statute law, and "Imperial" statute law on the succession to the Crown afford a good illustrative example. If they are part of the "Constitution of Canada," section 41(a) appears to apply. Otherwise, the federal "residuary" power appears to be available, enabling *unilateral* legislation.

Again, if section 4 of the Senate and House of Commons Act[40] (enacted under the authority of what is now[41] section 18 of the Constitution Act, 1867) governing the privileges, immunities, and powers of the Senate and House of Commons and their members, forms part of "the Constitution of Canada," it becomes necessary to consider the relative scope of sections 44 (empowering the federal parliament, subject inter alia to section 42, to "make law amending the Constitution of Canada in relation to . . . the Senate") and 42(1)(b) (providing that an "amendment to the Constitution of Canada in relation to" inter alia "(b) the powers of the Senate . . ." may be enacted *only* in accordance with the procedures prescribed in section 38(1)) of the Constitution Act, 1982). The two sections differ radically.

These may seem, to anyone save a specialist in Canadian public law, to be rather arcane illustrations. So I shall conclude this part of my discussion with a matter of obviously great importance—the constitutional position of the Supreme Court of Canada, which is the "General Court of Appeal for Canada" created by the Parliament of Canada pursuant to the Act of 1867. Section 101 of the Act of 1867 provides, "The Parliament of Canada may, notwithstanding anything in this Act, from Time to Time provide for the Constitution, Maintenance, and Organization of a General Court of Appeal for Canada, and for the Establishment of any additional Courts for the better Administration of the Laws of Canada."[42]

Whether the whole or any part of this plenary authority of Parliament to legislate as to the Supreme Court of Canada has survived the Constitution Act, 1982, is less than clear on the face of the latter act. The procedures for amending "the Constitution of Canada" as to matters pertaining to the Court, as these procedures are set out in the Constitution Act, 1982, are far more arduous than the unilateral federal power contemplated by the drafters of the Act of 1867. Under section 41 of the Constitution Act, 1982, an "amendment to the Constitution of Canada in relation to . . . (d) the composition of the Supreme Court of Canada" requires a proclamation by the Governor General authorized by the Senate and House of Commons—or by the Commons alone under section 47(1)—and by the legislative

40. CAN. REV. STAT., ch. S-8 (1970).
The Senate and the House of Commons respectively, and the members thereof respectively, hold, enjoy and exercise,
    (a) such and the like privileges, immunities and powers as, at the time of the passing of the *British North America Act, 1867,* were held, enjoyed and exercised by the Commons House of Parliament of the United Kingdom, and by the members thereof, so far as the same are consistent with and not repugnant to that Act; and
    (b) such privileges, immunities and powers as are from time to time defined by Act of the Parliament of Canada, not exceeding those at the time of the passing of such Act held, enjoyed and exercised by the Commons House of Parliament of the United Kingdom and by the members thereof respectively.
41. The original section 18 of the British North America Act, 1867, 30 & 31 Vict., ch. 3 (U.K.), was repealed and replaced by the Parliament of Canada Act, 1875, 38 & 39 Vict., ch. 38 (U.K.), § 1.
42. British North America Act, 1867, 30 & 31 Vict., ch. 3 (U.K.), § 101.

assembly of *every* province. Under section 42(1), an "amendment to the Constitution of Canada in relation to . . . (d) subject to paragraph 41(d), the Supreme Court of Canada" requires a proclamation by the Governor General authorized by the Senate and House of Commons—or by the Commons alone under section 47(1)—and resolutions of the legislative assemblies of at least *two-thirds* of the provinces that have, in the aggregate, according to the then-latest general census, at least fifty percent of the population of all the provinces.

It is beyond discussion that, prior to the commencement of the Constitution Act, 1982, the Parliament of Canada, under section 101 of the Act of 1867, had legislative authority to make, by simple federal statute, whatever provision it might have thought fit as to the composition of the Supreme Court of Canada, its jurisdiction, or any other aspect of its existence.[43] The Constitution Act, 1982, does not purport, in express terms, to repeal section 101 of the 1867 Act, whether in whole or in part. Indeed, the former Act's section 53(1), read with the schedule, expressly continues the whole Act of 1867 in force, with exceptions not now material.

The Parliament of Canada has, of course, provided for the constitution and organization of the Supreme Court of Canada. Most of its legislation on the subject is to be found in the Supreme Court Act,[44] some of the most important provi-

---

43. *See, e.g.,* Attorney-Gen. of Ontario v. Attorney-Gen. of Canada, 1947 A.C. 127 (P.C.); Crown Grain Co. v. Day, 1908 A.C. 504, 506 (P.C.).
44. CAN. REV. STAT., ch. S-19 (1970).

THE COURT

3.   The court of common law and equity in and for Canada now existing under the name of the Supreme Court of Canada is hereby continued under that name, as a general court of appeal for Canada, and as an additional court for the better administration of the laws of Canada, and shall continue to be a court of record.

THE JUDGES

4.   The Supreme Court shall consist of a chief justice to be called the Chief Justice of Canada, and eight puisne judges, who shall be appointed by the Governor in Council by letters patent under the Great Seal.
5.   Any person may be appointed a judge who is or has been a judge of a superior court of any of the provinces of Canada, or a barrister or advocate of at least ten years standing at the bar of any of the provinces.
6.   At least three of the judges shall be appointed from among the judges of the Court of Appeal, or of the Superior Court, or the barristers or advocates of the Province of Quebec.
7.   No judge shall hold any other office of emolument either under the Government of Canada or under the government of any province of Canada.
8.   The judges shall reside in the National Capital Region described in the schedule to the *National Capital Act* or within twenty-five miles thereof.
9.   (1) Subject to subsection (2), the judges hold office during good behaviour, but are removable by the Governor General on address of the Senate and House of Commons.
     (2) A judge ceases to hold office upon attaining the age of seventy-five years.

SESSIONS AND QUORUM

25.   Any five of the judges of the Supreme Court shall constitute a quorum and may lawfully hold the Court.
26.   It is not necessary for all the judges who have heard the argument in any case to be present in order to constitute the Court for delivery of judgment in that case, but in the absence of any judge, from illness or any other cause, judgment may be delivered by a majority of the judges who were present at the hearing.
27.   (1) Any judge who has heard the case and is absent at the delivery of judgment, may hand his opinion in writing to any judge present at the delivery of judgment, to be read or announced in open court, and then to be left with the Registrar or reporter of the Court.

sions of which are set out below. Other provisions pertaining to the Court are to

(2) A judge who has resigned his office, or who has ceased to hold office under section 9 shall, within six months thereafter, for the purposes of this section, be deemed to be absent at the delivery of judgment in any case heard by him in which judgment has not been delivered during his tenure of office.

28. (1) No judge against whose judgment an appeal is brought, or who took part in the trial of the cause or matter, or in the hearing in a court below, shall sit or take part in the hearing of or adjudication upon the proceedings in the Supreme Court.

(2) In any cause or matter in which a judge is unable to sit or take part in consequence of this section, any four of the other judges of the Supreme Court constitute a quorum and may lawfully hold the Court.

29. Any four judges constitute a quorum and may lawfully hold the Court in cases where the parties consent to be heard before a court so composed.

30. (1) Where at any time there is not a quorum of the judges of the Supreme Court available to hold or continue any session of the Court, owing to a vacancy or vacancies, or to the absence through illness or on leave or in the discharge of other duties assigned by statute or order in council, or to the disqualification of a judge or judges, the Chief Justice, or, in his absence, the senior puisne judge, may in writing request the attendance at the sittings of the Court, as an *ad hoc* judge, for such period as may be necessary, of a judge of the Federal Court, or, should the judges of that court be absent from Ottawa or for any reason unable to sit, of a judge of a provincial superior court to be designated in writing by the Chief Justice or in his absence by any acting chief justice or the senior puisne judge of such provincial court upon such request being made to him in writing.

(2) Unless two of the judges of the Supreme Court available fulfil the requirements of section 6, the *ad hoc* judge for the hearing of an appeal from a judgment rendered in the Province of Quebec shall be a judge of the Court of Appeal or a judge of the Superior Court of that Province designated as above provided.

APPELLATE JURISDICTION

35. The Supreme Court shall have, hold and exercise an appellate, civil and criminal jurisdiction within and throughout Canada.

41. (1) Subject to subsection (3), an appeal lies to the Supreme Court from any final or other judgment of the highest court of final resort in a province, or a judge thereof, in which judgment can be had in the particular case sought to be appealed to the Supreme Court, whether or not leave to appeal to the Supreme Court has been refused by any other court, where, with respect to the particular case sought to be appealed, the Supreme Court is of the opinion that any question involved therein is, by reason of its public importance or the importance of any issue of law or any issue of mixed law and fact involved in such question, one that ought to be decided by the Supreme Court or is, for any other reason, of such a nature or significance as to warrant decision by it, and leave to appeal from such judgment is accordingly granted by the Supreme Court.

(2) Leave to appeal under this section may be granted during the period fixed by section 64 or within thirty days thereafter or within such further extended time as the Supreme Court or a judge may either before or after the expiry of the thirty days fix or allow.

(3) No appeal to the Supreme Court lies under this section from the judgment of any court acquitting or convicting or setting aside or affirming a conviction or acquittal of an indictable offence or, except in respect of a question of law or jurisdiction, of an offence other than an indictable offence.

(4) Whenever the Supreme Court has granted leave to appeal, the Supreme Court or a judge may, notwithstanding anything in this Act, extend the time within which the appeal may be allowed.

42. Notwithstanding anything in this Act, the Supreme Court has jurisdiction as provided in any other Act conferring jurisdiction.

JUDGMENT FINAL AND CONCLUSIVE

54. (1) The Supreme Court shall have, hold and exercise exclusive ultimate appellate civil and criminal jurisdiction within and for Canada; and the judgment of the Court is, in all cases, final and conclusive.

(2) Notwithstanding any royal prerogative or anything contained in any Act of the Parliament of the United Kingdom or any Act of the Parliament of Canada or any Act of the legislature of any province of Canada or any other statute or law, no appeal lies or shall be brought from or in respect of the judgment of any court, judge or judicial officer in Canada to any court of appeal,

be found in the Rules[45] made under the Act, and in other statutes, numbering perhaps two dozen, such as the Bankruptcy Act[46] and the Criminal Code,[47] which latter includes the sections on Supreme Court jurisdiction also set out below.[48]

---

tribunal or authority by which, in the United Kingdom, appeals or petitions to Her Majesty in Council may be ordered to be heard.

(3) *The Judicial Committee Act, 1833*, chapter 41 of the statutes of the United Kingdom of Great Britain and Ireland, 1833, and *The Judicial Committee Act, 1844*, chapter 69 of the statutes of the United Kingdom of Great Britain and Ireland, 1844, and all orders, rules or regulations made under those Acts are repealed in so far as they are part of the law of Canada.

SPECIAL JURISDICTION

References by Governor in Council

55.   (1)   Important questions of law or fact concerning

(a) the interpretation of the *British North America Acts;*

(b) the constitutionality or interpretation of any federal or provincial legislation;

(c) the appellate jurisdiction as to educational matters, by the *British North America Act, 1867*, or by any other Act or law vested in the Governor in Council;

(d) the powers of the Parliament of Canada, or of the legislatures of the provinces, or of the respective governments thereof, whether or not the particular power in question has been or is proposed to be exercised; or

(e) any other matter, whether or not in the opinion of the Court *ejusdem generis* with the foregoing enumerations, with reference to which the Governor in Council sees fit to submit any such question;

may be referred by the Governor in Council to the Supreme Court for hearing and consideration; and any question concerning any of the matters aforesaid, so referred by the Governor in Council, shall be conclusively deemed to be an important question.

(2) Where a reference is made to the Court under subsection (1) it is the duty of the Court to hear and consider it, and to answer each question so referred; and the Court shall certify to the Governor in Council, for his information, its opinion upon each such question, with the reasons for each answer; and the opinion shall be pronounced in like manner as in the case of a judgment upon an appeal to the Court; and any judge who differs from the opinion of the majority shall in like manner certify his opinion and his reasons.

(3) Where the question relates to the constitutional validity of any Act that has heretofore been or is hereafter passed by the legislature of any province, or of any provision in any such Act, or in case, for any reason, the government of any province has any special interest in any such question, the attorney general of the province shall be notified of the hearing, in order that he may be heard if he thinks fit.

(4) The Court has power to direct that any person interested, or, where there is a class of persons interested, any one or more persons as representatives of such class, shall be notified of the hearing upon any reference under this section, and such persons are entitled to be heard thereon.

(5) The Court may, in its discretion, request any counsel to argue the case as to any interest that is affected and as to which counsel does not appear, and the reasonable expenses thereby occasioned may be paid by the Minister of Finance out of any moneys appropriated by Parliament for expenses of litigation.

References by Senate or House of Commons

56.   The Court, or any two of the judges thereof, shall examine and report upon any private bill or petition for a private bill presented to the Senate or House of Commons, and referred to the Court under any rules or orders made by the Senate or House of Commons.

45.   Rules of the Supreme Court of Canada, CON. REG. CAN., ch. 1512 (1978). (New Rules of the Supreme Court of Canada, made on Jan. 11, 1983, will be valid only so far as consistent with the Constitution Act, 1982. *See* SOR/82-74, 117 Can. Gaz. 380 (1983).)

46.   CAN. REV. STAT., ch. B-3, §§ 164-67 (1970).

47.   CAN. REV. STAT., ch. C-34 (1970).

48.   618.   (1)   A person who is convicted of an indictable offence and whose conviction is affirmed by the court of appeal may appeal to the Supreme Court of Canada

(a)   on any question of law on which a judge of the court of appeal dissents, or

(b)   on any question of law, if leave to appeal is granted by the Supreme Court of Canada within twenty-one days after the judgment appealed from is pronounced or within such extended time as the Supreme Court of Canada or a judge thereof may, for special reasons, allow.

(2)   A person

It is important to note that *none* of these statutory provisions—not those in the Supreme Court Act nor those in the Criminal Code—are *enumerated* as part of the "Constitution of Canada" in the schedule of the Constitution Act, 1982. Yet section 53(1) of the latter Act, as shown above, does not make that enumeration exhaustive. If, and to the extent that, any or all of the provisions in question *are* part of the "Constitution of Canada," they can, clearly, be altered only in compliance with the elaborate formulae prescribed in sections 41(d) and 42(1)(d) of the Constitution Act, 1982. Indeed, in the cases of sections 6 and 30(2) of the Supreme Court Act, concerning judges from Quebec,[49] quoted earlier, it is at least arguable that section 43 of the Constitution Act, 1982, applies prima facie; if so, there arise difficult questions as to the nature of section 43 and its relationship to the other procedures—both generally and in the specific matter of the Supreme Court of Canada. Would repeal of section 6 of the Supreme Court Act be possible: (i) by unilateral federal statute under section 101 of the Act of 1867? (ii) by the procedure prescribed by section 41(d) of the Constitution Act, 1982? (iii) by the procedure prescribed by section 42(1)(d) of the Constitution Act, 1982? (iv) by the procedure prescribed by section 43 of the Constitution Act, 1982?

To argue that *none* of the federal statute law dealing with the Supreme Court of Canada forms part of the "Constitution of Canada" is to say, in effect, that Parliament may continue to legislate on the subject exactly as it pleases; and that its power under section 101 of the 1867 Act to do so cannot be taken away save by the elaborate methods newly prescribed by Part V of the Constitution Act, 1982. This can scarcely have been what the eight "opposing" premiers had in mind when they signed their "April Accord"[50] from which sections 41(d) and 42(1)(d) were taken. Yet this construction is not, on its face, an impossible one.

On the other hand, if *all* federal statute law on the subject of the Supreme Court of Canada forms part of the "Constitution of Canada," it is not obvious why amendment of any of the Rules of the Supreme Court of Canada is not equally subject to the procedure prescribed by section 42(1)(d) of the Constitution Act,

---

1982. One such rule provides, "The covers of the appellants' factum shall be coloured buff and the covers of the respondents' factum shall be coloured green."[51] Such a position would be tantamount to holding that sections 41(d) and 42(1)(d) of the Constitution Act, 1982, have impliedly repealed so much of section 101 of the Act of 1867 as concerns the "General Court of Appeal for Canada." The rule of statutory construction pertaining to implied repeal was perhaps best stated by Rt. Hon. Dr. Lushington in *The India (No. 2)*:

> What words will constitute a repeal by implication it is impossible to say from authority or decided cases. If, on the one hand, the general presumption must be against such a repeal, on the ground that the intention to repeal, if any had existed, would have been declared in express terms; so on the other, it is not necessary that any express reference be made to the statute which is to be repealed. The prior statute would I conceive be repealed by implication, if its provisions were wholly incompatible with a subsequent one, or, if the two statutes together would lead to wholly absurd consequences, or if the entire subject-matter were taken away by the subsequent statute. Perhaps the most difficult case for consideration is where the subject-matter has been so dealt with in subsequent statutes, that, according to all ordinary reasoning, the particular provision in the prior statute would not have been intended to subsist, and yet if it were left subsisting no palpable absurdity would be occasioned.[52]

The Supreme Court of Canada will likely be disposed to adopt an intermediate position, attributing to some of the federal statutory provisions a "constitutional" character, and to others not. This would give an entrenched status to the essential elements of the court's character, without involving the inconvenience which an implied repeal of the pertinent portion of section 101 would entail. On the other hand, it would show very clearly just how uncertain in law is the phrase "the Constitution of Canada" as it appears in Part V of the 1982 Act.

The phrase "the constitution of the province" appears in section 45 of the Constitution Act, 1982, which provides that, subject to section 41, "the legislature of each province may exclusively make law amending" it. Section 45, of course, establishes a distinct amending procedure in its own right, and it will be convenient to treat it as such. Suffice it for the moment to say that the "constitution of the province," roughly speaking, is the body of law governing the provinces' executive and legislative institutions.

Are the phrases "Constitution of Canada" and "constitution of the province" mutually exclusive? Arguably, they are not. In my view, the constitution of every province is part of the "Constitution of Canada" as that phrase appears in Part V of the 1982 Act. The heading of Part V, which embraces section 45, is indeed "Procedure for Amending Constitution of Canada." And there is other textual evidence pointing in the same direction. Thus section 45 is subordinated to section 41 and section 41(c) refers to section 43—notably, to section 43(b). This appears to imply that a constitutional provision respecting the use of the English and French languages can, at one and the same time, be both part of the constitution of a province and also part of the Constitution of Canada.

---

51. Rules of the Supreme Court of Canada, CON. REG. CAN., ch. 1512, R. 32(2) (1978). Under the new Rules (*supra* note 45) "the cover of the intervener's factum shall be blue": Rule 39(2). Is this validly enacted?

52. 167 Eng. Rep. 345, 346 (Adm. 1864).

This issue is of considerable importance in determining how far the various procedures of Part V are mutually exclusive: in particular, how far sections 38 and 45 are mutually exclusive. I shall return to this question in section X.

IV

THE AMENDING PROCEDURES AND THE PARTICIPANTS

A. The Amending Procedures

I propose to denominate the amending procedures established by Part V of the Constitution Act, 1982, as follows: (i) the "general" procedure (section 38, with which may be read section 42); (ii) the "unanimous consent" procedure (section 41); (iii) the "special arrangements" procedure (section 43); (iv) the "unilateral federal" procedure (section 44); and (v) the "unilateral provincial" procedure (section 45). The first two descriptions are suggested by the marginal notes to the statute; the others are of my own choosing.

Before proceeding to analyze each amending formula individually, I shall first consider some attributes common to all of them.

B. The Participants

1. *The Crown.* The Sovereign or her representative (federally, the Governor General of Canada and provincially, the Lieutenant Governor of the province) is a necessary participant in all the amending procedures of Part V. The "unilateral" procedures contemplate Acts of Parliament of Canada[53] and of the provincial legislatures.[54] In each such instance royal assent, given personally by the Sovereign or through her representative, is legally indispensable.[55] The other amending procedures of Part V, sections 38(1), 41, and 43, all require a "proclamation issued by the Governor General under the Great Seal of Canada."

In the Canadian constitutional system—at the federal level at any rate—both supreme executive power and coordinate legislative power are vested *directly* in the person of the Sovereign,[56] and are exercisable by her representative only by delegation.[57] It thus appears asymmetrical, and even unseemly, for Part V to confer upon the subordinate directly—rather than initially upon the principal—the ultimate lawmaking power: the power of enactment of constitutional amendments after the necessary consents have been secured.

---

53. Constitution Act, 1982, 1982 ch. 11 (U.K), Sch. B § 44.

54. *Id* § 45.

55. *See* Constitution Act, 1867, 30 & 31 Vict., ch. 3 (U.K.), §§ 17, 55-57, 91 (requiring assent, expressly or by inference, for federal legislation); *id* §§ 58-59, 64-65, 69-90, 88 (for provincial legislation). The same result follows for the provinces admitted since 1867 in virtue of the enactments and other instruments establishing them. *See also* In re Initiative and Referendum Act, 1919 A.C. 935, 944-45 (P.C.); Liquidators of Maritime Bank of Canada v. Receiver-General of New Brunswick, 1892 A.C. 437, 444 (P.C.).

56. *See* Constitution Act, 1867, 30 & 31 Vict., ch. 3 (U.K.), §§ 9, 17, 91.

57. The Governor-General appears to derive his authority to assent to bills directly from the statute; its exercise, however, is subject at least to the Sovereign's control by instruction, and probably to restriction by prerogative instrument. *See* Constitution Act, 1867, 30 & 31 Vict., ch. 3 (U.K.), § 55. *See* Scott, *Entrenchment by Executive Action: A Partial Solution to "Legislative Override",* 4 SUPREME COURT L. REV. 303 (1982).

No doubt, in contemplation of law the act of the Governor General in amending the Constitution of Canada is the act of the Sovereign.[58] Yet there are serious questions as to whether the Sovereign *could* act *personally*; whether a federal statute (enacted, for example, under section 45) could empower the Sovereign to act personally; and whether the Sovereign could, as a matter of law, impose restrictions upon the power of her subordinate to make constitutional amendment proclamations. However these problems be resolved (and even assuming the resolution most favourable to the status and dignity of the Crown), it seems most objectionable that the Sovereign's position should be impaired in this disrespectful way, which was in my view quite deliberate.

Section 48 shows some concern about the proprieties in that it imposes its novel (and unnecessary) duty upon the Queen's Privy Council for Canada to *advise* issuance of a proclamation, and not upon the Governor General to *make* a proclamation—an act which he is, in consequence, legally free to refuse to do. It is an interesting question whether section 48 imposes an imperative duty—whether upon the Council as a body or upon its members—and, if so, at whose suit it is enforceable: "The Queen's Privy Council for Canada shall advise the Governor General to issue a proclamation under this Part forthwith on the adoption of the resolutions required for an amendment made by proclamation under this Part."[59]

2. *The Houses of the Parliament of Canada.* The concurrence of the House of Commons of Canada is an essential requirement of all the amending procedures of Part V, save only the "unilateral provincial" procedure.

What, then, of the upper house of the federal parliament, the Senate?[60] The Senate is, of course, in law a co-ordinate legislative body of the Parliament of Canada.[61] Indeed, its position as such cannot from now on be impaired save in accordance with section 42(1)(b) of the Constitution Act, 1982: that is, save through the "general" procedure of section 38(1). Accordingly, the Senate's concurrence is obviously necessary to any exercise of the "unilateral" federal amending power of section 44.

---

58. In Liquidators of Maritime Bank of Canada v. Receiver-General of New Brunswick, 1892 A.C. 437, the Privy Council held that, in the absence of express words to the contrary, the Crown must be presumed to be a necessary party to legislation. *Id.* at 443; *see also* Reference re Power of Disallowance, 1938 S.C.R. 71, 76 (Can.)("The act of a Lieutenant-Governor in assenting to a bill or in reserving a bill is an act of the Crown by the Crown's representative just as the act of the Governor General in assenting to a bill or reserving a bill is the act of the Crown."—per Duff, C.J.); In re Initiative and Referendum Act, 1919 A.C. 935 (P.C.).

59. Constitution Act, 1982, 1982 ch. 11 (U.K.), Sch. B § 48.

60. Senators, it will be recalled, are appointed by the federal executive government, and (if appointed after June 1, 1965) hold office until the age of seventy-five. (Senators formerly held office for life.) Representation is on a regional basis, with twenty-four Senators representing Ontario, twenty-four representing Quebec, twenty-four for the Maritime Provinces (ten each for Nova Scotia and New Brunswick, and four for Prince Edward Island), and twenty-four for the Western provinces (six each for Manitoba, British Columbia, Saskatchewan, and Alberta). Six have been added for Newfoundland, and one each for the Yukon Territory and the Northwest Territories.

On the position of the Senate of Canada, *see generally* Constitution Act, 1867, 30 & 31 Vict., ch. 3 (U.K.), §§ 17-18, 21-36, 53.

61. *Id.* §§ 17, 91.

The Senate's role in the other amending procedures—be they "multilateral"[62] or even in some cases "bilateral"[63]—has been reduced, by section 47, to a six-month delaying power:

> 47. (1) An amendment to the Constitution of Canada made by proclamation under section 38, 41, 42 or 43 may be made without a resolution of the Senate authorizing the issue of the proclamation if, within one hundred and eighty days after the adoption by the House of Commons of a resolution authorizing its issue, the Senate has not adopted such a resolution and if, at any time after the expiration of that period, the House of Commons again adopts the resolution.
>
> (2) Any period when Parliament is prorogued or dissolved shall not be counted in computing the one hundred and eighty day period referred to in subsection (1).

In the original proposal of October 2, 1980,[64] the Senate was given co-ordinate authority with the House of Commons where a referendum was to be employed;[65] but in other cases[66] the Senate was to enjoy only a ninety-day delaying power.

In the revised proposal of April 24, 1981, the Senate had full co-ordinate power in *all* cases. A beleaguered federal government was in no position to press forward to Westminster, not only against the opposition of eight provinces, but without the concurrence of the upper house in the traditional joint address to the Queen. Co-ordinate power for the Senate was in effect to be the price of the Senate's co-operation.

With the federal-provincial agreement of November 5, 1981, the Senate was no longer able, as a practical matter, to insist on retaining full co-ordinate authority in the whole constitutional amendment process, not even (perhaps *especially* not) where its own existence or constitution or powers were involved. On the other hand, subsections 42(1)(b) and (c) provide the Senate with a substantial degree of entrenchment.

3. *Provincial Legislative Assemblies*. All the procedures of Part V, save only the "unilateral federal" procedure, require the concurrence of bodies forming part of provincial "representative" legislatures. In the case of the three new-style formulae involving Governor Generals' proclamations—that is, the "general" procedure of section 38, the "unanimous consent" procedure of section 41, and the "special arrangements" procedure of section 43—the concurrence of the "legislative assembly" of one or more provinces is required. "Legislative assembly" is a term which ought to have been defined, particularly since the provinces are free under section 45 to have bicameral or multicameral legislatures and, indeed, largely free to prescribe the mode of selection of members of all or any of the bodies forming part of such legislatures. It would have been preferable to have attempted something along these lines:

> In Part V, the "legislative assembly" of a province is the only deliberative legislative

---

62. Constitution Act, 1982, 1982 ch. 11 (U.K.), Sch. B §§ 38(1), 41.

63. *See id.,* § 43. This assumes that § 43 does in truth create a distinct amending procedure. *See infra* Pt. VII.

64. *See supra* note 6, § 42.

65. *Id.* § 44, applying this rule to §§ 41(1) and 43.

66. *See supra* note 12, §§ 46, 47, 48 and 49.

body or the most numerous deliberative legislative body having at least full co-ordinate power, forming part of the provincial legislature.

Nevertheless, if the legislature includes one or more such bodies consisting only of elected representative members, the "legislative assembly" is that body, or the most numerous such body.

When two or more bodies qualify equally, and are equally numerous, any one may act to propose or to consent to a constitutional amendment, and all must act to withdraw or revoke it.

The last provincial legislative upper house disappeared from Canada on December 31, 1968, the day on which the Legislative Council of Quebec was abolished by a simple provincial statute,[67] enacted—under the authority of section 92.1 of the Act of 1867—by the Crown, the Legislative Council, and the Legislative Assembly. All Canadian provincial legislatures are now unicameral. Their single chambers are wholly elected; therefore, de facto, the term "legislative assembly" in Part V of the 1982 Act offers at present no difficulty of application.

Again, the term "legislature," where it appears in section 45 of the 1982 Act (the "unilateral provincial" amendment procedure, successor to section 92.1 of the 1867 Act) means the Sovereign, or her representative, acting with the other lawfully-prescribed elements of the provincial lawmaking process. Apart from the Sovereign's concurrence through royal assent, the law in every province requires, in order that a bill may become law, only due passage by the provincial legislative assembly. So, effectively, the term "legislature" in section 45 means, for the present, "Crown and provincial legislative assembly."

4. *The Referendum and Its Disappearance*. Under the federal proposals concerning constitutional amendment procedures, as they were referred to the Supreme Court of Canada on April 24, 1981, provincial consent to constitutional amendments could, in this scheme, be given by a majority of provincial legislative assemblies meeting stated criteria to ensure adequate representation of all regions (and concurrence of both Quebec and Ontario).[68] But provincial consent could alternatively be given by the Canadian electorate provided that the national refer-

---

67. An Act Respecting the Legislative Council, 17 Eliz. 2, ch. 9 (S. Que. 1968).
68. The essence of the federal proposals concerning constitutional amendment procedures, as those proposals stood on April 24, 1981, and as they were referred to the Supreme Court of Canada, may be seen in these two provisions:
    46. (1) An amendment to the Constitution of Canada may be made by proclamation issued by the Governor General under the Great Seal of Canada where so authorized by
        (a) resolutions of the Senate and House of Commons; and
        (b) resolutions of the legislative assemblies of at least a majority of the provinces that includes
            (i) every province that at any time before the issue of the proclamation had, according to any previous general census, a population of at least twenty-five per cent of the population of Canada,
            (ii) two or more of the Atlantic provinces, and
            (iii) two or more of the Western provinces.
    (2) In this section,
"Atlantic provinces" means the provinces of Nova Scotia, New Brunswick, Prince Edward Island and Newfoundland;
"Western provinces" means the provinces of Manitoba, British Columbia, Saskatchewan and Alberta.
    47. (1) An amendment to the Constitution of Canada may be made by proclamation issued

endum majority included also referendum majorities in provinces whose assemblies' consent would have sufficed as provincial approval. (The consent of the federal Houses would remain necessary in any event.)

By contrast, the constitutional amendment processes prescribed by Part V of the Constitution Act, 1982, all involve action by the Sovereign, or by the Governor General (presumably as the Sovereign's representative)—and by federal and provincial deliberative legislative bodies acting in various combinations.

Participation of the electorate directly through referendum—so prominent in the proposal of October 2, 1980,[69] and its ultimate revision of April 24, 1981[70]—has, in consequence of the November 5, 1981, agreement,[71] disappeared completely. This development is one of far-reaching significance.

During the course of public debate, no aspect of the federal proposal—not even the entrenchment of a charter of rights and freedoms—drew remotely as bitter a response from provincial authorities—from Newfoundland to Western Canada—as did the inclusion of the referendum process. Why?

The amending formula proposed in October 1980 and that which emerged in revised form in April 1981 both imposed stringent conditions as to the number and the grouping of provinces whose consent would be needed to effect constitutional amendments of various kinds. Most notably, these conditions controlled amendments bearing on the distribution of legislative powers as between the federal and provincial authorities. In particular, for a general amendment to become law, the consent of Quebec and Ontario would have been required (each having had, at some time, at least twenty-five percent of the population of Canada). Such a provision was an obvious euphemism for giving Quebec a veto and for conceding that whatever Quebec has, Ontario, too, must be given.

The federal government apparently expected—and in my view, rightly

---

by the Governor General under the Great Seal of Canada where so authorized by a referendum held throughout Canada under subsection (2) at which

    (a) a majority of persons voting thereat, and

    (b) a majority of persons voting thereat in each of the provinces, resolutions of the legislative assemblies of which would be sufficient, together with resolutions of the Senate and House of Commons, to authorize the issue of a proclamation under subsection 46(1).

have approved the making of the amendment.

(2) A referendum referred to in subsection (1) shall be held where directed by proclamation issued by the Governor General under the Great Seal of Canada, which proclamation may be issued where

    (a) an amendment to the Constitution of Canada has been authorized under paragraph 46(1)(a) by resolutions of the Senate and House of Commons;

    (b) the requirements of paragraph 46(1)(b) in respect of the proposed amendment have not been satisfied within twelve months after the passage of the resolutions of the Senate and House of Commons; and

    (c) the issue of the proclamation has been authorized by the Governor General in Council.

(3) A proclamation issued under subsection (2) in respect of a referendum shall provide for the referendum to be held within two years after the expiration of the twelve month period referred to in paragraph (b) of that subsection.

69. *See supra* note 6, § 42.
70. *See supra* note 12, § 47.
71. *See supra* note 13.

expected—the electorate, even in Quebec (perhaps *especially* in Quebec), to be more pliable than would be any elected provincial assembly in passing judgment on proposals from Ottawa for constitutional amendments. This would be particularly true where the balance of power within the federation was concerned. The voters would more readily give the consent of the province than would their provincial representatives.

After all, the Quebec electorate had, in the May 20, 1980, provincial referendum, refused the Parti Québécois provincial government its desired mandate to negotiate the independence of Quebec. Yet, on April 13, 1981, the same voters returned the same government to power, no less committed to its purpose of independence. This was a recent, and clear, demonstration of the way in which the Quebec electorate, speaking directly, could be expected to be more attached to, and sympathetic to, federal institutions than would a provincial legislature. But such a phenomenon would not be confined to Quebec alone. In *any* province, provincial legislators would probably cling to provincial jurisdiction with greater tenacity than would their electorate.

A difference in attitudes, flowing from their different positions, may naturally be expected between provincial voters and provincial representatives. But beyond this, the electoral system in itself may play an important psychological role in provincial legislators' attitudes toward constitutional amendments.

In Quebec that phenomenon can be expected to work in the following way. Of provincial political parties, the "more nationalist" party or parties will oppose "centralization" on principle. The "less nationalist" party or parties will oppose "centralization" out of fear that their opponents will effectively exploit the "national" or "provincial autonomy" issue. Moreover, elections often turn on "swing" votes: certain positions endanger marginal votes. Furthermore, non-French-Canadian voters—far more likely statistically to have a "federalist" political orientation—do not find the effect of their votes diluted in referenda; whilst, given their geographical concentration, their votes are greatly diluted in elections to the provincial legislature. All this points to referenda as being more favourable to federal interests than are provincial legislative assemblies.

Although Mr. Trudeau and his colleagues may not have worked the theory out quite so fully as this, they clearly perceived that: (1) at least in the Canadian political context, a referendum, inserted in the amending formula as an alternative means of securing the necessary provincial consents, would be an element of flexibility; (2) the more rigid the amending formula in other respects, the more this element of flexibility was needed; and (3) the flexibility derived from a referendum would be favourable to federal interests, particularly as no referendum could be held without the consent of the Senate and House of Commons of Canada.[72]

The provincial premiers and the federal opposition leader grasped the implica-

---

72. The October 2, 1980 scheme marked the first appearance of the referendum in the text of a proposed amending formula. This author suggested something similar in September 1964. Wishing to alleviate the rigours of the proposed "Fulton-Favreau Formula" (requiring unanimous provincial consent for most important constitutional amendments), this author advanced the idea that, in any amending

tions of the referendum element from the start. Of the eight premiers who opposed the October 1980 package, virtually all made a special point of attacking the referendum specifically, or of attacking the package generally with the referendum obviously in mind. The language was sometimes envenomed, and the complaint was that the referendum was "centralizing." It was indeed more "centralizing" than a formula without it. Provincial autonomy was not safe in the hands of provincial electors—at any rate, it was much less safe than in the premiers' own hands. Whatever in Mr. Trudeau's proposals might by any possibility have survived the Supreme Court's decision of September 28, 1981, the referendum could never have done so. In fact, it did not.

C.   Initiation of Amending Procedures

All the amending procedures may be "initiated" by any of the participating legislative chambers. The "unilateral" procedures—assuming bicameralism or multicameralism—will of course be subject to the normal rule that bills may be introduced in any of two or more co-ordinate legislative bodies. For the other procedures of Part V of the Constitution Act, 1982, section 46(1) makes it explicit that "[t]he procedures for amendment under sections 38, 41, 42 and 43 may be initiated either by the Senate or the House of Commons or by the legislative assembly of a province."

The power of a provincial legislative assembly to "initiate" constitutional amendments by resolution seems far more likely to be effective than the power, given to an American state legislature by Article V of the United States Constitution, to apply for the calling of a convention, even though the constitutional language seems to impose a duty upon Congress to comply with such a request from the legislatures of two-thirds of the states. Of course, the Canadian federal Houses can ignore provincial resolutions—just as the provincial assemblies can ignore those coming from Ottawa. But, as a matter of comity, the formal proposal of an amendment by a resolution enjoying legal status seems to command the attention of the other participants, and to demand at least due consideration. It will be interesting to see whether the federal government will feel obliged to provide parliamentary time to debate resolutions coming from provincial assemblies.

D.   Revocation of Resolutions of Assent

Section 46(2) of the 1982 Act settles in the affirmative the question—which otherwise would sooner or later have had to be litigated—whether resolutions of assent to amendments are revocable before the making of the amendment. That section provides that "[a] resolution of assent made for the purposes of this Part may be revoked at any time before the issue of a proclamation authorized by it."[73]

---

formula, "*provincial* consent should be capable of being given alternatively by the *voters* of the province . . . ." *See Editor's Diary,* 12 McGILL L.J. 337, 342-43 note (1966-67).

Nothing came of the suggestion. In this century, the federal Liberal Party has been rather effective in getting, and keeping, federal power in Canada. It is astounding to see how slow it has been to grasp an idea at once so likely to advance federal interests and so very obvious.

73.   Constitution Act, 1982, 1982 ch. 11 (U.K.), Sch. B § 46(2).

V

The "General" Procedure

The marginal note to section 38 of the 1982 Act suggests that this formula be styled the "general procedure" for amending the Constitution of Canada:

> 38. (1) An amendment to the Constitution of Canada may be made by proclamation issued by the Governor General under the Great Seal of Canada where so authorized by
>
> > (a)   resolutions of the Senate and House of Commons; and
> >
> > (b)   resolutions of the legislative assemblies of at least two-thirds of the provinces that have, in the aggregate, according to the then latest general census, at least fifty per cent of the population of all the provinces.
>
> (2) An amendment made under subsection (1) that derogates from the legislative powers, the proprietary rights or any other rights or privileges of the legislature or government of a province shall require a resolution supported by a majority of the members of each of the Senate, the House of Commons and the legislative assemblies required under subsection (1).
>
> (3) An amendment referred to in subsection (2) shall not have effect in a province the legislative assembly of which has expressed its dissent thereto by resolution supported by a majority of its members prior to the issue of the proclamation to which the amendment relates unless that legislative assembly, subsequently, by resolution supported by a majority of its members, revokes its dissent and authorizes the amendment.
>
> (4) A resolution of dissent made for the purposes of subsection (3) may be revoked at any time before or after the issue of the proclamation to which it relates.

A.   Necessary Number of Consenting Provincial Assemblies.

An amendment under section 38 requires the consent of two-thirds of the provinces' legislative assemblies. For the moment, that means seven. This at least *formally* explains the apparent (implied) abrogation[74] of Parliament's pre-existing unilateral legislative power to create new provinces.[75] This power could conceivably have been employed to create additional provinces precisely in order to facilitate passage of constitutional amendments under the new procedure. (American history seems to offer at least one close precedent.[76]) Even so, the provisions of section 38(2) would surely have given adequate protection to most of the basic provincial interests. It is a fair guess that the Trudeau government did not resist curtailment of federal legislative power to create new provinces because the federal authorities could henceforth more easily resist pressure for the creation of new provinces in the north. The resources of the north are thus more likely to remain a "national" asset with a bigger share remaining for the existing provinces.

---

74. *See* Constitution Act, 1982, 1982 ch. 11 (U.K.), Sch. B §§ 42(1)(f), 42(2).

75. *See* Constitution Act, 1871, 34 & 35 Vict., ch. 28 (U.K.), § 2.

76. The state of West Virginia appears to have been created by Congress to further the cause of suppressing the Confederate rebellion against the United States. *See, e.g.,* A. McLaughlin, A Constitutional History of the United States 634-38 (1935). A rump government of "Virginia" at Wheeling was recognized as giving the consent of Virginia to the cession of the territory from which Congress erected the new state of West Virginia in the summer of 1863.

The thirteenth amendment to the U.S. Constitution was proposed by Congress on January 31, 1865. West Virginia, the sixth state to ratify, did so three days later, on February 3, 1865, and it was recognized as one of the twenty-seven ratifying states when ratification was complete on December 6, 1865. In itself, this does not prove that West Virginia was erected specifically to ratify the thirteenth amendment. But it seems that West Virginia was erected to co-operate, and did co-operate, with Congressional purposes as regards the Confederacy.

B. Required Character of Consenting Provincial Assemblies.

Since by its terms the provinces whose assemblies' consent is needed for an amendment must include "provinces that have, in the aggregate, according to the then latest general census, at least fifty percent of the population of all the provinces," population statistics are needed to ascertain compliance with section 38. The 1976 and 1981 Census figures are these:[77]

TABLE 1
POPULATION OF CANADA BY PROVINCES AND TERRITORIES

PROVINCE OR TERRITORY	1976 Census	1981 Census
Alberta	1,838,037	2,237,724
British Columbia	2,466,608	2,744,467
Manitoba	1,021,506	1,026,241
New Brunswick	677,250	696,403
Newfoundland	557,725	567,681
Nova Scotia	828,571	847,442
Ontario	8,264,465	8,625,107
Prince Edward Island	118,229	122,506
Quebec	6,234,445	6,438,403
Saskatchewan	921,323	968,313
Yukon Territory	21,836	23,153
Northwest Territories	42,609	45,741
	22,992,604	24,343,181
[Provinces only	22,928,159	24,274,287]

C. Treatment of Provinces on a Uniform Basis.

The rules governing the number and character of the provinces whose assemblies' consent is needed for an amendment under section 38 can be said, with a plausibility formerly impossible, to put all provinces on an "equal" footing or to apply "fair" or "uniform" criteria. The veto power sought to be conferred upon Quebec and Ontario[78] has been eliminated. It had formerly been accepted that a "veto" could not be refused to Quebec and that whatever Quebec had, Ontario, too, must be given. Needless to say, this was increasingly resisted in western Canada, where some of the provinces began to assert a claim to the like veto. In the end, the power of "dissent" replaced the veto.

D. Majorities Required to Pass Resolutions Derogating from "the legislative powers, the proprietary rights or any other rights or privileges of the legislature or government of a province."

Section 38(2) requires that the resolutions which it contemplates be passed by "a majority of the members of" each of the Senate, the House of Commons, and the legislative assemblies required under subsection (1). It is notable that no similar express condition is to be found in subsection (1) which speaks only of "resolu-

---

77. For the 1976 figures, see 1981 CANADIAN ALMANAC & DIRECTORY 955 (1981). The 1981 Figures have been informally furnished by Statistics Canada, a federal government agency.

78. *See, e.g., supra* note 68.

tions of the legislative assemblies . . . ." As a matter of historical fact, it appears that no difference was in truth intended by the federal parliamentary draftsman, but that provincial legal advisers would not agree to the elimination of the extra phrase.

Of course, a majority of *some* sort is obviously needed to carry *any* resolution, even one under section 38(1). Normally a statutory quorum will be required,[79] and the question will then be decided by a majority of persons present and voting.[80] In the Senate of Canada, the Speaker has an original vote, but no casting vote;[81] elsewhere, he usually has a casting vote to be exercised on equal division only.[82] The addition of the extra words "a majority of the members of" involves a prima facie presumption that they are not superfluous, and that they produce a different legal result from that which obtains where (as in section 38(1)) they are not used. If this principle of statutory construction is applied, the question is: what is the special or additional requirement which they add? The only obvious explanation can be that a majority of the *whole membership* of the house is needed to pass resolutions derogating from provincial powers. It remains an open question as to how vacancies are to be taken into account.

The rule of statutory construction is not an inflexible one, and it may be that the courts will decline to construe section 38(2) as creating a class of resolutions which require special majorities of the entire membership of the body. Indeed, uniformity could also be achieved (though justified only with difficulty) by a judicial construction imposing the more stringent, rather than the less stringent, rule in all cases.

Those who may wish to embark on the process of constitutional amendment would do well to secure a judicial clarification at the earliest opportunity. Otherwise lengthy legislative efforts may prove abortive. Indeed, one of the serious practical embarrassments which would result from distinguishing the majority normally required by section 38(1) from the majority specially required by section 38(2) is that the sponsor would be forced from the outset of any journey of amendment, either to secure the special majority in *every* case, or to judge correctly whether the proposed amendment falls outside the requirements of section 38(2) so that the lesser, "normal" majority suffices. If there are two rules and two kinds of majority, one can readily envisage how perplexed parliamentary officers and legal advisers will be when they are faced with a resolution which has been "passed" by the normal majority only, and they must decide what to do next.

E.   "Dissent" as a Substitute for Veto.

Subsections 38(3) and (4) of the Constitution Act, 1982, create and regulate a

---

79. *See* Constitution Act, 1867, 30 & 31 Vict., ch. 3 (U.K.), §§ 35, 48, (Houses of Parliament); *id.* §§ 87-88 (provincial legislatures). Quorum requirements are also to be found in instruments creating the several provinces and in the provincial statutes.

80. *See id.,* §§ 36, 49, 87-88. Instruments creating the individual provinces and provincial statutes also contain such requirements.

81. *Id.* § 36.

82. *Id.* §§ 49, 87-88.

mechanism whereby the legislative assembly of a province can "dissent" from a proposed amendment "that derogates from the legislative powers, the proprietary rights or any other rights or privileges of the legislature or government of a province" (and can later revoke its "dissent"). Outright veto of constitutional amendments has instead become veto of their application to a particular province. The outright veto had been conceded—at least where provincial rights and powers were to be impaired—to *all* provinces in the Fulton Formula[83] and the Fulton-Favreau Formula[84] of the sixties. The veto had been effectively limited to Quebec and Ontario in later proposals.[85]

The implications of this substitution were summarized in Mr. Trudeau's phrase "chequerboard Canada." He opposed and resisted it strongly. Although the provision for dissent allows either geographically-selective centralization or decentralization, we shall probably see the former. Were past historical attitudes to be projected into the future, federal jurisdiction would tend to *expand* with respect to provinces other than Quebec. A "special status" for Quebec could emerge. In Quebec, even amongst French-Canadian nationalists, there seems to be some uncertainty as to whether this would be a good thing. Would it, for example, underscore the necessity, desirability, or feasibility of Quebec independence?

It should be noted that the problem, discussed above, as to the meaning of the phrase "resolution supported by a majority of" members, recurs in respect of the passage[86] or revocation[87] of a provincial assembly's resolution of dissent. While provincial representatives in Winnipeg in March 1981 had worked out a formula requiring a *two-thirds* majority of a provincial assembly to carry a resolution of dissent, the eight premiers—apparently after late-night negotiations—reduced this in their April 16, 1981, Ottawa proposal[88] to "a majority of the Members." The moving force, it appears, was Premier René Lévesque of Quebec, who, in the April 13, 1981, provincial general election—three days earlier—had been returned to power with eighty of the one hundred and twenty-two seats in the Quebec "National Assembly"—two seats short of a two-thirds majority.

F.   Compensation to Dissenting Provinces.

Outright veto of a constitutional proposal to transfer a matter from provincial to federal jurisdiction would, *ex hypothesi*, prevent the constitutional change from

83.   *Reprinted in* 12 McGILL L.J. 576 (1966-67).
84.   *Reprinted in* 12 McGILL L.J. 579 (1966-67).
85.   This was accomplished through the euphemism of giving a veto to every province "that at any time before" the "issue" of a proclamation of amendment "had, according to any previous general census, a population of at least twenty-five percent of the population of Canada": Art. 49, CANADIAN CONSTITUTIONAL CHARTER, being a draft produced by the Constitutional Conference at Victoria, B.C., June 14-16, 1971, reproduced as Appendix B to the FINAL REPORT of the Special Joint Committee of the Senate and of the House of Commons on the Constitution of Canada (Ottawa, 1972) at 106. *See* provisions to the same effect in the drafts of October 2, 1980 (*supra* note 6), §§ 41(1)(b)(i) and 42(1)(b); and April 24, 1981 (*supra* note 12), §§ 46(1)(b)(i) and 47(1)(b).
86.   Constitution Act, 1982, 1982 ch. 11 (U.K.), Sch. B § 39(3).
87.   *Id.* subsections 39(3), (4).
88.   *See* CANADIAN NEWS FACTS, Vol. 16, No. 7, at 2490-91, and No. 8, at 2498 (1981).

occurring at all. "Dissent," on the contrary, is simply an "opting-out," and given the existence of the present ten provinces, up to three can do so without blocking passage of the amendment. For these "dissenting" provinces there are obvious fiscal consequences, since they will continue to support expenditures which the participating provinces will have transferred to the federation. Section 40 of the 1982 Act serves to minimize such consequences by providing, "Where an amendment is made under subsection 38(1) that transfers provincial legislative powers relating to education or other cultural matters from provincial legislatures to Parliament, Canada shall provide reasonable compensation to any province to which the amendment does not apply." Section 40 is restricted in scope, covering only "education or other cultural matters." This restriction is a principal point of objection by the Quebec government.

Section 40 suggests the following questions. First, what is a "transfer"? Does creation of a *concurrent* federal power suffice to bring section 40 into operation? Second, what are "cultural" matters? (This genus includes "education" with "other cultural matters.") Third, what, for that matter, is "education"? (Formal instruction only?) Fourth, is there a continuing obligation, subject to reassessment from time to time? Fifth, how far is the reasonableness of the compensation judicially reviewable? Finally, does section 40 create a statutory obligation enforceable by law?

G.   Minimum and Maximum Time Period for the Operation of the "General" Procedure.

Section 39 reads as follows:

39.   (1) A proclamation shall not be issued under subsection 38(1) before the expiration of one year from the adoption of the resolution initiating the amendment procedure thereunder, unless the legislative assembly of each province has previously adopted a resolution of assent or dissent.

(2) A proclamation shall not be issued under subsection 38(1) after the expiration of three years from the adoption of the resolution initiating the amendment procedure thereunder.

In effect section 39(2) imposes a maximum time period of three years. (*Quaere* whether one of the federal or provincial houses can "re-initiate" an already-pending proposal before the expiry of the three years.) On the other hand, section 39(1) is clearly designed to give each provincial assembly reasonable leisure to decide whether or not to dissent, and reasonable opportunity, if it so chooses, to dissent under section 38(3) before a proclamation is made under section 38(1)—for dissent is *only* possible, under section 38(3), "prior to the issue of the proclamation to which the amendment relates." Effectively, a minimum deliberative period of a year is available to each assembly in which it can act one way or the other. If so much as one province's assembly declines, or fails, to act either way, the amending process can be delayed for the full year. This may become serious in cases of urgency. Indeed, the power to delay, when others are anxious to move forward, can itself be used in bargaining.

H. Special Matters Reserved Exclusively to the "General" Procedure.

"An amendment to the Constitution of Canada in relation to" a series of important matters can, under section 42(1), be made only under section 38(1). Under section 42(2), the power of dissent does not apply in such cases. Thus section 42(1) does not create a distinct amending procedure. It specifies cases where subsection 38(1) applies and excludes the application of subsections 38(2), (3) and (4). In a sense it creates a variant of the general procedure. It should be noted, however, that sections 46(1) and 47(1) do speak of section 42[89] as creating a distinct procedure in its own right.

Although the effect of section 42(1) is essentially straightforward, it does give rise to some intricate problems, such as the meaning of the phrase "the territories" in section 42(1)(e). For example, if it were sought to extend all or some provinces' boundaries seaward, the proper application, respectively, of section 42(1)(e) and section 43 of the Constitution Act, 1982, and of section 3 of the Constitution Act, 1871,[90] would pose difficult questions.

VI

THE "UNANIMOUS CONSENT" PROCEDURE

Section 41 of the Constitution Act, 1982, reads as follows:

41. An amendment to the Constitution of Canada in relation to the following matters may be made by proclamation issued by the Governor General under the Great Seal of Canada only where authorized by resolutions of the Senate and House of Commons and of the legislative assembly of each province:

(a) the office of the Queen, the Governor General and the Lieutenant Governor of a province;

(b) the right of a province to a number of members in the House of Commons not less than the number of Senators by which the province is entitled to be represented at the time this Part comes into force;

(c) subject to section 43, the use of the English or the French language;

(d) the composition of the Supreme Court of Canada; and

(e) an amendment to this Part.

It should be noted that section 41(e) imposes the requirement of using the "unanimous consent" procedure for any amendment to the provisions of Part V itself.

Although generally straightforward, section 41 seems bound to give rise to some important problems. First, the effect of section 41(d) (along with that of section 42(1)(d)) on Parliament's legislative authority over the Supreme Court of

---

89. 42. (1) An amendment to the Constitution of Canada in relation to the following matters may be made only in accordance with subsection 38(1):

(a) the principle of proportionate representation of the provinces in the House of Commons prescribed by the Constitution of Canada;

(b) the powers of the Senate and the method of selecting Senators;

(c) the number of members by which a province is entitled to be represented in the Senate and the residence qualifications of Senators;

(d) subject to paragraph 41(d), the Supreme Court of Canada;

(e) the extension of existing provinces into the territories; and

(f) notwithstanding any other law or practice, the establishment of new provinces.

(2) Subsections 38(2) to (4) do not apply in respect of amendments in relation to matters referred to in subsection (1).

90. *See supra* note 29 & accompanying text.

Canada has already been noted.[91] Second, it is less than clear just how much of the law relating to the Crown is covered by section 41(a): that is, what is meant by the "office" of the Sovereign and those of her representatives.

VII

THE "SPECIAL ARRANGEMENTS" PROCEDURE

Section 43[92] appears to be the Rubik's Cube of the Constitution Act, 1982, and in this instance no booklet is available to offer quick solutions. Although it was doubtless drafted as an independent procedure in its own right—and is referred to as such in sections 46(1) and 47(1)—it is possible to treat it as simply attaching a condition upon the exercise of section 38, and requiring the consent of affected provinces in certain cases. So read, section 43 could arguably be said to serve the purpose of avoiding the anomaly which would seem to arise in some cases from the application of section 42. For example, an amalgamation of Nova Scotia, New Brunswick, and Prince Edward Island into a new province might otherwise be possible through section 38(1) (read with section 42(1)(d), which carries a *non obstante* clause), without these provinces being able to "dissent."[93] Notwithstanding the appeal of reading section 43 to obviate such anomalies, it is probably, on balance, an independent amending procedure. If so, it is the least satisfactory of those enumerated in Part V.

It is a condition for the application of section 43 that the provision being subjected to amendment must be one "that applies to one or more but not all, provinces." However, it is neither necessary nor sufficient that the amendment itself will have such a restricted application. On the other hand, so long as one chooses, as the formal object of one's amendment, an existing constitutional provision—*any* existing provision—"that applies to one or more but not all provinces," there is nothing in the language of section 43 to require that the amendment *itself* be in any way germane to the subject matter of the provision being amended. Unless, therefore, the scope of section 43 is confined by judicial construction, the results could be perfectly bizarre. Almost any sort of special constitutional arrangement could be made with the concurrence of the federal authorities and those of the one or more provinces to which it would apply.

The language of section 43 also raises a more immediate question: By what legal means within the Constitution of Canada could Quebec be established as a sovereign independent state?

---

91. *See* text accompanying notes 44-52 *supra*.

92.   43. An amendment to the Constitution of Canada in relation to any provision that applies to one or more, but not all, provinces, including (a) any alteration to boundaries between provinces, and (b) any amendment to any provision that relates to the use of the English or the French language within a province, may be made by proclamation issued by the Governor General under the Great Seal of Canada only where so authorized by resolutions of the Senate and House of Commons and of the legislative assembly of each province to which the amendment applies.
Constitution Act, 1982, 1982 ch. 11 (U.K.), Sch. B.

93. *See id.* § 42(2).

VIII

THE "UNILATERAL FEDERAL" PROCEDURE

The Constitution Act, 1982, integrates directly into the scheme of Part V what may be called "unilateral federal" and "unilateral provincial" amending procedures.[94] Section 44 of the 1982 Act provides: "Subject to sections 41 and 42, Parliament may exclusively make laws amending the Constitution of Canada in relation to the executive government of Canada or the Senate and House of Commons." Section 44 gives no power to alter the federal lawmaking process, as defined in the 1867 Act by section 17 and the opening words of section 91, through the *subtraction* of any of its elements. Nor does it appear to afford power to *add* further elements—be they other actors or other formalities—as conditions of valid legislation. Section 44 appears to allow unilateral federal statutory amendments to the existing individual elements of the federal parliament—the Crown, the Senate, and the House of Commons—whose continued existence section 44 presupposes; even this power is subject to severe restrictions.[95]

The Canadian Bill of Rights[96]—which, it seems, is to be allowed to stand on the federal statute book—enumerates various fundamental rights and freedoms, and provides that:

> Every law of Canada shall, unless it is expressly declared by an Act of the Parliament of Canada that it shall operate notwithstanding the *Canadian Bill of Rights*, be so construed and applied as not to abrogate, abridge or infringe or to authorize the abrogation, abridgment or infringement of any of the rights or freedoms herein recognized and declared.[97]

---

94. The "unilateral federal" procedure of section 45 is the recognizable successor to section 91.1 of the amended 1867 Act (since 1949 the first item in the list of legislative powers of the Parliament of Canada):

> The amendment from time to time of the Constitution of Canada, except as regards matters coming within the classes of subjects by this Act assigned exclusively to the Legislatures of the provinces, or as regards rights or privileges by this or any other Constitutional Act granted or secured to the Legislature or the Government of a province, or to any class of persons with respect to schools or as regards the use of the English or the French language or as regards the requirements that there shall be a session of the Parliament of Canada at least once each year, and that no House of Commons shall continue for more than five years from the day of the return of the Writs for choosing the House: Provided, however, that a House of Commons may in time of real or apprehended war, invasion or insurrection be continued by the Parliament of Canada if such continuation is not opposed by the votes of more than one-third of the members of such House.

British North America Act, 1867, 30 & 31 Vict., ch. 3 (U.K.), § 91.1 (as amended by British North America (No. 2) Act, 1949, 12, 13 & 14 Geo. 6, ch. 81 (U.K.)). This earlier provision has been repealed and replaced by Section 44 of the 1982 Act. The language of section 44 creating the unilateral federal procedure is framed in terms distinctly narrower than those of its predecessor, section 91.1 of the amended 1867 Act. However, in view of the highly restrictive construction placed upon the latter by the Supreme Court of Canada in the *Senate Reference*, the difference may not be very large in terms of actual legal results.

Reference re Legislative Authority of Parliament to Alter or Replace the Senate, 102 D.L.R.3d 1 (Can. 1979). The court held: (1) that section 91.1 of the 1867 Act did not enable the Parliament of Canada to abolish the Senate or alter its essential characteristics, *id.* at 18; (2) that "Canada" in section 91.1 referred to the "juristic federal unit" rather than to the country generally (thus rendering nugatory some enumerated exceptions to the section), *id.* at 12; and (3) that the federal parliamentary structure, at least in its essential respects, was also excepted by implication, *id.* at 13. In my view, the soundness of the Court's opinion is more than doubtful. For the most part, the difficulties created by the *Senate Reference* will disappear under the new constitutional regime.

95. *See* Constitution Act, 1982, 1982 ch. 11 (U.K.), Sch. B §§ 41-42.

96. Act for the Recognition and Protection of Human Rights and Fundamental Freedoms, 8 & 9 Eliz. 2, 1960 CAN. STAT. ch. 44, Part I.

97. *Id.* § 2.

Only federal laws, of course, are affected,[98] and in the absence of the required *non obstante* clause, a "law of Canada" which conflicts with the Canadian Bill of Rights is inoperative to that extent.[99] In effect, the Canadian Bill of Rights has been read as a statute providing a guarantee that some or all provisions of any given federal Act, even though the bill has been duly passed by the Senate and Commons of Canada and assented to in the Queen's name, cannot operate as law without the additional formality of a *non obstante* clause.[100]

It is not easy to bring such a guarantee within the power conferred by section 44 of the Constitution Act, 1982. On the other hand, would the guarantee, if valid and in force before April 17, 1982, not continue until competently repealed? If such is the case, how could the guarantee competently be repealed?

IX

The "Unilateral Provincial" Procedure

The unilateral provincial procedure of section 45 of the 1982 Act is framed in terms much wider than those of section 44: "Subject to section 41, the legislature of each province may exclusively make laws amending the constitution of the province."[101]

The exclusion from the provincial amending power of the office of the Queen—even so far as it may be considered part of the provincial constitution—is, under the terms of section 41(a), no longer left to inference from the exclusion of the office of her representative, the Lieutenant Governor. Furthermore, in view of section 41(c), a constitutional guarantee of language use[102] can be treated as forming part of the relevant provincial constitution without involving the consequence that it is unilaterally amendable by the provincial legislature. It is no longer necessary to the entrenchment of the provision that it be held to be part of the general constitution of the country as opposed to part of the constitution of the province.[103] That expedient may, however, be necessary to rationalize entrenchment of the new Charter as it concerns subjects of provincial jurisdiction.

---

98. Section 5(2) of the same Act provides:

The expression of "Law of Canada" in Part I means an Act of the Parliament of Canada enacted before or after the coming into force of this Act, any order, rule or regulation thereunder, and any law in force in Canada or in any part of Canada at the commencement of this Act that is subject to be repealed, abolished, or altered by the Parliament of Canada.

Act for the Recognition and Protection of Human Rights and Fundamental Freedoms, 8 & 9 Eliz. 2, 1960 Can. Stat. ch. 44, § 5(2).

99. *See* Regina v. Drybones, 9 D.L.R.3d 473, 482 (Can. 1969).

100. Such a guarantee was, arguably, within federal legislative power under the terms of section 91.1 of the amended 1867 Act, though it is hard to see how this can be reconciled with the restrictive construction given to section 91.1 in the *Senate Reference*. *See supra* note 94, for discussion of *Senate Reference*.

101. The "unilateral provincial" procedure of section 45 is the recognizable successor to section 92.1 of the 1867 Act, although there are some points of difference:

92. in each Province the Legislature may exclusively make laws in relation to Matters coming within the Classes of Subjects next herein-after enumerated; that is to say,—

1. The Amendment from Time to Time, notwithstanding anything in this Act, of the Constitution of the Province, except as regards the Office of Lieutenant Governor . . . .

102. *See, e.g.,* Constitution Act, 1867, 30 & 31 Vict., ch. 3 (U.K.), § 133.

103. *See* Attorney-Gen. of Quebec v. Blaikie, 101 D.L.R.3d 394, 401 (Can. 1979); Attorney-Gen. of Manitoba v. Forest, 101 D.L.R.3d 385, 388-89 (Can. 1979).

Section 45, in terms and by authority,[104] confers a general power to deal with the constitution and organization of provincial institutions—legislative, executive, or other—subject to the position of the Sovereign and her representative, the Lieutenant Governor, protected by section 41(a). Grammatically, at any rate, section 45 is wide enough to permit the provincial legislative institutions, however they may be lawfully constituted at any time, to reconstitute those very institutions with the utmost freedom. The old issue affecting its predecessor, section 92.1— that is, whether any implied limitations circumscribe that freedom—seems to continue.[105] The question arises, for example, whether a referendum can lawfully be established as an *alternative*—or even as a *substitute*[106]—lawmaking authority alongside, or in place, of the provincial representative legislature, or whether the referendum can be imposed as a superadded condition necessary for the valid enactment of all legislation, or of legislation of some defined classes.[107] Another such question is whether—so long as the law presently in force is carefully respected—additional houses can be added to the representative legislature or special majorities can be required in the legislative houses or, for that matter, in the referenda.

X

RELATIONSHIPS AMONG AMENDING PROCEDURES

A principal question raised by Part V is how far the various procedures which it creates are mutually exclusive. Despite the appearance of the word "only" in section 43, and the word "exclusively" in sections 44 and 45, these sections, it is submitted, ought not to be read so as to make them exclusive of section 38.

---

104. *Cf.* Attorney-Gen. of Quebec v. Blaikie, 101 D.L.R.3d at 400 (construing § 92.1 of the Act of 1867).

105. The Constitution Act, 1982, 1982 ch. 11 (U.K.), Sch. B, through its section 53(1) and Schedule Item 17, effects the repeal of section 7(1) of the Statute of Westminster, 1931, 22 Geo. 5, ch. 4 (U.K.). This may affect the continuing applicability of section 5 of the Colonial Laws Validity Act, 1865, 28 & 29 Vict., ch. 63 (U.K.), to the extent (if any) that the aforesaid section 7(1) had otherwise preserved its operation where amendments to the British North America Acts were concerned.

Section 5 of the Colonial Laws Validity Act, 1865, which in terms grants power to representative colonial legislatures to amend the colonial constitution in certain respects, was one of the constitutional bases for colonial legislation on "manner and form" of lawmaking. *See infra* note 107.

106. *See* In re Initiative and Referendum Act, 1919 A.C. 935 (P.C.), *affirming* Re Initiative and Referendum Act, 32 D.L.R. 148 (Man. 1916). There, the Privy Council, strictly speaking, left this question open. The Council construed the provincial referendum scheme (in my view, *magis ut pereat quam valeat*) as dispensing with the Lieutenant Governor's participation, and so struck the scheme down as violative of section 92.1 of the British North America Act, 1867, 30 & 31 Vict., ch. 3 (U.K.).

The broader reasons of the Manitoba Court of Appeal in the decision below—taking a generally restrictive view of section 92.1 and apparently barring a referendum as a substituted legislative process, 32 D.L.R. at 153, have recently been cited (without express approval or disapproval) by the Supreme Court of Canada. Reference re Legislative Authority of Parliament to Alter or Replace the Senate, 102 D.L.R.3d 1, 14 (Can. 1979).

See generally Scott, *Constituent Authority and the Canadian Provinces*, 12 McGILL L.J. 528 (1966-67).

107. *See generally* Attorney-General of New South Wales v. Trethowan, 1932 A.C. 526 (P.C.), *affirming* Attorney-General of New South Wales v. Trethowan, 44 C.L.R. 394 (Austl. 1931), *affirming* Trethowan v. Peden, 31 N.S.W. St. R. 183 (S. Ct. N.S.W. 1930).

The Privy Council's decision turned essentially on the Colonial Laws Validity Act, 1865, 28 & 29 Vict., ch. 63 (U.K.), § 5, and thus may be of marginal value in Canada today. *See supra* note 105. The decisions of the Australian courts, however, are based on much wider grounds.

Mutual exclusivity *inter se* of the various procedures of Part V, where it does not result from the very nature of the provision (as it does in the case of section 41), is of mischievous consequence, and should be avoided so far as possible.

It is important that, to the extent that the terms of two or more provisions overlap, they be read as concurrent *pro tanto.* In particular, as between *more* comprehensive provisions (such as section 38) and *less* comprehensive ones (such as section 43), it appears desirable that they be read whenever possible as standing in a hierarchy, so that the former stands to the latter as the "more difficult" to the "less difficult." Compliance with the former would be ipso facto compliance with the latter. Otherwise it may prove impossible to include, in a single proposed amendment and as a single package, a single provision having effects upon different parts of the constitution.

Both of the "unilateral" amending procedures, sections 44 and 45, purport, in terms, to confer "exclusive" powers. But "exclusive" of what? That the powers conferred by sections 44 and 45 are, in principle, "exclusive" of one another is certain. It is no less certain that each of these two powers is, in principle, equally exclusive of *all powers*, however arising, belonging to the other level of government. Moreover, the powers of each province are, of course, exclusive of those of any other province.

In my view, however, sections 44 and 45 ought *not* to be held to be in any sense exclusive of the *other* amending procedures of Part V. It would be of mischievous consequence for an amendment, merely because it has an impact upon the federal executive government, or the Senate, or the House of Commons, to be invalid as an encroachment upon the "exclusive" powers of section 44, even though the amendment has duly complied with the requirements of another prima facie appropriate procedure—for example, section 38. (Indeed, section 41 *requires* the "unanimous consent" procedure to be employed; and section 42 *requires* the "general" procedure to be employed, for certain amendments dealing with federal institutions.)

Moreover, the internal provincial constitutions ought properly to be regarded as part of the "Constitution of Canada" as that term appears in Part V of the Constitution Act, 1982.[108] If so, the various "bilateral" and "multilateral" procedures of Part V are not excluded from effecting amendments to matters contemplated by section 45. This can be inferred from section 41(e), which allows section 45 *itself* to be amended by the "unanimous consent" procedure. The unanimous consent procedure can thus be used first to amend section 45, and then to alter the provincial constitution. If so, it should be possible to compress the two stages into one, and to amend a provincial constitution directly through the use of section 41.[109] While this is not of great practical consequence—since the concurrence of the provincial assembly is required in any event—it does point to the conclusions that provincial constitutions are part of the "Constitution of Canada," and that Part V procedures other than section 45—notably section 38—can be used to

108. *See supra* Pt. III.
109. McCawley v. The King, 1920 A.C. 691 (P.C.).

amend them. Of course, the power of "dissent" furnished by section 38(3) would be available in such cases.

If Article V of the United States Constitution had come before a meeting of Canadian federal and provincial legal advisers, a provincial representative would immediately have insisted upon the addition, at the end of the Article, of something like the following words: "or of the application to such State of the benefit of this proviso." That, I think, explains a great deal about the way in which Part V of the Constitution Act, 1982, is drafted. Indeed, it shows, basically, how we in Canada write and read legislation.

THE AMENDING PROCESS IN CANADA AND THE UNITED STATES: A COMPARATIVE PERSPECTIVE

WALTER DELLINGER*

For 115 years the basic written constitution of Canada had been a statute of the United Kingdom Parliament, the British North America Act of 1867 (BNA) and its amendments.[1] On April 17, 1982, Queen Elizabeth II brought these acts home to Canada in a ceremony celebrating the recent passage by the United Kingdom Parliament of the Canada Act of 1982.[2] The Canada Act was the final amendment by the Parliament in London of the BNA Act; this basic document will henceforth be a wholly domestic Canadian law, amendable by Canada alone without the unseemly necessity of petition to the parliament of a foreign government.

Passed two years after the American Civil War, the British North America Act united the British colonies of Canada (Ontario and Quebec), Nova Scotia, and New Brunswick into a new federated nation. The BNA Act provided the basic constitution of Canada, allocating authority between the federal and provincial governments. As a statute of the United Kingdom, however, it could be changed only by the Parliament in London. In practice amendments have been made upon (and only upon) formal request by the government of Canada.[3]

For half a century, efforts have been made to "patriate" the Canadian Constitution: that is, to terminate the formal power of the United Kingdom Parliament to change the BNA and to make its provisions a part of the law of Canada, amendable by processes wholly Canadian. And for half a century these efforts were unsuccessful, for the Canadian federal government and the governments of the ten Canadian provinces were unable to agree upon a formula for amending the constitution once it became part of Canadian law and no longer subject to revision by the United Kingdom Parliament.[4]

Finally, in November 1981, after months of intense controversy, the Canadian federal government and nine of the ten provinces reached agreement on a future amending process.[5] In spite of the objections of Quebec, the Parliament of the

---

* Professor of Law, Duke University.

I wish to thank my colleague Donald Horowitz for his helpful comments and Kathryn Battuello and Teresa Reichert for their assistance on this article.

1. British North America Act, 1867, 30 & 31 Vict., ch. 3.
2. Canada Act, 1982, ch. 11.
3. *See* P. HOGG, CONSTITUTIONAL LAW OF CANADA 18-20 (1977).
4. *See generally* G. FAVREAU, THE AMENDMENT OF THE CONSTITUTION OF CANADA ch. III (1965) (discussing the federal-provincial conferences and meetings of 1927, 1935-36, 1950, 1960-61, and 1964).
5. Montreal Gazette, Nov. 6, 1981, at 1, col. 5.

United Kingdom responded to a "Joint Address to the Queen" from the Canadian Senate and House of Commons by enacting, in March 1982, the Canada Act.[6] This final London amendment to the BNA Act converted it into the Constitution Act of Canada[7] and added the agreed upon formula for effecting future constitutional amendments through Canadian procedures.[8]

That the dispute over a future Canadian amendment formula was the critical issue preventing for so long the patriation of the Canadian Constitution should not be surprising. In a federal system of powers divided between the central government and provincial (or state) governments, the two most critical issues are the initial allocation of powers between the two levels of government, and the location of power to change that allocation in the future.[9] It may indeed be said that legal "sovereignty" resides in that combination of bodies with power to effectuate changes in the fundamental law. The amending power can alter whatever delicate balance has been achieved in constructing a federal system. Thus the amending power is the most delicate of issues.

Once a genuine consensus is achieved on the proper relationship between central and provincial authority, agreement on an amendment process follows naturally, as it did in the United States in 1787.[10] Where there is no agreement on the proper allocation of authority, or (more fundamentally) no agreement on the desired level of unity within the society, as has been the case in Canada, agreement on a wholly satisfactory amendment process becomes impossible. Though an amendment formula may seem to be a relatively small aspect of a constitutional system, it is in fact the fulcrum of future power. Debates over the allocation of authority for future constitutional change become, as they did in Canada, debates over the desired level of unity in the society. Until a substantial consensus is reached on the underlying questions of nationhood, no satisfactory agreement can be reached on a process of amendment.

Why did it take half a century of struggle to agree upon an amendment formula for Canada? And how successful was the effort? This comparative look at the American and Canadian amendment processes, their evolution, and prospects, will attempt to shed some light on these questions.[11]

I

THE EVOLUTION OF THE AMERICAN AMENDMENT PROCESS

The coming together of the American colonies into a single nation was more difficult than we can easily now imagine. John Adams, at the Continental Congress in 1775, spoke of "[f]ifty gentlemen meeting together all strangers, . . . not

6. Canada Act, 1982, ch. 11.
7. Constitution Act, 1982, pt. 7, § 52(2), Sched. B (Can.).
8. *Id*. pt. 5.
9. Pearson, *Introduction* to G. FAVREAU, *supra* note 4, at vii.
10. *See infra* pp. 286-87.
11. Since this paper was delivered to the Duke-McGill Conference on April 27, 1982, at least three books have been published concerning the reformed Canadian Constitution. *See generally* E. McWHINNEY, CANADA AND THE CONSTITUTION 1979-1982 (1982); D. MILNE, THE NEW CANADIAN CONSTITUTION (1982); and P. HOGG, CANADA ACT 1982 ANNOTATED (1982).

acquainted with each other's language, ideas, views, designs. They are therefore jealous of each other—fearful, timid, skittish."[12] While to us they stand at the beginning, initiating a history, Garry Wills notes that "they saw themselves as defenders of a history accomplished; taking risks that might end, rather than launch, a noble experiment."[13] They came as representatives of legislative assemblies a century old; indeed, the Virginia House of Burgesses had held an unbroken sequence of sessions for over one hundred and fifty years. The colonies were more trading rivals than partners.[14] The physical distances were vast, and land travel between colonies was an arduous undertaking. None of the Massachusetts delegates had ever seen Philadelphia.[15]

The American colonies fought the war as allies, not as a union. At war's end they confederated as thirteen governments under Articles of Confederation, each retaining its "sovereignty, freedom, and independence"[16] except as expressly delegated to a Congress of limited authority, in which each state voted as a state and cast a single vote.[17]

Of the many problems which beset this Confederation, ("We are fast verging to anarchy and confusion," wrote Washington to Madison)[18] the overriding constitutional difficulty was that no alteration designed to remedy its other defects could be made without the unanimous consent of all the parties to the Articles of Confederation.[19] And unanimity on proposed amendments was impossible to achieve.

Change could thus be made only under a new constitutional order. Even though the instructions to the Constitutional Convention in Philadelphia were limited to proposing alterations in the Articles of Confederation, it was apparent from the outset that nothing less than a wholly new constitution would be proposed.[20] Since unanimity was required for alterations in the Articles of Confederation, and unanimity could not be achieved, a new Constitution was to take effect when ratified by nine of the thirteen states. It was understood, however, that no state could be forced into the newly constituted nation without its consent. The new Constitution would take effect when ratified by nine states—but only as a union of those states which chose to ratify.[21]

From the outset of the Philadelphia Convention, the delegates recognized the

---

12. John Adams, Remarks at the Continental Congress (1775), *quoted in* G. WILLS, INVENTING AMERICA 34 (1979).

13. G. WILLS, INVENTING AMERICA 38 (1979).

14. 2 R. MIDDLEKAUFF, THE GLORIOUS CAUSE 27-28 (1982).

15. G. WILLS, *supra* note 13, at 46.

16. ARTICLES OF CONFEDERATION art. II (1778).

17. *Id*. art. V.

18. Letter of George Washington to James Madison, November 5, 1776, copy on file, Perkins Library, Duke University.

19. ARTICLES OF CONFEDERATION art. XIII (1778).

20. The Virginia Resolutions, introduced by Edmund Randolph on the third day of the Constitutional Convention, proposed sweeping changes. *See* 1 THE RECORDS OF THE FEDERAL CONVENTION OF 1787, at 20-23 (M. Farrand ed. 1937) [hereinafter cited as 1 FARRAND].

21. "The Ratification of the Conventions of nine States, shall be sufficient for the Establishment of this Constitution between the States so ratifying the Same." U.S. CONST. art. VII.

need to create a process by which future revision would be a genuine possibility.[22] The amendment process represented, in a sense, the domestication and taming of the right to revolution which had been proclaimed by the colonists. The early state constitutions legitimated the right of revolution by proclaiming the right to "reform the old or establish a new government." (Maryland, 1776).[23] Most early state constitutions did not, however, contain any definite procedures by which reform or reformation could be accomplished. As Judge Jameson noted,

> [T]he doctrine of the Revolution, that governments were founded by the people, and could be amended by them as they should think fit, was erroneously understood to warrant tumultuous assemblages of citizens, without legal authority, to dictate to the government not only its current policy, but amendments of the fundamental law.[24]

The inclusion of specific amendment procedures can thus be seen as part of the conservative thrust of much of the work of the Convention. The inclusion of a specific amendment procedure emphasized that changes of fundamental law were henceforth to be made only in accordance with modes sanctioned by the document itself, and thus served to confine the right to revolution within prescribed legal procedures.

Throughout the summer of 1787, the delegates at the Philadelphia Convention constructed the basic framework of American federalism. Only in the closing days of the Convention—*after* the difficult task of achieving consensus on the delicate balance of state and national power had been completed—was agreement reached on an amendment formula.[25]

The Convention did not find it difficult to agree upon the method for ratifying any proposed amendments: after considering a requirement for unanimous ratification, and one that would have required ratification by two-thirds of the states, the Convention settled upon three-fourths of the states as the proper number to agree to any proposed amendment.[26] The more critical question was whether the national Congress should be given the exclusive authority to propose amendments. And if there should be some method free of congressional control for *proposing* amendments for state ratification, what should that method be?

Unlike the Canadian experience, in which every suggested amendment formula required the assent of the national parliament for all amendments, the American framers found it particularly difficult to decide whether Congress should have the power to veto amendments desired by the states. The Virginia Resolutions, presented at the outset of the Convention by John Randolph, stated "that provision ought to be made for the amendment of the Articles of Union whensoever it shall seem necessary, and that the assent of the National Legislature ought

---

22.   Section 13 of the Virginia Resolutions provided that "provision ought to be made for the amendment of the Articles of Union whensoever it shall seem necessary . . . ." 1 FARRAND *supra* note 20, at 22.

23.   3 F. THORPE, THE FEDERAL AND STATE CONSTITUTIONS, COLONIAL CHARTERS, AND OTHER ORGANIC LAWS (1909).

24.   J. JAMESON, CONSTITUTIONAL CONVENTIONS 548 (4th ed. Chicago 1887) (1st ed. n.p. 1866).

25.   For a discussion of the evolution of Article V at the Constitutional Convention see Dellinger, *The Recurring Question of the "Limited" Constitutional Convention,* 88 YALE L.J. 1623, 1624-1630 (1979).

26.   2 THE RECORDS OF THE FEDERAL CONVENTION OF 1787, at 555 (M. Farrand ed. 1937) [hereinafter cited as 2 FARRAND].

not be required thereto."[27]

Midway through its deliberations, however, the Convention considered giving to Congress the sole power to propose amendments to the states for ratification. This was not acceptable to Mason of Virginia who had earlier stated that "[i]t would be improper to require the consent of the Natl. Legislature, because they may abuse their power, and refuse their consent on that very account."[28] One tentative proposal would have given Congress the authority to propose amendments whenever (1) Congress thought amendment necessary or (2) whenever two-thirds of the states thought amendment necessary.[29] Even this version was objectionable to Mason who feared that

> As the proposing of amendments is in both modes to depend, in the first immediately, and in the second, ultimately, on Congress, no amendments of the proper kind would ever be obtained by the people, if the Government should become oppressive, as he verily believed would be the case.[30]

Some delegates believed the proposal avoided this difficulty by permitting two-thirds of the states actually to draft a proposed amendment which Congress would be required automatically to submit to the state legislatures for ratification.[31] Such a system would have allowed proposed amendments to be made by a process of state legislative initiation and state ratification which would not require any national forum to approve the substance of the change. This was unsatisfactory to nationalists such as Alexander Hamilton who expressed the concern that "[t]he State Legislatures will not apply for alterations but with a view to increase their own powers— . . . ."[32] Various framers thus feared lodging exclusive power over amendment proposals in Congress. Others were apprehensive about any process by which the state legislatures could both propose and ratify amendments without the approval of a body designed to reflect the national interest.

The solution to this dilemma was one of the pragmatic compromises that mark the Constitution. In addition to providing that amendments may be proposed by Congress, the final version also required Congress to summon a Constitutional Convention whenever two-thirds of the state legislatures applied for one. Such a convention would be, like Congress, a deliberative body capable of assessing, from a national perspective, the need for constitutional change and drafting proposals for submission to the states for ratification. At the same time it would *not* be Congress, and therefore would not pose the threat of legislative self-interest blocking needed reform of Congress itself.

Having agreed upon alternative methods for proposing amendments (Congress, or a national convention summoned at the request of two-thirds of the states) and alternative methods for ascertaining the assent of three-fourths of the states (ratification by state legislatures or by conventions in each state) the Convention had completed its work on Article V, which read, in its final form:

---

27. 1 FARRAND, *supra* note 20, at 22.
28. *Id.* at 203.
29. 2 FARRAND, *supra* note 26, at 559.
30. *Id.* at 629.
31. *Id.* at 629-30.
32. *Id.* at 558.

> The Congress, whenever two thirds of both Houses shall deem it necessary, shall propose Amendments to this Constitution, or, on the Application of the Legislatures of two thirds of the several States, shall call a Convention for proposing Amendments, which, in either Case, shall be valid to all Intents and Purposes, as Part of this Constitution, when ratified by the Legislatures of three fourths of the several States, or by Conventions in three fourths thereof, as the one or the other Mode of Ratification may be proposed by the Congress . . . . [33]

A detailed commentary on Article V will follow later in this article, allowing for a comparison with the Canadian procedures to be described below. Nevertheless, it is worth noting here a few of the more salient points about the American amendment article. Nowhere in the American Constitution (except perhaps in the original provision for selection of two United States Senators by the legislature of each state)[34] is its federal character more pronounced. Each state counts as one in the amendment process. Unlike the presidential selection process,[35] Article V does not provide for the "votes" of each state to be weighted by population. Nor is there any requirement that those states approving an amendment contain even a bare majority of the national population.

What is critical is approval by the designated body (state legislature or state convention) in the requisite number of states —not the degree of national popular support. How much popular support a proposed amendment needs varies enormously depending upon whether it is supported or opposed principally in small or large states. An amendment opposed by the 12 smallest states containing (1980) 3.8 percent of the national population will not be valid unless it is approved by 38 states with 96 percent of the national population. On the other hand, an amendment favored by the 38 less populous states would be ratified despite the opposition of states with nearly 60 percent of the national population. Since a constitutional convention is to be summoned at the request of two-thirds of the states, a convention can be called at the instance of states with 32 percent of the national population (the 34 smallest) to propose amendments which will be effective if ratified by states with 41 percent of the population (38 smallest).[36]

The proposed Equal Rights Amendment, on the other hand, has been ratified by states with 70 percent of the national population. If ratified by the two next most likely states, Illinois and Florida, it would have been ratified by states with 80 percent of the national population and still not be a part of the Constitution. Thus, populations of states needed to approve a proposed constitutional change can vary (in 1980) from 41 percent to 96 percent depending upon whether the proposal is supported by smaller or larger states.

These are factors of which the framers of Article V were not unaware. Population variations in 1787 were similar; some amendments could be ratified with the

---

33. U.S. CONST. art. V.

34. *Id*. art I, § 3, cl. 1.

35. *Id*. art II, § 1, cl. 2.

36. U.S. Dept. of Commerce, Bureau of the Census, POPULATION PROFILE OF THE UNITED STATES: 1980, Current Population Reports, Population Characteristics Series P-20, No. 363, issued June 1981 Table 6.

In contrast, the Canadian amending formula requires that the ratifying provinces contain at least 50% of the national population in order for an amendment to be ratified.

support of states with less than half the population, and others fail even though supported by states with over 90 percent of the population.[37] These figures reflect an inevitable conflict between the underlying principles of federalism and democracy (in the sense of control by national popular majority). The important federal principle embodied in Article V is that the assent of each state is fully as significant as that of any other state. A citizen of Delaware or Utah thus has a far greater voice in the amendment process than one in California or New York. The equality relevant to the process of amendment under Article V is the equality of states in a federal union, and not that of individual citizens.

The second salient characteristic of Article V is the attempt to provide mechanisms of constitutional change free of the control of existing governmental institutions. Although every amendment to date has been proposed by the United States Congress, and every successful amendment but one ratified by state legislatures, the framers included alternative mechanisms both for proposing and for ratifying amendments. As noted above, amendments can be proposed by a national constitutional convention free of congressional control. To be sure, such a convention can be held only upon the petition of state legislatures; once properly convened, however, such a convention can, in the view of many scholars, determine its own agenda and submit for ratification whatever amendments it deems appropriate.[38]

The framers provided as well for a method of ratification that would allow amendments to be made over the opposition of state legislatures. By giving to Congress the power to submit proposed amendments to conventions in each state, rather than to the state legislatures, the possibility of a reform which restricts the power of existing state legislatures is preserved.

The "convention of the people" was a familiar device in the eighteenth century.[39] It now seems archaic, and the use of either a national convention for proposing amendments or state conventions for ratification are at present fraught with difficulties and uncertainties too complex for full discussion here. The convention device was nonetheless an imaginative effort to address a universal problem of constitutional amendment procedures: how to provide the means of reforming existing governmental institutions, when the only institutions readily

---

37. One amendment proposed by Congress has failed to become part of the Constitution even though ratified by states with more than three-fourths of the national population. The first amendment proposed by Congress, as part of the package which was to become the Bill of Rights, would have changed the representation in Congress so as to provide a guarantee of more representatives in proportion to population than was the case under the original Constitution. This apportionment amendment was ratified by ten states—all but Delaware, Massachusetts, Georgia, and Connecticut. The ratifying states contained 79.6% of the national population. W. LIVINGSTON, FEDERALISM AND CONSTITUTIONAL CHANGE 234 (1956). Thus an amendment favored by two-thirds of both Houses of Congress, and states with nearly 80% of the population, failed for lack of the required number of state ratifications.

In 1790, the ten larger states had 92.7% of the population; the four smallest states which could preclude amendments from being ratified, had only 7.3% of the population. See HEADS OF FAMILIES, FIRST CENSUS OF THE UNITED STATES: 1790 (Government Printing Office, 1908).

38. See Dellinger, supra note 25; Dellinger, Who Controls A Constitutional Convention? — A Response, 1979 DUKE L.J. 999. For the contrary view, see Van Alstyne, Does Article V Restrict the States to Calling Unlimited Conventions Only? — A Letter to a Colleague, 1978 DUKE L.J. 1295; Van Alstyne, The Limited Constitutional Convention — The Recurring Answer, 1979 DUKE L.J. 985.

39. See generally G. WOOD, THE CREATION OF THE AMERICAN REPUBLIC, 1776-1787, at 306-43 (1969).

available for proposing and ratifying amendments are those already in existence, and possibly in need of reform themselves. (As shall be seen, this is a difficulty for the new Canadian amendment process as well.)[40]

Having settled upon a future amendment formula, the Philadelphia delegates were faced with a more immediate problem of constitutional revision: how to bring into being the proposed constitution itself. The Convention, summoned only to propose changes in the Articles of Confederation, had outrun its limited mandate. The amendment process under the articles, requiring unanimous consent of all 13 states, did not promise to be successful. In seeking legitimacy for the new constitutional system, the delegates felt considerable discomfort about the "revolutionary" action of discarding an old order in a manner not sanctioned by the existing Articles. Elbridge Gerry of Massachusetts urged "the indecency and pernicious tendency of dissolving in so slight a manner, the solemn obligations of the articles of confederation"[41] and suggested that if nine out of thirteen can dissolve the existing compact, "[s]ix out of nine will be just as able to dissolve the new one hereafter."[42] Alexander Hamilton also expressed misgivings about allowing nine states "to institute a new Government on the ruins of the existing one."[43] They nonetheless decided not to submit the Constitution to the existing Congress for approval or disapproval, but merely to lay before Congress the draft Constitution, and to provide that the Constitution would take effect, upon the ratification of nine states, in those states which chose to ratify.[44] In a critical decision, it was determined that the Constitution would be placed for ratification not before the existing legislatures of the states, but before conventions of delegates chosen by the people for the express purpose of ratification or rejection.[45] In this way, the new Constitution would not falter at the hands of state legislative bodies whose power was being significantly diminished by the proposed document.

The ratification of the proposed constitution was nonetheless a difficult and intensely contested process; the outcome was precariously close in the essential states of Virginia[46] and New York.[47] Critical to the success of ratification was the proponents' campaign promise to make early resort to the new amendment process to add a Bill of Rights to the original document.[48]

In spite of the close division over its adoption, the Constitution has provided a stable structure of government for nearly two centuries. The Article V revision process has contributed to that stability, permitting twenty-six amendments to be made in response to changing conceptions of public good and private rights. The

---

40. *See infra* p. 300.

41. 2 FARRAND, *supra* note 26, at 561.

42. *Id.*

43. *Id.* at 560.

44. *Id.* at 562-63.

45. *Id.* at 475-78.

46. The Virginia Convention voted for ratification by a vote of 89-79. 3 THE DEBATES IN THE SEVERAL STATE CONVENTIONS ON THE ADOPTION OF THE FEDERAL CONSTITUTION, AS RECOMMENDED BY THE GENERAL CONVENTION AT PHILADELPHIA IN 1787, at 654-55 (J. Elliot 2d ed. 1937) [hereinafter cited as ELLIOT'S DEBATES].

47. The New York Convention voted to ratify by a vote of 30-27. 2 ELLIOT'S DEBATES 413.

48. *See generally* R. RUTLAND, THE BIRTH OF THE BILL OF RIGHTS 159-89 (1955).

Article V amendment process is now itself a subject of renewed controversy. After reviewing the evolution of the new Canadian amendment process, this paper will conclude with a comparative assessment of the Canadian and American approaches to constitutional revision.

II

THE EVOLUTION OF THE CANADIAN AMENDMENT PROCESS

The passage in 1867 of the BNA Act by the Parliament in London served to unite several former colonies into a dominion under the name of Canada. It did not, however, create a truly independent nation. Canada was to a significant extent still a British colony, subordinate to London in foreign affairs and subject still to the power of the imperial Parliament to enact statutes controlling in Canada. The evolution of Canada into an independent nation has been a gradual one.

Although the BNA Act conferred a substantial measure of authority for self-government on Canada, established the central and provincial governments and defined their respective authorities, it did not include any provision by which Canadian authorities could amend those allocations of power or make other changes in the BNA Act without recourse to the United Kingdom Parliament.

The reality of independence for Canada was achieved over the ensuing years. A signal step was the enactment by the U.K. Parliament of the Statute of Westminster in 1931.[49] The statute provided that hereafter no statute of the United Kingdom would extend to a dominion "unless it is expressly declared in that Act that that Dominion has requested, and consented to the enactment thereof."[50] The Act further granted to each dominion the power to repeal or revise any imperial statutes which had previously been passed and applied to the dominion.[51]

Had the Statute of Westminster said no more, the federal Canadian Parliament could have revised, on its own authority, the provisions of the BNA Act, without the consent or participation of the Canadian provinces. The division of authority between the central and provincial governments, established by the BNA Act, could thus have been altered at the will of the federal government. The Canadian provincial governments insisted upon the inclusion of a clause protecting them from this threat. The result was a provision preventing any alteration by Canada alone of the BNA Act.[52]

Canada was thus left, as it had been since 1867, with no means for altering its

---

49. Statute of Westminster, 1931, 22 Geo. 5, ch. 4.
50. *Id.* § 4.
51. No law and no provision of any law made after the commencement of this Act by the Parliament of a Dominion shall be void or inoperative on the ground that it is repugnant to the law of England, or to the provisions of any existing or future Act of Parliament of the United Kingdom, or to any order, rule or regulation made under any such Act, and the powers of the Parliament of a Dominion shall include the power to repeal or amend any such Act, order, rule or regulation in so far as the same is part of the law of the Dominion.
Id. § 2(2).
52. *Id.* § 7(1) provides that "Nothing in this Act shall be deemed to apply to the repeal, amendment or alteration of the British North America Acts, 1867 to 1930, or any order, rule or regulation made thereunder."

basic constitutional document except through enactments by the United Kingdom Parliament. Subsequent revision of the BNA Act by the imperial Parliament in 1949 granted to the Canadian House of Commons and Senate authority to make constitutional changes affecting only the federal government.[53] Changes affecting the distribution of powers between the federal and provincial governments continued to be possible only by action of the imperial Parliament. The convention was clearly established, however, that the United Kingdom Parliament would act only at the request and with the consent of Canada.

As Stephen Scott has noted, the settled convention regarding London amendments to the BNA Act was that a joint address by the Senate and House of Commons of Canada was both (1) a necessary and (2) a sufficient condition for action by the imperial Parliament for the exercise of its remaining legislative authority over Canada.[54] The critical issue *within* Canada became the question of the extent of consent by the provincial governments required before the Canadian federal parliament applied to London for a constitutional change.

A White Paper, issued by the Canadian Federal Ministry of Justice in 1965, stated that as a general principle "the Canadian Parliament will not request an amendment directly affecting federal-provincial relationships without prior consultation and agreement with the provinces."[55] The Paper went on to note, however, that the "nature and degree of provincial participation in the amending process . . . have not lent themselves to easy definition."[56]

The pre-1982 amendment process for changes affecting federal-provincial relationships was thus defective in two respects. First, the process was ambiguous, in that it was unclear what degree of provincial consent was necessary to make legitimate a request by the federal parliament for constitutional change. As subsequent events in Canada have vividly demonstrated, a constitutional amendment process needs to be precise and unambiguous if true legitimacy is to attach to the fundamental law and to its revision. Secondly, the need to resort to the imperial Parliament for changes in basic Canadian law, however formal that process, was a symbolic vestige of colonialism.

The obvious solution was for Canadian authorities to agree upon a wholly domestic amendment formula, and to submit such a formula to the United Kingdom Parliament for enactment as the final London amendment to the BNA Act. This would confer full and final authority on Canadian domestic institutions over the Canadian Constitution and accomplish what has come to be known as "patriation" of the constitution.

The struggle to find an agreeable formula for patriating the Canadian Constitution contained two distinct elements, each relevant to a study of constitutional change:

---

53. British North America Act, 1949, 13 Geo. 6, ch. 81.
54. Scott, *Opinion Submitted to the Foreign Affairs Committee of the House of Commons of the United Kingdom on the Role of the United Kingdom Parliament in Relation to the British North America Acts,* 26 McGILL L.J. 614, 615 (1981). *See* Scott, *Law and Convention in the Patriation of the Canadian Constitution,* 62 PARLIAMENTARIAN 183 (1981).
55. G. FAVREAU, *supra* note 4, at 15.
56. *Id.*

(1) the disagreement over the content of the future amendment formula, and

(2) the disagreement over the proper level of provincial consensus required for this last United Kingdom amendment—the one which would result in a new amendment formula for Canada.

The government of Canada and the governments of the ten provinces attempted unsuccessfully to reach agreement on a constitutional amendment formula in the course of ten federal-provincial conferences held in 1927, 1931, 1935, 1950, 1960, 1964, 1971, 1978, 1979, and 1980.[57] The assumption of these conferences seems to have been that a future amendment formula would be submitted to London for enactment only when it was agreed to by the federal government and the governments of all ten provinces. One distinguished scholar, writing in 1956, stated that although there was no certain degree of provincial consent necessary to make an application to London for more routine changes, it was "clear that an amendment providing for a general procedure of amendment will not be enacted without the consent of all the provinces."[58]

After the federal-provincial conference of 1980 failed to reach unanimous agreement on any of the major issues, however, the federal government of Prime Minister Trudeau boldly introduced a joint resolution in the federal parliament to send to London a patriation package—with or without provincial agreement.[59] The government's proposed resolution would ask the Queen to lay before the imperial Parliament a measure changing the BNA Act into the Constitution Act of Canada, with future power to amend that act in Canada, and including an entrenched Bill of Rights and a provision giving greater control over natural resources to the provinces. The premiers of eight of the ten provinces announced their opposition to the submission of this package to London.[60] In significant measure, opposition was based upon the inclusion of a Charter of Rights which would limit the authority of provincial legislatures.

Although many provinces objected as well to the amendment part, which essentially gave a veto to Ontario and Quebec, it would likely have been possible to obtain provincial agreement on simple patriation with some compromise amendment formula. Since it would have been difficult to obtain future ratification of an entrenched Bill of Rights under *any* of the suggested domestic amendment formulas, however, the federal government insisted on treating patriation, an amendment formula, minority language rights, and an entrenched Charter of Rights (which Trudeau strongly favored)[61] as a package.

Other papers in this volume will deal in some detail with the political and legal controversy created by these proposals; only a brief discussion is necessary here. For more than a year major controversy ensued in both Canada and England. In Canada the issue was the legality or propriety of the federal government's pro-

57. Reference Re Amendment of the Constitution of Canada, 125 D.L.R.3d 1, 103 (Can. 1981) (citing G. BEAUDOIN, LE PARTAGE DES POUVOIRS, EDITIONS DE L'UNIVERSITÉ D'OTTAWA 346 (1980).

58. W. LIVINGSTON, *supra* note 37, at 105.

59. *See* The Globe and Mail (Toronto), Apr. 15, 1982, at 4, col. 1; *see also id*. at 5, col. 3.

60. *See* The Globe and Mail (Toronto), Apr. 15, 1982, at 5, col. 3.

61. *Id*. at 10, col. 1.

ceeding with a request to the United Kingdom Parliament for a fundamental change in the constitutional structure of Canada, when the request was opposed by eight of the ten provincial governments. In London, the issue was whether the United Kingdom Parliament should not even "sniff at the package"[62] before proceeding to automatic enactment, or whether that Parliament should "look behind" the anticipated legislative request from the Canadian federal government and take note of provincial opposition.[63]

In a proceeding brought by three of the opposing provinces, the constitutionality of proceeding with the request was challenged in the courts, and ultimately, in the Supreme Court of Canada. In *Reference Re Amendment of the Constitution of Canada*[64] the Court held, 7-2, that as a matter of strict law, there was no legally enforceable requirement that the concurrence of the provinces be obtained before the Canadian federal Parliament submitted its request to the United Kingdom Parliament.[65] This did not terminate the matter, however, for the Court went on to consider whether there was a custom "amounting to a convention of the constitution" that provincial consent be obtained. And the Court held 6-3 that there was indeed such a convention.[66]

The notion of a "convention" of the constitution is not a familiar one to American lawyers. "Conventions" in Canadian law are unwritten "rules of the constitution which are not enforced by the law courts," but which have been accepted over time by political institutions.[67] A minority of three Justices found no basis for inferring the existence of the convention suggested by the provinces:

> The degree of provincial participation in constitutional amendments has been a subject of lasting controversy in Canadian political life for generations. It cannot be asserted, in our opinion, that any view on this subject has become so clear and so broadly accepted as to constitute a constitutional convention.[68]

The majority of the Canadian Supreme Court, however, noted that no modern amendment had been requested by the federal government which limited the powers of the provinces without first obtaining provincial consent, and concluded that this practice had become a convention of the constitution.[69] The Court declined to specify how much provincial concurrence was constitutionally (conventionally) required, noting only that the support of two of ten provinces was insufficient: "[I]t will be for the political actors, not this Court, to determine the degree of provincial consent required."[70]

To one trained in American law, the most striking facet of the federal government's unsuccessful position in the *Reference* case was the irony of its twin arguments that (1) a reform which could not be accomplished by the Canadian

---

62. *See* Hogg, *Commentaries: Amendment and Patriation,* 19 ALTA L. REV. 369, 371 (1981).
63. Kershaw, *The Canadian Constitution and the Foreign Affairs Committee of the U.K. House of Commons, 1980 and 1981,* 62 PARLIAMENTARIAN 173, 175 (1981).
64. 125 D.L.R. 3d 1 (Can. 1981).
65. *Id.* at 22.
66. *Id.* at 89.
67. P. HOGG, *supra* note 3, at 7.
68. Reference Re Amendment of the Constitution of Canada, 125 D.L.R.3d 1, 115 (Can. 1981).
69. *Id.* at 94, 107.
70. *Id.* at 103.

Parliament alone could be accomplished at its request by action of the imperial Parliament in London; and (2) action by the imperial Parliament, by settled convention, is a pure formality. No one suggested that the Canadian House of Commons and Senate could, acting alone, liberate Canada from the constraints of the BNA Act and enact a major reform of Canadian federalism. The 1949 amendment to the BNA Act, granting to the Canadian federal Parliament the authority to make constitutional changes "except as regards matters coming within the classes of subjects by this act assigned exclusively to the Legislatures of the provinces . . ."[71] by express exception continued what was clear before: the federal legislature should not be permitted, on its own, to make constitutional changes affecting the provinces. But while conceding that the Canadian Parliament could not make these changes, the Trudeau government asserted that the unilateral submission to the United Kingdom Parliament was proper. Since the inhibition on unilateral action by the Canadian Parliament was based upon the very *real* consideration of the federal nature of Canada, it is difficult to see how an additional action (U.K. legislation) that the government itself argued was *without substance* could provide a suitable basis for constitutional reform. If the United Kingdom Parliament had retained "real" legislative discretion over Canada, then one could accept the notion that London could choose to do at Ottawa's request that which Ottawa could not do alone. The heart of Ottawa's argument in London, however, was that the U.K. Parliament was obligated, by settled convention, to rubber stamp without question whatever it received from the federal government of Canada. Trudeau's proposed procedure thus represented a triumph of form over substance, a resort to legal fiction that seems out of place in the process of constitutional revision.

And so it appeared to the majority of the Canadian Supreme Court. The constitutional convention inferred by the Court from past practice—that the Canadian Parliament will not seek from London an amendment directly affecting federal-provincial relationships without first securing the agreement of the provinces—was necessary to protect the basic federal principle of Canada, and to "prevent the anomaly that the [Canadian] House of Commons and Senate could obtain by simple resolutions what they could not validly accomplish by statute."[72]

The Court's judgment was in the nature of an advisory opinion. There would have been no judicial interference if the federal government had proceeded unilaterally to submit its controversial package to London, and had sought automatic enactment by the U.K. Parliament.[73]

In the aftermath of the Court's declaration, however, an agreement was struck between the federal government and nine of the ten provinces. In exchange for provincial support, the federal government made several fundamental changes in its constitutional reform package, including (1) the addition of a provision permitting the legislature of a province to "override" provisions of the Charter of Rights by express declaration that a particular act would not be subject to the Charter,

---

71. British North America Act, 1949, 13 Geo. 6, ch. 81, § 1(1).
72. Reference Re Amendment of the Constitution of Canada, 125 D.L.R.3d 1, 106 (Can. 1981).
73. *Id*. at 48-49, 84-85.

and (2) the substitution of an amendment formula preferred by most of the provinces.[74]

With support of nine provincial governments, the new constitution was sent, by Joint Address to the Queen, from the Canadian Parliament to London, where it was enacted by the British House of Commons by a vote of 334-44. The royal assent of the Queen was given on March 29, 1982.[75] The ensuing royal pageant in Ottawa, which made the transfer of authority official, was boycotted by the Premier of Quebec who marched instead in a protest demonstration through the streets of Montreal.[76]

The government of Quebec alone continued to challenge the submission of the new compromise to London. Even if unanimity of the provinces was not required (the Canadian Supreme Court had spoken only of "substantial consent"),[77] Quebec argued in a new court challenge that *its* approval was essential since it represented a distinct society within Canadian federalism.[78] The Quebec claim was unanimously rejected by the Quebec Court of Appeals a week before the patriation ceremony.[79] The Quebec court noted that although "certain provinces are superior to others in land surface, population and resources, . . . legally speaking they are all on the same footing." The BNA Act, the court said, "give[s] the smaller provinces the same powers as the bigger provinces."[80]

To what extent does the dissent of the Quebec government deprive the reformed constitution of legitimacy? As noted above, it was not thought appropriate in 1787 to bring under the authority of the new American Constitution any state which had not chosen to ratify.[81] Quebec's objection means that the government of a province with one-fourth of Canada's people, the seat of its French and Catholic culture, did not agree to the reformed constitutional order of which it is now a part. Set against these concerns, however, are the following considerations.

First, the Quebec government's stated objections to the reformed constitution in its final form appear to be minor indeed, at least to one viewing from a distance. The provincial government of Quebec objected to a Charter of Rights which would limit its legislative authority; in its final version, however, the Charter can be overridden by a province under the authority of section 33, which provides that "the legislature of a province may expressly declare in an Act . . . that the Act or a provision thereof shall operate notwithstanding a provision included in [the principal sections] of this Charter."[82] Thus, none of these provisions need apply in Quebec so long as its legislature is willing expressly to declare them inapplicable.

Quebec objected as well to the amendment formula, but again on quite narrow

---

74. Montreal Gazette, Nov. 4, 1981, at 1, col. 6.

75. P. Hogg, *supra* note 11, at 3.

76. N.Y. Times, Apr. 18, 1982, at 1, col. 2.

77. Reference Re Amendment of the Constitution of Canada, 125 D.L.R.3d 1, 103 (Can. 1981).

78. *See* Re Attorney General of Quebec, 134 D.L.R. 3d 719, 727 (Que. Ct. App. 1982).

79. *Id.*

80. *Id.* at 726.

81. *See supra* p. 290.

82. Constitution Act, 1981, pt. 1, § 33(1), sched. B (Can.).

grounds.[83] The final formula (as will be noted in greater detail below) permits any province whose legislature objects to an amendment approved by the federal government and seven provinces to "opt-out" of the amendment.[84] Furthermore, if any amendment transfers educational or cultural responsibilities from the provinces to the federal government, a province which rejects the application of the amendment within its borders will be entitled to "reasonable compensation."[85] The Quebec government wanted "full" compensation and to have the provision apply to all amendments, not just those transferring educational or cultural matters.

Finally, Quebec objected to the provision relating to Minority Language Educational Rights,[86] from which a province may not opt-out. The principal provision of this section, however, is declared by the Constitution Act to be ineffective in Quebec until the Quebec National Assembly by affirmative act chooses to have it apply.[87] The remaining sections make only a minor incursion into Quebec's existing treatment of its Anglophone minority.

In sum, the fundamental provisions of the reformed constitution will continue to be those of the British North America Acts. Very little of substance in the revisions themselves will be applicable in Quebec without its consent. There was no guarantee, when the Canadian nation was formed in 1867, that the imperial Parliament would alter its BNA Act only with the consent of Quebec. If the agreement of nine of ten provinces and the federal parliament (including, it should be noted, almost all the Quebec representatives to that body)[88] satisfies the federalist convention calling for provincial concurrence, Quebec's claim of illegitimacy does not seem substantial. The fundamental disagreement of Quebec's separatist provincial government may in fact be with the 1867 BNA Act itself, rather than with the recent reformation of the constitution.

III

THE CANADIAN AMENDMENT PROVISIONS: A COMPARATIVE ASSESSMENT

Perhaps as a reflection of the complex politics of Canadian federalism, the new domestic amendment procedures are unusually complicated. The basic structure includes the following provisions:

(1) A few parts of the constitution can be amended only with unanimous consent of the Canadian Parliament and the legislative assembly of every province. These provisions include the office of the Queen, the right of a province to a certain number of members in the House, the composition of the Canadian Supreme Court, and, significantly, any amendment of the Amendment Part itself;[89]

---

83. *See* The Globe and Mail (Toronto), Apr. 15, 1982, at 2, col. 5.
84. Constitution Act, 1981, pt. 5, § 38(3), sched. B (Can.).
85. *Id*. § 40.
86. Constitution Act, 1981, pt. 1, § 23, sched. B (Can.).
87. Constitution Act, 1981, pt. 7, § 59(2), sched. B (Can.).
88. Montreal Gazette, Dec. 3, 1981, at 1, col. 5.
89. Constitution Act, 1981, pt. 5, § 41, sched. B (Can.).

(2) Parliament acting alone can alter provisions relating to the executive government of Canada or to parliament itself, except with respect to those matters noted above which require unanimous consent, and certain other fundamental provisions, such as the principle of proportionate representation of the provinces in the House of Commons;[90]

(3) The legislative assembly of a province may alter its own provincial constitution, except for those few matters noted above which require unanimous consent;[91] and

(4) The amendment of any provision that applies to one or more, but not all, provinces may be made upon the agreement of the federal parliament and each province to which the amendment applies.[92]

Each of the provisions noted above deals with special situations. The basic amendment provision applicable to most amendments will be a version of the "Vancouver formula."[93] Under this basic provision, an amendment may be made upon the concurrence of the Senate and House of Commons, and the legislative assemblies of two-thirds of the provinces that have, in the aggregate, at least fifty percent of the population of all the provinces.[94] Where an amendment derogates from the rights of a province, it must be passed by the House and Senate, and in the requisite number of legislative assemblies, by a majority of the members rather than by a mere majority of those present and voting.[95] Any amendment requiring the assent of the appointed federal Senate can be passed without the consent of that body, if repassed by the House of Commons after 180 days have elapsed.[96] Unlike the discarded "Victoria formula" under which Ontario and Quebec would each have had a permanent veto over amendments to the constitution, the new provisions grant to no single province the special status of a veto.

Perhaps the most interesting provision of the Amendment Part, however, is section 38(3) which states that any amendment which derogates from the proprietary rights of a province, or from the legislative or governmental powers of a province "shall not have effect in a province the legislative assembly of which has expressed its dissent by resolution adopted by a majority of its members prior to proclamation of the amendment."[97] The possible ramifications of this provision will be considered below.

An evaluation of the Canadian amendment procedures should perhaps begin by noting that its detailed provisions answer several perplexing questions that Article V of the American Constitution has left to speculation and, more recently, controversy. Article V confers upon Congress the power to propose amendments, and upon the states the power to ratify. It is silent, however, as to how long an

---

90. *Id*. § 44.

91. *Id*. § 45.

92. *Id*. § 43.

93. *See* McConnell, *Cutting the Gordian Knot: The Amending Process in Canada,* LAW & CONTEMP. PROBS., Summer 1981, at 195, 214-15.

94. Constitution Act, 1981, pt. 5, § 38(1), sched. B (Can.).

95. *Id*. § 38(2).

96. *Id*. § 47(1).

97. *Id.* § 38(3).

unratified amendment remains viable, and as to whether a state which has ratified an amendment may subsequently change its mind and rescind its ratification. In *Dillon v. Gloss*[98] the Supreme Court held that Congress had the implicit power to set a time limit for the consideration of an amendment by the states. Left unanswered in *Dillon* was whether Congress could subsequently extend that time, as Congress undertook to do as the proposed Equal Rights Amendment neared its original seven year deadline.[99] Consideration of the Equal Rights Amendment has been further complicated by the purported rescission by several previously ratifying states.[100] Particularly perplexing is the fact that there appears at present to be no definitive mechanism for ascertaining the validity of time extensions or rescissions. And however these questions should be resolved, their mere existence casts a substantial cloud over the amendment process, and threatens to deny a proper sense of legitimacy to future amendments.

Part V of the Canadian Constitution Act has the virtue of answering these questions. Amendments may be initiated by either a provincial government or the national parliament. Once initiated, an amendment remains open for ratification, or dissent from the application of the amendment within a province, for at least a year, unless before that time every province has adopted a resolution of assent or dissent.[101] A proposed amendment lapses unless ratified by the requisite number of assemblies within three years of the adoption of the resolution which initiated the amendment procedure.[102]

The Canadian provision clearly endorses the concept of rescission: "A resolution of assent made for the purposes of this Part may be revoked at any time before the issue of a proclamation authorized by it."[103] Similarly, a province which has dissented from the application of a proposed amendment may reverse itself and assent to the amendment.[104] Even after proclamation of a new amendment, a previously dissenting province may decide to accept the amendment and have it apply within the province.[105] Once a province has assented to an amendment, however, and the amendment has been proclaimed, that province may not thereafter "opt-out" of application of the amendment. No provision, at least, is made for such a reversal after adoption of an amendment and assent by a province; in light of the explicit treatment of all similar issues, silence in this instance is best construed as a denial of power.

The Canadian Constitution also avoids what appears to be a philosophical conundrum under the American amendment process.[106] A proviso to Article V states that no state shall be deprived of its equal suffrage in the Senate without its consent. Can this be amended? That is, could three-fourths of the states first

---

98.   256 U.S. 368, 373, 376 (1920).
99.   H.R.J. Res. 638, 95th Cong., 2d Sess., 92 Stat. 3799 (1978).
100.   *See* Idaho v. Freeman, 529 F. Supp. 1107, 1114 (D. Idaho 1981), *appeal pend'g sub nom.* National Org. for Women, Inc. v. Idaho, 102 S. Ct. 1272 (1982).
101.   Constitution Act, 1981, pt. 5, § 39(1), sched. B (Can.).
102.   *Id.* § 39(2).
103.   *Id.* § 46(2).
104.   *Id.* § 38(3).
105.   *Id.* § 38(4).
106.   *See* Linder, *What in the Constitution Cannot Be Amended?*, 23 ARIZ. L. REV. 717 (1981).

amend Article V by deleting this proviso, and then by three-fourths deprive some states, without their consent, of equal representation in the Senate? Could it be done in one step? Or is it implicit that the equal suffrage provision, which requires the consent of every adversely affected state, is not subject to amendment under Article V? Canada now answers these and similar questions by providing that the Amendment Part is itself unamendable—except with the concurrence of *every* province and the federal parliament.[107] The amendment clause thus provides special protection to certain very fundamental matters, such as the office of the Queen, by first providing, in its Amendment Part, for revision of such basic norms only by unanimous consent, and then by locking in this safeguard by rendering the amendment process itself subject to change only by unanimous agreement.

In one major respect, however, the Canadian Constitution seems unduly rigid. It affords little or no possibility of reforming those existing institutions of government which play a critical role in the amendment process. No amendment of any kind can be enacted, for example, without the concurrence of the Canadian House of Commons. This precludes any reform of that institution not desired by its members. Moreover, in a system of parliamentary government, it effectively precludes any amendment not approved by the Prime Minister. The concurrence of seven provincial assemblies is also required, which again, under parliamentary government, means that the concurrence of the provincial premiers is an essential step to every reform.

The central role of existing institutional bodies in the amendment process will serve to narrow substantially the range of future constitutional discourse. No future reform of provincial government which runs counter to the vested interest of the existing institutions is conceivable. One way to have avoided the permanent roadblock of existing legislative assemblies would have been to provide for ratification by referendum, as is done in Switzerland and Australia,[108] requiring, for example, a majority vote in seven of ten provinces, as well as a national majority, for enactment of an amendment. As an alternative to referenda, the American approach of ratification by specially elected conventions in every province might have been considered.[109] Unlike a referendum, a convention offers the possibility of being a deliberative body. It is not affected, moreover, by institutional self-interest, and since its members are elected for the express purpose of approving or disapproving a proposed amendment, there is substantial popular input into its determination.[110] (The one American experience with ratification by conventions, rather than by state legislatures, came in 1933. The twenty-first amendment, which repealed prohibition, was sent to, and ratified by, conventions in each state.

---

107. Constitution Act, 1981, pt. 5, § 41(e), sched. B (Can.).

108. *See* W. Livingston, *supra* note 37, at 319-22.

109. Article V of the Constitution provides that an amendment proposed by Congress "shall be valid to all Intents and Purposes, as Part of this Constitution, when ratified by the Legislatures of three fourths of the several States, *or by Conventions in three fourths thereof,* as the one or the other Mode of Ratification may be proposed by the Congress." U.S. Const. art. V (emphasis added). The Supreme Court held in United States v. Sprague, 282 U.S. 716, 730 (1931), that "The choice . . . of the mode of ratification, lies in the sole discretion of Congress."

110. *See* Dellinger, *Another Route to the ERA,* Newsweek, Aug. 2, 1982, at 8.

In that instance, there was very little deliberation. The state conventions met and quickly endorsed the preferences of the voters who had selected delegates on the basis of whether a particular candidate favored ratification or rejection of that one proposal.)[111] Since the Canadian Amendment Part can itself be amended only by agreement of the national government and every legislative assembly, any reform of those institutions seems effectively precluded.[112]

Some have hoped to see in the reformed Canadian Constitution an occasion for national renewal and a reversal of the centrifugal forces at work in Canada.[113] In some respects the Constitution Act may indeed exert a positive force for Canadian nationalism. A Charter of Rights, even though it may be overridden by a provincial assembly determined to do so, nonetheless articulates a set of rights to which Canada aspires for its citizens and which are national rights that one has as a Canadian. Mobility and minority education rights, though less complete than some wished, likewise set forth aspirations that there be one Canada in which every Canadian can feel welcome.

Casting a shadow over the reformed constitution, however, is the critical section permitting dissenting provincial governments to preclude the application within their borders of future amendments to the constitution.[114] Long opposed by Trudeau as a measure which would lead to a "checkerboard constitution" and foster national disintegration, the opting-out provision will, at a minimum, preclude future amendments which might have permitted evolving *Canadian* principles to be applied throughout the country.

As one reviews the twenty-six amendments to the American Constitution, it is interesting to consider what impact such a provision would have had. It would not have precluded the Bill of Rights[115] in its initial application to the federal government alone, nor the amendment limiting the President to two terms,[116] nor that which established rules for presidential succession.[117] Almost all of the other amendments, however, have at least in part served the function of bringing an evolving national consensus to bear upon a section or states which were not in step with that consensus. Several had meaningful application only in states which would have exempted themselves had they had the opportunity: the thirteenth amendment,[118] abolishing slavery, is the most profound example; the twenty-fourth,[119] abolishing a poll tax used only in a few non-ratifying states, is another. The fourteenth amendment,[120] which sought to guarantee equality of rights to

---

111. For a compilation of the records of the state conventions ratifying the 21st amendment, see E. BROWN, RATIFICATION OF THE TWENTY-FIRST AMENDMENT TO THE CONSTITUTION OF THE UNITED STATES (1938).

112. For the suggestion that Canada should utilize the process of initiative and referendum in the amendment process, see Hogg, *The Theory and Practice of Constitutional Reform*, 19 ALTA. L. REV. 335, 349-51 (1981).

113. *See, e.g.*, THE TASK FORCE ON CANADIAN UNITY, A FUTURE TOGETHER (1979) at 17.

114. Constitution Act, 1981, pt. 5, § 38(3), sched. B (Can.).

115. U.S. CONST. amends. I-X.

116. *Id*. amend. XXII.

117. *Id*. amend. XXV.

118. *Id*. amend. XIII.

119. *Id*. amend. XXIV.

120. *Id*. amend. XIV.

freedmen, imposed national standards on a subcommunity. Without it, it is difficult to imagine the full integration of the South into the national economy. The termination, through a nationally imposed amendment, of the South's extreme racial conflict has been a necessary precondition to its economic ascendency. Prohibition,[121] women's suffrage,[122] and the proposed Equal Rights Amendment, while less striking examples, have nonetheless had in part the function of applying a national consensus to areas of dissent from that consensus. The ability to apply amendments to dissenting states has thus played a significant role in the evolution of a sense of America as a single nation.

The provision permitting a province to "opt-out" of an amendment functions in some respects like a provision requiring unanimous consent for amendments. The preservation of federalism requires, of course, that the provinces or states have some critical role to play in any amendment process. The requirement of unanimity, however, is one more closely associated with confederacies than with federal systems.

As Professor Livingston reminds us, the formal institutions of federalism "are only the surface manifestations of the deeper federal quality of the society" which subtends them.[123] The inescapable fact is that Canada is a society of weak national loyalties, described by one observer as "almost totally lacking in a genuinely shared set of symbols, heroes, historical incidents, enemies, or even ambitions."[124] An amendment process which reflects the decentralized quality of such a society is neither good nor bad. It is only accurate.

---

121. *Id*. amend. XVIII (1787, repealed 1933).
122. *Id*. amend. XIX.
123. W. LIVINGSTON, *supra* note 37, at 2.
124. Meisel, *Canadian Parties and Politics,* in CONTEMPORARY CANADA 135 (R. Leach ed. 1968), *quoted in* A. LIJPHART, DEMOCRACY IN PLURAL SOCIETIES 128 (1977).

CONSTITUTION ACT, 1982

The Constitution Act, 1982, is not the whole of Canada's Constitution. It is an act adding to the body of Canadian constitutional law and amending parts of the British North America Act, 1867 (now retitled the Constitution Act, 1867), and other earlier documents. What follows is the English language version of the Constitution Act, 1982 (Schedule B). Schedule A, which is omitted here, contains the French language version of the act. Schedule I, referred to in Sections 52 and 53, lists item by item the earlier constitutional documents being amended and/or renamed. It also has been omitted here.

THAT, WHEREAS in the past certain amendments to the Constitution of Canada have been made by the Parliament of the United Kingdom at the request and with the consent of Canada:

AND WHEREAS it is in accord with the status of Canada as an independent state that Canadians be able to amend their Constitution in Canada in all respects;

AND WHEREAS it is also desirable to provide in the Constitution of Canada for the recognition of certain fundamental rights and freedoms and to make other amendments to that Constitution;

A respectful address be presented to Her Majesty the Queen in the following words:

TO THE QUEEN'S MOST EXCELLENT MAJESTY:
MOST GRACIOUS SOVEREIGN:

We, Your Majesty's loyal subjects, the House of Commons of Canada in Parliament assembled, respectfully approach Your Majesty, requesting that you may graciously be pleased to cause to be laid before the Parliament of the United Kingdom a measure containing the recitals and clauses hereinafter set forth:

An Act to give effect to a request by the Senate and House of Commons of Canada

Whereas Canada has requested and consented to the enactment of an Act of the Parliament of the United Kingdom to give effect to the provision hereinafter set forth and the Senate and the House of Commons of Canada in Parliament assembled have submitted an address to Her Majesty requesting that Her Majesty may graciously be pleased to cause a Bill to be laid before the Parliament of the United Kingdom for that purpose.

Be it therefore enacted by the Queen's Most Excellent Majesty, by and with the advice and consent of the Lords Spiritual and Temporal, and Commons, in this present Parliament assembled, and by the authority of the same, as follows:

1.   The *Constitution Act, 1982* set out in Schedule B to this Act is hereby enacted for and shall have the force of law in Canada and shall come into force as provided in that Act.

2.   No Act of the Parliament of the United Kingdom passed after the *Constitution Act, 1982* comes into force shall extend to Canada as part of its law.

3.   So far as it is not contained in Schedule B, the French version of this Act is set out in Schedule A to this Act and has the same authority in Canada as the English version thereof.

4.   This Act may be cited as the *Canada Act*.

SCHEDULE B

PART I

CANADIAN CHARTER OF RIGHTS AND FREEDOMS

Whereas Canada is founded upon principles that recognize the supremacy of God and the rule of law:

Guarantee of Rights and Freedoms

1.   *The Canadian Charter of Rights and Freedoms* guarantees the rights and freedoms set out in it subject only to such reasonable limits prescribed by the law as can be demonstrably justified in a free and democratic society.

Fundamental Freedoms

2.   Everyone has the following fundamental freedoms:
    (a) freedom of conscience and religion;
    (b) freedom of thought, belief, opinion and expression, including freedom of the
        press and other media of communication;
        (c) freedom of peaceful assembly; and
        (d) freedom of association.

Democratic Rights

3.   Every citizen of Canada has the right to vote in an election of members of the House of Commons or of a legislative assembly and to be qualified for membership therein.

4. (1) No House of Commons and no legislative assembly shall continue for longer than five years from the date fixed for the return of the writs at a general election of its members.

    (2) In time of real or apprehended war, invasion or insurrection, a House of Commons may be continued by Parliament and a legislative assembly may be continued by the legislature beyond five years if such continuation is not opposed by the votes of

more than one-third of the members of the House of Commons or the legislative assembly, as the case may be.

5.   There shall be a sitting of Parliament and of each legislature at least once every twelve months.

Mobility Rights

6. (1)Every citizen of Canada has the right to enter, remain in and leave Canada.

(2) Every citizen of Canada and every person who has the status of a permanent resident of Canada has the right
  (a) to move to and take up residence in any province; and
  (b) to pursue the gaining of a livelihood in any province.

(3) The rights specified in subsection (2) are subject to
  (a) any laws or practices of general application in force in a province other than those that discriminate among persons primarily on the basis of province of present or previous residence; and
  (b) any laws providing for reasonable residency requirements as a qualification for the receipt of publicly provided social services.

(4) Subsections (2) and (3) do not preclude any law, program or activity that has as its object the amelioration in a province of conditions of individuals in that province who are socially or economically disadvantaged if the rate of employment in that province is below the rate of employment in Canada.

Legal Rights

7.   Everyone has the right to life, liberty and security of the person and the right not to be deprived thereof except in accordance with the principles of fundamental justice.

8.   Everyone has the right to be secure against unreasonable search or seizure.

9.   Everyone has the right not to be arbitrarily detained or imprisoned.

10.   Everyone has the right on arrest or detention
  (a) to be informed promptly of the reasons therefor;
  (b) to retain and instruct counsel without delay and to be informed of that right; and
  (c) to have the validity of the detention determined by way of *habeas corpus* and to be released if the detention is not lawful.

11.   Any person charged with an offence has the right
  (a) to be informed without unreasonable delay of the specific offence;
  (b) to be tried within a reasonable time;
  (c) not to be compelled to be a witness in proceedings against that person in respect of the offence;
  (d) to be presumed innocent until proven guilty according to law in a fair and public hearing and by an independent and impartial tribunal;

(e) not to be denied reasonable bail without just cause;

(f) except in the case of an offence under military law tried before a military tribunal, to the benefit of trial by jury where the maximum punishment for the offence is imprisonment for five years or a more severe punishment;

(g) not to be found guilty on account of any act or omission unless, at the time of the act or omission, it constituted an offence under Canadian or international law or was criminal according to the general principles of law recognized by the community of nations;

(h) if finally acquited of the offence, not to be tried for it again and, if finally found guilty and punished for the offence, not to be tried or punished for it again; and

(i) if found guilty of the offence and if the punishment for the offence has been varied between the time of commission and the time of sentencing, to the benefit of the lesser punishment.

12.   Everyone has the right not to be subjected to any cruel and unusual treatment or punishment.

13.   A witness who testifies in any proceedings has the right not to have any incriminating evidence so given used to incriminate that witness in any other proceedings, except in a prosecution for perjury or for the giving of contradictory evidence.

14.   A party or witness in any proceedings who does not understand or speak the language in which the proceedings are conducted or who is deaf has the right to the assistance of an interpreter.

Equality Rights

15. (1) Every individual is equal before and under the law and has the right to the equal protection and equal benefit of the law without discrimination and, in particular, without discrimination based on race, national or ethnic origin, colour, religion, sex, age or mental or physical disability.

(2) Subsection (1) does not preclude any law, program or activity that has as its objective the amelioration of conditions of disadvantaged individuals or groups including those that are disadvantaged because of race, national or ethnic origin, colour, religion, sex, age or mental or physical disability.

Official Languages of Canada

16. (1) English and French are the official languages of Canada and have equality of status and equal right and privileges as to their use in all institutions of the Parliament and government of Canada.

(2) English and French are the official languages of New Brunswick and have equality of status and equal rights and privileges as to their use in all institutions of the legislature and government of New Brunswick.

(3) Nothing in this Charter limits the authority of Parliament or a legislature to advance the equality of status or use of English and French.

17. (1) Everyone has the right to use English or French in any debates and other proceedings of Parliament.

(2) Everyone has the right to use English or French in any debates and other proceedings of the legislature of New Brunswick.

18. (1) The statutes, records and journals of Parliament shall be printed and published in English and French and both language versions are equally authoritative.

(2) The statutes, records and journals of the legislature of New Brunswick shall be printed and published in English and French and both language versions are equally authoritative.

19. (1) Either English or French may be used by any person in, or in any pleading in or process issuing from, any court established by Parliament.

(2) Either English or French may be used by any person in, or in any pleading in or process issuing from, any court of New Brunswick.

20. (1) Any member of the public in Canada has the right to communicate with, and to receive available services from, any head or central office of an institution of the Parliament or government of Canada in English or French, and has the same right with respect to any other office of any such institution where

      (a) there is a significant demand for communications with and services from that office in such language; or

      (b) due to the nature of the office, it is reasonable that communications with and services from that office be available in both English and French.

(2) Any member of the public in New Brunswick has the right to communicate with, and to receive available services from, any office of an institution of the legislature or government of New Brunswick in English or French.

21. Nothing in sections 16 to 20 abrogates or derogates from any right, privilege or obligation with respect to the English and French languages, or either of them, that exists or is continued by virtue of any other provision of the Constitution of Canada.

22. Nothing in sections 16 to 20 abrogates or derogates from any legal or customary right or privilege acquired or enjoyed either before or after the coming into force of this Charter with respect to any language that is not English or French.

Minority Language Educational Rights

23. (1) Citizens of Canada

      (a) whose first language learned and still understood is that of the English or French linguistic minority population of the province in which they reside, or

      (b) who have received their primary school instruction in Canada in English or French and reside in a province where the language in which they received that instruction is the language of the English or French linguistic minority population of the province,

have the right to have their children receive primary and secondary school instruction in that language in that province.

(2) Citizens of Canada of whom any child has received or is receiving primary or secondary school instruction in English or French in Canada, have the right to have all their children receive primary and secondary school instruction in the same language.

(3) The right of citizens of Canada under subsections (1) and (2) to have their children receive primary and secondary school instruction in the language of the English or French linguistic minority population of a province

(a) applies wherever in the province the number of children of citizens who have such a right is sufficient to warrant the provision to them out of public funds of minority language instruction; and

(b) includes, where the number of those children so warrants, the right to have them receive that instruction in minority language educational facilities provided out of public funds.

Enforcement

24. (1) Anyone whose rights or freedoms, as guaranteed by this Charter, have been infringed or denied may apply to a court of competent jurisdiction to obtain such remedy as the court considers appropriate and just in the circumstances.

(2) Where, in proceedings under subsection (1), a court concludes that evidence was obtained in a manner that infringed or denied any rights or freedoms guaranteed by this Charter, the evidence shall be excluded if it is established that, having regard to all the circumstances, the admission of it in the proceedings would bring the administration of justice into disrepute.

General

25.   The guarantee in this Charter of certain rights and freedoms shall not be construed so as to abrogate or derogate from any aboriginal, treaty or other rights or freedoms that pertain to the aboriginal peoples of Canada including

(a) any rights or freedoms that have been recognized by the Royal Proclamation of October 7, 1763; and

(b) any rights or freedoms that may be acquired by the aboriginal peoples of Canada by way of land claims settlement.

26.   The guarantee in this Charter of certain rights and freedoms shall not be construed as denying the existence of any other rights or freedoms that exist in Canada.

27.   This Charter shall be interpreted in a manner consistent with the preservation and enhancement of the multicultural heritage of Canadians.

28.   Notwithstanding anything in the Charter, the rights and freedoms referred to in it are guaranteed equally to male and female persons.

29.   Nothing in this Charter abrogates or derogates from any rights or privileges guaranteed by or under the Constitution of Canada in respect of denominational, separate or dissentient schools.

30.   A reference in this Charter to a province or to the legislative assembly or legislature of a province shall be deemed to include a reference to the Yukon Territory and

the Northwest Territories, or to the appropriate legislative authority thereof, as the case may be.

31.   Nothing in this Charter extends the legislative powers of any body or authority.

Application of Charter

32. (1) This Charter applies
       (a) to the Parliament and government of Canada in respect of all matters within the authority of Parliamant including all matters relating to the Yukon Territory and Northwest Territories; and
       (b) to the legislature and government of each province in respect of all matters within the authority of the legislature of each province.
    (2) Notwithstanding subsection (1), section 15 shall not have effect until three years after this section comes into force.

33. (1) Parliament or the legislature of a province may expressly declare in an Act of Parliament or of the legislature, as the case may be, that the Act or a provision thereof shall operate notwithstanding a provision included in section 2 or sections 7 to 15 of this Charter.
    (2) An Act or a provision of an Act in respect of which a declaration made under this section is in effect shall have such operation as it would have but for the provision of this Charter referred to in the declaration.
    (3) A declaration made under subsection (1) shall cease to have effect five years after it comes into force or on such earlier date as may be specified in the declaration.
    (4) Parliament or a legislature of a province may reenact a declaration made under subsection (1).
    (5) Subsection (3) applies in respect of a re-enactment made under subsection (4).

Citation

34.   This Part may be cited as the *Canadian Charter of Rights and Freedoms*.

PART II
RIGHTS OF THE ABORIGINAL PEOPLES OF CANADA

35. (1) The existing aboriginal and treaty rights of the aboriginal peoples of Canada are hereby recognized and affirmed.
    (2) In this Act, "aboriginal peoples of Canada" includes the Indian, Inuit and Metis peoples of Canada.

PART III
EQUALIZATION AND REGIONAL DISPARITIES

36. (1) Without altering the legislative authority of Parliament or of the provincial legislatures, or the rights of any of them with respect to the exercise of their legislative

authority, Parliament and the legislatures, together with the government of Canada and the provincial governments, are committed to

(a) promoting equal opportunities for the well-being of Canadians.

(b) furthering economic development to reduce disparity in opportunities; and

(c) providing essential public services of reasonable quality to all Canadians.

(2) Parliament and the government of Canada are committed to the principle of making equalization payments to ensure that provincial governments have sufficient revenues to provide reasonably comparable levels of public services at reasonably comparable levels of taxation.

PART IV
CONSTITUTIONAL CONFERENCE

37. (1) A constitutional conference composed of the Prime Minister of Canada and the first ministers of the provinces shall be convened by the Prime Minister of Canada within one year after this Part comes into force.

(2) The conference convened under subsection (1) shall have included in its agenda an item respecting constitutional matters that directly affect the aboriginal peoples of Canada, including the identification and definition of the rights of those peoples to be included in the Constitution of Canada, and the Prime Minister of Canada shall invite representatives of those peoples to participate in the discussion on that item.

(3) The Prime Minister of Canada shall invite elected representatives of the governments of the Yukon Territory and the Northwest Territories to participate in the discussions on any item on the agenda of the conference convened under subsection (1) that, in the opinion of the Prime Minister, directly affects the Yukon Territory and the Northwest Territories.

PART V
PROCEDURE FOR AMENDING CONSTITUTION OF CANADA

38. (1) An amendment to the Constitution of Canada may be made by proclamation issued by the Governor General under the Great Seal of Canada where so authorized by

(a) resolutions of the Senate and House of Commons; and

(b) resolutions of the legislative assemblies of at least two-thirds of the provinces that have, in the aggregate, according to the then latest general census, at least fifty per cent of the population of all the provinces.

(2) An amendment made under subsection (1) that derogates from the legislative powers, the proprietary rights or any other rights or privileges of the legislature or government of a province shall require a resolution supported by a majority of the members of each of the Senate, the House of Commons and the legislative assemblies required under subsection (1).

(3) An amendment referred to in subsection (2) shall not have effect in a province the legislative assembly of which has expressed its dissent thereto by resolution supported by a majority of its members prior to the issue of the proclamation to which the amendment relates unless that legislative assembly, subsequently by resolution supported by a majority of its members, revokes its dissent and authorizes the amendment.

(4) A resolution of dissent made for the purposes of subsection (3) may be revoked at any time before or after the issue of the proclamation to which it relates.

39. (1) A proclamation shall not be issued under subsection 38(1) before the expiration of one year from the adoption of the resolution initiating the amendment procedure thereunder, unless the legislative assembly of each province has previously adopted a resolution of assent or dissent.

(2) A proclamation shall not be issued under subsection 38(1) after the expiration of three years from the adoption of the resolution initiating the amendment procedure thereunder.

40.   Where an amendment is made under subsection 38(1) that transfers provincial legislative powers relating to education or other cultural matters from provincial legislatures to Parliament, Canada shall provide reasonable compensation to any province to which the amendment does not apply.

41.   An amendment to the Constitution of Canada in relation to the following matters may be made by proclamation issued by the Governor General under the Great Seal of Canada only where authorized by resolutions of the Senate and House of Commons and of the legislative assembly of each province:
  (a) the office of the Queen, the Governor General and the Lieutenant Governor of a province;
  (b) the right of a province to a number of members in the House of Commons not less than the number of Senators by which the province is entitled to be represented at the time this Part comes into force;
  (c) subject to section 43, the use of the English or the French language;
  (d) the composition of the Supreme Court of Canada; and
  (e) an amendment to this Part.

42. (1) An amendment to the Constitution of Canada in relation to the following matters may be made only in accordance with subsection 38(1):
    (a) the principle of proportionate representation of the provinces in the House of Commons prescribed by the Constitution of Canada;
    (b) the powers of the Senate and the method of selecting Senators;
    (c) the number of members by which a province is entitled to be represented in the Senate and the residence qualifications of Senators;
    (d) subject to paragraph 41(d), the Supreme Court of Canada;
    (e) the extension of existing provinces into the territories; and
    (f) notwithstanding any other law or practice, the establishment of new provinces.

(2) Subsections 38(2) to (4) do not apply in respect of amendments in relation to matters referred to in subsection (1).

43.   An amendment to the Constitution of Canada in relation to any provision that applies to one or more, but not all, provinces, including
  (a) any alteration to boundaries between provinces, and
  (b) any amendment to any provision that relates to the use of the English or the French language within a province,

may be made by proclamation issued by the Governor General under the Great Seal of Canada only where so authorized by resolutions of the Senate and House of Commons and of the legislative assembly of each province to which the amendment applies.

44.   Subject to sections 41 and 42, Parliament may exclusively make laws amending the Constitution of Canada in relation to the executive government of Canada or the Senate and House of Commons.

45.   Subject to section 41, the legislature of each province may exclusively make laws amending the constitution of the province.

46. (1) The procedures for amendment under section 38, 41, 42 and 43 may be initiated either by the Senate or the House of Commons or by the legislative assembly of a province.

   (2) A resolution of assent made for the purposes of this Part may be revoked at any time before the issue of a proclamation authorized by it.

47. (1) An amendment to the Constitution of Canada made by proclamation under section 38, 41, 42 or 43 may be made without a resolution of the Senate authorizing the issue of the proclamation if, within one hundred and eighty days after the adoption by the House of Commons of a resolution authorizing its issue, the Senate has not adopted such a resolution and if, at any time after the expiration of that period, the House of Commons again adopts the resolution.

   (2) Any period when Parliament is prorogued or dissolved shall not be counted in computing the one hundred and eighty day period referred to in subsection (2).

48.   The Queen's Privy Council for Canada shall advise the Governor General to issue a proclamation under this Part forthwith on the adoption of the resolutions required for an amendment made by proclamation under this Part.

49.   A constitutional conference composed of the Prime Minister of Canada and the first ministers of the provinces shall be convened by the Prime Minister of Canada within fifteen years after this Part comes into force to review the provisions of this Part.

Part VI
Amendment to the Constitution Act, 1867

50.   The *Constitution Act, 1867* (formerly named the *British North America Act, 1867*) is amended by adding thereto, immediately after section 92 thereof, the following heading and section:

Non-Renewable Natural Resources, Forestry Resources and Electrical Energy

92A. (1) In each province, the legislature may exclusively make laws in relation to
   (a) exploration for non-renewable natural resources in the province;
   (b) development, conservation and management of non-renewable natural resources and forestry resources in the province, including laws in relation to the rate of primary production therefrom; and

(c) development, conservation and management of sites and facilities in the province for the generation and production of electrical energy.

(2) In each province, the legislature may make laws in relation to the export from the province to another part of Canada of the primary production from non-renewable natural resources and forestry resources in the province and the production from facilities in the province for the generation of electrical energy, but such laws may not authorize or provide for discrimination in prices or in supplies exported to another part of Canada.

(3) Nothing in subsection (2) derogates from the authority of Parliament to enact laws in relation to the matters referred to in that subsection and, where such a law of Parliament and a law of a province conflict, the law of Parliament prevails to the extent of the conflict.

(4) In each province, the legislature may make laws in relation to the raising of money by any mode or system of taxation in respect of
(a) non-renewable natural resources and forestry resources in the province and the primary production therefrom, and
(b) sites and facilities in the province for the generation of electrical energy and the production therefrom,
whether or not such production is exported in whole or in part from the province, but such laws may not authorize or provide for taxation that differentiates between production exported to another part of Canada and production not exported from the province.

(5) The expression "primary production" has the meaning assigned by the Sixth Schedule.

(6) Nothing in subsections (1) to (5) derogates from any powers or rights that a legislature or government of a province had immediately before the coming into force of this section.

51.   The said Act is further amended by adding thereto the following Schedule:

"The Sixth Schedule: Primary Production from Non-Renewable Natural Resources and Forestry Resources

1.   For the purposes of section 92A of this Act,
(a) production from a non-renewable natural resource is primary production therefrom if
(i) it is in the form in which it exists upon its recovery or severance from its natural state, or
(ii) it is a product resulting from processing or refining the resource, and is not a manufactured product or a product resulting from refining crude oil, refining upgraded heavy crude oil, refining gases or liquids derived from coal or refining a synthetic equivalent of crude oil; and
(b) production from a forestry resource is primary production therefrom if it consists of sawlogs, poles, lumber, wood chips, sawdust or any other primary wood product, or wood pulp, and is not a product manufactured from wood."

Part VII
General

52. (1) The Constitution of Canada is the supreme law of Canada, and any law that is inconsistent with the provisions of the Constitution is, to the extent of the inconsistency, of no force or effect.

(2) The Constitution of Canada includes

(a) the *Canada Act*, including this Act;

(b) the Acts and others referred to in Schedule I; and

(c) any amendment to any Act or order referred to in paragraph (a) or (b).

(3) Amendments to the Constitution of Canada shall be made only in accordance with the authority contained in the Constitution of Canada.

53. (1) The enactments referred to in Column I of Schedule I are hereby repealed or amended to the extent indicated in Column II thereof and, unless repealed, shall continue as law in Canada under the names set out in Column III thereof.

(2) Every enactment, except the *Canada Act*, that refers to an enactment referred to in Schedule I by the name in Column I thereof is hereby amended by substituting for that name the corresponding name in Column III thereof, and any British North American Act not referred to in Schedule I may be cited as the *Constitution Act* followed by the year and number, if any, of its enactment.

54.   Part IV is repealed on the day that is one year after this Part comes into force and this section may be repealed and this Act renumbered, consequential upon the repeal of Part IV and this section, by proclamation issued by the Governor General under the Great Seal of Canada.

55.   A French version of the portions of the Constitution of Canada referred to in Schedule I shall be prepared by the Minister of Justice of Canada as expeditiously as possible and, when any portion thereof sufficient to warrant action being taken has been so prepared, it shall be put forward for enactment by proclamation issued by the Governor General under the Great Seal of Canada pursuant to the procedure then applicable to an amendment of the same provisions of the Constitution of Canada.

56.   Where any portion of the Constitution of Canada has been or is enacted in English and French or where a French version of any portion of the Constitution is enacted pursuant to section 55, the English and French versions of that portion of the Constitution are equally authoritative.

57.   The English and French versions of this Act are equally authoritative.

58.   Subject to section 59, this Act shall come into force on a day to be fixed by proclamation issued by the Queen or the Governor General under the Great Seal of Canada.

59. (1) Paragraph 23(1)(a) shall come into force in respect of Quebec on a day to be

fixed by proclamation issued by the Queen or the Governor General under the Great Seal of Canada.

(2) A proclamation under subsection (1) shall be issued only where authorized by the legislative assembly or government of Quebec.

(3) This section may be repealed on the day paragraph 23(1)(a) comes into force in respect of Quebec and this Act amended and renumbered, consequential upon the repeal of this section, by proclamation issued by the Queen or the Governor General under the Great Seal of Canada.

60.   This Act may be cited as the *Constitution Act 1982*, and the Constitution Acts 1867 to 1975 (No. 2) and this Act may be cited together as the *Constitution Acts, 1867 to 1982*.

INDEX

Kent, 160, 161

King, Mackenzie, 20n, 57–58

Kirby, Michael, 153

Lafontaine, Louis, 46, 47

Langevin, Hector, 101

Language Rights, Canada: and Alberta, 21; and British North America Act, 1867, 6–7, 16, 178, 218; and Canada Act, 1982, 206–8; and Canadian Bill of Rights, 178–79; and Canadian Charter of Rights and Freedoms, 208–9; and Manitoba, 21, 180–83; and New Brunswick, 21, 185–87, 208; and Ontario, 187–88; and Quebec, 190–206, 210–13; and Saskatchewan, 21. See also Education Rights, Canada

Lapointe, Ernest, 20

Laskin, 178, 256

Laurendeau, Andre, 22

Laurier, Wilfred, 19

Laurin, Camille: and La Politique Québécois de la Langue Française, 197–98, 210; and The Quebec School: A Responsible Force in the Community, 214, 217–18

Lesage, Jean, 24, 177

Levesque, René: attack by, of Canadian Charter of Rights and Freedoms, 154; call by, for legislation for French unilingualism, 192; as force in negotiations for provincial dissent, 273; opposition by, to reformed constitution, 154–55, 207; on significance of Supreme Court of Canada in federal-provincial conflict, 61; support by, for building French-Canadian nation, 51–52; support by, of language rights for francophones, 52

Lincoln, Abraham, 41–42

Livingston, W., 302

Lloyd, 118

London Resolutions, 150

Loranger, T. J. J., 17

Louis XIV, 43

Lowenstein, 159

Lower, A., 19

Lower Canada, 44–45, 53

Lushington, 262

McConnell, 225n

Macdonald, John A.: on Canadian nationalism, 47; on centralized union, 14, 15, 95n; constitutional intentions of, hindered by provincial demarcations, 104; on federal disallowance of provincial enactments, 54–55; as leader of the party of confederation, 48–49, 106; and the "Macdonaldian Constitution," 19

MacEachen, Allen, 112, 130n, 131, 140n

McInnis, E., 44, 45, 46

McRae, 140

McRuer Report, 32

Madison, James, 285

Mallory, J., 23n, 107

Manitoba: education rights in, 183–85; government of, will not use override of Canadian Charter of Rights and Freedoms, 157; language rights in, 180–83; place of, in representative tax system and total provincial income equalization formulas, 126, 127, 129, 130, 131, 134, 135, 139, 140, 141, 143

Manitoba Act, 1870, 180–82, 183, 184

Mansfield, Lord, 180–81

Marshall, Alfred, 103

Mason, 287

Massachusetts Bay Company, 37

Melvin, 137

Monnin, 181, 182

Montreal Gazette, 48

Moore, A., 120

Moore, Milton: on anomalies of representative tax system, 132–33; on macroeconomic approach to equalization, 117, 122

Morgan, Edmund S., 36, 38

Morin, Jean-Marie, 214

Morin-McNab Ministry, 47

Morton, W.: on federal-provincial conflict and the British North America Act, 1867, 16; on Lord John Russell and the Durham Report, 45; on the Quebec Act, 1774, 44

Mowat, Oliver, 17–18, 31

Municipal governments, Canada, 158

National Adjustment Grants, 116

Natural Resources Revenue: and federal-provincial conflict over control of, 61, 64–65n, 109–10, 138; as significant factor in equalization formulas, 117–20, 125–26, 128, 130–32, 136–43, 147; taxing of, as established in British North America Act, 1867, 110, 136–37; taxing of, as established in Constitution Act, 1982, 109–10, 137–38

New Brunswick: education rights in, 186; language rights in, 185–87, 208; place of, historically, in equalization formulas, 113–15; place of, in representative tax system and total provincial income equalization

CONTRIBUTORS

KEITH ARCHER is completing the doctoral program in political science at Duke University. He has received an appointment as assistant professor of political science at the University of Calgary.

CLARK R. CAHOW, professor of history, university registrar, and assistant provost at Duke University, has directed a number of Exxon educational projects on financing higher education and has been a member of the College Board Services Commission. His publications include articles on management information systems in higher education, the relevancy of the Bakke decision, and studies of mental institutions. His interest in constitutional change has led to a new constitutional history course at Duke.

PAUL DAVENPORT, whose publications on investment productivity and industrial policy have appeared in a number of Canadian and Australian journals, has also given many testimonials and radio interviews with reference to the Quebec economy, energy policy, federal tax policy, and unemployment. In 1981 he received a major grant from the Social Sciences and Humanities Research Council to study federal-provincial economic relations. He has been professor of economics at McGill University since 1973.

WALTER E. DELLINGER, professor of law at Duke, was on leave during 1980–81 in order to serve as Special Counsel and Professor in Residence for the U.S. Department of Justice. He served as associate dean and/or acting dean of the Duke Law School from 1974 to 1978. He has published on constitutional law, criminal process, and civil procedure. His advice on the constitutional process has been sought by a number of federal agencies, and he presently holds a Rockefeller National Humanities grant to write a book on constitutional change: the process of amendment.

ALLAN KORNBERG taught at the University of Michigan and Hiram College before coming to Duke as professor of political science. His research on comparative legislative behavior, comparative party systems, and Canadian and American political behavior is represented in many books and articles. Two volumes, with Harold Clarke and William Mishler, were published in 1982: *Political Support in Canada: The Crisis Years* and *Representative Democracy in the Canadian Provinces*.

DANIEL LATOUCHE, a graduate in political science from the University of Montreal and the University of British Columbia, has been associate professor of political science and director of the French Canada Studies Program of McGill since 1970. He was formerly an editorial writer for the daily *Montreal Matin* and has served as constitutional adviser to the Prime Minister of Quebec (1978–80).

RICHARD H. LEACH is a professor of political science at Duke University and director of the Canadian Studies Center. He has published and edited many books on American, Canadian, and Australian comparative federalism, American political thought, and public administration. His articles in a number of journals discuss interstate compacts, urban affairs, educational policies, and metropolitan area governance.

JAMES R. MALLORY is R. B. Angus Professor of Political Science Emeritus at McGill. He served for three years as chairman of the Social Science Research Council of Canada and as vice president of the Canadian Political Science Association. His many publications include *Social Credit and the Federal Power in Canada* (Toronto, 1964 and 1976) and *The Structure of Canadian Government* (Toronto, 1971).

A. KENNETH PYE, professor of law and director of international studies at Duke, came to Duke University from Georgetown University. He served as dean of the Law School from 1973 to 1976. He has held visiting professorships in Germany, India, and Australia. His writing has focused on criminal law, use of troops in civil disturbances, and legal education. He has held a number of posts in the American Bar Association, the Association of American Law Schools, and the Council for International Exchange of Scholars.

FILIPPO SABETTI is associate professor of political science at McGill University. He has published a number of articles on local politics and policy analysis and is currently coediting with Harold M. Waller a special issue of *Publius* on Canadian federalism. His ongoing research interests are political crises and policy outcomes in unitary and federal systems.

STEPHEN A. SCOTT is a member of the law faculty at McGill University and of the bar of the Province of Quebec. His doctoral dissertation at Oxford was "The Prerogative of the Crown in External Affairs and Constituent Authority in a Commonwealth Monarchy." He wrote opinions on various constitutional questions published with *Report of the Commission of Inquiry on the Position of the French Language and on Language Rights in Quebec* (Gendron Commission, 1972). His latest opinions on Bill C-60 appeared in the *Canadian Bar Review* 587 and on the role of the U.K. Parliament in relation to the British North America Act in the *McGill Law Journal* 26 (1981).

WILLIAM TETLEY was elected MNA for the Notre-Dame-de-Grace in 1968. He spent eighteen months in the Opposition in the Quebec National Assembly. Elected again in 1970 and 1973, he became Minister of Revenue for six months and Minister of Consumer Affairs, Cooperatives and Financial Institutions for five years. His government studies include a report on foreign investment in Quebec. He is now professor of law at McGill University, author of *Marine Cargo Claims* (Carswell and Stevens 1966), the second edition of which (Butterworths 1978) is to be translated and published in Russian and Japanese.

WILLIAM G. WATSON is assistant professor of economics at McGill University. He holds a B.A. from McGill and a Ph.D. from Yale. He teaches public sector economics and has published on commercial, industrial, and fiscal policy. He is currently writing a book on the growth of taxation and public expenditure in the OECD countries in the post–World War II period.

PSE/AH   O/E/A 840TS (1-3)

Davenport